P9-DGI-434

Data Warehouse: Practical Advice from the Experts

Joyce Bischoff and Ted Alexander

Sid Adelman   Denis Kosar
Peter Brooks   John Ladley
Marie Buretta   Trina LaRue
Brenda Castiel   Jay Marquez
Howard Fosdick   Terry Mason
Susan Gausden   Edward M. Peters
Dave Gleason   Jack Sweeney
Paul Hessinger   Pete Uhrowczik
Martin Hubel   Colin White
          Richard Yevich

Foreword by John A. Zachman

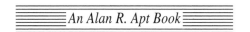

An Alan R. Apt Book

Prentice Hall
Upper Saddle River, New Jersey 07458

Library of Congress Cataloging-in-Publication Data

Bischoff, Joyce
    Data warehouse: practical advice from the experts/Joyce Bischoff,
Ted Alexander
    p.   cm.
    Includes bibliographical references and index.
    ISBN: 0-13-577370-9
    CIP data available upon request

Publisher: Alan Apt
Editor: Laura Steele
Production editor: Sharyn Vitrano
Editor-in-chief: Marcia Horton
Managing editor: Bayani Mendoza DeLeon
Copy editor: Patricia Daly
Cover designer: Marjory Dressler
Director of production and manufacturing: David W. Riccardi
Creative director: Paula Maylahn
Art director: Heather Scott
Manufacturing buyer: Donna Sullivan
Editorial assistant: Toni Chavez
Compositor: Preparé Inc. / Emilcomp srl

 © 1997 by Prentice-Hall, Inc.
Simon & Schuster / A Viacom Company
Upper Saddle River, New Jersey 07458

All rights reserved. No part of this book may be
reproduced, in any form or by any means,
without permission in writing from the publisher.

The author and publisher of this book have used their best efforts in preparing this book. These efforts
include the development, research, and testing of the theories and programs to determine their
effectiveness. The author and publisher make no warranty of any kind, expressed or implied, with
regard to these programs or the documentation contained in this book. The author and publisher shall
not be liable in any event for incidental or consequential damages in connection with, or arising out of,
the furnishing, performance, or use of these programs.

The cover drawing, "The Data Warehousing Process", by Paul Hessinger, copyright 1997, Vision UnlimITed
is used with permission.

Printed in the United States of America

10   9   8   7   6   5   4   3   2   1

ISBN 0-13-577370-9

Prentice-Hall International (UK) Limited, *London*
Prentice-Hall of Australia Pty. Limited, *Sydney*
Prentice-Hall Canada Inc., *Toronto*
Prentice-Hall Hispanoamericana, S.A., *Mexico*
Prentice-Hall of India Private Limited, *New Delhi*
Prentice-Hall of Japan, Inc., *Tokyo*
Simon & Schuster Asia Pte. Ltd., *Singapore*
Editora Prentice-Hall do Brasil, Ltda., *Rio de Janeiro*

To Ken, Jim, and Kathy
—Joyce Bischoff

To Carole and M. J.
—Ted Alexander

Trademarks

This book contains direct and indirect references to products and/or designations used by sellers to distinguish their products. Every effort has been made to identify all trademarks and we regret any omissions or oversights. The following products and/or designations are claimed as trademarks by their respective companies:

ADABAS and NATURAL are registered trademarks of SOFTWARE AG.

ADW (now called KEY: Plan) is a trademark of Sterling Software, Inc. (formerly owned by Knowledgeware).

AIX, AS/400, CICS, Data Guide/2, DataJoiner, DataPropagator, DB2, DB2/MVS, DB2/2, DB2/6000, Data Interpretation System (DIS), Distributed Relational Database Architecture (DRDA), ESCON, IBM, IMS, Information Warehouse (IW), Lotus Notes, OS/2, MVS, MVS/ESA, MVS/XA, Parallel Sysplex, QMF, S/390, RACF, SearchManager, Visualizer, Visual Warehouse, VSAM, and VTAM are trademarks or registered trademarks of IBM Corporation.

Arbor and Essbase are registered trademarks of Arbor Software Corporation.

Brio and BrioQuery are trademarks or registered trademarks of Brio Technology, Inc.

Business Objects and Mercury are trademarks or registered trademarks of Business Objects, Inc.

BYNET is a trademark of NCR Corporation.

CA-ACF2, CA-Datacom, CA-IDMS, and CA-Top Secret are registered trademarks of Computer Associates International, Inc.

Cognos and PowerPlay are registered trademarks of Cognos, Incorporated.

Cross Access is a trademark of Cross Access Corporation.

DEC, DECNET, and VMS are trademarks of Digital Equipment Corporation.

Distributed Computing Environment (DCE) is a trademark of Open Software Foundation, Inc.

Eco Net and Eco Tools are trademarks or registered trademarks of Compuware Corporation.

Enterprise Data Access/SQL and EDA/SQL are trademarks or registered trademarks of Information Builders, Inc.

ExpressNet is a trademark of American Express.

GroundWorks and Terrain are trademarks or registered trademarks of Cayenne Software, Inc. (Formerly Bachman Analyst and Bachman/Database Administrator).

Group 1 Software is a trademark or registered trademark of Group 1 Software, Inc.

Hewlett-Packard (HP) is a trademark of Hewlett-Packard Company.

IA Decision Support Suite is a trademark of Information Advantage, Inc.

Information Engineering Facility and IEF are trademarks of Texas Instruments, Inc.

Informix is a registered trademark of Informix Software, Inc.

Intel, Pentium, and Pentium Pro are trademarks or registered trademarks of Intel Corporation.

KEY:Plan is a trademark of Sterling Software (formerly Knowledgeware's ADW).

Lotus, 1-2-3, and Lotus Notes are trademarks of Lotus Development Corporation.

Macintosh is a registered trademark of Apple Computer, Inc.

Microsoft, Access, Excel, Open Database Connectivity (ODBC), Powerpoint, SQL Server, Windows, Windows NT, Windows 3.1, and Windows 95 are trademarks or registered trademarks of Microsoft Corporation.

Novell and NetWare are registered trademarks of Novell, Inc.

OmniReplicator is a trademark of Praxis International, Inc.

ORACLE is a registered trademark of Oracle Corporation.

Patrol is a trademark or registered trademark of BMC Software, Inc.

PLATINUM Data Shopper, PLATINUM InfoPump, PLATINUM Repository, and PLATINUM Forest and Trees are trademarks or registered trademarks of Platinum Technology, Inc.

Postalsoft is a trademark or registered trademark of Postalsoft, Inc.

PowerBuilder is a registered trademark of Powersoft Corporation.

Prism Solutions, Inc., Prism Warehouse Manager, and Prism Directory Manager are trademarks or registered trademarks of Prism Solutions, Inc.

Program Maintenance Standard Solutions (PMSS) is a trademark of ADPAC Corporation.

Quicken is a trademark of Intuit, Inc.

Red Brick and Red Brick Warehouse are trademarks or registered trademarks of Red Brick Systems.

R&O, Rochade, and Rochade Repository are trademarks or registered trademarks of R&O: The Repository Company.

SPARCluster, Solaris, and Centerplane/Gigaplane are registered trademarks of SUN Microsystems, Inc.

SYBASE, SYBASE IQ, SYBASE SQL Server, Replication Server, and SQL Anywhere are trademarks or registered trademarks of Sybase, Inc.

SYNCSORT is a trademark of SYNCSORT, Inc.

Tandem is a trademark of Tandem Computers, Incorporated.

Teradata is a trademark of NCR Corporation.

Tuxedo is a registered trademark of UNIX System Laboratories, Inc.

UNIX is a registered trademark and is licensed exclusively through X/Open Company Limited.

Vality is a registered trademark of Vality Technology, Inc.

X-Windows is a registered trademark of the Massachusetts Institute of Technology.

Foreword

This is one book that truly lives up to its subtitle: *Practical Advice from the Experts.* I do not think I have ever read a book that was written from such a depth of experience. There are many different authors, many different styles, and many different topics, areas of specialization, and perspectives, but the one common thread is that every chapter virtually oozes with an aura of authority, which only comes from the sobriety of emerging unscathed from a brush with potential catastrophe and the euphoria of great accomplishment.

The chapters that comprise this book are written by authors who have lived through the reality of data warehouse implementations, who have emerged successfully, and who have learned what works and what does not. It is a book that is worthy of being read by every serious information professional, whether involved in data warehousing or not. It is a book that addresses the reality and the practicality of operating a business and its systems in the complex and ever-changing Information Age.

I was impressed with the forthrightness and honesty of the book. The editors and authors are not merely marketing to you, telling you what you *want* to hear. They are advising you, giving you the benefit of their hard-earned successes, telling you what you *need* to have a positive data warehouse experience. If you follow this wealth of advice, you are virtually guaranteed of deriving the value of these substantive concepts wherever and whenever you implement them.

Although it was from my close friend Bill Inmon that I (along with many) learned about data warehouse, I am sure there were others who were "inventing" the concept at the same time, because data warehouse is clearly an idea whose time has come. It is representative of Thomas Kuhn's *Theory of Scientific Revolutions,* in which Kuhn observed that inventions are a function of the times as opposed to a function of the personalities who invent them. Similarly, Peter Chen, Charlie Bachman, Bob Brown, and Clive Finkelstein (and, I am sure, others that I do not know personally) were simultaneously inventing data modeling. Data warehouse is indeed a function of the times.

The history of data processing is rife with the perspective that the value of computers in business enterprises is attributable to their ability to process repetitive transactions faster and more accurately than can humans. Therefore, it is not surprising that the vast majority of implemented systems are devoted to on-line transaction processing or OLTP. The value of the data historically has been significant only insofar as it is required to complete a transaction. Therefore, data architecture has been a complete, universal nonissue and has been perceived to take too much time and cost too much money.

It is only when the complexity and dynamics of the Information Age business environment place a high premium on management's ability to see what is happening in and to the enterprise that the values and semantic quality of the data become a business issue, not a technical issue. At that juncture, the disparities and discontinuities of the legacy implementations (that is, the absence of data architecture) become an albatross around the information community's neck, driving the enterprise frustration levels beyond control while escalating the time and costs of system maintenance.

Someone had to figure out a way to compensate, after the fact, for this lack of data architecture by creating a virtually integrated database, populating it with currently available real legacy data, and attempting to reconcile the physical disparities and semantic discontinuities to whatever extent possible and make the existing data usable for management purposes, beyond simply processing transactions. Data warehouse was inevitable.

I am describing this historical context for data warehouse to observe that anyone who is building a data warehouse and ignores the data architecture issue clearly does not understand the problem. A data warehouse that is not derived from an enterprise data model is simply one more legacy file and ultimately will further contribute to the enterprise's disappointment and frustration with its information systems.

In reading this book, I was impressed to note that not a single author succumbed to the temptation to suggest extracting data from legacy files to create a data warehouse without first building a logical data model and, beyond that, understanding the enterprise implications of the model—that is, data architecture. This is some strong evidence that this book is filled with advice from knowledgeable people, advice that leads you to successful enterprise experiences of these vital concepts, not just advice that leads to expedient implementations, independent of their business and technical validity or utility.

The genius of data warehouse is twofold. First, it is the recognition that we could create an architected environment and move the output (decision support) processing into the new environment (data warehouse) without having to rewrite all the input (transaction) processing systems. Second, it establishes the possibility of creating a three-schema environment comprised of a conceptual schema (logical data model), an internal schema (legacy files), and an external schema (data warehouse) in which the many-to-many ($m \times n$) maintenance relationships of the legacy files could be reduced to many-to-one-to-many ($m + n$) of the three-schema environment. It is significant to note that both of these benefits accrue only if a logical data model is an integral part of the data warehouse project.

Looking beyond these short-term benefits, the next logical step in the data warehouse evolution would be to rebuild, incrementally, transaction by transaction, the input (transaction) processing systems to support and directly feed an architected (operational data store) environment and, over time, system by system, completely eliminate the legacy with all of its inherent discontinuities, maintenance problems, and costs. However, this would imply building the logical data model with the intent to derive both a transaction processing physical database (operational data store) as well as a decision support physical database (data warehouse) and, further, to persistently synchronize these two implementations of the same logical data model.

Therefore, the immediate value of the data warehouse is satisfaction of management's short-term demands for integrated visibility into the enterprise and its environment while reducing the maintenance burden of the existing systems. This could be invaluable to both management and IT in reducing stress levels and improving management and IT collaboration in the challenging transition into a knowledge-based society.

On the other hand, the long-term value of data warehouse could be utilization of an operational data store to provide a perpetual migration path out of the legacy systems into an architected environment designed to accommodate high rates of enterprise change. This has enormous significance to an Information Age enterprise, whose very existence is dependent on its ability to respond to the dynamics of its marketplace. I have heard it strongly argued that the new entrants (competitors), regulatory changes, existing competition, and general market demands are going to force the legacy to be rewritten. It is only going to be a matter of time, and the question is, Will the legacy merely be re-written, or will it be architected for change? My observation is that data warehouse is the key to architecting and migrating to a new environment, and architecture, in turn, is the key to data warehouse and assimilating high rates of change.

Whether looking at the immediate, short-term benefits of data warehouse or, from my perspective, the far greater migration implications of the long-term benefits, responsible people could only advise building a data warehouse based on an enterprise data model.

Data Warehouse: Practical Advice from the Experts is filled with chapters written by knowledgeable, responsible people. It is a tribute and testimony to the wisdom and experience of successful implementors, and it discusses a great variety of issues ranging from developing the business case through designing large databases, implementing security facilities, and administering the warehouse after it is installed.

On a serious, cautionary note, I am concerned that the subject of data warehouse is extremely vulnerable these days. It is hard to pick up an industry publication or a vendor brochure without a laudatory note on data warehouse and its potential for solving all the enterprise's information problems. This is reminiscent of what happened with CASE, Repository, and ADCycle or, before that, artificial intelligence, expert systems, or mini-computers etc., etc. There is nothing wrong with CASE, Repository, or ADCycle and all the rest, but when *anything* becomes a panacea, it is inevitable that the grand, unrealistic expectations simply cannot be met. The typical market backlash against an exposed "silver bullet" is a devastating reaction that tends to obfuscate or dissipate substantive and vital concepts in the process. My perception is that in 1997, data warehouse is such a panacea candidate. The antidote to the usual, "Well, *that* didn't work!" reaction is a substantive infusion of reality and a major proliferation of notable successes.

Data Warehouse: Practical Advice from the Experts is exactly that infusion of reality, and I urge you to read with diligence, follow this advice, and produce a plethora of notable successes. Every one of us must ensure the ongoing vitality and viability of the data warehouse approach.

This book is clearly the result of quality thinking and enormous effort on the part of Joyce Bischoff and Ted Alexander, who pulled together a comprehensive, realistic statement of the state of the art in data warehouse. We may look back in a few years and realize that they have made a major contribution to preserving the integrity of these valuable concepts for the generations of information professionals to come.

John A. Zachman
Glendale, California

Preface

Advances in information technology have brought us to the brink of achieving the ultimate information goal: to provide high-quality data to anyone who needs it, at any location, in a timely manner, at a reasonable cost. The evolution of information technology has taken us from the simpler days of batch processing and on-line transaction processing into the data warehouse, on-line analytical processing (OLAP), the Internet, and the Intranet. The journey has been swift and rarely without pain for those on its leading (and often bleeding!) edge.

This handbook for the data warehouse is designed to help technical managers, project managers, business analysts, systems designers, systems architects, database administrators (DBAs), data administrators (DAs), systems administrators, end users, and members of data warehouse project teams in all aspects of planning, designing, developing, implementing, and administering a data warehouse. It is also for students of computer science, information systems, and business administration. Vendors of data warehouse products may also find it of value in educating their staff and clients in the issues of implementing a data warehouse. It helps prepare people to progress toward the goal of providing any data, anywhere, anytime. The authors are consultants and users from various companies who have implemented hundreds of warehouses between them. They will share their experiences so that the reader may avoid some of the many pitfalls that await.

HOW TO USE THIS BOOK

This book contains six sections, which are designed to support a typical data warehouse project in approximately the sequence that the information will be needed by managers and the project team. It is suggested that everyone read the first three sections of the book to obtain a foundation for the warehouse project. Although readers may choose to read the whole book from beginning to end, it is not necessary to read the book in any particular order, and readers may use it as a reference when dealing with a particular aspect of a warehouse project.[*]

---

[*]For reader ease, a glossary of abbreviations is provided (see p. 403–413).

If the book is used in an academic setting, it would be most appropriate for advanced classes in computer science, information systems, or business administration. The course would emphasize the use of information to meet business objectives and present both business and technical issues that must be addressed to meet these objectives. In computer science and information systems classes, the book may be read from beginning to end. In a business administration class, Part One, Two, Three, and Six would be of greatest interest. If students have a technical background, they may optionally cover Parts Four and Five. Many universities offer classes to external students working in the field of information technology (IT). This book would be an ideal text for this type of class and could be presented from beginning to end.

A reference list is provided at the end of each chapter; references are cited in text using superscript numerals.

PART ONE: GETTING STARTED

This section provides a foundation for understanding the issues involved in building a successful warehouse. It establishes the vision of the data warehouse and discusses the alignment of business objectives with the data warehouse. It assesses the organizational impact and the need to work with end users in all phases of development. Practical advice from experienced users will be of value to those who are considering a data warehouse project. Part One will be of interest to technical managers, project managers, business analysts, information resource management personnel, and end users even before the data warehouse decision has been made.

PART TWO: PLANNING THE DATA WAREHOUSE

How have other people approached the building of a data warehouse? Is the methodology really different from that used in the on-line transaction processing (OLTP) environment? How should we plan a warehouse project? How can we cost justify the project? This part addresses the warehouse development methodology and discusses issues surrounding the planning of the pilot project. It will benefit project managers, designers, developers, and administrators who need to understand the differences in methodology and the iterative nature of warehouse development.

PART THREE: DATA: THE CRITICAL ISSUE

Data is the cornerstone of the data warehouse. Part Three begins with a study of data quality and moves on to a discussion of metadata in the warehouse. It discusses the experience of a major bank in developing its own user-oriented data directory, which will be of value to those who wish to develop their own directory or purchase a vendor product. The analysis and transformation of data that is moved from the legacy environment to the warehouse is a major concern because it may take more than half of all hours spent on the development of the warehouse. This part will be of interest to technical managers, project managers, business analysts, and information resource management personnel.

PART FOUR: DESIGN AND IMPLEMENTATION

We need to understand the technical architecture of the data warehouse before beginning the design process. Development of the data architecture and physical design will follow. This part discusses technical design options, including data replication, on-line analytical processing (OLAP), middleware, and parallel technology. This part will be of interest to database designers, application designers, and administrators.

PART FIVE: DATA WAREHOUSE ADMINISTRATION

Many warehouses have been implemented in a heterogeneous hardware and software environment, which presents many challenges. This part addresses the administrative issues that must be managed in a complex environment. It will be of particular interest to database administrators and system administrators.

PART SIX: TRENDS

Where will we go from here? What are the trends in data warehousing? This section will be of special interest to managers, business analysts, and members of the project team who are trying to build a foundation for the future.

ACKNOWLEDGMENTS

We would like to thank all of the authors for sharing their expertise through their contributions to this book. We would also like to thank them for their additional comments, suggestions, and other types of support that are too numerous to mention.

Sid Adelman	Sid Adelman and Associates, Sherman Oaks, CA
Peter Brooks	Coopers and Lybrand Consulting, Advanced Technology Group, Lexington, MA
Marie Buretta	President, Marie Buretta Inc., Princeton, NJ

Brenda Castiel	Senior Manager, Ernst and Young, Los Angeles, CA
Howard Fosdick	Fosdick Consulting, Inc., Villa Park, IL
Susan Gausden	Director, Brooklands Technology Limited, Weybridge, Surrey, United Kingdom
Dave Gleason	Senior Manager for Consulting and Offerings with PLATINUM Information Management Consulting (PIMC), a unit of PLATINUM Technology, Inc.
Paul Hessinger	Managing Director of Vision UnlimITed, Atlanta, GA
Martin Hubel	Martin Hubel Systems Consulting, Inc. Toronto, Canada
Denis Kosar	Vice President of Enterprise Information Architecture, Chase Manhattan Bank, New York, NY
John Ladley	META Group, St. Louis, MO
Trina LaRue	Senior Consultant, AT&T, Somerset, NJ
Jay Marquez	Senior Partner, The Praxium Group, Inc., Atlanta, GA
Terry Mason	Director, Brooklands Technology Limited, Weybridge, Surrey, United Kingdom
Edward M. Peters	Vice President and General Manager of the DataDirect Division of Intersolv, Inc.
Jack Sweeney	President and CEO, Intellidex Systems, Winthrop, MA
Pete Uhrowczik	Senior Technical Staff Member at IBM's Santa Teresa Laboratory
Colin White	DataBase Associates International, Morgan Hill, CA
Richard Yevich	Principal, RYC, Inc., Key Biscayne, FL
John A. Zachman	President, Zachman International, Glendale, CA

For more information about the authors and ways that you may contact them, their biographies are listed in the "Authors' Biographies" section (pp. 414–421).

We would also like to thank Alan Apt, Sharyn Vitrano, Mary Ann Telatnik, and Laura Steele, the editors at Prentice Hall, for their unwavering support throughout the project. We also owe a debt of gratitude to all of our authors, reviewers, and others who provided suggestions and support. In addition to the authors, this includes but is not limited to the following:

Chuck Ballard, IBM
James Bischoff, Bischoff Technical Services
Elizabeth Bortkiewicz, Information Bridges
David Christian, E. I. DuPont de Nemours
Jerrilyn Glanville, IBM
Joel Goldstein, Responsive Systems

Bernie Jeltema, Strategic Frameworks, Inc., and University of California
    (Irvine) Extension Program
David Liddell, IBM
Robert Manieri, Ford Electronics
Roger Miller, IBM
Anne Marie Smith, General Accident Insurance Company.

We also acknowledge the many professionals, too numerous to mention, who have
shared their warehouse experiences through their writing and speaking engage-
ments. Last, but not least, we are grateful for the opportunities we have had to share
the data warehouse journey with many clients, who have contributed directly or
indirectly to this book.

SUMMARY

This book is for readers who are critical players in the development of the data
warehouse in their organization. Although there are data warehouses in every
industry, some have been distinctly more successful than others. Some have
appeared to be successful at the start but failed later for a variety of reasons. Others
have been failures from the start. As the warehouse evolves, many organizational,
technical, and administrative changes must be addressed. The authors share a
wealth of experience in the following pages. It is our hope that readers will find the
political solutions, technical guidance, and direction to begin the journey toward a
successful data warehouse.

Joyce Bischoff
Ted Alexander

Contents

Data Warehouse:
Practical Advice from the
Experts

PART ONE

GETTING STARTED

"A journey of a thousand miles must begin with a single step."

Lao-tzu

There are many data warehouses across all industries that have met with varying degrees of success. Those that have been less than successful have usually failed to understand basic warehouse issues. This section provides practical advice from experienced users and consultants in the first stages of building a data warehouse.

Chapter 1, "Introduction to Data Warehousing" by Joyce Bischoff, presents an overall information strategy, defines basic data warehouse concepts and terminology, and provides a foundation for understanding data warehouse technology. Chapter 2, "A Renaissance for Information Technology" by Paul Hessinger, presents a visionary and motivational management framework. Hessinger discusses the renaissance that is occurring in the industry and the need for a renaissance state of mind to take advantage of the potential for warehouse development. He emphasizes the need for a data warehouse strategy that is strongly aligned with business objectives. He identifies critical success factors and outlines an action plan for achieving management objectives.

Chapter 3, "Organizational and Cultural Issues" by Sid Adelman, discusses the issues that must be addressed in a successful data warehouse. Adelman addresses the issue of building an appropriate infrastructure to support the warehouse and lists 10 criteria for a successful data warehouse. He describes changing roles and responsibilities and the shift in the power structure that may occur with a warehouse implementation.

Chapter 4, "Working Effectively with End Users" by Joyce Bischoff, carries the organizational issues one step further. Many warehouses have failed because users were not properly involved in all phases of implementation. The level of end-user involvement in each phase of the project will vary depending on the type of warehouse project. Bischoff presents suggestions for involving users throughout the planning, design, implementation, and administration of the warehouse. One thing is certain: The warehouse will probably fail if users are involved only after the warehouse is implemented.

In Chapter 5, "The Seven Deadly Sins," Denis Kosar presents a list of things *not* to do when building a warehouse. These suggestions come from his real-world experience in building a large warehouse at a major New York bank.

In Chapter 6, "Real-World Data Warehousing: The Management Challenge," Howard Fosdick analyzes the most common reasons for failure of data warehouse projects and presents a checklist of classic errors of data warehouse projects.

Introduction to Data Warehousing

1

Joyce Bischoff

Bischoff Consulting, Inc.
Hockessin, Delaware

"No man sees far, the most see no further than the end of their noses."

Thomas Carlyle

It is important to consider the basic strategies that provide a business foundation for the development of a data warehouse. There are four levels of analytical processing that must drive the evolution of the data warehousing process. Data warehouses are not an end in themselves but merely a step on the path to the information data superstore.

STRATEGIC DELIVERY OF INFORMATION

In the never-ending quest to access *any* information, anywhere, anytime, an architecture is needed that includes data from both internal and external sources in a variety of formats. It must include operational data, historical data, legacy data, subscription databases, and data from Internet service providers. It must also include easily accessible metadata. Today's businesses require the ability to access and combine data from a variety of data stores, perform complex data analysis across these data stores, and create multidimensional views of data that represent the business analyst's perspective of the data. Furthermore, there is a need to summarize, drill down, roll up, slice, and dice the information across subject areas and business dimensions.

The Problem

These objectives cannot be met easily because data is scattered in many types of incompatible structures. A lack of documentation has prevented us from integrating older legacy systems with newer systems. Although database administrators have long advocated the design of well-documented integrated databases that may be shared across artificial application lines, most organizations have failed to heed the advice. The result is that analysts cannot perform ad hoc analysis across applications without first creating integrated data structures.

The Internet has opened up additional business opportunities needing nontraditional categories of information. The World Wide Web has provided us with magazines, travel, professional communication, games, shopping information, and a new set of adventures for everyone. Vendors are consolidating data from many sources into accessible databases and selling access through the Internet. Although the data and its relationships have not been standardized and defined in data directories, search engines have been developed to identify related information. The use of different search engines with the same criteria may yield different results. The need exists for improved Internet software and more accurate and accessible metadata across multiple organizations if we are to address this problem.

ANALYTICAL PROCESSING REQUIREMENTS

Information systems need to support at least four levels of analytical processing in modern organizations. The first level consists of simple queries and reports against current and historical data and is usually accomplished with spreadsheets, query, and reporting tools. The second level goes deeper and requires the ability to do "what if" processing across dimensions of a data store. If labor costs increase by 5% next year and sales remain constant, how will profits be affected? Again, the use of spreadsheets, query tools, and database technology will permit this question to be answered.

At the third level of analysis, the need is to step back and analyze what has previously occurred to bring about the current state of the data. Why was there a sudden increase in the sale of cough syrup in the Northeast during the month of January while other regions remained constant? Was there a particularly effective marketing campaign in the Northeast? Was there an epidemic of influenza? Have any competitors gone out of business? The answer to these queries requires complex processing of internal and external data. The increasing need for external data plays a role in this level of querying. A credit card firm might wish to be aware of potential job losses if a major firm downsizes its staff. The loss of jobs may affect the ability of credit card holders to pay their bills and increase the number of defaults. There is very little technology available today to support this type of automated analysis.

At the fourth level, what has happened in the past and what needs to be done in the future is analyzed to bring about a specific change. For example, if the goal is to increase profits by 5% next year, what conditions must change to achieve that objective? Furthermore, what business steps must be taken to implement the changes? The technology does not exist today to support this type of analysis and vendors are challenged to provide products to support this requirement. It is time that artificial intelligence is applied to products other than electronic games to improve the competitiveness of businesses.

INFORMATION DATA SUPERSTORE (SUPER DATA WAREHOUSE)

Organizations should begin to position themselves now to move into an overall architecture that will eventually support all levels of data access and analysis against internal and external data in a variety of formats. The term *information data super-store* (IDSS) was introduced in a paper by Bischoff and Yevich[1] to define the architecture needed to support the far-ranging requirements of the four levels of analysis across internal and external data. It includes access to legacy systems, operational data stores, data warehouses, data marts, database service providers, and Internet and Intranet Web Servers. The IDSS might also be called a *Super Data Warehouse* because it is much more than today's warehouse.

Virtual warehousing techniques can provide access to data in any storage location and provide views across diverse data stores through a semantic map that shields the end user from its specific physical location. Industry standards that promote interoperability will permit interoperability between applications and databases and may become more prevalent with the evolution of the IDSS.

The IDSS architecture highlights major changes in analytical processing that must occur if all of these diverse data stores are to be exploited. In addition to the aforementioned general analysis requirements, users would like to ask questions that require heterogeneous joins across multiple business organizations. For example, what is the lowest mortgage rate for a 20-year fixed rate mortgage with a particular credit rating? Where can I buy the least expensive Mercedes within 100 miles of a customer's home?

Although there is not enough coordination of data or technology to implement the full IDSS today, vendors are challenged to provide effective products. The need to join data on fields with a common meaning that have slightly different definitions is a requirement. For example, social security numbers might be stored with dashes in one table, spaces in another, and a nine-digit numeric field in still another table. Fuzzy logic or artificial intelligence is also needed to allow recognition that these are essentially the same. Sequential Query Language (SQL) needs to be modified to support this type of processing. The constant unloading and reformatting required to standardize and integrate every file, especially those that reside outside of our own organization, can no longer be tolerated. Although this may be theoretically possible within organizations, it is not possible to control external databases.

Another missing product is a dynamic, active, unstructured data directory that will support cross-organizational data access. One possible approach would involve the movement of critical, user-oriented metadata into the system catalogs of relational or postrelational (object-oriented) DBMSs. The basic description of each table and column, its source, and relationships might be stored at the most basic level in a relational catalog. This would fit into the original relational theory developed by E. F. Codd[2] and would allow users or applications to access the data directly without use of a specific directory. It would still allow each vendor's repository or directory product to access the data in a standard format and integrate it with the extensible capabilities of specific vendor products. This would require cooperation of both relational database management system (RDBMS) vendors and dictionary/repository vendors. Some dictionary/directory vendors might see this move as usurping their territory, but this need not happen. The rich functionality provided by directory vendors could still remain in place and be further enhanced. They could continue to use their own proprietary structures while storing key end-user-oriented information only in the RDBMS.

In addition, a major change is occurring in the way business rules and constraints will be stored in relational or postrelational systems. For many years, programmers have written code to enforce business rules and constraints in application programs. Developers and administrators are beginning to include business rules and constraints as part of the database definition. These definitions are then enforced by the database engine and need not be included in programs. This improves data integrity and consistency and ensures that rules will be enforced uniformly.

There is a serious need for administrative tools that will ease the burden of both the data administration (DA) and data base administration (DBA) staffs. The maintenance of metadata in multiple repositories associated with various warehouse tools requires significant expertise and administration. The Metadata Coalition is working to ease the exchange of data between tools, but the administration of the movement of data will still be a problem. It is possible that triggers could be designed into various products to generate updates to other repositories automatically. The management of physical data stores with intelligent agents that notify the DBA when exception conditions occur must evolve even further to ease the DBA's burden.

The IDSS architecture also introduces a new layer, called the IDSS User Access Layer (UAL), which will encapsulate access code and allow information technology (IT) personnel to manage and optimize it. The IDSS UAL will work with the metadata manager when required to resolve data format differences and data location problems. The access layer will act either as a simple pass through layer or be fully involved when required. The IDSS UAL, when required, drives forward by "discussing" with the Metadata Manager to resolve any location or data difficulties. This is the true heart of the IDSS. Just as major client/server implementations have centralized declarative and procedural code (such as stored procedures and triggers) on servers, access code should be removed from the clients. This will allow IT personnel to integrate newer methods of dynamic and interpretive processing and utilize expert systems to great advantage.

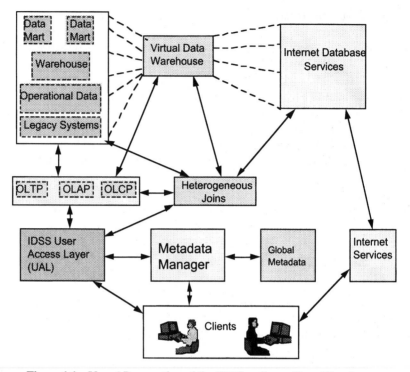

Figure 1.1   Users' Perspective of the IDSS or Super Data Warehouse.

The users' perspective of the IDSS is shown in Figure 1.1. Please note that the various constructs shown in the figure may be implemented on traditional servers, Intranet servers, or Internet servers.

Although all of the long-term goals of the IDSS cannot be met with today's technology, it is time to develop a strategy to build the basic constructs of the IDSS. These constructs must provide data integrity, flexibility, scalability, availability, and ease of use. Robust relational or postrelational database management systems should be used to ensure data integrity in a highly volatile environment while adhering to industry standards. Although it is always advisable to start small and grow, corporations should plan for enormous scalability in the selection of hardware, software, and applications. In today's world, it is not unusual for a data warehouse to double in size in the first six months. If applications and underlying software are discovered that will exceed technical limits when massive growth occurs, it will be expensive to accommodate increases in the number of users and quantity of data. The issue of connectivity is closely related to industry standards. IT departments must ensure that they have the tools necessary to connect client/server systems across the enterprise.

DATA WAREHOUSE TECHNOLOGY

There is a need to define basic terminology. John Ladley[6] has defined *data warehouse technology* as a set of methods, techniques, and tools that may be leveraged together to produce a vehicle that delivers data to end users on an integrated platform. Data warehouse technology is *not* a data warehouse. It is used to *create* a data warehouse, operational data store, or data mart stored on traditional servers, Intranet servers, or Internet servers. There is nothing unusual about the technology. The issue is one of applying technology to solve a business problem.

What Is a Data Warehouse?

Although decision support systems have been in existence for many years, it was not until the early 1990s that they were labeled data warehouses and top executives took notice of their business potential. The data warehouse means different things to different people. Some definitions are limited to data. Others refer to people, processes, software, tools, and data. Although the exact wording is different, they all have a common thread. W. H. Inmon[4] has provided the clearest definition of the data warehouse with the following definition:

> The data warehouse is a collection of integrated, subject-oriented databases designed to support the DSS (decision support) function, where each unit of data is relevant to some moment in time.

The data should be well defined, consistent, and nonvolatile in nature. Furthermore, the quantity of data should be large enough to support data analysis, querying, reporting, and comparisons of historical data over a longer period of time. The data warehouse is one piece of the approach used to meet the overall objectives stated previously. It is not a product and cannot be bought. It must be built, one step at a time.

There are successful warehouses in every industry with many subject areas. An informal survey has shown that many warehouses support the sales and marketing functions. All companies need to understand the demographic characteristics of their customers. After they understand current customers, they may want to find out who is *not* buying their products. Data is often purchased from external sources and brought into the warehouse for this type of analysis. The warehouse may then be used to provide lists of potential customers for marketing purposes. Other warehouses may provide data for client tracking, financial analysis, claims associations, fraud analysis, and other purposes. The warehouse must provide a framework to support the merging of operational data, informational data, external data, departmental data, and personal data. Just as a blueprint is needed to build a house, a technical framework is required to build a warehouse that will evolve into the IDSS.

Because many companies work with averages in analyzing customer information, some companies have questioned the need for detail data in the data warehouse. Although preliminary analysis may provide important information, there may be a need to drill down into the detail data to obtain information needed to gain competitive advantage. It should be noted that average companies work with averages. The superstars differentiate themselves by paying attention to the details. They may need to slice and dice the data in different ways to obtain a deeper understanding of their customer base and other data.

The data warehouse must be user driven. Some companies have tried to build large warehouses without user involvement and have failed. They thought that they understood user requirements based on the existing backlog of requests. Unfortunately, many users give up asking for new data and functionality because of delays in meeting their requests. The backlog is only the tip of the iceberg.

Need for a Separate Environment

But why does the data warehouse require a separate environment? Why can't decision support functions perform against the operational environment? Although operational systems exist to support the day-to-day business functions, the data warehouse is used for analysis, decision making, and informational purposes. The legacy operational environment is inadequate in many respects. If infinitely fast hardware and perfectly efficient software were used, only one environment might (theoretically) be required. Unfortunately, in the real world, hardware and software constraints may prevent meeting performance objectives of both operational and decision support objectives in the same environment.

In addition, the type, quantity, and quality of data contained in the legacy environment is usually inadequate for decision support. The warehouse is often used to analyze trends over a long period of time. Operational systems contain only the data needed to meet day-to-day business requirements, while data warehouses contain a larger quantity of historical data for informational purposes. Warehouse data must be consistent, integrated, well defined, and time stamped, and the legacy environment usually fails in this respect. There is also a need to merge operational data, external data, and personal data in ad hoc queries. Most operational systems are not positioned to meet this objective.

In addition, the type of access is different. In an operational environment, users know what they need and they will access a small number of rows in a single transaction. In the warehouse, there are large sweeps of data because thousands or millions of records may be retrieved to answer a single query. Considering the answer obtained in one query, the user may decide to analyze the data in another way. One frustrated database administrator complained about the warehouse users: "They don't even know what they want! How can I provide it?" This is a good question. The answer is to provide a flexible data architecture and database design coupled with metadata and the infrastructure to support rapidly changing user requirements.

What Is an Operational Data Store?

An operational data store (ODS) provides the basis for operational processing and may be used to feed the data warehouse. It has been defined by Inmon, Imhoff, and Battas[5] as an architectural construct that is

- Subject oriented
- Integrated (i.e., collectively integrated)
- Volatile
- Current valued
- Comprised of only corporate detailed data.

Data in the ODS is organized around subjects such as customer, product, order, policy, claim, etc. It is fed by the legacy systems and contains data that has been cleansed, transformed, and integrated. Multiple applications may share the data with updating occurring in only one place in the ODS. The ODS has been effective in organizations that are trying to move their legacy systems into an integrated environment. One large telecommunications company is consolidating customer information from hundreds of legacy files into a single, shared ODS, which the company personnel refer to as a data warehouse because they are using it for both operational and informational purposes. The usual definitions say that the ODS contains data used for operational purposes, while the data warehouse contains data used for informational purposes. Because of advances in technology, the lines are becoming blurred between the ODS and the data warehouse, and many organizations are using the data in this manner. An ODS is an optional construct that may or may not be present in the architecture of a particular organization. As an alternative, many companies move detail data directly into the warehouse and do not allow it to be updated in the on-line environment.

The differences between the two environments are summarized in Figure 1.2. In examining this figure, it is obvious that the differences between the two environments are significant. In the warehouse, the unit of work is usually much larger than that found in the operational environment. It is also unpredictable in terms of frequency. Because of this, the impact of ad hoc queries with large numbers of users may be unacceptable in a heavy production environment. Improvements in hardware and software have allowed some merging of the environments, and it is best to consider the definitions as guidelines rather than hard and fast rules.

Data Marts

There has been much vendor hype on the subject of data marts. A data mart is a data warehouse that has been designed to meet the needs of a specific group of users. It may be large or small, depending on the subject area. The planning, design, and implementation issues are the same as those found in any phase of warehouse

Issue	Operational	Warehouse
How built	One application at a time in the legacy environment or one subject area at a time in the ODS	One or more subject areas at a time
Requirements	Known	Vague
Critical to	Daily business operation	Management decisions that may affect profitability
Data access	Smaller numbers of rows retrieved in a single call	Large sets of data scanned to retrieve results
Tuning	Highly tuned for frequent access to small amounts of data	Tuned for infrequent access to larger quantities of data
Data volume	Volume needed for daily operation	Larger volume needed to support statistical analysis, forecasting, ad hoc reporting, and querying
Data retention	Data retained to meet daily requirements	Data retained longer to support historical reporting, comparison, analysis, etc.
Data currency	Must be up to the minute	Usually represents a static point in time; usually important that data does not change minute by minute
Data availability	High availability may be needed	Usually does not require as high availability as the production environment unless worldwide access is necessary
Unit of work	Small, manageable, predictable unit of work	Large, unpredictable, highly variable unit of work
Design priority	High performance	Flexibility

Figure 1.2   Operational versus Warehouse Characteristics.

implementation. The issues of metadata, data architecture, data cleanup, consistency, integrity, accessibility, and administration are the same as those encountered in the warehouse. Since the considerations are basically the same, this book will not address the concept of data mart as a separate issue. A data mart may or may not be designed with corporate accessibility and standards in mind. A word of caution: Sooner or later, the data in a data mart will probably be of interest to persons outside the original group of users. When a data mart is built, it should consider corporate standards for hardware, software, networking, database management systems, and naming conventions. There are a few vendors and consultants who would like to get around IT by marketing directly to the end users and implementing without IT involvement. Under these conditions, a data mart may become an expensive, isolated island of information that will be inaccessible to others in the corporation. Even if a data mart is developed independently of IT, it is in the corporate interest that data be positioned for general accessibility.

Vendors have found that selling data marts directly to end users is an easy sale. Corporate IT departments should be aware of these situations and try to work directly with the vendors and users during all phases of data mart implementation. No data mart is truly isolated. Sooner or later, someone from another group will ask for data in a local data mart. If it has been implemented without regard for IT standards, it may be difficult to access the data. It is vital that data marts be built with corporate standards for hardware, operating systems, networks, databases, naming conventions, metadata, etc.

Data Flow in a Single Organization

Figure 1.3 shows the flow of data across the data stores found in many companies. Data from legacy systems must be cleansed, transformed, and integrated before it is moved into operational data stores, a data warehouse, or a data mart. The sequence in which the ODS, data marts, or data warehouses are built is optional and will depend on business requirements. A data mart is often an easy place to begin using data warehouse technology. For performance reasons, many shops try to keep only a minimum amount of data in the ODS. Data warehouses may or may not contain detail data. One problem with the classical definitions of ODS, data warehouse, and

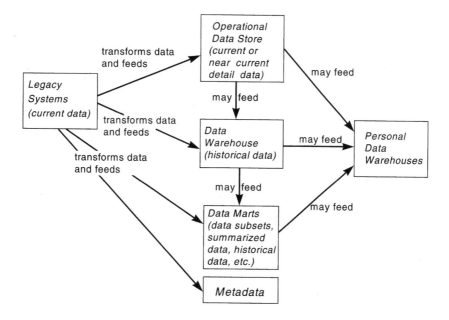

Figure 1.3   Data Flow within a Single Organization.

data mart is that detail data may be stored redundantly in all three data stores. For very large databases, redundant storage can be extremely expensive. Some shops, such as the major telecommunications firm described previously, opt to store detail data only in the ODS and place summarized data only in the data warehouse. Personal data warehouses may be fed from the ODS, data warehouse, or one or more data marts. Philosophically, data in personal data warehouses is personal in nature, and its usability and validity are controlled by the user. Although there may be automatic backups of personal data warehouses, the IT staff is not responsible for its status. Personal data is just that—personal. It should not be allowed to flow back into the other structures without IT procedures to ensure its integrity.

Need for Metadata

Users should be empowered to meet their own information needs. This requires that they know *what* data exists, *where* it is located, and *how* to access it. Legacy operational systems usually fail on this point as well. For many years, data analysts have promoted the use of dictionaries and repositories with databases that are properly designed and documented. Unfortunately, most organizations have not listened, and as a result, there is now a wealth of undocumented data in legacy systems. No matter what type of flexible query tool is provided, the tool alone is not the answer. A body of well-documented metadata is needed in addition to a tool.

SUMMARY

This chapter describes an overall architecture called the information data superstore or super data warehouse that should serve as a foundation for warehouse development. It has defined the various constructs found within that framework and noted the strategic importance of driving toward that framework in the development of operational data stores and data warehouses. Data warehousing has been described as a journey rather than a destination, and an understanding of the road map is vital to reaching that elusive destination.

REFERENCES

[1] BISCHOFF, J. and YEVICH, R., "The Superstore: Building More than a Data Warehouse." *Database Programming and Design*, September 1996.

[2] CODD, E. F., "A Relational Model for Large Shared Data Banks," *CACM,* 13, No. 6, June 1970.

[3] CODD, E. F., CODD, S., and SALLEY, C., "Providing OLAP (On-line Analytical Processing) to User-Analysts: An IT Mandate," E. F. Codd & Associates, 1993.

[4] INMON, W. H., *Building a Data Warehouse,* QED Technical Publishing Group, 1992.

[5] INMON, W. H., IMHOFF, C., and BATTAS, G., *Building the Operational Data Store,* John Wiley and Sons, New York, 1996.

[6] LADLEY, JOHN, "Operational Data Stores: Building an Effective Strategy," *Data Warehouse: Practical Advice From the Experts,* Prentice Hall, Englewood Cliffs, NJ, 1997.

A Renaissance
for Information Technology

Paul Hessinger

Vision UnlimITed
Atlanta, Georgia

> "If you have built castles in the air, your work need not be lost. That is where they should be. Now, put foundations under them."
>
> *Henry David Thoreau*

D ata warehousing is an idea whose time has come. Within the context of general business trends relative to the use of information and IT, this chapter creates a broad vision for data warehouse opportunities. The themes of strategy alignment and business intelligence are key to effective data warehouse strategies. The former provides the beginning of the business context for a data warehouse. The latter is the ultimate raison d'être for the data warehouse. Each will be discussed. This chapter also outlines some critical success factors and basic action items that should be included in a data warehouse strategy.

The chapter concludes with an emphatic process perspective, which suggests that, for many organizations, how data is viewed as a business resource and made available to knowledge workers is at least important as the technical characteristics that describe what a data warehouse is. Simply put, a data warehouse is a collection of logically related data (databases). Data warehousing is the process by which data that is important to the enterprise is identified, analyzed, collected, and made available to the enterprise. (See Chapter 1 for an in-depth definition and discussion of the term *data warehouse.*)

THE RENAISSANCE AND ITS VISIONARIES

For many IT professionals, data warehousing signifies a rebirth of interest in, if not a powerful affirmation of, the fundamental tenets of data and database management. For other IT professionals, data warehousing is the coalescence of old enterprise data architecture practices with new, multidimensonal data modeling techniques that, perhaps, more closely model how information is needed and used in the context of data-intensive business processes. For many business analysts and decision makers, a data warehouse is the product of enlightened innovation by information engineers in the IT organization who are focused on better enabling report and query/decision support/executive information systems.

A data warehouse is at the crossroads of client/server architecture and the Internet. From a home page, a knowledge worker effortlessly, if not transparently, can access a server that houses an aggregation of data, which, in turn, is refreshed on a periodic basis with data extracted from other servers and legacy databases. A renaissance is occurring that is driven by the data warehousing paradigm and is empowered by the passionate pursuit of the inter- and intranetworked enterprise by IT professionals who, whether they realize it or not, are renaissance people.

Market Leaders

For many enterprises, the renaissance is part of a (re)visioning effort in which they attempt to establish or extend market leadership. Some organizations have focused on operational excellence, product or service innovation, and customer intimacy. The experience of acknowledged market leaders, such as American Airlines, American Express, Federal Express, Sprint, WalMart, and many others, confirms that each of the aforementioned three disciplines has a powerful information technology dimension.

Data warehouses, either in conceptual terms or in implementation reality, are at the core of many market leadership efforts. Data-based projects range from specialized data boutiques on a home page on the World Wide Web (Web for short), to massive multidimensional data cubes residing on processing servers, to data mining projects that attempt to unlock secrets of market leadership by scouring the labyrinth of an enterprise's data resources.

A primary goal of a data warehouse is to increase the "intelligence" of a business process and the knowledge of workers involved in that process. The ability of product marketing executives to look at multiple dimensions of a product's sales performance—by region, by type of sales (retailer, catalog, etc.), by customer demographics—may enable better promotional efforts, increased production, or readjustments in product inventory and distribution. It can also stop the production of a product that simply is not selling. An airline conducts the vital process known as yield management by looking at time series of data about travel patterns on particular routes. That data can be blended with data on current demand for seats as well as competitive fare data. This can result in adjustments of fares of specific seats on specific flights on specific dates.

The preceding example suggests two important points. First, data warehousing is not just about open-ended, blue sky speculation. It enables an enterprise to take an a priori approach (based on experience further based on data) to pursuing operational excellence, customer intimacy, and profitability. Second, data warehouses can and should contain linkages of some form to transaction-based, operational systems. These provide a source of data for warehouses. Additionally, they are a point of impact if warehouse-based analysis indicates that the efficiency of a business process can be adjusted via an update to an operational database.

Change Masters

At the core of the renaissance in IT and effective data warehousing is the challenge of change. Rosabeth Moss Kanter, in her book *The Change Masters*,[1] provides insights into a renaissance person she describes as a "change master." A modern renaissance involves the right people in the right place at the right time. Kanter describes the right people as those "that move beyond an organization's established practices." The right places are "integrative environments that support innovation and encourage the building of coalitions to implement visions." The right times are "those moments in the flow of organizational history when it is possible to reconstruct reality on the basis of accumulated innovations to shape a more productive and successful future."

The experiences of early adopters of data warehousing point to the guiding influence of change masters. These are managers and technicians who were prepared to innovate with new technologies, such as on-line analytical processing (OLAP) tools and multidimensional databases. They were just as ready to continue employing RDBMSs as warehouses for data and time-honored methods for modeling information, such as entity-relationship (ER) models.

The change management initiative extends beyond IT and pure technology issues to the information behavior of the enterprise from a process perspective and to a broad spectrum of users of data warehouses. The phrase "a fool with a tool is still a fool" is far less a pejorative than it is a strong warning to data warehouse architects and administrators to define and manage the processes that will allow end users to articulate their information requirements as well as to access and interact with data warehouses. Within a process context, a tool becomes just that and not the equivalent of "hammer to a child, for whom the whole world is a nail." Information behavior encompasses the degree to which true sharing of information on both an intra- and interenterprise basis is encouraged—if not rewarded—by an organization. Information hoarding looms large as an obstacle to effective data warehousing and business intelligence systems.

Kantor's change masters "deal in symbols and shared understandings as well as techniques and trappings of their own specialties . . . [and] operate on a symbolic as well as a practical level choosing out of all possible 'truths' those that are needed at the moment to allow the next step to be taken, to help people operate integratively, bridging multiple realities and reconceptualizing activities to take account of new ideas." With just a modicum of reflection on the intent of object-oriented modeling and repository technologies, the value of "symbols and shared understandings" and helping "people operate integratively" suggests an alignment between renaissance attributes and enabling techniques and tools for data warehousing.

Management is at the heart of being a renaissance person, of leading an enterprise's data warehousing initiatives. What attributes define a renaissance IT person? A humanist, technologist, a visionary, a pragmatist, passionate, and a person who is analytical, ambitious, and focused on effectiveness. Those qualities must cut across job descriptions and provide common denominators for the IT professionals who will seize the day in data warehousing—from the chief information officer (CIO) to the data administrator to the information architect to the engineer to the ultimate beneficiary of an "information-at-your-fingertips" strategy. The increasingly ubiquitous enterprise knowledge worker herself or himself can participate in, if not drive, a renaissance for IT.

Informating

As a new millennium approaches, the compelling vision of "information at your fingertips" (a casual utterance of Bill Gates in the early 1990s) represents not just the potential for data warehousing. It may well be a critical success factor for enterprises that will either recognize and leverage the informating power of data resources or be left behind as an age of electronic commerce emerges, as physical marketplaces are obviated by virtual, IT-based market*spaces. Informating* can be defined as "focusing on the information dimension of any process." Automating focuses on the tasks involved in a process. It often obscures the former because of the complexities involved in computerizing a manual process. By focusing on the information dimension, without necessarily rushing to automate the process, businesses have seen data-based improvements in analysis and decision making.

An enterprise's ability to put information about its products, services, and transactions with its customers at their fingertips will provide sustainable competitive advantage and vital business intelligence for new offerings and more profitable, if not expanded, relationships with those customers. Already, data warehouses are not just enhancing internal decision support efforts but are also extending an enterprise's information value chain to external entities (i.e., customers, suppliers, etc.).

The effectiveness of IT processes for enterprise information access and decision support (informating) as well as the automation of core, transaction-intensive business processes has emerged as a critical success factor. An enterprise's ability to achieve ongoing, dynamic alignment between business and IT strategies is a clear demarcation between organizations that are using information for competitive advantage and those that are struggling to find the on-ramps to the information superhighway, let alone use information strategically. The objective of business intelligence systems is simultaneously a business issue and a technology opportunity, a logical extension of client/server architecture and a new generation of decision support systems.

Data Awareness

Data warehouses are key to an enterprise's ability for executives, business analysts, and customer service personnel to access required data for frequently encountered decision support and customer-related processes. Multidimensional views of financial information, customer demographics, buying patterns, and value/supply chain data—derived from operational databases with varying degrees of frequency and detail—provide new evidence that knowledge is power or what you don't know *can* hurt you, in competitive *dis*advantage terms. The power lies in an ability of data warehouses to structure data access that is synchronized with core, cross-functional business processes and their supporting transaction processing applications, but without putting undue performance stress on OLTP systems and their supporting databases.

A data warehouse can be tightly focused on a key performance metric, with data succinctly extracted from operational systems to give managers a strategic window through which to view that performance metric and adjust business plans and processes accordingly. Leveraging enterprise data can also involve a more broadly focused effort in which a collection of data warehouses is provided to analysts to support "what if" decision support scenarios.

In a 1993 *Harvard Business Review* article, Richard Nolan makes an analogy between commercial airlines "flying by wire" and IT organizations.[2] In today's state-of-the-art commercial airlines (e.g., Boeing 777, Airbus 340, or MD11), pilots are in effect flying an "informational representation" of the airplane. In kind, IT organizations must focus on allowing managers to "manage by wire," to manage informational representations of the enterprise. As we fly across country or across an ocean, little do we realize that data warehouses are providing the basis for high performance and safe travel and providing the ability to monitor performance data from the operating systems of the aircraft, thereby making mid-course corrections to avoid turbulence, when needed. So it is with the potential for data warehouses to support "managing by wire" by leveraging key business data.

With the growing presence of the information superhighway, enterprises are, in fact, extending the boundaries of information access to allow direct customer access to data. American Express's data warehouse, ExpressNet, is available via America Online as well as through direct connects with American Express (AmEx). ExpressNet allows card holders to view their credit card status, drill down through several levels of transaction detail, and download selected data into their own personal data warehouse in Quicken or an Excel spreadsheet. Federal Express's Internet home page and an America Online link allow a customer to check the status of a package by accessing a "package tracking data warehouse." For technical accuracy, but mindful of not being overly dogmatic, it should be pointed out that the

FedEx example is conceptually a data warehouse. For FedEx, it is an extension of their overarching commitment to the information logistics infrastructure for their core business processes. Whether or not it is really a data warehouse application is not a key point. The ability to improve the effectiveness of a business process by warehousing data, and thus by making sure that data is accessible, is the lesson to be learned as an organization defines its strategies for the effective use of data.

In both cases, as well as in many others, the bottom-line business significance to an information-at-your-fingertips capability is reduced support costs as an enterprise outsources some of its information-intensive customer support processes directly to its customers via data warehouses. Architecturally, it is important to note the relationship between the data warehouse and key OLTP systems, which are the originating source of the data. In the AmEx example, there is a more static frequency to the transfer of data between the warehouse and the operational data store. In the FedEx example, it is more a real-time and lower volume of data that each tracking request involves.

Beyond that lies a somewhat less tangible but still vital benefit of customer intimacy: using IT and data resources to make a customer feel as if he or she has a unique, personalized relationship with the vendor, a vendor that is easier to do business with in part because of an effective information exchange/access capability. Think of how easy it has become to access bank and credit account status via touch tone telephone; even the IRS provides a data warehouse to tell you the status of your tax return.

The 1995 CSC/Index Group survey of key issues clearly indicates that the number 3 issue for the 603 companies surveyed is "organizing and utilizing data." It is an essential dimension of effective customer service, order management and product distribution, and supply chain management, which were the target processes for more effective IT enablement and business process automation. Organizing and utilizing data is the essence of an enterprise data warehouse program.

REPOSITORIES

There is another, equally vital, dimension to organizing and utilizing data: repositories. Here is still another dimension of a renaissance, a rebirth of interest, and a renewed recognition of the business significance of fundamental IT processes: information resource management (IRM), or data administration.

In the early 1980s, Dr. E. F. "Ted" Codd saw the business significance of the RDBMS model.[3] Organizations were finally beginning to have strategic success in integrated transaction processing via venerable DBMS technologies such as IMS or IDMS. Just prior to the advent of IBM's DB2, Codd said, in a quiet voice that spoke volumes, "You may think that defining the meaning of data is simple, *but it is not.*" Unfortunately, that subtle exhortation fell on many deaf ears as organizations presumed that the apparent simplicity of the relational model would, in turn, simplify defining the meaning of data.

In another compelling *Harvard Business Review* article, Thomas Davenport signals the critical nature of data. He writes, "Technocratic solutions often specify the minutiae of automation machinery while disregarding how people actually go about acquiring, sharing and making use of information."[4] He further elaborated that "the problem of multiple information meanings may indicate a healthy rebirth of interest in information management."[5]

Fundamentally, as both these eminent industry gurus suggest, it is an issue of managing metadata—the meanings (the plural is important) and interrelationships of key business data—at the core of business processes. Without a repository and a repository management program (i.e., data administration), Codd's observations represent a sink hole that will work against the success, if not ensure the failure of, data warehouses that allow business users to utilize data that is well defined, organized, and managed.

Data management is the foundation of an enterprise's information value chain. The repository is an essential aspect of effective data warehousing. Repository management becomes a key IT process for organizing and utilizing metadata in support of data warehouse and more traditional application development projects. Metadata warehouses hold the key to the enterprise context and information content of core business processes. Repositories provide the basis for managed connectivity between processes, tools, and databases. The metadata warehouse is the core of a data logistics system, the infrastructure for an enterprise's data warehouses, and, ultimately, an enterprise's business intelligence systems.

A repository is a collection of "artifacts," the objects of fundamental importance to automating and informating key business processes. Object modeling methods and tools are providing more effective, more integrated ways of representing data and process models. The repository is the storage point for these models. It is also the data store for the technical definitions of the data and process (metadata) that allow the object models to be translated into design specifications for applications. Whether the applications are enabled with object-oriented (OO) technology or powerful reporting and query tools for advanced decision support systems, the repository provides the coordination point for an enterprise's data resources.

Still dubious about the value of repositories? Think about walking into a library with a topic in mind but no specific book that addresses it—or with a specific book but without all the metadata. Think about how easy the "card file"—a repository—makes it to find the book.

In a more commercial context, consider the *Official Airlines Guide (OAG)*, which has built its business by building and selling a data warehouse and a repository at the same time. Data is drawn from the monthly operational schedules of commercial airlines, which define the data needed to plan and book an air travel itinerary. Today, access to the *OAG* comes in hard copy and electronic copy, via touch tone telephone or downloaded to a workstation. Electronic commerce is an effective approach for making data a source of revenue. From retail to financial services, the marketplace abounds with examples of how being "data aware" can lead to data as a "ware" through access to data warehouses.

IT organizations are finding that data warehouses provide a powerful enabler of business process (re)engineering. One example is the case study of how AT&T successfully reengineered its billing process by applying information quality principles and establishing information warehouses to make the billing process more information based, responsive, and accurate.[6]

Max Hopper, retired CIO of AMR (the parent company of American Airlines), writes in a 1995 *Computerworld* editorial,

> The specter of entropy casts a dark shadow over the efficient flow of information. . . . It's time to reexamine the very fabric of our companies' business information—the data elements from which it is derived. That involves revising the enterprise data dictionary to establish a unique one-to-one correspondence between the term we use to describe a data element and the meaning related to a key attribute of our business. . . . Perhaps the awareness that some companies at the cutting edge of IT [information technology] are honing their data dictionaries will inspire others to sharpen their data saws.[7]

At the cutting edge of managing and leveraging business data lies the emerging power of data warehousing technology. Organizing and utilizing metadata is a critical success factor for an enterprise's data warehouse strategy. Nolan, in "Managing by Wire," emphasizes the business significance and architectural importance of managing metadata using objectories and making "information at your fingertips" a reality by building and deploying data warehouses.

> Like a plane at mach speed, a company must be able to respond to threats in real time. Top managers have to view information and IT in a new light. Rather than investing in isolated IT systems—such as e-mail, reservation systems or inventory control systems—a company must invest in IT capabilities that enable it to "manage by wire." The ideal implementation uses an enterprise model to represent the operations of the entire business.

In other words, the repository is used to store and manage an ever-changing enterprise model and the data warehouse is used to organize and make available business data.

A STRATEGY FOR BUILDING A DATA WAREHOUSE

An organization's size is not among the criteria that determine the need for data warehousing. Before your organization launches into developing and implementing a data warehouse, begin the process by evaluating your enterprise against a set of key indicators.

Need Indicators

- The organization is in a changing, highly competitive marketspace.
- There is the desire to be well informed about and intimate with customers.

- There are opportunities for information-based products or services that can generate revenue and/or improve efficiency.
- Commonly used and related enterprise data is stored in many different places and systems.
- The organization is plagued by the "same-data-only-different" syndrome.
- True decision support systems are required.
- Users want more effective ad hoc data querying and reporting.
- There is a need for an information logistics infrastructure.

Action Steps

If most or all of the aforementioned key factors apply to your organization, it is time to take action.

- Verse management and its clients in the trends and directions of other organizations. Emphasize the importance of organizing and utilizing data to support cross-functional systems that provide linkages with customers and suppliers in the context of overall information.
- Develop a visionary-oriented mission statement for a data warehouse program. Include specific considerations to support the mission statement. Look for immediate, relatively narrow "proof of concept" opportunities that are tightly aligned with key enterprise goals.
- Revitalize and reskill the data administration function. Establish a strong and ongoing information architecture that explicitly recognizes the fundamental importance of data but also provides a business process context for the use of that data in strategic informating activities. A data architecture is an essential part of the overall architecture that defines the blueprints for various data warehouse implementations, ranging from a data warehouse that actually supports an operation to massive, multidimensional "data cubes" that support "what if" analyses and decision support.
- Adopt object-oriented business process modeling methods and tools and draft an object repository, or objectory (an extension of the repository concept that is more an object management and configuration management tool than just a metadata storage point), foundation for the storage and management of the metadata and process definitions that object models represent. Link the use of the objectory to other key IT processes, such as application development, application/system management, and, of course, data warehouse projects.
- Define a portfolio of tools that will provide reporting, querying, and decision support system (DSS) functions and executive information system (EIS) applications that will access data warehouses. In today's market, there is a significant amount of overlap among these tools (some are true functional overlaps, others are "marketecture or brochureware"). Apply performance modeling tools to client/server deployment of specific data warehouse projects that look

at network bandwidth and data staging frequencies in particular. Do not forget to manage expectations; database sizes and access volumes are often underestimated and can cause user dissatisfaction.

Realistic vision with a pragmatic business rationale for a data warehouse project is the first key to success. Having a common data vocabulary throughout the enterprise is essential; define the meanings of key business entities, such as customers and revenue. These terms do not and should not have to mean just one thing. There must be an enterprise focus on effective information behavior, which most often is manifested (either well or poorly) in terms of how information is presented and how it is shared. Multidimensional, object-oriented thinking about the business must be encouraged. The use of automated modeling tools in the context of joint application design (JAD) sessions with the target users of data warehouses will facilitate this as well as assist in understanding and architecting the data to be stored in a warehouse. An "always-complete-yet-never-done" esprit de corps should dominate the actual construction and deployment of a data warehouse. The incremental, iterative evolution of a data warehouse is key to its sustained efficacy.

A Process Framework for Data Warehousing

Increasing user experience with data warehouses suggests that the data warehousing process perspective is a dominant one in successful projects. The process framework has three fundamental tenets (see Figure 2.1):

1. A business process and the accompanying information subject(s) provide the context for a specific data warehousing project
2. The project is initiated with a clear business value proposition with a statement of expectation(s) for both tangible and intangible benefits to be achieved. The value proposition is authored by an executive who ideally is the owner of the target business process and who becomes the chief advocate of the project.
3. The target user community for the data warehouse is clearly identified so that within the process the users' current information behavior can be modeled and their basic requirements for one or more business intelligence tool(s) can be defined early in the process.

The process assumes that there is some form of an enterprise data architecture that provides a content framework for data warehousing projects. At the base technology level, RDBMSs provide the physical housing of operational databases and often informational data warehouses. Database management system technology is the linkage between data architecture and infrastructure technology. The infrastructure provides metadata management via repository technology, which plays an integral role at each stage of the model/build/deploy process.

It is imperative that a broader perspective on the infrastructure be established early in the data warehousing effort. At a high level this includes middleware to

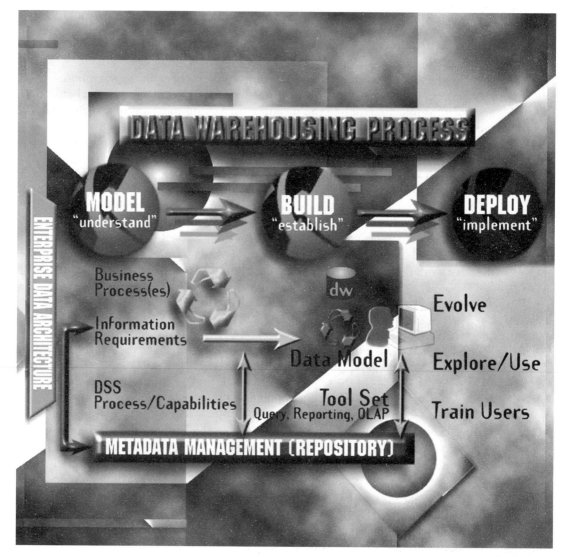

Figure 2.1

provide connectivity between the data warehouse(s) and applications such as OLAP and EIS. Additionally, the infrastructure would include data cleansing, extraction, and movement tools. These tools come in various forms and can be tightly related to the RDBMS platform or extensions of a repository solution. Other technologies, such as a help desk, should be incorporated into the support infrastructure.

A Charter for the Data Warehousing Effort

With the established framework and foundation components, a three-stage data warehousing process is summarized as follows:

- *Model.* In the simplest terms, take the time to understand a business process, the information requirements of that process, and the decisions that are currently made within that process (i.e., information behavior).
- *Build.* Establish requirements for tools that suit the types of decision support that the targeted business process involves and a data model that helps further define information requirements. Then decompose them into data specifications and the actual data store, which represents either a data mart or a more comprehensive data warehouse.
- *Deploy.* Implement relatively early in the overall process the nature of the data to be warehoused and the various business intelligence tools to be employed; begin with training users. The deploy stage explicitly contains a time during which users explore both the repository (to understand data that is and should be available) and early versions of the actual data warehouse. This can lead to an evolution of the data warehouse, which involves adding more data, perhaps extending historical periods from which data is extracted, or returning to the build stage to expand the scope of the data warehouse through the data model.

Therefore, an effective data warehousing process involves context, content, and coordination. Figure 2.2 summarizes some of the key points within the model/build/deploy process, which focuses on these three issues.

IBM, seldom given credit for being an innovative organization, in "Information Warehouse Framework" (IBM announcement letter 291-471, September 11, 1991) announced its product strategy and provided compelling content for a data warehouse mission statement.

> Today ... IBM introduces ... a set of database management systems, interfaces, tools and facilities that manage and deliver reliable, timely, accurate and understandable business information to authorized individuals for business decision making. Products ... provide access to data wherever it is located in the enterprise, on IBM systems or on systems from other vendors.
>
> First steps ... determine what data to make available to knowledge workers ... [and] require a careful inventory of data currently held by the enterprise, [and determine] new data that can be derived. ... The success ... depends on the degree to which it captures and synthesizes the significant data activity of the entire enterprise. ... It requires a coherent business model ... [and] the very act of researching and creating the model may bring to light problem areas which when corrected will lead to greater enterprise efficiency. ... A methodology is essential.

Effectiveness of The Data Warehousing Process - Key Points.....

References: Peter Drucker's "Effectiveness is 'Doing the Right Things Right'"; Stephen Covey's "7 Habits of Highly Effective People"

"Begin with the end in mind; Put first things first"

CONTEXT

- A data warehouse project *must* be aligned with relatively specific business objectives with at least a basic 'estimate' of the business value that will be created by the project
  - ◆ Tangible benefits such as reduced customer service costs from allowing customers to directly access data in a warehouse
  - ◆ Less tangible benefits such as more rapid and/or accurate decision making
- An Enterprise Data Architecture provides the context for mapping data to and across core business processes supported by a data warehouse
- Encourage multidimensional 'thinking' about information related to cross-functional business processes

"Be proactive ; Seek first to understand then to be understood"

CONTENT

- Do *not* begin the information and data modeling effort by asking 'what data' the user(s) want - ask about the 'metrics' and/or decision making/analytical criteria that data is required to support
- Establish the value of metadata and a repository to the end user(s) *early* in the process
- Focus on a common vocabulary for the business processes and the information objects/entities that will be described by data in both the repository and the warehouse(s)
  - e.g. : defition(s) of revenue may vary based upon the user and business process referencing 'revenue' (a repository supports this) and based upon whether marketing or financial data (which warehouse)is required
- Emphasize an iterative approach to modeling the data and building the warehouse... *an 'always complete yet never finished' mindset*

"Synergize; Continuously sharpen the saw"

COORDINATION

- Data Administration must play an influential role at every stage of the process coordinating the technical and non-technical efforts in deploying a data warehouse that provides the right content in the right business process context to the right users at the right times
- An effective data warehouse project is NOT about choosing the 'right' tool; however, effective tools are a critical success factor and end users need to be involved in selecting the tool(s) that are most appropriate to the information retrieval/analysis/decision support that a data warehouse will support (one data warehouse may be more focused on one of those three tasks and the choice of a tool should reflect that - i.e. basic query versus report writer versus an OLAP tool)
- Train users early in the process in both the metadata and tools

Figure 2.2 Effectiveness of the Data Warehousing Process.

Therein lies the opportunity and the challenge in pursuit of aligning business strategies with data warehousing strategies to achieve true and effective business intelligence for the virtual enterprise in the new millennium.

SUMMARY

A renaissance is under way, driven by continued advances in IT. The Web best symbolizes these advances. From a business perspective, the value of information is rivaling the value of tangible products and services as the virtual enterprise moves rapidly from vision to reality. Data warehousing provides a catalyst for aligning what the business needs in an information strategy with what IT can actually produce. A data warehousing process framework was provided; for many organizations, a similar process has amounted to a cathartic experience. It can be a powerful force in transforming bold visions into solid realities.

Data warehousing is a journey. Look toward the end of the journey, but seize the day in terms of the tremendous opportunities that today's technologies afford for putting information at the fingertips of knowledge workers and customers anywhere at any time. Never lose the renaissance perspective that applies so well to data warehousing: The journey *is* the reward.

REFERENCES

[1] KANTER, ROSABETH MOSS, *The Change Masters: Innovation for Productivity in the American Corporation*, New York, Simon & Schuster, 1983.

[2] NOLAN, RICHARD, " Managing by Wire," *Harvard Business Review*, September-October 1993, p. 122.

[3] CODD, E. F., *The Business Significance of the Relational Model,* Midwest DB/DC Users Group Conference, Chicago, October, 1981.

[4] DAVENPORT, THOMAS, "Saving IT's Soul: Human-centered Information Management," *Harvard Business Review*, March-April 1994, p. 119.

[5] DAVENPORT, THOMAS, "Saving IT's Soul: Human-centered Information Management," *Harvard Business Review*, March-April 1994, p. 122.

[6] STEPHEN COVEY, *Seven Habits of Highly Effective People,* New York, Fireside Press, Simon & Schuster, 1990.

[7] MAX HOPPER, "Time to Sharpen the Saw," *Computerworld*, February 20, 1995, p. 95.

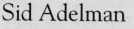

Organizational and Cultural Issues

Sid Adelman

Sid Adelman and Associates
Sherman Oaks, California

"A good way for ineffective people to cling to power in an organization is by creating a monopoly on information."

Scott Adams, The Dilbert Principle

There are few guarantees in life, but the failure to address the organizational and cultural issues that are imposed by the data warehouse is guaranteed to result in failure. Unfortunately, the existing conditions in most IT organizations are not favorable to the success of the data warehouse.

THE CURRENT SITUATION

Most organizations do not understand the value of their own data; the problem is not confined to IT. Because the value is not recognized, access to the data is not provided. Data is an extremely valuable asset, but only if it is used.

Responsibility for the quality of data often is not identified. IT frequently abdicates responsibility, assuming that users have the sole charge. Users naively believe that IT will keep them from entering incorrect data. Data quality is a topic that is rarely addressed in a serious and comprehensive manner. (For more information on data quality, see Chapter 10).

Most IT shops do not have an organization in place with either the skills or assigned responsibilities that would support the data warehouse. For example, few installations have the data dictionary/repository skills and people to support the data warehouse. Most IT installations are not aware of the resources to support the data warehouse. These resources include people, software, hardware, and infrastructure. When estimates have been calculated, many important resources are overlooked or not mentioned for fear of driving up the cost estimates.

Data is not shared or is only shared reluctantly. Users often feel that the data that supports their activity is their own province. Withholding data may give them power that they only share reluctantly. The decision not to share data is often justified by stories of data that has been misused or misinterpreted by those outside a department.

Users understand their data to varying degrees. Data is often poorly documented, so although some users may have an instinctive understanding of the data, these instincts are not prevalent and not consistent even across their own department.

Reports are inconsistent, and the effort to resolve the disparity among reports is both time consuming and frustrating. This problem is found at all levels in the organization up to and including the board of directors. It has been reported that boards of directors spend time arguing over reports that disagree. These disparities are often the result of inconsistencies in data definitions, timing (e.g., does the term *month-end* mean the last Friday in the month or the last day of the month?), the correction of known errors that appear in some reports and not in others, and special spins put on the data to enhance departmental results. The net result of lack of understanding and inconsistent reports is that users do not trust their reports or the underlying data. This results in time wasted verifying the reports or a key decision not made due to concern over the validity of the data supporting the decision.

Finally, many enterprises continue to be organizationally challenged. The same factors that result in a failure to deliver quality operational systems will often mean that data warehouse projects will also fail. However, the data warehouse is somewhat less complex than operational systems, and a clever project manager may be able to insulate the data warehouse project from a dysfunctional IT department.

CULTURAL IMPERATIVES

For the data warehouse to be successful, certain conditions must be in place. It is the users who must choose the data they need. While IT may facilitate the process, the users must determine which columns, which rows, what timeliness, what aggregation, what historical data, and what derived data they need. The data warehouse cannot be static. The architecture of the data warehouse must be flexible enough to incorporate requirements not included in initial phases as well as requirements users have not yet dreamed of.

The users must trust the data, but this trust can only come from their own verification of the data. This trust, if it does develop, will come slowly and will be accompanied by a move to a mindset of quality in both the user and IT camps. This mind-set will include the understanding that quality is everyone's business and must be addressed at every step of development and operation.

User expectations must be clearly understood and documented. These expectations include response time, scheduled completion dates, what data users will have available to them, ease of access, and the level of help users should expect from IT. These expectations should also address how much involvement is required from the user departments. Dates and capabilities should never be promised if they cannot be delivered.

SUCCESS CRITERIA

There are at least ten criteria for success in data warehousing:

1. The data warehouse must be able to satisfy the users' requirements, even when they are unable to articulate their needs.
2. The data warehouse must make a significant contribution to the success of the business (e.g., better decision making that results in more sales, higher productivity, and greater profit).
3. The organization must have the ability to establish project governance. In an environment where the data warehouse is seen to be effective there will always be too many projects demanding attention and priorities must be cleverly determined.
4. The data warehouse is perceived by upper management as making a significant contribution to the business (if management does not recognize the benefits, the data warehouse will be a failure).
5. The users embrace the system and actively use it (the best data warehouse in the world is worthless if the users never access it).
6. The benefits are not exceeded by the costs.
7. An adequate budget must be in place. The data warehouse does not come cheap. The funds must be in place to staff the project, to purchase some new software and hardware, and to provide adequate training for both IT and to the users.
8. The proper skills must be in place and must be dedicated to the data warehouse project.
9. The implementation of the data warehouse must not cause other problems that overshadow the benefits (e.g., severely affecting the performance of critical on-line systems).
10. A reasonable schedule must be established. A successful project is one that is completed on schedule. Too often, inadequate time is allotted for a data warehouse project, especially considering that some activities are being performed for the first time.

ORGANIZATION ROLES AND RESPONSIBILITIES

The data warehouse implementation team should have a good reputation with both IT and the users, a reputation earned from the successful delivery of other systems. Members of this team must also have a good relationship with the users. Otherwise the users will give them neither the time nor the right people necessary to make the project a success.

Definitions of roles and responsibilities are important only in that all the required roles are understood and assigned. Assignments can easily be forgotten or overlooked. The designations in this section are only a sample. Organizations will want to change these assignments and the names of the roles to correspond to those within their enterprise, but in the process they will want to be assured that all roles are assigned and that overlapping responsibilities are clearly understood and the primary responsibility identified. However, a title alone is not sufficient. Each of these roles requires significant training and experience. A number of these roles will appear in more than one functional area, indicating a potential for joint responsibility.

End User (Client)

The following is a true story. A large manufacturer developed a data warehouse but chose not to involve the end users. IT implemented a large, robust database brimming with data with excellent access potential through state-of-the-art front-end query tools. The missing components were the end users. There were no queries generated outside the IT department. Since the users were not involved, they were not interested in what was perceived to be an IT project.

Users will have different levels of interest in writing their own queries. Some will be anxious to write queries, while others will only use predefined or canned queries. The organization must decide who will write the initial predefined queries as well as new predefined queries, but these queries are usually written by power users, user liaisons, end-user support, and IT application developers.

End users must be sold on the data warehouse and on accepting the following responsibilities:

- Identify data requirements (this is not a one-time process).
- Provide data definitions.
- Own the data—be responsible for determining security, access, update capability, required levels of availability and performance.
- Perform governance to identify priorities for implementation.
- Determine the form of the data (detailed, summarized, aggregated, derived, and historical).
- Validate the quality of data under end-user ownership.
- Validate the accuracy of reports and queries produced from the data warehouse.
- Identify transformation rules for data migrating from legacy systems to the data warehouse.

Strategic Architecture

Strategic architecture may be seen as apart from the data warehouse projects and not necessary for the initial data warehouse implementation. In fact, its role may be critical for long-term success. Data warehouse is not just an isolated delivery of a data warehouse subject area, but it involves how access to data supports the overall goals of the enterprise. As such, strategic architecture would have the following responsibilities:

- Determine and validate the goals and objectives of the data warehouse and assure that they conform to the goals and objectives of the enterprise.
- Develop the data warehouse architecture, including standards, products, and suites of tools.
- Set priorities based on the strategic direction of the organization.

Data Warehouse Project Manager

There are those on the turnip truck who feel that the technology is all that is needed for success, that a data warehouse project should manage itself. Those with some experience understand that a project manager is crucial. The project manager should be well connected, have a good track record, and have experience in managing projects. His or her job would include the following:

- Assume overall responsibility for the data warehouse.
- Estimate the costs and benefits of the data warehouse.
- Act as a quality reviewer throughout the project.
- Help with project planning, determining deliverables, and establishing time frames.
- Plan for the integration of the data from other (and future) operational systems into the data warehouse.
- Plan for the incorporation and integration of external data sources.
- Measure the benefits of the data warehouse, measure the cost, and provide management with information on cost justification.
- Make recommendations on ways to improve the data warehouse.

User Liaison

The user liaison could come from either IT or from the user departments. The job of the user liaison may vary, depending on personal background. The most successful user liaison usually has a mix of both backgrounds. The user liaisons will work closely with the project team in four major areas of responsibility:

1. Gather requirements from end users.
   - Identify subject areas (financial, human resources, customer services, regional data, etc.).
   - Determine the client set for each subject area—who will be accessing each subject area.
   - Identify data requirements for each subject area.
   - Identify new data requirements.
   - Determine the form of the data (detailed, summarized, aggregated, derived, or historical).
   - Validate the quality of data.
   - Identify transformation rules for the data coming from the legacy systems.
   - Perform governance to identify priorities for implementation.
2. Monitor the implementation of the data warehouse infrastructure.
   - Provide clients' requirements for the selection of the required architecture for the data warehouse environment.
   - Help with project planning, determining deliverables, and establishing time frames.
   - Help establish criteria for end-user query tool selection.
   - Participate in training clients in the use of query tools.
   - Educate new clients in the existence and content of existing data warehouse data.
   - Identify data inconsistencies and establish processes to resolve the inconsistencies.
   - Communicate new requirements to IT.
3. Work to improve data quality.
   - Provide definitions of data.
   - Identify data quality problems, redundancies, inconsistencies, and their sources.
   - Communicate programming change requirements to IT that would improve data quality.
4. Perform acceptance testing—are the front-end tools, canned queries, client query environment, and so on performing as expected and producing accurate results?

End-User Support

End-user support must understand that not all users have the same computer desires or capabilities. Users run the gamut from power users to PC novices, and the different levels of users must be dealt with differently. Condescension is not appreciated by the power users, and the novices must be sensitively taught to use the system. If they are thrown into the pool without learning to swim or without a life jacket, they will not drown, but the system will.

End-user support is the most visible group encountered by the end users. If this encounter is not satisfactory, the end users will stop using the system and the data warehouse will be failure. End-user support must be at the proper level so that users will not be discouraged because there is no one to answer their questions or to help them through a difficult problem. This role is often demeaned and dismissed as an unimportant help desk function. With the data warehouse, this role needs to include far more capabilities and responsibilities:

- Manage and administer query libraries.
- Evaluate front-end query tools.
- Monitor query performance.
- Train end users—determine training requirements, evaluate training delivery options and schedules, coordinate and administer classes and teach classes, and create manuals (handbooks, reference guide, user manuals for accessing data).
- Provide a help desk, supporting the standard end-user query tools.
- Perform acceptance testing—are the front-end tools, canned queries, client query environment, and so on performing as expected and producing accurate results?
- Create canned queries.
- Coordinate the integration of tools, software, and operating systems (e.g., spreadsheets, Windows, end-user query tools).
- Install and replicate desktop computers, front-end tools, middleware, and support software, including spreadsheets and operating systems.
- Understand the data in the data warehouse.
- Complete familiarity with the query tools.

Data Administration

Data administration (DA) has not had much influence in most IT organizations in the United States, but the data warehouse suggests a number of new responsibilities for which DA is uniquely qualified, which gives, DA the opportunity to make a major contribution to the entire enterprise. The data warehouse may breathe new life into this important but unappreciated job. The ultimate success of the data warehouse will, in large part, be determined by how well DA carries out the following roles and responsibilities:

- Consult with project teams modeling data warehouse data and modeling legacy data.
- Model the data.
- Ensure the quality and integrity of the data warehouse model.
- Align data warehouse information requirements with data warehouse models.
- Manage the models.
- Provide internal support and vendor management of the data modeling tool.

- Administer, manage, and control the repository, including who is allowed to access, update, create, and delete repository objects.
- Handle the process of bringing the metadata from the data models into the repository.
- Provide internal support and vendor management of the repository.
- Interface with the DBA, including keeping the logical and physical models synchronized.
- Facilitate joint end-user/IT data modeling sessions to determine data warehouse requirements.
- Be jointly responsible, with application development, for the selection of which legacy data to use when there are multiple sources.
- Handle both internal support and vendor management of the repository.

Data Analyst

The data analyst could come from application development, or this could be a sub-role of data administration. In either case, the following roles are important and need to be performed:

- Act as a technical design specialist.
- Build business rules into data warehouse tools.
- Look for opportunities for reuse and integration of data.
- Map operational data to data warehouse models.
- Build and implement data and metadata into the data warehouse.

Application Developer

Application development often is most familiar with the source data and so should be heavily involved with identifying source data. While the migration and transformation tool vendors represent that this process requires little, if any, application programming involvement, experience has shown that, except for trivial transformations, serious application code needs to be written. The following are roles that application development would perform:

- Participate in determining the meaning of each data source and the meaning of each data warehouse column.
- Write the more complex queries that are beyond the capabilities of end users.
- Feed information back to application development on what the data warehouse could provide as a source of data for operational reports.
- Identify what data should be migrated to the data warehouse.
- Assess the current systems' data.
- Develop and maintain models of business requirements.

- Be responsible for computation formulas in the transformation process.
- Be jointly responsible, with data administration, for the selection of which legacy data to use when there are multiple sources.

Security Office

Many organizations have an office or group responsible for security. The data warehouse presents many old security capabilities as well as a number of new security options and challenges—the challenge is to make information easily available to the right people and to restrict unauthorized access. Security options (imbedded in most of the software that will be used in the data warehouse) are only effective if they are understood and properly selected and implemented. The security office would have responsibility for the following:

- Educate users on the need for security and help them understand their role in establishing security requirements.
- Determine who should have authority to read, create, update, and delete specific data.
- Establish strategies, design approaches to security, develop policies, and implement security procedures.
- Determine the security requirement.
- Explore the security capabilities of the DBMS and strategize the implementation of various security options with DBA.
- Explore the security capabilities of the end-user query tools and strategize about security options with end-user support (or the owner of the front-end tool).
- Explore the security capabilities of the migration tool and repository and application development tools, and strategize about security options.
- Administer security procedures (granting and revoking authority).

For more information on security, see Chapter 26.

Database Administration

Most of the roles and responsibilities of the DBA are not a departure from traditional functions, but the amount of work is significant—especially as the databases get very large and are distributed and as performance becomes a problem. It is not that they do not know how to do the work, it is just that the quantity of work is substantively greater. The roles and responsibilities for the DBA include the following:

- Interface with DA, including keeping the logical and physical models synchronized.
- Generate the physical database design for the data warehouse.
- Participate in migrating data from the legacy systems to the data warehouse.

- Responsible data warehouse performance.
- Monitor database performance:
  - Database tuning
  - SQL tuning in combination with end-user query tool tuning
  - Resource control in the DBMS (governor)
  - Database reorganization
- Handle database backup and recovery.
- Implement database security (the information on what security to administer would come from the security office, which would also determine access to databases).
- Responsible for distributing data and deploy distributed data warehouses.
- Manage the DBMS vendor.
  - Determine the best use of the product
  - Deal with software problems
- Understand how the end-user query tool accesses the DBMS. In so doing, deal with performance and usability/productivity issues.

For more information on database administration, see Chapter 25.

Technical Services

Since the data warehouse will, most likely, be accessed over a network, the network administrator would be responsible for network design and for the performance and availability of the network. For convenience, network design and administration have been included in technical services.

Technical services is responsible for establishing the infrastructure that is the foundation for building the other data warehouse components. There are seven major roles in the creation of the data warehouse infrastructure:

1. Establish data warehouse technical architecture in conjunction with other groups.
   - DBMS evaluation of each hardware and software platform
   - Utility evaluation and selection (e.g., performance monitoring)
   - Tools validation
   - Warehouse management
     - Migration tools
     - Repository
   - Evaluation of end-user query tools
   - Investigation of new technologies
   - Integration of data warehouse software
   - Validation of existing architecture
2. Develop capacity plans.
   - Network
   - Servers

- Platforms
- DBMS
- DASD

3. Monitor performance.
   - Network
   - Servers
     - Platforms
     - DBMS
     - DASD
   - Evaluate query performance.
   - Monitor compliance with performance service-level agreement.

4. Develop contingency plans for disaster recovery and monitor availability.
   - Network
   - Server
     - Platform
     - DBMS
     - DASD
   - Monitor compliance with availability service-level agreement.

5. Recommend approaches to network connectivity.
   - Network protocols
   - Client to server gateway

6. Manage installation and maintenance.
   - Hardware
   - System software

7. Perform acceptance testing—are the front-end tools, canned queries, client query environment, and so on performing as expected and producing accurate results?

The large number of roles may give the reader the impression that hordes of workers are necessary to implement the data warehouse. In fact, the most successful projects have been executed by a small team of people who are smart, trained in their respective roles, motivated, dedicated to the data warehouse project, and well managed.

CHOOSING THE INITIAL DATA AND DEPARTMENT

The rule of thumb is that if the first project is successful, there will be an opportunity for a second project. If the first is a failure, the second project manager may have a chance to resurrect the data warehouse project.

The most important contributor to success is the frame of mind of the department manager whose department will be using the system. The ideal candidate is a person who is accepting of problems and setbacks, takes them in stride, and does not use these problems as an excuse to kill the project. This candidate also understands the benefits of data warehouse, understands the costs and resources that must be devoted to the project, and is already planning how his or her department will use the system.

The project itself should be of a reasonable size, large enough that the organization can learn from the experience and large enough that the results will not be discounted. It is important that the initial project makes a significant contribution to the business. It should be neither a throwaway nor simply a proof of concept. It should *mean* something.

The first project should be one that anticipates significant use. It is impossible to guess the usage in a decision support environment, but it is possible to know that a system will serve no useful purpose, that only one or two people will ever be interested in using it, or that its ongoing cost may be prohibitive. Avoid systems that are useless, unpopular, and not cost effective.

Now for a reality check. Politics usually force the choice of a first project. The project manager rarely has the latitude to choose the first project. In fact, the data warehouse project team is often forced to implement multiple subject areas concurrently.

ESTABLISHING AN INFRASTRUCTURE

A data warehouse requires certain additional software, procedures, organization, and management attention. Some of this infrastructure can be developed as the data warehouse is being implemented; others are best to have in place early on.

The first component (usually not included in an infrastructure) is management commitment. Along with this commitment comes budget and the allocation of scarce resources (excellent people are the most scarce). Management commitment from the users includes access to key personnel, without whom it would be impossible to understand user information requirements.

A key component of the infrastructure is the architecture, the blueprint, the strategy that defines how the various components of the data warehouse will be selected, used, controlled, and fit together. This architecture includes the use of a data dictionary/repository and data modeling and the incorporation of data standards.

While a primary goal of the data warehouse is easy access to enterprise data, the goal must be tempered with controls that only allow access to data by authorized personnel. Data warehousing has the potential for serious and widespread data security violations. Security procedures assume that data has been categorized and ownership has been established. Security also demands that access correctly differentiates between detailed and summarized data. The distribution of data exacerbates the problem even more. As part of the infrastructure, security requirements and the administration of security must be firmly in place.

The infrastructure must provide for user friendly access to data. This would be a combination of a user friendly front end, good training, predefined queries, and a strong support structure that would help the user in times of trouble.

It is critical for the organization to know how well the data warehouse is performing and who is using it (who, how much, which data). Performance measurements can provide the information to tune the system and thus help provide acceptable performance. The usage data can tell departmental management if and how well the system is being used.

TRAINING USERS

Training for users will include some or all of the following:

- Front-end query tools
- Understanding of the data
- Use of the data dictionary/repository
- Use of data models
- Use of predefined queries
- Development of ad hoc queries
- Procedures to request data that have not yet been loaded into the data warehouse
- Organizational structure and support (getting help)
- Testing procedures for queries.

Described as just-in-time training, training should be scheduled just prior to the users getting their hands on the system. If much time goes by between the training and availability, users will lose both knowledge and enthusiasm.

It has been shown that when users understand the data being used in the workshops (where they get hands-on training), they identify more easily with the concepts and learn better. If their own data (i.e., the data from their own department) is used, they move to the front of their chairs and are intent on learning a capability that gives them access to their data.

While it is more costly and labor intensive, some organizations have successfully used mentors during workshops. Mentors have been assigned to each student and were able to answer questions as they arose. This process kept the students more focused and led to better-trained users. This technique also helped the users bond with individuals from IT.

CHANGE IN THE POWER STRUCTURE

The data warehouse will result in a change in the organization's power structure, especially within IT. While the implementation of the data warehouse should result in an increase in prestige and position for IT, any change will invariably result in someone losing power. Those expecting to lose power will probably fight any change and may fight the data warehouse itself.

The group most likely to lose power is application development. Some of their functions, such as providing reports for the users, could be drastically diminished. Depending on the new organization, their liaison relationship with the users could also be impacted. End users may now turn to others in the organization for answers.

ISSUES TO BE RESOLVED

For the data warehouse to be successful, some key issues must be resolved:

- Is the value of information understood? If information is not perceived as important, no budget or other resources will be assigned to the project.
- Are departments willing to share data? The data warehouse can be implemented in a nonsharing environment, but the benefits to the enterprise will be far less than in an organization where departments access the same data. A sharing environment usually requires the availability of metadata that accurately defines the data's meaning. Sharing also means far fewer extract and load programs and less DASD dedicated to the data warehouse.
- Has the data warehouse been justified? This means measuring costs and benefits and selling and reselling the data warehouse internally.

Specific Steps

While no environment is perfect, there are a number of problem conditions that could spell doom for the data warehouse. However, there are a number of specific steps that can be taken to mitigate existing problem conditions.

If the mission and the objectives for the data warehouse have not been defined, identify the sponsor of the data warehouse, insist (strongly recommend) that the mission and objectives be defined prior to any serious activity, and develop a sample set of missions and objectives and propose this to the data warehouse sponsor.

The mission and objectives of the data warehouse may not map to those of the enterprise. If there are no explicit enterprise objectives, there are probably assumed objectives to which most people in the enterprise would subscribe. These should be documented and mapped to the data warehouse objectives. If enterprise objectives exist but the data warehouse does not support them, rethink the goals and objectives of the data warehouse.

If the skills are not in place to support the data warehouse, define the functional responsibilities of data administrators, database administrators, application developers, and user liaisons. Define the skill levels required for each of these positions. Sell management on the need to have skilled people on the data warehouse team and sell management on the need to have these people sufficiently dedicated to the project.

If an adequate budget has not been allocated, compile industry publications, presentations, etc. that indicate what a data warehouse will normally cost. Watch out for those who give figures for selected subsets of the effort or who disregard costs assumed by non-IT departments. Itemize each of the project's costs. Do not pad the numbers, but do not underestimate just because the true cost may paralyze management. If the numbers are too high, consider a smaller project or one that does not require big-ticket items (e.g., a new DBMS, other expensive software, or major new hardware).

If there is no strong, well-placed, and reasonable user sponsor, go slowly, make a list of sponsors that match the aforementioned criteria, and put the strongest ones on top. Research their decision support requirements and determine which problems could be well served by the data warehouse. Invite sponsor 1 to lunch, sell that user on the data warehouse, outline what would be needed from that sponsor and from his or her department, and ask for that person's sponsorship. If sponsor 1 is not agreeable, invite sponsor 2. When only *The User From Hell* is left, stop and do something else.

If the primary users of the data warehouse are not computer literate, budget more money for user support. Allow more time for the target volumes to be achieved and readjust expectations for success. Revamp the training so as not to frighten the students. Provide mentors in the training process. Develop a more comprehensive set of predefined queries and be sure to choose an extra user friendly front end (choose *warm and fuzzy* over *power and function*).

If the data warehouse is seen as a power grab by the data warehouse implementation team, first be sure it is not a power grab and make the application developers an integral part of the data warehouse team. After they have been properly trained, make the application developers the primary contact with the users.

If the users have unrealistic expectations for the data warehouse, be honest. Do not misrepresent what the users will be getting, their required involvement, the costs, or the schedules. Never be coerced by anyone to accept unrealistic time frames or budgets. Document what the users will be getting and when (some installations ask the users to sign this document). Continue to remind the users of what they will be getting and when. If a user is unwilling to accept legitimate estimates, give someone else the opportunity to work with that user.

If the CIO's brother-in-law (a.k.a. an unmotivated incompetent) is being proposed to play a key role, respectfully decline. The most important determinant of success is the quality of the data warehouse team.

SUMMARY

Any serious implementation of a data warehouse takes technical skills and planning. It takes hardware, software, and budget. But more important are the organizational and cultural issues. Unless these are addressed, the project is doomed to failure.

Other issues, such as technical problems, can almost always be resolved, while organizational problems can administer a fatal blow to the data warehouse project and its potential success in the organization.

REFERENCES

ADELMAN, SID, "People Oriented Issues," *Database Programming and Design,* June 1995.

BELCHER, LLOYD W., and WATSON, HUGH J., "Assessing the Value of Conoco's EIS," *MIS Quarterly,* September 1993.

BOULDIN, BARBARA M., *Agents of Change,* Englewood Cliffs, NJ, Prentice Hall, 1989.

HORROCKS, BRIAN, and MOSS, JUDY, *Practical Data Administration,* Herefordshire, Great Britain, Prentice Hall International, 1993.

IVES, BLAKE, JARVENPAA, SIRKKA L., and MASON, RICHARD O., "Global Business Drivers: Aligning Information Technology to Global Business Strategy," *IBM Systems Journal,* Vol. 32, No. 1, 1993, pp. 143–161.

JONES, CAPERS, *Applied Software Measurement,* New York, McGraw-Hill, 1991.

KEEN, PETER G. W., "Information Technology and the Management Difference: A Fusion Map," *IBM Systems Journal,* Vol. 32, No. 1, 1993, pp. 17–39.(C/S)

LOOSLEY, CHRIS, "Look Before You Leap," *Database Programming & Design,* June 1994, pp. 23–25.

MORTON, MICHAEL S. SCOTT, *The Corporation of the 1990s: Information Technology and Organizational Transformation,* New York, Oxford University Press, 1991.

OUELETTE, L. PAUL, *How to Market the I/S Department Internally: Gaining the Recognition & Strategic Position You Merit,* New York, AMACOM, American Management Association, 1992.

PARKER, MARILYN, BENSON, ROBERT J., with TRAINOR, H. E., *Information Economics,* Englewood Cliffs, NJ, Prentice Hall, 1988.

ROTHSTEIN, MICHAEL F., and ROSNER, BURT, *The Professional's Guide to Database Systems Project Management,* New York, John Wiley & Sons, 1990.

SIMSION, GRAEME, *Data Modeling Essentials: Analysis, Design, and Innovation,* New York, Van Nostrand Reinhold, 1994.

SOWA, JOHN F., and ZACHMAN, JOHN A., "Extending and Formalizing the Framework for Information Systems Architecture," *IBM Systems Journal,* Vol. 31, No. 3, 1992, pp. 590–616.

TEOREY, TOBY J., *Database Modeling and Design,* San Mateo, CA, Morgan Kaufmann Publishers, 1990.

VAN DEN HOVEN, JOHN, "End-user Access Tools: Self-serve Data?" *Database Programming & Design,* August 1993, pp. 42–49.

VON HALLE, BARBARA, and KULL, DAVID, *Handbook of Data Management,* Boston, Auerbach, 1993.

WATSON, HUGH J., RAINER, R. KELLY, and FROLICK, MARK N., "Executive Information Systems: An Ongoing Study of Current Practices," *International Information Systems,* April 1992.

YOURDON, EDWARD, *Decline & Fall of the American Programmer,* Englewood Cliffs, NJ, Yourdon Press, 1993.

ZACHMAN, J. A. "A Framework for Information Systems Architecture," *IBM Systems Journal,* Vol. 26, No. 3, 1987, pp. 276–292.

Working Effectively with End Users

4

Joyce Bischoff

Bischoff Consulting, Inc.
Hockessin, Delaware

"The customer is always right."

H. Gordon Selfridge

End users are the alpha and omega of the data warehouse. The ultimate success of a data warehouse will be measured by the end-user community, and the relationship between IT personnel and end users should be considered at the inception of the warehouse project. There are two extremes: In the first scenario, end users may develop their own data, possibly with the help of a consulting firm; in the second, IT plays a major role in developing a traditional warehouse. Although success may be achieved in different ways, an appropriate balance of involvement from IT and the user community is critical.

SCENARIO I: DATA MART WITH LITTLE OR NO IT INVOLVEMENT

Many vendors are pushing the development of data marts with little or no involvement from IT. In some shops, IT has moved so slowly that users have taken the lead and developed their own data marts. From the vendor's perspective, it is a great marketing opportunity and usually results in satisfied users. This may be a two-edged sword. Although it can meet user needs quickly, sooner or later the data contained in the data marts may be of interest to other areas of the company. If standard names and definitions have not been used and the architecture used in the data mart is incompatible with corporate standards, there will be problems. If an organization has a group of users that want to move ahead on their own, IT should consider reorganizing its priorities to work with the users on the project. If IT is not involved, the data mart may become an isolated island of information that is of little value to the rest of the corporation. When there is reasonable assurance that the data is of interest only to a specific group of individuals, it may be worthwhile to allow it to be developed independently. Naming standards and metadata issues should still be addressed.

The old adage of "Pay me now or pay me later" still applies. There are numerous query tools and virtual data warehouse approaches that try to solve this problem but, in the long run, it would be easier and cheaper to solve it during development. (See Chapter 21 for details.)

SCENARIO II: TRADITIONAL WAREHOUSE

There are several approaches to the traditional warehouse. Some companies have taken the attitude that they know what is best for the users and can design a warehouse based on the backlog of service requests. What these companies fail to realize is that the "official" service requests represent only the most pressing needs and may be the tip of the proverbial iceberg. In addition, these requests may represent only the most vocal, assertive users. Frustrated users whose past needs have been unmet may have given up asking for service long ago. Companies that have built data warehouses with inadequate user involvement have struggled with questions such as these:

- Now that we have a data warehouse, how do we convince our users to use it?
- Why do our users complain so much about the wonderful data warehouse that has been built for them?
- Why does the discussion surrounding the warehouse seem to be "us versus them"?

At the start of a project, consideration should be given to the "right" amount of user involvement, which may vary with different companies and different projects. In some cases, users are happy to provide a project sponsor and business requirements, participate in all project team meetings (no matter how technical), manage implementation issues from a business perspective, take responsibility for training their own personnel, etc. In other shops, they are willing to provide a project sponsor and business requirements but want to delegate as much detail as possible to IT personnel on the project team.

As a general rule, users have a better sense of ownership for the project when they are involved in the details. Unfortunately, users face time pressures in their jobs and cannot always devote the amount of time that the project team might prefer. An appropriate balance must be reached between the absolute minimum amount of involvement required for success and the amount of time that the user community can afford to devote to the project.

PROJECT SPONSOR

The sponsor of a warehouse project should come from the user community and be highly enough placed in the organization to be able to run interference when problems occur. Many of the problems with the first warehouse project are political in nature and may be solved efficiently under these circumstances. The author knows of more than one shop that has insisted that the project sponsor come from within IT because user sponsorship is perceived as a loss of control. Without a project sponsor from the user community, successful warehouse projects are the exception rather than the rule. This author feels that shops that take this approach, even if the project sponsor is the vice president of IT, will decrease the probability of success. If the vice president has a strong user advisory group that is truly behind the project, the problem may be lessened, but it is difficult to think of a reason that a project would be more successful with a high-level IT sponsor than with a user sponsor. Joint sponsorship might also be considered.

GATHERING REQUIREMENTS AND MANAGING EXPECTATIONS

In the initial phase of the project, the users and the IT Department should work closely together to determine the project scope and detailed requirements. An official alliance between users and IT is the basis for a successful warehouse project: Users establish the need, and IT provides the technical expertise to solve the problem. It is important to manage user expectations at the start of the project. Do not tell them that they will be able to submit every imaginable query and obtain quick answers. Be sure that they understand that a query that analyzes millions of rows of data may not return a response with subsecond response time. If a query does a great deal of work, it may take time. With the latest technical advances in parallel processing, this is steadily improving, but users should not be given unrealistic expectations.

In one shop, the IT Department tried to develop a sales and marketing warehouse that failed because of inadequate product and customer information. They thought that the users did not want to be bothered with further discussions of requirements and data analysis because they had complained about their level of service for so long. They were confident that IT could produce a warehouse based on past requests for service. Unfortunately, previous requests did not reflect what users *really* wanted. Surely, IT departments should know better than to attempt projects with this attitude since it has brought IT a bad reputation and consistent trouble over the years.

COST JUSTIFICATION PROCESS

After a project has been selected and a project sponsor from the business community has been identified, the process of business justification will begin. The user perspective is important in this process. If IT handles this process independently, the cost justification may be biased toward cost saving in the IT department. By its nature, the data warehouse will bring more autonomy to the user community, and extra work will come with it. In many cases, IT personnel will justify the data warehouse because they can see an offloading of ad hoc reports to the user community. This will certainly result in more satisfied users, but there will be a shift in the workload for both departments. (See Chapter 8 for details.)

END-USER INTERFACE TO THE WAREHOUSE

Warehouses can be built with various levels of service and technical complexity. A data warehouse may range from a simple query and reporting system designed to offload the production environment to a sophisticated data warehouse providing capabilities for browsing, drill-down, data mining, OLAP, etc. Users may range from novices to power users, and the tools and expected usage of the different user types will vary correspondingly.

The end user's view of the data warehouse may consist of ad hoc query tools, reporting tools, analytical tools, spreadsheets, multidimensional databases, purchased or custom developed decision support applications, OLAP, and/or data mining tools. Although IT must provide technical expertise and ensure technical compatibility with the hardware and software environment, users should play a role in the selection of tools, development of applications, and planning for user training. In more than one shop, there have been arguments when users preferred to continue use of existing query and reporting tools rather than accept IT's newly selected warehouse tools. This type of argument can waste time and cause ill will on a project. If the tool that is currently in use will work with the DBMSs that will be used in the warehouse, it is worthwhile to consider keeping the tool, in addition to the new tools. Also, IT should not try to select user tools without user participation. Since there is no "one size fits all" warehouse tool, most successful warehouses are equipped with a selection of tools to meet a range of user requirements.

END-USER TOOLS

There are many different kinds of users with differing tool requirements. One group of users may only need a strong reporting tool, but others may wish to perform statistical analysis or advanced data mining with a multidimensional database. The functionality and the learning curves may vary considerably. It should not be assumed that engineers or scientists will require the same type of tool as market or financial analysts. Since IT's objective may be to meet as many needs as possible with a single tool, IT personnel often choose a tool with the greatest functionality, which may imply the longest learning curve. The type of usage should be carefully considered. Those who use the warehouse infrequently may be more interested in simplicity than advanced functionality. (See Chapter 27 for more details on this topic.)

DATA: THE CRITICAL ISSUE

Users need to gather, analyze, and report on business information if they are to help the organization gain competitive advantage. Although most companies have a wealth of legacy data, it is worthless if its existence is unknown, it cannot be found, or it cannot be understood outside the context of an application. Furthermore, it is useless if it is incorrect.

Users must play a role in the development of a data model for the subject areas to be included in the warehouse. They are the only ones who can provide accurate business definitions and will need to answer business questions during data analysis and modeling. In many cases, there is a lack of documentation in legacy applications, and the application's users are the only ones who can provide information about the legacy data.

An effective warehouse documentation strategy should be developed with the end users. In some shops, IT personnel have been known to gloss over the need for data definitions. They think that an understanding of the data is intuitive and that users will understand the meaning when they see the data name. For initial warehouse implementations with a small group of power users, this may be true. In the long run, however, nothing could be further from the truth. Although the initial group of users may be able to get by without documentation, the addition of new users and expansion of the types of data in the warehouse becomes a problem. As soon as the group is expanded, the need for well-documented data becomes greater. Unfortunately, if IT personnel did not pay attention to this initially, they may continue to ignore it.

A major hospital developed a successful data warehouse with patient information that was used by six to eight analysts. For the first three years, it was successful because there was a stable group of analysts who were long-term employees and really knew the data. Because the warehouse was used successfully in analyzing patient care, there was a strong desire to expand the data and the user community. After analyzing the situation, IT personnel decided that it was hopeless to build on the existing warehouse because of inflexible database design and lack of metadata. They started from scratch and were able to build a well-documented warehouse with a wealth of experience behind them.

Ideally, a user-oriented data directory will be available and its contents will be created with a business perspective, rather than the technical perspective that is found in most data dictionary/repository products. Users should play an active role in the development and review of the directory. Some data directory products will provide descriptions of components of a warehouse, including tables, standard spreadsheets, reports, and queries. Examples include IBM's Data Guide 2,™ Platinum's Data Shopper,™ Prism's Directory Manager,™ and others. They will usually allow drill-down through the metadata to spreadsheets, reports, queries, or applications and permit the user to launch the program from the directory. Some data directory products will accept input that has been extracted from another dictionary or repository product. Other products may provide an acceptable view into an all-purpose dictionary/repository. Unless a product permits a view into the directory that includes only data available to warehouse users, it can be confusing. If users are required to learn to use a full function repository, including various versions and technical information, there will be problems. Products need a limited view for end users. (See Chapter 12 for more information.)

DESIGN REVIEWS

Users should participate in appropriate design reviews. Since an accurate data model will be the foundation for the warehouse, the users' role in reviewing the data model is important. Decisions regarding summary levels, indexing, integrating external data, or development of an appropriate star or snowflake schema will depend on expected usage, and the end user is the most reliable source for this information. During the physical design review, these issues will be addressed. Although it is often difficult to include users in a physical design review, it can be productive if there is a willing user. (See Chapter 20 for more information.)

BUILDING THE FRAMEWORK

A data warehouse cannot be bought. It must be developed with an architecture that is flexible enough to meet current and future unknown requirements. It may contain global data that is accessible across the organization, or it may consist of a series of data marts designed to meet the needs of a specific work group or department.

The physical components of the warehouse may include detail data, summary data, external data, replicated data, specialized subsets, and multidimensional databases at a global warehouse level or data mart level. In theory, if processors and networks were infinitely fast, all user requests could be met by accessing detail data. Although the new parallelism at the hardware and software level has brought us closer to realizing this objective, it is still necessary to consider summaries, subsets, and multidimensional databases to meet the objective. The need must be determined according to the expected usage of various levels of data. Only the users can provide information regarding their expected usage. Although some people say, "We have no idea how our users will access the data," this may not be completely correct. An initial analysis should give some idea about summary levels or specialized subsets that may be required. Since the warehouse is dynamic in nature, it will be necessary to respond with new levels in the architecture as user requirements change.

USER PERSPECTIVE ON CUSTOM APPLICATIONS

IT must be as creative as possible in the development of custom applications. In one large financial organization, the IT department built a prospective customer database with approximately 50 million potential customers in five related DB2 tables. Users wanted to search the database for potential customers with specific characteristics and were unhappy with the performance. For example, they might want to produce a mailing list for all males over 40 years of age who drive a red Porsche and have one or more dogs. Furthermore, the list might be generated by running against only one table on indexed fields or might require a five-way join on fields that might or might not have compatible indexes. When first implemented, the application produced satisfactory response time about 80% of the time. The remaining 20% of the time produced scans that ran from a few minutes to 18 hours. No matter how it is viewed, analyzing a potential 50 million related records in five tables requires a great deal of work.

Users and IT worked together to solve the problem in several ways. First, a judgment was made in the application program regarding the query's runtime. If the query ran against one or more tables with compatible indexed fields, the program would allow it to run immediately. If it specified nonindexed fields, it would generate a message to the user suggesting that the query would run faster if certain indexed fields could be specified. In some cases, the user would modify the query. If the user decided to submit it anyway, the program would return a message to the user saying that the query could not run immediately but would be run overnight and the answer would be available in the morning. It would also ask the user to confirm the query request.

In some cases, the program found it difficult to determine if the expected runtime was reasonable. In these cases, the program would run the SQL EXPLAIN command and analyze the results internally. If an acceptable access path was available, the program would run the query immediately; otherwise, it would generate a batch job to be run during off-hours. This is *not* a suggestion to build EXPLAIN into warehouse applications. This was only practical because the query load was light and the time to run EXPLAIN was not excessive *for this application*. The recommendation is to be as creative as possible in solving problems that occur.

USER TRAINING

Early in the project, an assessment should be made regarding the computer literacy of the user community for the pilot project. Users range from novices to power users, and training requirements will vary accordingly. In addition, each user may use the available set of tools in a different way, depending on the job function.

Users will need appropriate training in the use of front-end tools; use of the data directory; use of data models and metadata; development and use of ad hoc and canned reports, queries, spreadsheets; and use of custom applications. Last, but not least, they must be given an understanding of the actual data structures that they will be using on a regular basis. Experienced warehouse developers believe that the average user cannot initially understand more than about 20 tables and their inter-relationships. Users should be given a manageable number of tables and training in the use of these tables. It is not enough to give users training in the front-end tools and use of the data directory.

Conducting training classes with the actual warehouse tables pays large dividends in user success. This may be achieved in two ways: (1) Customize standard classes so that exercises are performed against actual warehouse data, or (2) plan a follow-up class that occurs soon after the class and that will include training in the data structures and data access. In many standard classes, exercises are carefully planned to use increasingly complex problems, and the cost of customizing these exercises to use actual warehouse tables is prohibitive. In these cases, it is suggested that the formal classes be followed by a special class using the tool against actual data.

Users will need an overview of the data warehouse, which may be provided by an in-house training group or an outside vendor. Many users ask, "Why are you developing a warehouse? What's in it for me? Furthermore, why should it take so long and cost so much simply to move a bunch of data from the legacy systems?" The overview class should address these issues (and a host of others) and emphasize the quality, consistency, and integrity that will be available in the new warehouse and what is involved in the transformation of data and population of a data directory. It helps if real examples of inconsistent data can be pulled from existing files and shown in the class. An understanding of the data issues will help everyone.

If there is a standard suite of desktop products and a help desk is in place, planning for training and ongoing support will be simplified. In any case, basic and advanced training for all standard front-end tools must be available.

An understanding of the meaning and use of metadata and the data directory must also be provided. It is not enough to give users training in the front-end tools and use of the data directory. It is helpful if the data directory can be populated with the actual data that will be available in the warehouse.

User training should also include testing of query results. User friendly query languages can be very forgiving and return answers to incorrect queries. Because such languages return an answer, a user may believe that the answer is correct. Users have also been known to compare "apples and oranges" from different tables in the belief that they are they same. Training should include techniques for determining the correctness of query results.

Users must understand how to work with IT to improve query performance. This author's favorite slogan is, "If you're happy with the warehouse and its performance, tell your friends. If you're unhappy, tell us and we'll try to fix the problem." Users need to understand that managing performance requires cooperation between users and IT. This is where a solid alliance between users and IT pays off. Users must also be educated to understand that large queries may involve a considerable amount of work and may result in a lengthy response time. Learning to work with IT to improve performance is critical.

Moving Data into Personal or Work Group Databases

Although the shared global warehouse contains a wealth of data, it is not always most efficient to work directly in that environment. Sooner or later, users will want to extract data from the global warehouse and move it into a personal or work group database or spreadsheet. This has a double benefit: Some of the query load is moved to smaller platforms, and the data is closer to the users where they may work with it on their own desktop. Training should include the following:

- How to identify needed data
- Tools and procedures that may be used to move data efficiently
- Selecting the time of day for moving data
- Issues involved with sharing personal data with coworkers (integrity, point in time, completeness of the data)
- Impact of updating corporate or departmental data in a personal database.

TESTING AND VALIDATION

In keeping with the philosophy of an alliance between IT and the end users, a plan should be developed that will allow end users to play a critical role in testing and validating the warehouse. If a warehouse is delivered to the users without their involvement in the testing and validation of the data, they may be reluctant to share their opinions.

In a major manufacturing company, the warehouse had been in place for about three years and was unsuccessful. Performance was poor, data structures were difficult to understand, and data definitions were less than user friendly. Users were so unhappy that they refused to use the system. A project was developed to correct the deficiencies. At first, users refused to participate because they felt it would be a waste of time. The team took a new approach (for their organization) and assured the users that nothing would go into production without their approval. They made the users an official part of the team. They selected a small group of users for the testing period and encouraged them to use it to its fullest capability. Because they had been told that nothing was final, users felt comfortable in providing feedback to the team. After several iterations, the warehouse was successful and opened up a continuing easy communication between IT and the users that carries over to this day.

CHANGING USER REQUIREMENTS

Meeting changing user requirements is much like trying to hit a moving target. After the warehouse has been in use for a period of time, users will begin to realize its potential. IT is inevitable that they will require changes or enhancements. Changes may be required for any of the following reasons:

- Data may have been defined incorrectly.
- Data may have incorrect values because of poor transformation or derivation.
- Performance may be poor.
- Users recognize the need for additional data.
- Users may need data from past periods to perform trend analysis.

Enhancements may be needed because the user has dared to ask questions that were inconceivable before the warehouse was developed and needs additional subject areas or additional fields in existing tables. IT should consider developing a process for managing change in the warehouse. The process should not be a burden and should not be as complex as the change request process that is in place for the production environment. For example, the addition of a single field to one table should not be a big problem if it has a reliable source. IT should also consider establishing a process for tracking current usage and determining new requirements.

MEASURING USER SATISFACTION

After the warehouse is implemented, there should be a formal evaluation of user satisfaction. The first evaluation will probably help to tune the infrastructure and introduce new requirements. At this time, it is very important for the IT group to respond with enthusiasm so that the users will feel that a team spirit is present. IT should be certain not to respond by saying, "We'll put it on the backlog and get to it in six months." User satisfaction should be evaluated on a regular ongoing basis, not only after the first implementation.

SUMMARY

Users are critical to every aspect of design and development of the data warehouse. They should be involved in selecting the project, gathering requirements, defining data, justifying cost, selecting end-user tools, developing custom DSS applications, handling design reviews, designing procedures for accessing and moving data to personal warehouses, testing and validation, and developing processes for managing changing requirements and measuring user satisfaction. A proper balance of involvement from IT and the user community is critical. With appropriate user involvement in all phases of the warehouse project, success may be assured.

CHAPTER 5

The Seven Deadly Sins

Denis Kosar

Chase Manhatttan Bank
New York, New York

"If you built it without a sponsor, they definitely won't come."

Kosar

T his chapter will discuss the things (what I call the seven deadly sins) to avoid when embarking on a data warehouse project. The reason they are considered deadly is because any one of these sins, when committed, can lead to the death of your data warehouse. The advice contained in this chapter is the result of my experiences in developing two data warehouses for a major New York bank. It is my hope that the information contained in this chapter will assist you in both the planning and implementation of a data warehouse.

The challenge associated with providing information access to the end user is not a new one. In the late 1970s, an attempt was made to solve this problem with the introduction of the information center, which required a dedicated computer and heavy resource consumption both in hardware as well as personnel. The mid-1980s featured the data reengineering approach to relational technology. This approach proved to be too complex and often raised performance issues due to the way data was accessed. In the 1990s, the answer appears to be data warehousing. Building a data warehouse requires that IT management understand what must be done, as well as how to do it.

SIN NUMBER ONE: "IF YOU BUILD IT, THEY WILL COME."

The first sin deals with having blind faith, thinking everyone will come and use the data warehouse just because it is there. It is a failure of not recognizing the importance of having a clear set of business objectives and a business sponsor or champion for the data warehouse. If you saw the movie *Field of Dreams*, you know that a farmer built a baseball field in the middle of an Iowa corn field. This by itself was not really strange. The farmer, however, was motivated by a voice he heard telling him, "If you build it, they will come." The data warehouse cannot simply be built with the hope that someone will come and use it. There must be a clear mission, strategy, and plan.

Why are data warehouse projects started? There are times when a data warehouse project is started simply because the CIO just came back from a seminar or stumbles across the idea in a magazine or article. Sometimes it is approached as a strategic project simply because someone wants to add it to their resume. Most of the time, when data warehouse projects are started, the IT organization may not have a true business sponsor or a clear definition of what their business requirements are. Both are very important in developing a data warehouse strategy. As is often said, the road to hell is filled with good intentions. The motivation behind the effort may be initially based on a clear need or genuine desire to help the organization. However, once the project gets under way, a documented set of requirements and a set of business objectives should be developed.

To be truly effective, the planning process should embrace an enterprise approach. However, under no circumstances should the first phase of the project include the total scope of the enterprise. The project must be phased in by modules (containing the process and the necessary data to support them). This approach depends on the size of the enterprise and how decentralized the functional areas are within the organization. If your organization is large and decentralized, it will be difficult to implement a total enterprise solution. You should, however, try to address any issues that will have an impact on the total organization, such as customer indicative data, product, organization, and finally credit data. Regardless of the scope of the initial phase of the data warehouse, this data will have a major impact on the total enterprise, and data conflict issues must be settled before the project can move forward.

It is naive to believe that the data warehouse alone will enable the management team to make better business decisions. The requirements should clearly document, with examples, how this will occur. Success must be something that is quantifiable and should clearly be measurable. As mentioned earlier, it is extremely important to have a business sponsor or champion to help in the justification of the data warehouse. When chosen, the business sponsor should come from a functional area of the enterprise designated as the introductory user. It should be an area of the organization that will derive a direct benefit from the effort.

Care must be taken when choosing the data warehouse sponsor. The sponsor must fully believe in what is to be accomplished and recognize its importance to the business. The sponsor must also understand how using the data warehouse will allow decisions to be made that will have a positive impact on the future of the organization. In addition, the sponsor must have a good understanding of the data that will be loaded into the warehouse. When the going gets tough (and it definitely will get tough), your sponsor must weather the storm and stay onboard even when the outlook seems bleak. Early on in the project, make sure the data warehouse requirements are clearly defined and that time has been taken in finding the right sponsor.

SIN NUMBER TWO: DATA WAREHOUSE ARCHITECTURAL FRAMEWORK

The second is the sin of omission concerning the data warehouse architecture. This sin is of a grave nature because it affects one of the most important success factors, which is the need for an architectural framework for the data warehouse. Such a framework can be likened to the blueprints used when constructing a building or a house. Whatever architecture is decided on, it will be used over and over during the life of the project because it will drive the basic components of the design and usage of the data warehouse. From the architecture, it can be determined how data will be loaded, how it will be accessed, and how it will be delivered. (For a more in-depth view, see Chapter 7.)

When deciding on an architecture, many things have to be considered. The number of end users and functional areas, the diversity and volume of data, the refresh cycle, and the storage and access complexities are only a few. Any or all of these things can influence the architecture of the data warehouse. The following example can be used as a template to assist in understanding the development of the architectural framework. Figure 5.1 depicts three discrete layers or tiers in the data warehouse architecture: information acquisition, information storage, and information delivery.

Information Acquisition

This layer is responsible for the gathering, refining, cleansing, and aggregating the data from the existing production or legacy systems. The data should be accurate and provide a common meaning, since it will be utilized across lines of business to facilitate decision making. During the analysis of the feeder systems, certain applications will be designated as the system of record. This means that the most reliable application will be used as the source for specific data loading. For example, when loading customer indicative data, make sure its source is the customer information file (CIF). If there is more than one such file, make sure the difference is only the update cycle and not the actual values associated with it.

Since the primary responsibility of this architecture layer is to provide data consolidation and integration, it is important that the software be designed and developed in a generic way, especially if this is an enterprise data warehouse. Standardization is important because it provides flexibility when implementing future requirements and integrating additional feeder systems data into the data warehouse.

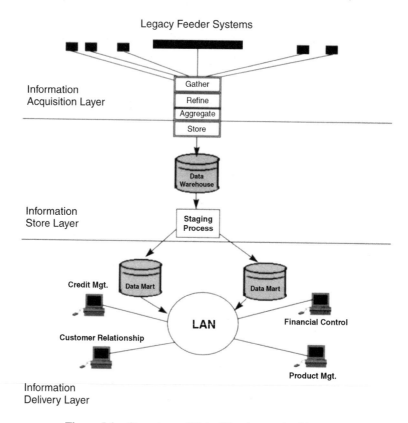

Figure 5.1   Overview of Data Warehouse Architecture.

Information Storage

This layer provides the single logical information store that contains point-in-time data. This data will normally be stored at the most granular level, and denormalization of the physical design will be kept to a minimum. Here we try to keep the physical design as close to the data model as possible. This is important in providing the ultimate flexibility to satisfy the design requirements.

Using the framework in Figure 5.1, the information store layer is a holding area for the data. If we use the manufacturing industry as an example, it would be a real warehouse containing the nuts and bolts that will be used to assemble a final product. In this example, it will become the information that will be available on the information delivery layer. Since a data warehouse must store many different views of business data, a single design would have a negative impact on the performance service levels necessary to support the integrated delivery requirements. It is because of this that we conclude that an important attribute of the data warehouse is flexibility. The architecture must therefore leverage the information delivery layer to accomplish this.

Information Delivery

This layer is the part of the architecture that will support a common set of presentation and analytical tools. It will provide a common look and feel through reports and queries made available on intelligent workstations. This is the architecture layer that provides the business with the end product, information. This is the part of the data warehouse that the end user will interface with and is the primary point of contact.

As earlier mentioned, in the information store, the data warehouse must provide the ultimate in flexibility. In Figure 5.1, the data mart concept is used as the vehicle for the delivery of information to the desktop. It is a subset of the data warehouse that stores only the necessary data for a particular set of business functions. It is in the specific format and level of granularity that the business user requires. For example, a data field called customer revenue is normally maintained on a monthly basis at the information store layer. A functional area called Financial Control requires that it be summarized on a year-to-date level. The data is derived from the summarization of all monthly values stored in the data warehouse and made available in the information delivery layer. For this to be accomplished, the data warehouse would also store the summarization or derivation rules necessary. In the example, there are four discretely different data marts: financial control, product management, customer relationship, and credit management. Each area may have different data requirements associated with their business functions. At the same time, they might also share common data, such as customer number, customer name, or customer credit rating.

In retrospect, the data warehouse architecture should consist of all three layers. Data must be acquired or gathered, loaded into the warehouse for storage, and, finally, made available to the business. If any one of these functions is missing, then the data warehouse is not completing the functions that it was designed to perform.

SIN NUMBER THREE: DOCUMENTING ALL ASSUMPTIONS AND CONFLICTS EARLY

In any data warehouse development project, it is important that all assumptions, conflicts, and issues are identified and documented up front. Sin number three is underestimating the importance of documenting your assumptions and conflicts early. It is typically during the feasibility or requirements phase of the project that questions are identified and documented. The answers to these questions, because of their nature, are critical to the development of the data warehouse. The following questions are typically asked by the team at the start of the data warehouse development project:

- *How much data should be loaded initially into the warehouse?* The answer should be, as much as is required to support the preliminary requirements and business functionality. This will, however, depend on how the implementation is phased and how many users will access the data. Typically, the implementation phase might be based on the data load sequence or the data subject area (customer, product, risk management, revenue/expenses, etc.). These subject areas are the building blocks of the data warehouse and will have a major impact on the implementation phases. Remember the fallacy of "If you build it, they will come." Data storage and load cycles are very expensive. If you put too much data out there, it may become underutilized or, worse, not used at all.

- *What is the level of data granularity?* This identifies if the data will be stored at a detailed level, summarized level, or both. This will be documented in your architecture document and will drive a number of other issues. It will have an impact on whether derived data is calculated each time for queries or stored in the data warehouse. If it is stored, will it be available in the main warehouse or derived and brought down to the delivery layer each time? Remember that there is a need to provide flexibility for future use and data integration.

- *How often must the data be refreshed?* The refresh cycle is another critical question that must be answered. It could be daily, interdaily, weekly, or monthly. It may also be all the aforementioned depending on the specific type of data in question. Customer indicative data might be refreshed monthly, whereas the revenue or credit-related data might be refreshed weekly or daily depending on the OLAP requirements designated by the business. The refresh schedule will also depend on the update schedules of the operational systems that are the source of the data.

Another key question might be, "On what platform will the data warehouse be developed and implemented?" The answer to these questions will typically be contained in your architecture document. This will depend on many things: the refresh cycle, the data volume, the complexity of the legacy information acquisition process, the access requirements, and the tools available. It should now be evident that it is important to do this early in the project. During the development process, the data warehouse development team will constantly refer back to the architecture document for direction and guidance. This will indeed become the warehouse blueprint or architectural drawing, so make sure it is accurate and complete.

SIN NUMBER FOUR: METHODOLOGY AND TOOLS

The fourth is the sin of methodology and tool abuse. Building a data warehouse is much different from building a system. Therefore, it requires a different methodology and set of tools. This section will identify the need for a different methodology and describe the generic tools required during the data warehouse development cycle. (For a more in-depth overview, see Chapter 27.)

Methodology

The methodology chosen will be driven by many things. Some of these are contained within the corporate culture, and some are not. The choices available might be influenced by the information acquisition or extraction approach being used. There are many tool vendors who provide their own methodology along with the actual tool kit. The choice of methodology might also depend on the legacy technology that is being used by the operational systems. If the legacy application was written in Software AG's ADABAS and the 4GL language NATURAL, the decision might be to use the same program language for the legacy data capture. This would minimize the learning curve during development. Some of the choices available can be as formalized as information engineering or may be just the use of structured techniques, such as process modeling and data modeling. Whatever methodology is chosen, some data modeling technique should and must be used to ensure that the data warehouse will reflect the business data requirements. (For more details on methodology, see Chapter 9.)

Data Warehouse Tools

The project manager will find that the type and number of tools contained in the tool kit will depend on the technical environment, corporate culture, and methodology chosen. Data warehouse tools can be categorized into four discrete groups: analysis tools, development tools, implementation tools, and delivery tools. Be aware that the tool categories identified are predicated on the use of the architectural framework described in Figure 5.1. An attempt will be made to include some examples of tool vendors currently available in the marketplace. This is not a complete list but only a sample of available tools.

Analysis Tools   These tools are used during the analysis phase, specifically when the current operational environment is being studied. They assist in the identification of data requirements, the primary data source for the information acquisition layer and building the data model. To make this section more meaningful, I will disclose the tools I used while building a data warehouse for a major international bank.

CASE tools:	Computer-aided software engineering (CASE) tools are used for data/process modeling (e.g., Texas Instruments, IEF; Bachman, Analyst tool; Knowledgeware, ADW). I used the Bachman Analyst and the DBA tool.
Scanners:	These will scan language copy code for file or database definitions or procedure code to identify data usage (e.g., Platinum, Cobol Scan; R&O; Adpac, Cobol Scanner). I used a third-party scanner from a consulting firm.

Data repositories: Stores all metadata loaded during analysis and design phases (e.g., Platinum's Repository, R&O's Repository, MSP's Repository). I used a third-party repository from a consulting firm.

Development Tools   These tools will assist the developer during code generation for the information acquisition, data cleansing, data integration, and loading of the data warehouse data.

Code generators: These are used with case tools to generate application code, developed from process models (same as CASE vendors).

Data repositories: Storage for all metadata loaded during development phase (e.g., Platinum's Repository; R&O's Repository; MSP's Repository).

Implementation Tools   These tools assist in the actual cleansing, consolidation, and loading of the data warehouse. There are vendors who will provide a methodology and implementation tools for data cleansing, data replication, and integration of legacy data. If the project team chooses, some of these tools can be developed in-house using fourth-generation-level (4GL) languages. If this is the case, then the scope of the development tools will increase. We already had a system in place for data cleansing and consolidation that was written in Natural II, a 4GL sold by Software AG. With the advent of more master extract files being used by larger corporations, this approach seems to be occurring more often because corporations have seen the need for this type of home-grown system in gathering, consolidating, and cleansing data.

Data acquisition tools: These are used for the data warehouse gather process, data cleansing, data replication, and data consolidation (e.g., IBM, Prism, Platinum).

Information store tools: These are used to load data into the data warehouse (e.g., IBM, Prism, Platinum).

Delivery Tools   These tools will assist in data conversion, data derivation, data loading, and reporting for the delivery platform, provided the project team uses a different platform for delivery.

Data loader: Converts data from the host computer and loads it on the delivery platform for reporting and/or queries (e.g., IBM, Prism, Platinum). Once again, we used Natural II to convert and summarize the data before downloading it to the data mart environment.

Data glossary: The data glossary provides the end user, in business terms, the ability to identify what data is in the ware-

	house (e.g., IBM, R&O, Prism, Platinum). We developed our business glossary using Lotus Notes.
Query and reporting:	These tools provide on-line and batch reporting functions, either canned or ad hoc (e.g., Platinum's Forest & Trees, Brio's Brio Query, IBM's Visualizer). We used Lightship from Pilot Software Inc.

Figure 5.2, shows an example of how tools are used during the analysis and design phases of the project. It should first be noticed that the example is using the architectural components of information acquisition, information store, and information delivery as functional groupings to describe the tools' usage. These tools would be used to support analysis, requirements, and logical design.

Within the acquisition function, language scanners are used to capture and document data files, database definitions, data elements, and files within the current legacy environment. The strawman data model is also loaded into the repository from the case tool.

The store function is used to capture what was scanned in from the legacy environment into a data repository or dictionary tool. From the data files and database definitions, data elements, column names, and descriptions are loaded. The strawman data model will contain logical data entities, attributes, relationships, and business rules pertaining to data used in the organization.

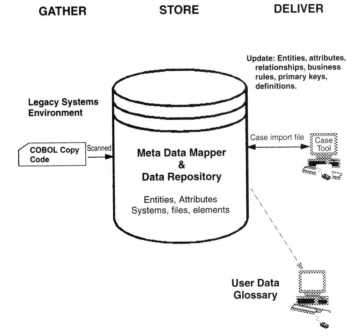

Figure 5.2 Data Analysis Tool Environment.

The deliver function will provide the delivery of this metadata (data about data) to the project team and end users. This is achieved because of the bidirectional interface between the data repository and the CASE tool. Finally, a user data glossary is made available to the business user. This contains a definition for all common business terms used within the functional organization.

SIN NUMBER FIVE: DATA WAREHOUSE LIFE CYCLE

The fifth sin is the sin of life-cycle abuse. This is a failure to realize the difference between the data warehouse life cycle (DWLC) and the system development life cycle (SDLC). Many are already familiar with the SDLC when building application systems. This life cycle typically deals with the development of OLTP systems. These systems are, by definition, on-line transaction processors and are normally the mission-critical applications in the organization.

There is another type of application called the OLAP systems. This application is normally used with the data warehouse for decision support or EIS. The DWLC is used to support OLAP application development. Figure 5.3 identifies the phases associated with the DWLC. For each phase a brief description is provided. You will notice that the life cycle is ongoing. It is continuous in nature. (For a more in-depth view, see Chapter 9.)

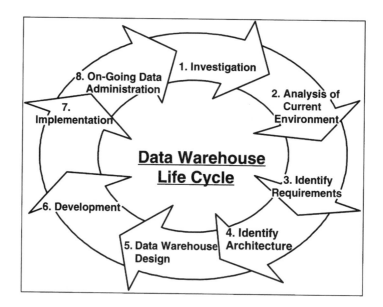

Figure 5.3 Data Warehouse Life Cycle.

Investigation Phase

The preliminary investigation is conducted by the team to identify the need or justification for the data warehouse. It is also during this phase that a business sponsor is selected and a mission statement for the data warehouse is developed. The primary deliverable is an investigation report, which contains the statement of the assumed business opportunities, the mission statement, the name of the business sponsor, the business areas to be initially supported, and a recommendation to move forward.

Analysis of Current Environment Phase

During this phase, the legacy data in the production systems is analyzed and documented. Within each application system, once the functional areas and the business sponsor are identified, a list of master files is obtained for review and analysis. Within each master file, every data field is reviewed and cataloged. An attempt is then made to acquire a business definition and document the size and data type (date, amount, name, etc.). If a CASE tool is used, existing data models and database definitions are scanned into the data dictionary or repository. An effort is made to identify the primary key for each master file and/or database record. An analysis across master files is then conducted to identify data field synonyms. These are fields that have different names but mean the same thing. An example of this might be `Customer-id`, `Cust-nbr`, and `Client-no`. We will discuss this process in greater detail when we get to Sin Number 6, Resolution of Data Conflicts. The main deliverables produced in this phase are a data inventory catalog, a business definition, and a synonym report.

Identify Requirements Phase

During this phase, an effort is made to identify the business requirements associated with the use of the data warehouse. These requirements should support only the use of the initial business area and nothing more. Remember the phrase, "If you build it, they will come." It is important that we focus on this and only this. It is very time consuming and expensive to load more data than is initially required early in the project. The first phase must be turned over to the business area on time and within budget. The deliverable from this phase is the requirements document.

Identify Architecture Phase

During this phase, the data warehouse architecture is developed by the team. Using the requirements from the previous phase, the data warehouse architecture is developed by the team. In addition, a development methodology and tool kit is decided on. A platform analysis project may have to be completed to identify what topography the data warehouse will be developed and implemented on. The phased deliverables are normally contained in the architecture document. However, among other things, this document usually contains a methodology and tools section, a topography section, and a section on data principles.

The topography section will describe the data warehouse platform, as well as how data will be loaded and accessed. Examples of data principles are as follows: Data must be kept at its most granular level in the warehouse. Data will never be cleansed or corrected on-line within the warehouse. It must be corrected in the information acquisition layer through a batch update function. Once data is loaded into the data warehouse, it is considered the information bible of the business organization.

Data Warehouse Design Phase

During this phase, the actual design of the data warehouse is produced. Using the results of the analysis, requirements, and architecture phases, both the logical and physical designs are completed. The phase deliverables that are produced by the team are the data model, physical database design, and a logical to physical mapping document that identifies complete mappings of each and every entity in the data model to the corresponding table name in the data warehouse. An example of this might be that the CUSTOMER entity is mapped to the CUSTINFO table.

Development Phase

During this phase, the data warehouse is defined by the database administrator and, if appropriate, the necessary process code for the information acquisition, information store, and information delivery layers of the architecture. Programs must be developed and tested for data cleansing, data integration, and data loading. The major phase deliverables are data warehouse definitions, program code, test data, and user acceptance and quality assurance plans.

Implementation Phase

During this phase, the data warehouse is actually implemented by the project team. The phase deliverables consist of some of the following: production data warehouse, first data load for data warehouse, backup and recovery procedures for database, user procedures, and training manuals and computer run books.

Data Administration (Ongoing)

This phase of the life cycle has as its primary function the monitoring of data changes from the feeder systems. Specifically, this is affectionately called data administration. This function is responsible for the administration of the metadata that is associated with the data warehouse.

Since the data loaded into the data warehouse is gathered from the legacy data taken from the operational systems, it is constantly subject to change. Changes made to the operational system files and databases are normally made without the knowledge of the warehouse development team. Because of this, the data administration or data architecture group is normally responsible for monitoring all changes and, if appropriate, ensuring that any impacts are integrated into the data warehouse.

This process would include data derivation or data transformation formulas and any additional data elements or database columns. It would also include any changes made to existing data elements that affect size, length, or data types. When changes are identified, they are discussed with the business analysis team, the DBA group, and the project manager to assess the impact. The phase deliverables are data inventory reports, change memos, and various impact analysis reports produced by a data dictionary or repository.

SIN NUMBER SIX: DATA ANALYSIS AND RESOLUTION OF DATA CONFLICTS

One of the most difficult phases in the DWLC is data analysis and the resolution of data conflicts. The sixth sin is ignorance concerning the resolution of data conflicts. One should not underestimate the importance of the resolution of data conflicts during the analysis phase. Often an effort is made to try to justify the need for a data warehouse simply because data quality issues may arise. (For a more in-depth overview, see Chapter 10.) Inconsistent data may have an impact on decisions made by a company's EIS. Business decisions need to be made on a daily basis, and often customer profitability or revenue tracking systems may uncover inconsistent data. These inconsistencies often occur because of data quality in the legacy systems. Data element names are sometimes misnamed or improperly defined or lack documentation of the transformation rules.

It simply is not enough to identify problems associated with data quality issues. Be prepared to deal with the hard issues associated with data resolution conflicts. There is a natural tendency for people and organizations to be protective of their applications and data. It is at this time that most of the grunt work is done in the trenches. An analysis of the current application environment must be conducted to identify the best data sources available. Once chosen, these applications should be identified as the system of record. They should be the system whose data is in the most correct state. As such, that system should be tagged as the best source for the data warehouse load. Each organization may have very different challenges ahead. If the data warehouse requires the loading of customer revenue data, it may be necessary to consolidate all customer sales data across product lines. The analytical process requires a review of all customer, transaction, and product files and documentation of key data elements, such as customer ID, product ID, and transaction ID. During this process, you will be surprised with the different sizes, formats, and values associated with the same data field. In short, data conflicts will be identified and must be resolved. You must sometimes take the largest size field and use it to store data in the data warehouse.

Indicative customer data, such as customer name, address, and telephone number, will have to be analyzed to identify the system of record. Often, the time associated with the update cycle must be taken into account. This can cause an impact to the refresh cycle for the data warehouse and should be considered carefully.

The major tasks associated with this phase of the project are as follows:

1. Identify key files and systems.
2. Catalog each field with definitions in a data repository or dictionary.
3. Build a strawman data model.
4. Identify synonyms concerning data fields (same meaning, different name.)
5. Map all input data fields to business names in data model.
6. Update and normalize the data model as required for data warehouse.

SIN NUMBER SEVEN: LEARNING FROM MISTAKES

Sin number seven is wasting knowledge learned from the mistakes made during the data warehouse project. During the first data warehouse project, many mistakes will be made. It is important that when they are made, they are documented so that the lesson is learned. With this in mind, the data warehouse implementation strategy should be phased. In this way, there will be more data quality and control activities during each phase. Quality assurance is a key success factor concerning the development of the warehouse. Once data is loaded in the data warehouse, the assumption should be that it is correct. By this we mean that it contains the correct values and has been sourced from the system of record. When the project has multiple phases, mistakes made in a prior phase can be documented and not repeated in the next. If this strategy is used, a strong data warehouse can be built with lasting benefits.

SUMMARY

In conclusion, remember a data warehouse is not simply a super database made available to the business for questions and answers. It is really a strategy that consists of an architecture, a development methodology, a tool set, a data model, a database, a business sponsor, and a life cycle. As long as the seven sins are not committed and these things are religiously followed, the developers will produce a successful data warehouse implementation.

Real-World Data Warehousing: The Management Challenge

6

Howard Fosdick

Fosdick Consulting, Inc.

"We must rediscover the distinction between hope and expectation."

Ivan Illich

For many companies, data warehousing represents an entire new dimension in the usefulness of information systems. For the first time, companies are able to unlock the value of their historical data. They not only retrieve this data, but use it to project future trends, sales, needs, and markets. They make management and marketing decisions based on "slicing and dicing" the data and viewing it from many different angles. Such benefits explain why *data warehousing*, a term that showed up in industry trade magazines in 1993, has already translated into widespread project activity.

Unfortunately, practical experience shows a downside to data warehousing. While seemingly every company has a data warehouse project, there have been many qualified successes and several outright failures in implementing this technology. The lure of tremendous value added at many companies has been comprised by IT's difficulty in successfully bringing home data warehouse projects.

What can be learned from projects thus far? This chapter describes common problems in initial data warehouse projects and how to avoid them. It is based on experiences in data warehousing at several companies. Understanding the causes of failure for past projects (and addressing them head on) increases the chances for the success of your own effort.

THE CAUSES OF FAILURE

Examination of data warehouse projects shows that difficulty centers on these areas:

1. Failure to understand the data warehouse concept
2. Management issues
3. Design issues
4. Sizing issues
5. Technical issues.

As sometimes happens in the early stages of IT' adaptation of new technology, the most daunting challenges with data warehousing are not technical issues. They involve, instead, the difficulty of understanding and managing the new technology. While some companies blame technical problems for the failure of their data warehouses in fulfilling the high hopes they may have had for them, conceptual, design, and management issues are the root causes of the problems. This chapter focuses on these areas of misunderstanding that commonly cause data warehouses to fall short of their potential.

WHAT IS A DATA WAREHOUSE?

At this early time in the evolution of data warehouses, it is not surprising to find many projects floundering due to basic misunderstanding concerning what a data warehouse is. What does surprise, however, is the size and scale of projects that have failed due to such basic misunderstandings. In many cases, these large projects were the first data warehouse projects to be implemented at their respective companies. Or worse, they were the first client/server project at the company. This is a classic mistake in project management: taking on a large project as the first of its kind, rather than initially tackling a smaller project. In the data warehouse arena, smaller, departmental data warehouses are called data marts. They are ideally suited to be the first implementation of this technology at a company.

Many companies err by not defining exactly what a data warehouse is, the business problems it will solve, and the uses to which it will be put. As always, any term in the computer industry that proves its usefulness quickly becomes ill defined, due to purposeful misuse of the term by software and hardware vendors, consultants, industry analysts, and the like. However, the term *data warehouse* has several identfiable progenitors. As one example, in his several books on the topic, Bill Inmon provides a crisp, clear definition of the data warehouse.[1,2] (See Chapter 1 for details.) He defines a data warehouse as databases that support decision making and that are

1. Subject-oriented
2. Integrated
3. Time-variant
4. Nonvolatile.

Comparing these defining parameters to warehouses in your own experience quickly shows why some data warehousing projects flounder. Subject-oriented databases require database design. Some companies do not formally design their data warehouse databases at all. They informally evolve these databases. Sometimes they evolve outward from core OLTP or operational systems. Other companies evolve them from existing DSS that were not intended specifically for data warehousing. Either case spells trouble. Subject databases are organized or designed around the essential entities of the business and require data-driven design. This rarely results from adapation or evolution of existing OLTP file structures and databases. Nor is it likely to result from older DSS data stores, which often represent file extracts and database dumps, rather than well-designed, independently maintained, subject databases.

The term *integrated data* means that some design process or methodology was followed to create the data warehouse databases. Consistency in naming conventions, keys, relationships, encoding, and translation can only be achieved by design. Subject databases and the high degree of integration required by the data warehouse underline the reality that only companies that plan on, budget for, and follow through on a rather large design effort can successfully build a data warehouse.

The term *time-variant* data means that the data warehouse design organizes data by various time periods. This is fundamental to deriving value from temporal data analysis. Warehouse data is often summarized by period—for example, by months, quarters, or years.

Stating that data warehouse data is nonvolatile means that it is not updated in real time. Typically, data is staged into a data warehouse on a nightly or weekly basis. This staging may involve complicated extraction, summarization, accumulation, and aging procedures. Once the data is in the warehouse, it is not updated directly by users. There is no data in the warehouse whose periodicity is such that it must be updated during the day or in real time. The decisions that are made predicated on warehouse data can easily tolerate approximations of that data. Real-time nth degree accuracy is important for operational decisions, but not for data warehouse decisions.

Many companies have difficulty because they permit real-time updates to their data warehouses. For example, one company insisted that it needed real-time updates because of the kinds of decisions that would be made through the warehouse. This simply showed that the company did not understand the role of the warehouse in decision making.

Another company turned on a replication server to propagate data automatically from its operational OLTP systems to the data warehouse. Of course, this had the effect of near-real-time updates in the data warehouse databases. The company claimed that only a small number of updates were involved. Even so, it had a disastrous effect. First, read-only systems allow for a number of efficiency techniques that are not possible in updatable environments, even when only a small number of updates are involved. For example, read-only systems allow logging to be turned off, a major performance gain using most database management systems. Furthermore, large numbers of indexes can be set up for read-only systems and, of course, updating these indexes in real time represents major overhead. As a last example, the data transformation phase, through which data is accumulated, summarized, and analyzed during loading into the data warehouse, must now be done in real time. As seen in most successful warehouse projects, these data transformations are typically run as very large batch jobs during the night-time warehouse-building window. Doing them in the day is horribly inefficient. Dropping them in on top of user queries will be unacceptable. The entire value of the data warehouse hinges on its ability to provide speedy turnaround for a whole series of intensive queries. Running real-time updates is guaranteed to compromise the warehouse's responsiveness.

The kinds of information contained in the data warehouse include the following:

1. Old detail data
2. Current detail data
3. Lightly summarized data
4. Highly summarized data
5. Metadata (the data directory or guide).

The presence of old detail data means that the data warehouse designers must have a means of aging data. They must design a strategy as to when data is considered obsolete and enforce and implement it through some means of purging that data. They most decide, too, whether obsolete detail data is also eliminated from high-level summary statistics. An archival strategy may be needed for some warehouses, as well.

Detail data is a major problem for many warehouse projects because of its sheer volume. Selectivity criteria must be defined and put into place. Some warehouse projects flounder because designers fail to appreciate the impacts (and complexity) of managing large amounts of detail data. Large volumes force many design constraints. Designers' instincts may be to include all detail data (because then "we have it if we need it"), but this places a tremendous burden on performance techniques.

Summarized data relates to the requirement for lengthy data transforms or data manipulation when loading the data warehouse. This transform/load process may be long running and complicated. Big batch jobs are a part of most warehouses in their creation and maintenance in off-hours. Designing for the available batch window is key to success. Many of the programmers on warehouse projects come from client/server Graphical User Iterface (GUI) programming backgrounds. Desktop programmers often do not have sufficient exposure to batch processing to understand what is involved or the challenges of running large batch jobs. Often only those with mainframe experience truly appreciate what is required; but of course, managers staffing data warehouse projects often believe they must hire client/server programmers (read: "no mainframers"). It is important to include some experienced batch programmers or designers to meet the challenge of loading and transforming the data warehouse in a timely fashion.

Metadata is the users' guide to what is available in the warehouse and how to use it. Good analysis and design is essential to ensure that end users can employ the metadata to identify and retrieve the data they want in order to answer their questions. This challenge is often not understood by the technicians designing the warehouse. While wrapped up in intricate technical issues, they forget how important translation of the warehouse environment is into user terminology. Metadata must bridge the gap to the users' perspective, or else users will not take advantage of the warehouse.

Understanding the data warehouse concept is critical because so many companies declare their intent to create a data warehouse without understanding what it is. If the data warehouse were one of the many new technologies in our profession that sprung spontaneously from a new technology, this would be forgivable. But data warehousing evolved from DSS philosophy and techniques that have been practiced for a decade. Even worse, data warehousing has a recognized progenitor, and his writings, with their very detailed understanding and definition of the warehouse, are available to all. It is legitimate to modify or disagree with this definition, but not to embark on a major warehouse project without first understanding it. The sad fact is that some early data warehouse projects started with insufficient understanding of the term and its meaning. Some companies embark on certain failure by declaring their decision support system a data warehouse without noting the roles of summarized data and metadata, for example. Others simply term any DSS a data warehouse for political reasons to sell the project to management and secure its funding. In these cases, IT is cruising for the inevitable bruising that will occur when the mismatch between successful data warehouses and what it provides in its misnamed project is unmasked.

The data warehouse is well defined and documented. Understand this concept first, and then modify it (if necessary) for your own purposes.

MANAGEMENT ISSUES

The preceding discussion alludes to some key management issues. Let's discuss them now from the standpoint of managing the data warehouse project. While the present situation will change, the majority of data warehouse failures thus far have been management failures. Two factors lull IT management into a false sense of complacency. IT mentally associates warehousing with

1. Client/server technology
2. Rapid application development (RAD).

Client/server technology implies desktop programming in a software environment that is simpler to learn and easier to use than back in the days of hand-coded COBOL/CICS programming. Productivity is higher and entry-level skill requirements are lower. This intimately ties to the basic assumptions many have about RAD: Development should be quick and easy, iterative, and evolutionary. Gone are the days of intense, up-front design, good planning, and tight project management. "Users won't wait two years any longer for their applications to be developed, they want them now!"

While this last statement is certainly true, problems occur when management eliminates planning and design from data warehouse projects. Warehouses are typically large, complex undertakings. While they feature client/server architecture, easy-to-use GUI front-end tools for the users, and high-productivity desktop development environments for programmers, to assume that a good warehouse can casually be developed is dead wrong.

Some companies build small data marts, and these may fit the traditional model of two-tiered client/server development. Iterative development, evolving prototypes into production applications, and designless programming may work for relatively small data marts.

Scaling this attitude to databases in the gigabyte range, supporting unrestricted ad hoc queries and complex analysis, is a prescription for disaster. Data warehouses of significant size require significant up-front design work to implement properly. This planning and design encompasses several areas:

1. Database design
2. Design for preprocessed data
3. Design of the data load/transform processes
4. Metadata design
5. Design techniques used for very large databases.

Let's look at each area in turn. Data warehouse databases must be subject oriented and integrated. How likely is it that databases have these features without a lengthy design effort? Or that such databases will naturally evolve as a result of an interative programming effort?

The answer, of course, is that such databases will almost certainly not result unless a project team spends significant time and effort in building them. Furthermore, the team requires the proper automated tools to design them. For some warehouse efforts, this means desktop-based GUI design tools. For others, it means large integrated CASE tools. In either case, management commitment in terms of the dollars to buy the tools, the training time to get the project team up to speed with them, and the work time for their use is essential. A warehouse project that skimps on any of the three because warehouses are quick client/server efforts risks databases that do not fulfill the requirements of the data warehouse.

Designing databases containing preprocessed data means building the warehouse such that period data can be sliced and diced on appropriate axes by users.

Given the volume of data in many warehouses, designing databases to meet this criteria will be time-consuming. The availability of preprocessed information is one key characteristic that distinguishes data warehouses from traditional DSS. The warehouse concept takes DSS design to the next step, a step that is fundamental to the usability of the warehouse. This step involves major planning and design, not the kind of effort that easily evolves in an unstructured environment without proper planning. Management must coordinate and structure the overall project plan so that this work gets done.

Key to proper design for preprocessed data is user interaction. Client/server applications are often designed with frequent user interaction at different points in the iterative project life cycle. This model excludes the advance design that is essential to the warehouse. Dynamically altering table design and definitions when gigabytes of data are involved is not realistic. The old-fashioned "waterfall" project design cycle, on which the project team spends lots of time with the users up front (before those users see much payoff), is unavoidable. In the IT industry, this approach is not popular (and with good reason). But large data warehouse projects require an up-front investment of time and effort to succeed. Their sheer size enforces discipline of the kind many client/server project managers prefer to avoid.

User interaction is key to good database design for the data warehouse. This is because the databases are specifically designed with certain queries and certain kinds of analyses in mind. (This is the essence of the denormalization, summarization, and aggregation typically required for warehouses to give prompt responses to user queries.) One of the biggest mistakes managers commit in directing warehouse projects is to omit user interaction and input in the project's requirements phase. The feeling is that IT cannot bother users with up-front involvement, that the warehouse is rather like a ballpark in a cornfield: "Build it and they will come." With large data warehouses, nothing could be further from the truth. Build a warehouse without knowledge of the actual queries users will run, and you build databases that require all sorts of tablespace scans. Thus, you build a warehouse in which user queries take hours to run. Once users get a taste of these long-running queries, they will surely abandon the warehouse before they even get a sense of how valuable it might be. This degenerates to a very different experience: "Build it and they will wonder why you did."

The process of building a successful data warehouse is the process of mutating many of the traditional features of "good" database design. These alterations can only be accomplished successfully with intimate knowledge of the kinds of queries and analyses users will make against the data warehouse.

Managers must also plan for the data loads necessary to build the warehouse databases. One activity that is almost always necessary is data cleansing. This can involve increasing the accuracy of data or, as is often the case, complicated matching of data from entirely different environments. A mechanism for accurately matching or normalizing keys may be required. The data transformations involved can be quite complicated. They can only be accomplished in projects of significant size by a concentrated, coordinated design effort. Data size and volume are again factors.

Loading a 20-gigabyte set of warehouse databases nightly by employing the same casual design approach that works well in iteratively putting up a much smaller application is unrealistic.

Metadata design is another area managers sometimes gloss over in unsuccessful warehouse projects. Metadata and the tools that access it are fundamental to users' ability to take advantage of the data in the warehouse. In the absence of such a data road map, the data warehouse locks data up as effectively as systems such as IMS did years before today's GUI tools were available. If you want to ensure that users do not use your data warehouse, leave out the directory. Few will find their way around in gigabytes of data without it.

Metadata is what turns raw data into useful information. Only with such a data guide can users find what they want, ask the questions they want, and do the analyses they want. However, metadata does not just happen. A winning combination of metadata directory and readily accessible end-user access tools only results from a well-thought-out design. Managers who do not plan on such an effort doom their data warehouses to failure.

Following iterative design principles, some managers ask, Why not just build the warehouse, then add metadata and its directory and tools later? This reasoning is seductive because it again hides the true cost involved in building a good warehouse. It pretends that the warehouse is something you can throw up in a couple months (at most) and that your users will derive immediate value from it without

---

CHECKLIST:
THE CLASSIC ERRORS OF DATA WAREHOUSE PROJECTS

- Company's first client/server project is a multi-gigabyte warehouse
- Management does not understand what a data warehouse is (subject-oriented, integrated, time-variant, non-volatile databases)
- Management launches the warehouse project without a crisp understanding of how users will use it
- Little or no database design is done
- Vague sizing projections (database size, number of users, resources consumed by typical queries, number of concurrent queries, RAM needed, CPU requirements, etc.)
- Users are not involved in defining the warehouse requirements
- Real-time updates are performed against the warehouse data (including "hidden updates" via replication or similar technologies)
- Database design techniques evolved specifically for data warehousing are not understood and employed
- Treat the large warehouse project as a small two-tier client/server application on a work group server
- The data warehouse is NOT isolated from OLTP or older DSS environments
- Failure to plan database transform/load steps to fit the batch window
- Metadata is not expertly crafted to the users' viewpoint

Figure 6.1

FAMOUS LAST WORDS

- "RAD techniques mean no design effort is necessary"
- "Just get me some GUI programmers; we don't need those high-priced, obsolete, back-end dinosaur technicians!"
- "Hey, it's just another client/server project"
- We can just add it onto our existing OLTP systems!"
- "I don't know what THEY do. But if we build this data warehouse, I know they'll find it invaluable!"
- "Well, at least I can add it to my resume…"

Figure 6.2

much effort on your part. Dream on. Building the metadata infrastructure can be done last, but some planning and preparation will be necessary to make it succeed. Adding it as a superstructure on top of the rest of the data warehouse (with no advance sense of what will be there) is problematic at best. In many cases, deferring metadata design and collection is merely a management excuse to avoid the exercise. But as in redesigning the warehouse databases to process typical user queries efficiently after the fact, users who confront a warehouse without a metadata superstructure from day 1 are not likely to tangle with the data warehouse again. User impressions form quickly and are no more subject to change (even in the face of new evidence) than are our first impressions of another person. If proper guides to the data are not in place from the start, IT may find it difficult to get funding to proceed any further with the data warehouse project.

Finally, managers must recognize the need for special techniques that apply to large database systems. Usually, warehouse data measures in gigabytes or even tens or hundreds of gigabytes. Without special high-technology approaches, manipulating such large data volumes becomes problematic. One example is in loading the data. Parallelization of the loads (into parallel partitions or tablespaces) will likely be required to perform the loads within the available batch window. Parallelization of queries may also be necessary. Individual queries may be broken up to run in parallel across parallel tablespaces, and multiple queries may be run simultaneously. All these cases require effort in planning, design, and implementation. Building large data warehouse databases and then deciding, after the fact, that parallel loads are required to meet batch windows will not work. DASD layout, adaptor layout, physical Data Definition Language (DDL) related to data storage and placement—all might need to be changed to parallelize loads after the fact. Few projects can take this kind of hit after it is discovered that loads do not work fast enough for success and then revise the environment to make them work fast enough. Parallel loads are just one example of the kinds of techniques that are required to work successfully with the large databases involved in most data warehouses.

The bottom line is that most data warehouses involve large data volumes and ad hoc queries and analysis of the type that will not meet user expectations without many special techniques unique to warehouse applications. Managers should not take a loosely managed, unstructured, ad hoc approach to resolving these problems. Low-end client/server applications and the quick iterative development approach embodied in RAD are wonderful new approaches, but they are limited in their applicability to large, complicated data warehouse databases. Managers should integrate some of the principles of these new approaches with the structured, coordinated management traditionally associated with very large projects.

Two other principles of data warehouse project management need to be mentioned: sizing and staff expertise. Managers often start with vague concepts of how the size of the data warehouse databases and user community will grow. Growth can be planned for, within some reasonable scope. But arbitrary or unplanned growth can wreak havoc. A gigabyte database perhaps can grow into a 10-gigabyte database without disruption. But can that 10-gigabyte database grow into 100 gigabytes? So often, data warehouse projects are sold to management and users as the ultimate "build it and they will come" project. But what if they do? Scaling a machine from 10 intense query users to dozens or hundreds can be impossible. Planning is called for. If you do not know what you are building, chances are that you will not build what it should have been.

Diverse staff expertise is required in building large warehouses. Back-end expertise in database design, system architecture, and database performance will be just as important as experience in desktop programming and GUI design. Assembling a flock of GUI programmers with two-tier experience is a great idea if it is accompanied by assembling highly technical personnel with some of the complementary skills mentioned here. Large-systems experience is essential, since serious data warehouses are inevitably large systems. Understanding how to map physical disk volumes to adaptors or channels, DASD to bus design, local area network (LAN) transfer rates to wide area networks (WANs), client processes to DBMS processes, tablespaces to physical volumes—all these highly technical skills have critical bearing on how well a large warehouse performs in quickly responding to user queries. The large warehouse is not another experience in quick deployment of a two-tier client/server project on a work group server.

SUMMARY

At this early date in the evolution of data warehousing, many projects experience difficulty because managers and designers fail to perceive the size, scope, and complexity of the challenge they undertake. Some of the skills of "traditional" IT, in planning, design, and up-front investment of time and effort, are necessary to bring home large data warehouse projects. Treating a multigigabyte data warehouse project as simply another two-tier, client/server project, in which unstructured RAD techniques can be applied for a quick success, shows more faith in media hype than actual experience. Data warehouses offer tremendous benefits to most organizations. With proper planning, funding, and project management, they can lead to entirely new uses of business computers.

REFERENCES

[1] INMON, W. H., *Using the Data Warehouse,* John Wiley & Sons, New York, 1994.
[2] INMON, W. H., *Building the Data Warehouse,* John Wiley & Sons, New York, 1993.

P A R T TWO

PLANNING THE DATA WAREHOUSE

"Our plans miscarry because they have no aim. When a man does not know what harbor he is making for, no wind is the right wind."

Seneca

This section discusses the planning of the data warehouse, with chapters on warehouse architecture, cost justification of the pilot project, and development methodologies. Although it is generally accepted that a data warehousing system helps organizations leverage their data assets to gain competitive advantage in the marketplace, there is not always agreement on what constitutes a data warehousing system. Chapter 7, "A Technical Architecture for Data Warehousing" by Colin White, clearly defines the architecture of a data warehousing system and describes in detail the functions performed by its various components. Although the initial implementation may not use all of the pieces of the architecture, it is helpful to understand the grand plan for data warehouses.

Since the business benefits may not always be known until after a warehouse is implemented, the process of cost justifying a data warehouse is an interesting combination of traditional and nontraditional thinking on the subject. Chapter 8, "Creating a Business Case" by Jay Marquez, describes the process of developing a business case for a data warehouse and provides real-world examples to help the reader through the process.

Chapter 9, "A Flexible Approach to Developing a Data Warehouse" by John Ladley, describes a methodology for developing a data warehouse or operational data store. Although existing methodologies may be used to guide traditional software projects, they must be adapted for data warehouse implementation. Ladley presents practical examples of applying the methodology to two different types of projects and suggests techniques for modifying the methodology to suit the project.

This section should give project managers much food for thought as the warehouse project begins.

A Technical Architecture for Data Warehousing

7

Colin White
DataBase Associates International
Morgan Hill, California

"When we build, let us think that we build forever."

John Ruskin

Although it is generally accepted that a data warehousing system improves end-user query, reporting and DSS capabilities and helps organizations leverage corporate data to gain competitive advantage in the marketplace, there is not always common agreement on what exactly constitutes a data warehousing system. The purpose of this chapter is to clarify matters by clearly defining the architecture of a data warehousing system and to describe in detail the functions performed by its various components.

The key components of a data warehousing system are shown in Figure 7.1.

- Design component, for designing warehouse databases
- Data acquisition component, for capturing data from source files and databases, and for cleaning, transporting, and applying it to data warehouse databases
- Data manager component, for creating, managing, and accessing warehouse data
- Management component, for administering data warehouse operations
- Information directory component, for providing administrators and business users with information about the contents and meaning of data stored in warehouse databases
- Data access component, for providing business end users with the tools they need for accessing and analyzing warehouse data
- Middleware component, for providing end-user tools with access to warehouse databases
- Data delivery component, for distributing warehouse data to other warehouses and external systems.

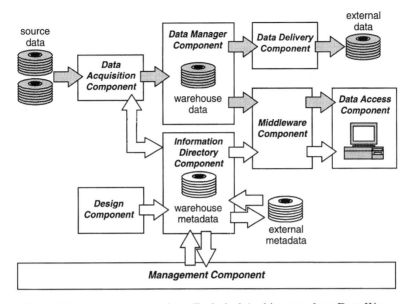

Figure 7.1 DataBase Associates Technical Architecture for a Data Warehousing System.

DESIGN COMPONENT

The design component is used by warehouse designers and administrators to design and define data warehouse databases. Additional factors that have to be considered when designing data warehouses (compared with designing operational databases) include the handling of summary and temporal (time-related) data. Some warehouse databases, particularly those for multidimensional data analysis, often involve denormalized database designs known as star schemas. Work group data modeling tools (W-CASE) are often used by the design component.

DATA ACQUISITION COMPONENT

The data acquisition component is used to develop and run data acquisition applications that capture data from source systems for applying to warehouse databases. Data acquisition applications are developed based on rules defined by the warehouse developer. These rules define the data sources from which the warehouse data will be obtained, and the data cleanup and enhancement to be done to this data before it is applied to warehouse databases.

Data cleanup may involve the restructuring of records or fields, removal of operational-only data, supply of missing field values, and checking of data integrity and consistency. Data enhancement may involve the decoding and translating of field values, addition of a time attribute (if one is not present in the source data) to reflect the currency of data, summarization of data, or the calculation of derived values.

Once the source data has be cleaned and enhanced, it is mapped to the target warehouse databases, transported to the data warehousing system, and applied to the appropriate warehouse databases. The application of data to the warehouse databases is done using data manipulation language statements (SQL, for example, in the case of a relational DBMS), or the load utility of the DBMS used to manage the warehouse.

The definitions created by the data acquisition component are often stored as metadata in the information directory component. Some products use this metadata to generate customized 3GL/4GL data acquisition programs. Other products use this metadata dynamically during data acquisition operations to manage the flow of data from source systems to the target data warehouse.

There are four main types of product that support data acquisition:

- *Code generators.* These create tailored data acquisition programs. The objective of these products is to generate tailored 3GL/4GL capture programs based on the data structure definitions, and cleanup and enhancement rules defined to the data acquisition component. This approach reduces the need for an organization to write its own 3GL data acquisition programs. These products are used for building warehouses that involve a large number of data sources and when there is significant data cleanup to be done.

- *Data replication tools.* Many database vendors market data replication products that capture changes to a source database on one system and apply the changes to a copy of the source database located on a different system. These replication products often do not support the copying of data from nonrelational files and databases, and often do not provide facilities for significant data cleanup and enhancement. These tools are used to build warehouses when the number of data sources and amount of data cleanup required is small.

- *Data pumps.* A data pump typically often runs on a different server from either the source or target database system. These products suck data into the pump server at user-defined intervals, clean and enhance the data, and then send (and apply) the results to the target warehouse database. Cleanup and enhancement is usually done based on a script or function logic defined to the pump server. These products are used to build small departmental warehouses, rather than large enterprise warehouses.

- *Data reengineering tools.* These tools are designed to handle data cleanup and enhancement. Some focus on structural changes to data, while others are designed to handle the cleanup of data content (for example, name and address data). In some cases, these products are used in conjunction with other data acquisition tools.

- *Generalized data acquisition tools and utilities.* These copy data from a source system to a target system. There are numerous other tools and utilities that support the movement of data from a source system to a target system, but they do not fit into one of the aforementioned categories. These products vary in performance and in their ability to support the data integration, cleanup, and enhancement requirements of a data warehousing system.

DATA MANAGER COMPONENT

The data manager component is used by other components in the data warehousing system to create, manage, and access warehouse data (and possibly metadata). The data manager employed by a data warehousing system is usually either an RDBMS or a multidimensional DBMS (MDBMS). RDBMSs are used for building large enterprise data warehouses or small departmental ones, while MDBMs are used for building small departmental data warehouses. Warehouse DBMSs have requirements over and above those for an operational OLTP applications. Key factors to consider here are scalability (database size, query complexity, number of users, number of dimensions, software exploitation of underlying hardware) and performance (utility operations and complex query processing). As query complexity and database size increases, data warehouses designers will need to consider the use of parallel hardware and parallel database software in order to obtain satisfactory performance.

MANAGEMENT COMPONENT

The management component consists of a set of systems management services for maintaining the data warehousing environment. These services include managing data acquisition operations, archiving warehouse data, backing up and recovering data, securing and authorizing access to warehouse data, and managing and tuning data access operations. At present, there are few tools designed explicitly for managing data warehousing systems, and most data warehouse administrators employ the facilities of the warehouse DBMS to perform these tasks.

INFORMATION DIRECTORY COMPONENT

The information directory component helps technical and business users access and exploit the power of a data warehousing system. It achieves this by providing a set of tools for the maintenance and viewing of warehouse metadata. This metadata may be created by warehouse developers and administrators during the warehouse design and development process, and/or may be imported from external products such as DBMS system catalogs, program libraries, CASE tools, and DSS tools. Metadata may also be created when doing data acquisition operations and when accessing warehouse data. The main elements of the information directory (see Figure 7.2) are the metadata manager, technical and business metadata, and the information assistant (sometimes called an information navigator).

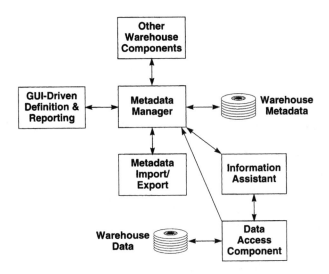

Figure 7.2   The Information Directory Component.

The metadata manager is used to maintain, export, and import warehouse metadata. To provide flexibility, the metadata manager should employ the services of a database management system and support metadata versioning. It should also have an external application program interface (API) and have a documented and user extendable metamodel.

Technical metadata contains information about warehouse data for use by warehouse designers and administrators when carrying out warehouse development and management tasks. These tasks include the design of warehouse databases, the definition of data acquisition rules, the building of data collections (a data collection is a set of data of interest to a specific user or group of users), the definition of the data deliveries to external products and users, and the management of authorization, backup and recovery, archiving, data delivery, data collections, data acquisition, and data access.

Technical metadata documents information about data sources, data targets, data cleanup rules, data enhancement rules, and data mapping between data sources and the warehouse databases. Most of the information is created when the warehouse designer defines the data sources and targets and the rules to be used when copying data into the warehouse. It may also be imported from an external system, such as a 3GL copybook library, DBMS system catalog, or CASE tool.

Technical metadata about the amount of data in the warehouse and the date it was created or updated should also be stored in the directory. Ideally, this information should be added by the tools employed to capture data from operational systems and apply it to the warehouse databases. Technical metadata about how end users access and use warehouse data should also be trapped and added to the directory to enable designers and administrators to tune and enhance the data warehouse.

Business metadata contains information that gives end users an easy-to-understand business perspective of the data in the warehouse. This information includes the mapping of business subject areas to technical metadata, details about predefined queries and reports, business terms and associated technical names, and details about the custodian of the data. The business metadata is usually created by the warehouse administrator—it may also be imported from external systems, such as CASE tools or decision support tools.

The information assistant provides warehouse end users with easy access to the business and technical metadata. It helps users discover what data exists in the warehouse and understand its business meaning. Some products also help users create, document, and/or run queries, reports, or analyses, and order data and/or information that cannot be found in the warehouse.

There are two main types of information directory product:

- Repositories and data dictionaries, which were initially designed for developing operational applications but are now moving in the direction of supporting business end users
- Business information directories, which are designed for data warehousing and which focus on business metadata and supporting business user access to a data warehousing system.

DATA ACCESS COMPONENT

The data access component provides the data access tools that enable end users to access and analyze warehouse data. These data access tools fall into the following categories:

- Query, reporting, and data analysis tools
- Multidimensional data analysis tools that access a relational DBMS
- Multidimensional data analysis tools that access a multidimensional DBMS
- DSS application development tools employing a 4GL or visual programming language.

MIDDLEWARE COMPONENT

The middleware component provides connectivity to warehouse databases from end-user data tools. Standard database middleware can be used to perform this task, but vendors are beginning to ship specialized middleware designed for a data warehousing environment. This specialized middleware is of two types:

- Intelligent data warehousing middleware, which provides a business view of warehouse data to end users and which monitors and tracks access to warehouse data

- Analytical servers, which improve the performance of multidimensional data analysis operations against relational DBMS data.

DATA DELIVERY COMPONENT

The data delivery component is used to distribute data collections to other data warehouses, and end-user products such as spreadsheets, local databases, and so forth. The content of the data collection is usually defined by the warehouse administrator, and the delivery schedule is defined using the information assistant facility of the information directory component. Delivery of data may be based on time of day or on the completion of an external event.

SUMMARY

There is more to data warehousing than just copying operational data into a separate informational database. A data warehousing system should provide a complete solution for managing the flow of information from existing corporate databases and external sources into end-user decision support systems. It should make it easy for business users to find out what information exists in the warehouse, and provide tools for accessing and manipulating that information.

Creating a Business Case

8

Jay Marquez

The Praxium Group
Atlanta, Georgia

"There's no such thing as a free lunch."

Milton Friedman

Creating a business case for a data warehouse with traditional methods is a difficult task because the real benefits of the warehouse may not be known until after the data warehouse has been built. Traditionally, when an enterprise develops a new information systems solution, it is with the intent of increasing productivity, reducing costs, improving the efficiency of particular business processes, or increasing user satisfaction. The benefits of these new information systems can be quantified and used in a pro forma cash flow statement. These statements can take various forms, such as payback or return on investment (ROI) documents. Basically, the costs are accumulated and subtracted from the sum of the benefits and the difference should be in favor of the benefits. Depreciation, income tax, and capital costs are included in the formula to determine the net cash flow of the project.

The benefits of a data warehouse are not as straightforward, but the gains can be quite substantial. An IDC study found an average ROI of over 400% at more than 60 organizations.[1] Many shops have had the luxury of introducing data warehouse projects without a full cost justification analysis because top management recognized the benefits of improved data accuracy, integration, and accessibility as well as increased user autonomy. They had an overriding business situation to address and were able to bypass an objective business case justification for the project. Although it is not uncommon to bypass the cost justification phase of the first data warehouse project, this approach has been limited to those enterprises that were adventurous or had significant amounts of research and development (R&D) funds. Now that top managers are recognizing the costs as well as the potential benefits, they often ask for an analysis of costs and benefits. This can provide an opportunity to demonstrate the potential value of the warehouse and bring individuals together from various departments at the start of the project. This chapter describes the process of creating a business case for typical data warehouse projects.

KEY TO JUSTIFYING A DATA WAREHOUSE

The key to justifying a data warehouse is to state clearly what the business issues are and how the data warehouse, with its data delivery mechanisms, can reap rewards for the business community. These rewards are varied for each individual enterprise, but they usually fall into one or more of the following categories: more intelligent decision making, improved customer service, enhanced asset/liability management, more business intelligence, and improved business processes. In other words, reaffirming that the data warehouse will turn the enterprise's data into a competitive tool will justify the development costs. As long as the data warehouse is aligned with the strategic and tactical direction of the enterprise, the key business managers and decision makers will fully endorse the effort and associated cost of a decision support solution.

BUILDING THE BUSINESS CASE

The business case must identify all the components that will affect or be affected by the building of a data warehouse. There will be an organizational impact, as described in Chapter 3, and the business case should consider the cost of building an infrastructure to support the warehouse. Many of these costs will not be repeated in future projects and will provide ongoing benefits for future projects. Above all, be honest with the costs associated with the data warehouse architecture. Everyone involved in this process, especially the executive sponsor, should have all the information needed to make the appropriate business decision. The easiest place to start is with the cost items:

- *Hardware purchase and/or lease.* This will entail identification of the costs of all hardware needed to construct the architecture, such as connectivity to the legacy systems, staging areas, the database servers, application servers, communication, networks (LAN and/or WAN), personal computers (PCs), laptops, and printers. Care must be taken in weighing the benefits between leasing and purchasing, so the legal and accounting departments of the enterprise must be involved.

- *Vendor software.* The list of software must be detailed enough for the entire data warehouse architecture (i.e., middleware, relational and/or multidimensional database management systems, query tools, application development tools, data analysis and transformation tools, etc.). The cost of a dictionary or directory should be considered. If there is an existing dictionary, is it suitable for users? If not, will a user-oriented directory be purchased? Some project teams have chosen to build a simple user-oriented directory as part of the project because of lack of funding in this area. The size of the client community should be estimated because many software costs are associated with licensing fees based on the number of concurrent users. Maintenance fees are an ongoing cost that must be highlighted because they continue after the warehouse is built.

- *In-house developed software.* Any software that must be written for the implementation of the data warehouse must be taken into consideration. These programs and utilities are usually the hardest to estimate but will take the majority of the time involved in setting up the data warehouse. Extraction and data cleansing programs are dirty jobs but will guarantee failure of the data warehouse endeavor if done poorly.

- *Installation and conversion.* Some of these costs, are buried with the purchase or leasing costs, but they are included here so that they will not be forgotten. This item also includes any changes to the existing hardware and software environment, such as more memory on servers, PCs, and printers; additional cabling to the legacy machines; and additional logic so legacy programs have more edits or cleansing routines.

- *Ongoing support.* The warehouse will create new roles as well as increase responsibility of the existing staff. These resources are expensive to train and retain. As part of the overall plan, the resource issue needs to be addressed. Ongoing support is crucial in terms of the usability of the data warehouse and helping the business community to exploit the information that is now at their fingertips. The cost of providing initial and ongoing training for clients and help desk personnel must be considered. The cost of responding to changing user requirements must also be considered.

- *Maintenance costs.* There is a high cost associated with continually maintaining the software and hardware within the architecture because new releases and functionality can affect the access of the data warehouse. In addition, there will be some risk because the maintenance release may conflict with the existing architecture or even expose problems in areas that were working.

The next set of components are the tangible and intangible benefits.

- *Cost reduction.* Elimination of manual tasks, batch reports, and staff can add to the benefits list. Be aware when dealing with people that a distinction should be made between those individuals that will be reassigned to other jobs and those who will no longer be needed. When itemizing the cost reduction of batch reports or jobs, include the savings of the reduction of CPU cycles, disk space, and paper as well as any peripheral jobs that are associated. There will be no real savings if the items being reduced are not released. Be honest about cost reductions. Since users will be performing many of the tasks that have been performed by technical personnel, there will be a shifting of certain costs from the IT staff to the user community.

- *Business community effectiveness.* The assumption is that the availability of information will allow business analysts to spend more time making decisions rather than looking for data to answer a given question. In one major company, the customer information that has been distributed in hundreds of separate files has been combined into an integrated operational data store as a foundation for the warehouse. This has eliminated the cost of redundant updating and enabled the company to analyze its customer base more effectively and devise more effective marketing plans and promotions. It has also allowed the company to be more responsive to customer problems and to offer potential new services when a customer calls in. In many credit card companies, the development of a warehouse has allowed data mining processes to identify buying patterns, which has saved millions of dollars in fraud prevention. It is sometimes difficult to predict the actual impact in this area.

The warehouse provides users with more autonomy, which can result in breakthrough ideas that have a major impact on the bottom line. The business value of being able to view company performance in a timely fashion from many different perspectives should not be overlooked.

- *Business revenue enhancement.* With the data warehouse in place and the tools to access it, the business community is expected to improve the bottom line or identify those areas that are costing the enterprise money. Whatever revenue improvement is quoted here must be tracked at the conclusion of the implementation phase of the data warehouse.

Timing of the various events can affect the cost of the data warehouse project. The costs start immediately and will continue until the project has ended. Any delay between the various phases can incur additional costs. The benefits will not be realized until the project has ended.

The last component to mention is risk. There are risks associated with the technology, infrastructure, resources, business community, and management. They cannot be minimized due to the immense impact they can have on the project. Be honest in the assessment of these risks, and be prepared to offer solutions.

BUSINESS ISSUES STATEMENT

Start the business case process by documenting the business issue(s) that will be resolved. The business issue(s) can be a specific problem, like detecting fraud, or the issue(s) can be in support of an enterprise's corporate goals. The business issue section will need to state these items:

1. Statement of the business issue to be resolved
2. Strategies to achieve the goals or address the issue(s)
3. Tactics that are to be used to implement the strategies
4. Performance metrics to measure the success of the tactics.

These items are stated in standard business terms so that everyone in the enterprise can understand what the issues are that will drive the design of the data warehouse. To help show the importance of these issues, the trends within the industry are also shown. The business trends will identify observations of the industry and contrast the trend with how the enterprise is doing. This contrast is important to illustrate where the enterprise stands relative to its competitors. If the information is well documented, it will be easier to identify the benefits.

Initial Subject Area

After this statement, the next task is to identify the initial subject area or areas that will be delivered in the warehouse. The subject area that is selected for implementation must have a data warehouse that is of a manageable size. The success of the project must be achievable and have a noticeable impact in the enterprise. For the first or pilot data warehouse, the goal is to have a small warehouse that can test the architecture in terms of integrating the data as well as delivering the information to the users within the business community.

For the subject area chosen, conduct an interview with key business managers and analysts to document their basic premises. These premises are written in three parts: observations, requirements, and key issues. The observations, requirements, and key issues are categorized by the degree of impact: high, medium, and low. The impact of each premise is measured by each department within the enterprise and the customer base that must be reached and maintained.

Current Information Technology Costs

The next task is to identify the current information technology costs of supporting the subject area's decision-making reports and applications. This will provide a basis for comparison of the new warehouse against the preexisting systems. The first step is to identify the costs of operational system development and maintenance. Next, identify database copies that exist and the number of extract programs that are run against them. If there is an existing DSS or EIS, estimate the ongoing cost. The last step is to identify what data conflicts and gaps exist and how this data fails to provide the information needed. The identity of the current process and costs will be used in a pro forma cash flow analysis.

INCOME AND EXPENSE CATEGORIES

The next step is to take the key issues and show which ones will have one of four income or expense categories:

1. Direct bottom line
2. Indirect bottom line
3. Organizational effectiveness
4. Organizational efficiency.

The direct bottom line category contains those key issues that will have a direct impact on the financial status of the business area. This category can be quantified by showing what costs or expenses can be reduced. The indirect bottom line is primarily the listing of those key issues that will improve the enterprise's capability to improve the bottom line. The effectiveness category includes key issues that will improve how the organization will be able to do its jobs or service its customers. The last category states the key values that demonstrate how efficient the organization will be.

EMPOWERING THE DECISION MAKERS

There are three key items that will empower the decision makers to make more informed decisions. Business analysts and managers will have direct access to the data warehouse. This will give them the capability to use their desktop PC to analyze the data using the familiar tools. Direct access will reduce the ad hoc reporting resources that a central information technology department provides. This reduction can be measured in terms of people, software, and hardware costs. The costs and tasks (i.e., setting up a help desk or increasing help desk staff, training, and user support, etc.) of empowering the users must be identified and listed.

The users can operate in a more iterative fashion in requesting information. This benefit will shorten the time needed to obtain information and allow users to respond more quickly to changing business conditions. Finally, by having direct access to the data warehouse with the ability to view data from many perspectives, users will have a better understanding of the information. This information will be better defined and cleansed and provide a more accurate view of the enterprise.

The second key will be the fact that the data will be distributed to the desktop by using PC-based technologies. The information can be used as a part of a workflow implementation or cross-functional idea exchange in a work group setting. This can be used to demonstrate how much more effective and efficient the business process can be.

The last key is that the users will be able to create their own programs and processes. They will have access to their own data and be able to transform it into information in a timely fashion. The information will provide immediate feedback about what is taking place within the enterprise. These three keys can be contrasted against the way things are being accomplished today.

BENEFITS ANALYSIS

At this point, the business case has shown what the business issues are and their importance to the enterprise and the customer base. The analysis of the tangible and intangible benefits is summarized to show how a data warehouse's information will affect each organization in the enterprise by increased effectiveness and efficiency.

ITERATIVE BUILDING

A data warehouse is built in an iterative manner to minimize cost and the disruption of the resources needed. The complete data warehouse architecture is usually too big a commitment to make. A complete data warehouse can involve a multimillion-dollar project with a completion term of two to three years. This is just too costly and too long to wait for the benefits to surface. The first iteration is the key to a successful implementation in that it sets a precedence of tangible benefits and success. Each subsequent iteration can occur in a quick and timely fashion without losing momentum.

Once the first iteration is decided, the database requirements are documented. This includes the origin of the data, the operational source and size, new requirements, and the data gaps or areas where the data quality can be improved. This will be required for each major entity and does not require a detailed analysis.

COST AND CASH FLOW ANALYSIS

The next steps are to do a cost analysis and a cash flow analysis. The cost analysis will show what the costs are to implement a particular architecture. The cash flow analysis is completed with best, worst, and expected cases. Risk assessment is included at this point.

FEEDBACK LOOP

The last part of this process is to provide a feedback loop to continue the benefits assessment and identify new requirements and refinements. To establish the data delivery requirements, sample queries must be gathered. These sample queries are written in English rather than any particular language. Each query must list what data will be needed, the rationale for the query, frequency of the requests, and how the data will be analyzed. A sample of the query will be shown for further clarification of what is needed. The client base is surveyed at the end of the first iteration to record the quantifiable results attained. Along with these results, positive or negative observations will be noted for future iterations.

REAL-WORLD CASES

CASE 1: Instinct

The central IT group and the business community were sure that a data warehouse would be beneficial but could not come up with a hard dollar amount in savings. IT and the business managers identified a subject area to be implemented and made sure that the cost was reasonable. Based on the success of the first project and actual cost savings generated, they were able to implement other subject areas and pursue additional warehouse projects. In other words, the first project was justified based on "gut feeling," but the results justified ongoing work.

CASE 2: Going with the Mission

In a large manufacturing organization, the IT group had a mission statement that was in synch with the business mission for the whole company. The business mission statement mentioned

- Reductions in time to get a product to market
- Identification of new markets
- Identification of potential new customers
- Improved market share, sales, and profits
- Improved communication across the company
- Optimized use of personnel
- Reengineered business processes.

IT's mission statement was based on the corporate mission and included objectives such as

- Reducing time spent maintaining corporate systems and supporting old technologies
- Shifting ownership of business information to the business community along with the tools and techniques needed for decision support.

A questionnaire was developed that could be used by the IT department in justifying new projects. Although it was useful for all projects, it was of special benefit to data warehouse projects because of the stated objective to shift ownership of information to the business community.

CASE 3: Business Necessity

In a large manufacturing organization, there were several divisions, each with its own sales team. There were certain cross-marketing agreements between the divisions, with the result that salesperson A, from division A, which manufactures widgets, might call on a client selling widget 1 and gadget 47. Salesperson B, from division B, which manufactures gadgets, might call on a client selling gadget 47, gadget 23, and widget 1. Due to lack of coordination, they might approach the same client on successive days, irritating the client and making poor use of salespeople.

A data warehouse was implemented that tracked sales plans by division, sales territory, salesperson, and prospective client. If salesman A and salesman B will be calling on the same client, the data warehouse made it possible to schedule calls so that they were spaced more effectively. It was possible to prevent overlap by multiple salespeople with the same client. The manufacturer was able to predict a potential gain in being able to present more products to the same client base with less irritation.

SUMMARY

A business case for a data warehouse requires a lot of effort in understanding the business climate and issues and is different from a traditional on-line transaction processing system. Once this business understanding is documented, the effort to present the issue(s) to the warehouse can be straightforward.

REFERENCES

[1] IDC Canada Ltd., Stephan Graham, Vice President of Software Research. Article in *Data Management Review,* June 1996, p. 39.

9

A Flexible Approach to Developing a Data Warehouse

John Ladley
META Group
St. Louis, Missouri

"When all else fails, read the directions."

Everyone's Grandfather

Developing a data warehouse (DW) or operational data store (ODS) is similar to other software projects. There are differences, however, whereby developing a DW or ODS departs from normal projects. ODS and DW are applications of data warehouse approaches (see Chapter 22). Many data warehouse efforts stutter when it comes to developing the project plan and managing the project because of these differences. Without some type of guidance, "tribal knowledge" fails project teams when they embark on a DW for the first time. Very few IT departments have a team experienced with data warehouse technology and approaches. DW projects are nearly always done in an iterative, rapid development mode. Rapid development requires a degree of rigor that many IT departments are unfamiliar with. Some type of documented process is needed to get by the departures from so-called conventional development methods.

A methodology is the formal definition of the processes required to bring an IT solution from an initial idea to a useful result. Methodology is also a concept that has great implications for IT organizations and businesses. A frequently used analogy is that IT methodologies can be thought of as cookbooks for doing software. But successful chefs do not seem to use cookbooks. Do great software developers need methodologies? Great chefs do use cookbooks, and great software projects do utilize a formally defined process or methodology.

Using a methodology does not imply following a described set of minutiae. A methodology exists to guide a software project. Every project is different. Like the great chef consulting a set of favorite recipes to create a new meal, the methodology is consulted to understand what is required for success and adapt to conditions that may vary from a perceived norm.

This chapter will present a set of examples that can be used as a guideline for developing data warehouse–based technology. A generic methodology will be used as a framework to present customized approaches to various types of DW projects. Each major step in the framework will be addressed from a "nuts and bolts" perspective. Rather than attempt to provide a methodology, each step is addressed from a perspective of "what to watch out for." Projects are contrasted and examples are provided to assist in determining how various projects differ in terms of activity and content and may require different application of techniques and methods.

Several assumptions are made so the chapter can concentrate on practical activities.

1. The projects used as examples have been approved.

2. You know what data warehouse and data warehouse technology (DWT) are (this always helps).

3. There is organizational support—business users and potential users of the DW are willing to supply expertise, buyin, and control the scope.

4. Data warehouse is seriously accepted as an information technology project. This sounds obvious, but some organizations have embarked on DW as an exercise in end-user computing.

The first guideline in developing the DW or ODS is that DW projects are iterative and done using RAD techniques. This means that the process

1. Relies heavily on short-term, tangible, iterative deliverables to indicate progress.

2. Accepts that all phases and activities will be time boxed. If the project experiences constraints that were not anticipated, scope is adjusted to ensure completion of value-added deliverables, or the time box is expanded.

3. Features high levels of user participation.

Figure 9.1 displays a generic methodology. The steps presented are iterative; each step provides more detail, and steps can be repeated. It is intended to be used as a framework for this chapter, and not as a full-blown detailed methodology. Each box represents a significant step that could or should happen during a DWT project.

This chapter will contrast two DWT projects by each step. Project 1 will be a relatively simple effort in scope, consisting of one subject area supporting a decision support system. Project 2, will be a multi-subject-area project with an operational component. Of course, there are many other possibilities, but these two examples cover the spectrum of applying the generic steps. The only area not significantly covered is the design and development of end-user access. This topic is covered in greater detail in other chapters.

Figure 9.1 illustrates the major components of a data warehouse project. Each box will be addressed in this chapter, in general and, then more specific terms. You can also approach this chapter by reading the descriptive portion of all sections before reviewing the comparative details.

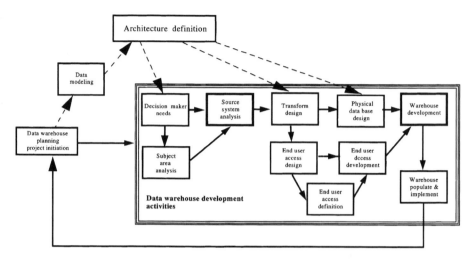

Figure 9.1 Generic Methodology.

DATA WAREHOUSE PLANNING: PROJECT INITIATION

Project teams have trouble starting a DW project for a variety of reasons. There is inexperience with formal approaches and lack of data warehouse experience. This planning activity is the most important aspect of the project, and key to initiating the project is classifying the project. This permits selection of the relevant tasks and activities. The project is classified and made comprehensible. There are three basic dimensions that can be used to assist in classifying the project:

1. What is the project scope? It includes determining the scope of the data (single or multiple subject areas), the role of technology (is there new technology involved?) and the temporal considerations (how fast do we need something of business value?).
2. What is the business reason? Is the project operational (i.e., requiring an operational data store) or decision support (i.e., requiring a data warehouse) in nature? What are the business drivers; what business problem is being solved?
3. Is the project tactical or strategic? Is the project being driven by business reasons that are responsive or proactive, that have short- or long-term consequences?

In addition to the plan, this activity produces

- Documented business drivers
- Scope of data
- Temporal scope
- Business reasons
- The overall approach

- Participants and their roles
- Assumptions and constraints
- Project management strategy.

There is really nothing new here. Like any other software project, a good plan provides an effective launch. Failure to do this will result in misdirected teams and missed requirements. In contrasting our two sample projects, we get the following:

STEP: DATA WAREHOUSE PLANNING: PROJECT INITIATION

	Project 1	Project 2
Business drivers	A competitive marketplace makes a financial organization realize it must begin to exploit the vast information contained in its daily activities. The enterprise is large in terms of assets, but has no ability to forecast its credit card use and profitability.	A major property and casualty insurer finds itself unable to deliver uniform billing statements for customers with multiple policies and complicated coverages. The competition is allowing customer access to account activity via an on-line query mechanism. The current environment produces billing information from a variety of systems. There is nearly a one-for-one correspondence between the potential source systems and insurance coverages. The project is really a consolidation effort, requiring data from a variety of sources to be mapped to a data model that will allow uniform reporting and user query.
Data scope	A single subject area is chosen—Credit Card.	Multiple subject areas, Revenue, Claims, and Customer involved.
Business reason	Decision support project to sell credit card activity, such as trends, demographics, etc., to organizations that honor the bank's credit card.	Operational support, consolidation of data, competitive pressure.
Classification	Strategic	Tactical
Temporal scope	3 to 6 months to add business value.	6 to 9 months for first deliverable; customers will be patient if progress is evident.
Technology scope	Recent corporate policy requires all new business software to be placed on client/server architectures.	Use existing technology for quick deliverables; new technology can be added later.

(continued)

STEP: DATA WAREHOUSE PLANNING: PROJECT INITIATION *(cont.)*

	Project 1	Project 2
Project approach	Highly iterative development of DW, ad hoc in use.	Divide the project into 6-month deliverables; then continue to deliver results incrementally.
Assumptions/ constraints	Staff available and dedicated; end users will accept ad hoc access initially.	Staff available and dedicated.
Roles	Sponsor Project manager Data modeler Business analysts Systems analysts Developers Users Subject matter experts	Sponsor Project manager Data modeler Business analysts Systems analysts Developers Users Subject matter experts
Steps selected	Modeling Decision maker needs Subject area analysis Source system analysis End-user (EU) access design EU access definition EU access development Transform design Physical database design Warehouse development Warehouse population and implementation	Modeling DSS Architecture Decision maker needs Subject area analysis Source system analysis EU access design Transform design Physical database design Warehouse development Warehouse population and implementation

ARCHITECTURE DEFINITION

The architecture steps entail developing the high-level plan or blueprint that establishes the technical and application infrastructure for DW and DSS. This step, or set of activities, is required when an organization if faced with overwhelming information needs. This occurs as a result of business reengineering exercises, or simply when the lack of integrated information affects operational as well as decision-making abilities. This step is also used when DWT is being used as the entry-level application for client/server.

The architecture definition step serves to divide the subsequent activities into manageable yet valuable steps. The project team should use techniques that map business requirements to subject areas or high-level information needs.

Initial sizing is done to guide equipment decisions and prepare benchmarks. The result of this activity is a high-level requirement for processing and storage.

Defining and preparing the technical environment is done when new equipment and software is in order. This is where equipment should be ordered and installed. The physical architecture should be defined in terms of its major components:

- *Source:* Where will the data come from, in terms of hardware and DBMS?
- *Transport:* What topology will the data be carried over?
- *Destination:* What hardware and DBMS is the data heading for?
- *Metadata:* How will data definitions, relationships, business rules, and transformations be stored and accessed?
- *Access:* How will the data be viewed by the end user?
- *Transform:* Is there a special tool required to transform the data and build Metadata?

Finally, the architecture activities attempt to ensure that the various components will work together.

STEP: ARCHITECTURE ACTIVITIES

	Project 1	Project 2
Applications architecture	Not required	The high-level requirements are placed into a prioritized list. The top three requirements are cross referenced with the three subject areas. It is discovered that a majority of customer needs can be met by concentrating on uniform billing reports. Therefore, an operational data store is proposed that will synchronize the various business activities. Reports and then queries will be released for use against the ODS.
Initial sizing	Sizing for this project can be done during subject area analysis. If there are no client/server components available, then initial sizing could be done to assist in server selection.	Logical quantities of the three subject areas are determined. The requirement is stated on a per month basis.
Technical environment defined	Due to the fact that client/server infrastructure must be supported, a new server is specified and acquired.	Not required initially.
Technical environment prepared	The new server is installed and prepared for use.	Not required initially.

DECISION-MAKER NEEDS

This step represents the conceptual design of data access and information requirements. Measurements of the project's business drivers must be identified. These are
turned into requirements for information, requirements for business processes, and
requirements for access to the data. If an architecture has been defined, this step is
executed based on priorities developed during the architecture activities.

Information requirements are developed by reviewing which primitive data
elements are required, as well as which data elements may be calculated or summarized. Business measures are developed and approved by appropriate business
personnel. Business requirements focus on business processes that may be supported or enabled by the new DW or ODS. Access requirements present the
processes that users desire to get to data. These requirements are presented in terms
of data content, access type (ad hoc, drill-down, etc.), and timing.

A preliminary prototype may be developed to assist in presenting access
requirements and verifying information and business requirements. If it fits, prototyping should be started as early as possible.

STEP: DECISION-MAKER NEEDS

	Project 1	Project 2
Information requirements	End users are surveyed to determine which information can be useful to sell or use to adjust credit policies within the bank.	Decision-maker needs here really mean what customers wanted to see, and supporting detail for internal users.
Business requirements	Process of selling information, types of information, and means of transmittal are defined.	Identify the process to be used when the new statements are issued and billing information is accessible immediately.
Access requirements	Determine the timing of providing information for ad hoc use, and the favored mode of data access.	Short-term report layouts are fine for this iteration; eventually, on-line query screens must be developed.
Prototype	A few formats of distributing the data are produced.	Present the reports and query screens as appropriate.

SUBJECT AREA ANALYSIS

During this step, the information requirements are refined. To accomplish this, the
level of detail required in the subject area is identified, the content of the subject
area is verified, and the DW data model is initiated. A subject area is rarely discrete
enough to present no overlap with other subject areas, so refining the scope is also
important. The team will confirm the scope and content of data required by verifying the subject area with the information requirements. If there is no data model
available, the subject area is modeled and normalized. If one exists, then the data

model for the data warehouse is started by extracting the subject area(s). The preliminary DW data model is a normalized model with preliminary summaries and measurements added and defined.

Subject area scope is delivered to establish firmly what is in the subject area for this project. (There may be entities within a subject area that are not part of a DWT project.) The level of detail required is determined in conjunction with delivering the preliminary summaries. Obviously, the components of any measurement or summarization are candidates for storage. The DW will be more useful in its early life if only summarized data is viewed, but inevitably the details are requested.

Preliminary summary tables are produced for several reasons. Most businesses cannot wait to evolve to summary tables. In addition, nearly all DW projects start with a business situation in which specific measurements and calculations are required. These measurements can be expressed in terms of dimensions and periodicity to begin with. For example, a measurement called total sales may need to be viewed by region (dimension) or by month (periodicity).

Domain values begin to appear in DWT projects at this point. As the model is developed, many data elements that are really codes, valid values, or other types of business parameters crop up. During modeling, new elements will have been uncovered that represent new codes or that correct codes that have become misused over the years. These are defined and added to the data model. If they do not crop up, the question needs to be asked, "Of what value is this project?" DWT requires mapping to an integrated model. If codes are simply being moved over, why is DWT the solution to the business problem? Related to domain values is the need for transformation tables (i.e., tables that associate two or more old codes to produce a new code). These can become very complex and not only affect development time, but also future DW maintenance requirements. Rarely does a DWT project have the luxury of adequate codes in the source systems, and populating and maintaining domain values can occupy a major part of DWT project resources.

STEP: SUBJECT AREA ANALYSIS

	Project 1	Project 2
Subject area scope	The Credit Card area is confirmed. Some elements, such as customer, seem to come from other subject areas, but are required to bring utility to the credit card.	The subject areas required to produce the first reports (Revenue, Claims, and Customer) are examined. An attempt is made to keep the data scope as tight as possible due to the complexity of converting multiple subject areas.
Level of detail required	To support summarization and trend calculation, daily activity by card holder is to be stored.	The customer is interested in data at a billing level. This allows the lowest level of granularity to be monthly for the revenue subject, but at an individual claim level for the loss side of the bill.

(continued)

STEP: SUBJECT AREA ANALYSIS *(cont.)*

	Project 1	Project 2
Preliminary summary tables	Given the ad hoc flavor of this effort, preliminary summaries are at first difficult to glean. However, scrutiny of the business requirements results in a preliminary activity by SIC (Standard Industry Code) and a geographic dimension. Periodicity is determined to be monthly.	Total billed by month, total claims per month are identified. The dimensions, however, are relatively simple—by customer.
DW data model	Ideally, the subject area is extracted from the corporate data model. The preliminary DW data model is the normalized model, with preliminary summaries and measurements added and defined.	Ideally, the subject areas are extracted from the corporate data model. If not, a potentially significant modeling effort is possible. An alternative would be to acquire an industry standard model from a consulting firm or warehouse tool vendor.
Domain values	Initially, it would seem that this project may not offer a lot of code or domain changes. Anything is possible, however. The limitation of one subject area will be a big help.	This project offers the potential for many domain values. It may be desirable to prioritize them as they are uncovered.

SOURCE SYSTEM ANALYSIS

This step determines where the data will come from. Systems and files that are candidates for providing data to the transformation process are scrutinized. They are evaluated in terms of integrity, quality of data, and operational problems. Timing of data is also an important consideration. At the end of this step, the source systems have been defined, a preliminary mapping completed, and refinements made to the data model as appropriate. This step is often trivialized. The team seems to know intuitively where to go to get the data. Due diligence is required, however. The most obvious system may be the one with the most data quality problems. A good rule of thumb is to start where the data enters the enterprise. Data sources that get farther away from this point will, by their nature, have had assumptions and calculations applied to them. Data sources at the point of entry may be the candidates with the most errors, or require the most transformation and cleansing. Evaluating where the data comes from is a serious activity.

Source candidates are listed (literally, a list of files that may be a candidate for system of record). This is really an initial screening. Many files may contain the right data element names, but not the data elements desired. Often, two or three systems will each offer a viable candidate.

The next step is the identification of integrity and operational problems. This acts as an additional screening. A file may contain data for what is required, but be riddled with processing exceptions and problems.

Evaluation is completed by weighing the quality, accuracy, and timeliness of the candidates. Each source system is rated as to the risks and advantages of its use. In addition to transformation, some data must undoubtedly be cleansed. The extent of potential cleansing is also weighed.

New attributes that were not originally required may be available in the source system. Conversely, there may be attributes required that cannot be found in candidate source systems. Update the data model accordingly.

More domains are created by exploring possible source systems. This will identify data elements that require transformation to new codes. These must be defined and added to the data model.

Metadata requirements, a critical component of DWT, are first addressed in this step. This is because preliminary mapping is occurring, as well as additions to the domain entities. The extent to which metadata is to be used and stored is determined. The DW data model is updated with additional elements from domains and metadata.

Historical availability is one area to explore in determining if the source system is the data. Many DW projects require that a history be developed. A source system may be ideal, but if a history conversion is required and none is available, it is scope reconsideration time.

The system of record is identified and documented. It should also be announced to other areas in information technology departments, such as legacy system maintenance. Nothing can slow down a DWT project more than an unforeseen change in the source file layout.

Preliminary mapping is accomplished once the source systems have been identified. It is effective to map critical data elements from the source file to the data model. (There are no physical tables to map to yet.) This gives the team an idea of transformation complexity. This may seem time consuming, but it will allow fine-tuning of the project schedule and scope if mapping problems are discovered now, rather than after physical tables are designed. Remember, iterative (RAD) approaches like this allow problems to be discovered, while time boxes and scope can be adjusted.

Control requirements are often overlooked in the building of data warehouse. That is, how do we ensure that all of the data got to where it was supposed to? Users will not trust anything that is transformed unless it can be absolutely proven. Many DW and ODS projects have failed due to this.

STEP: SOURCE SYSTEM ANALYSIS

	Project 1	Project 2
Source candidates	Given the granularity requirement and the singular nature of the data requirements the daily transaction file is designated the key source.	This project offers many candidates, probably from the on-line OLTP systems to large batch activity files, even perhaps general ledger files.
Integrity and operational problems	The single source of data is discovered to have minor integrity problems related to customer address and demographics.	Integrity and operational problems are causing some of the reporting shortfalls; therefore, a number of problems in the data are identified among the various candidate sources.
Evaluation	Since there is only one source, the evaluation recommends cleansing the minor problems that were discovered.	The multiple sources will create a long list of evaluation criteria and results. This task could actually take long enough to threaten the project schedule and could cause a scope or resource adjustment.
New attributes	It is doubtful, given the granularity of this type of system, that missing fields would be plentiful. If there are any, operational system changes are in order.	Given the slightly summarized nature of this ODS project, there may, surprisingly, be few new elements.
More Domains	As with attributes, Project 1 should not offer many new domains.	If experience doing DW and ODS is any proof, this aspect of source system analysis has the potential to create many new codes, especially codes requiring association of two or more old codes to create a new code.
Metadata requirements	Given that this is an ad hoc project, metadata that is accessible to advanced users will enhance the value of the DW, in addition to all of the other uses for metadata.	This project has multiple subject areas, so the metadata requirements should focus on the primary uses for metadata (i.e., source, mappings, business rules, change history, etc.). Metadata should be strongly considered for this project.
DW data model	Knowledge gleaned from discovering the source system, such as domains and new elements, is added to the DW data model.	Knowledge gleaned from discovering the source system, such as domains and new elements, is added to the DW data model.

(continued)

STEP: SOURCE SYSTEM ANALYSIS *(cont.)*

	Project 1	Project 2
Historical availability	Because this project is prospective, a historical conversion would not be required, and this activity could be skipped.	Because this project is prospective, a historical conversion would not be required, and this activity could be skipped.
System of record	This project would probably have an obvious system of record. There might be a limitation if the card transactions are in a proprietary format or are so voluminous that they preclude any kind of timely processing.	The files closest to the original creation of the data elements are designated. The system of record should also be announced to other areas in information technology departments, such as legacy system maintenance. Given the multiple sources that will probably be used for Project 2, this is a critical activity.
Preliminary mapping	This exercise will assist Project 1 in sizing up future efforts.	This may seem time-consuming for this project, given the multiple sources, but it will allow fine-tuning of the project schedule and scope if mapping problems are discovered now, rather than after physical tables are designed.
Control requirements	This is very important in establishing credibility for a project like Project 1, in which ad hoc users will have to trust the data.	This is mandatory for Project 2. Data will be transformed from old, but predictable operational systems. The new system must accurately fulfill the same expectations.

TRANSFORM DESIGN

Once the source systems are identified, the transform design step produces the processes for getting data from the source to its destination while maintaining accuracy and integrity. At this point, preliminary mapping has helped size up the extent of transformations. Determinations can now be made as to how to transform the data, what types of jobs or processes are required to execute the transformation, and how to summarize. If a DW management tool is available, it can begin to be used. Peripherally, data integrity issues are addressed, either by designing cleansing routines or making repairs to legacy systems. Interestingly, the design of mappings and jobs tends to generate a lot of documentation, so a DW management tool can prove invaluable for containing all of the information being generated at this point.

Transform specifications are the identification and design of routines for transforming data. A determination is made of whether to use a change data capture (CDC) or a snapshot approach. Depending on the approach and on the technology used to develop transformation routines, many modules may be defined, or only a few. It is rarely a case in which one subject area requires one or a few programs to transform data. Populating domain and code tables is likely to account for over 50% of the modules developed. Use and maintenance of code tables used for transformation (also called association tables) must be specified. Most environments need to run passes at multiple segments or files to build an entire subject area.

The determination and design of transform processes is an activity that must be taken seriously. The framework that runs the various transformation modules and programs is designed. Batch windows must be large enough, and some hardware platforms do not perform batch processing well. Another key determination for these jobs is if change data capture or snapshot processing is applied to the source files. The output of this activity should be job flows that include an idea of timing and duration.

Control design and audit routines are also specifically identified and designed in this step. There is automated control software available for some environments. If this is not available, modules to verify adequate passing of data and verification of transformation need to be designed. This activity could also produce manual control procedures if there is insufficient time to automate them. Interestingly, so much effort has been spent on developing on-line and client/server software in recent years that finding analysts who understand basic accounting controls, such as batch and hash totals, may be difficult.

In the summarization process, business measurements are identified. The project team should determine the types of required summaries for producing the data required by these measurements. Some summarization processes may resemble the control processes, so these efforts can be leveraged. The big decision for summary processing is where the summarization takes place. Do you summarize external to the warehouse, or within the warehouse once the granular data has made it there? One rule of thumb, besides the usual ones of performance, capacity, and so on, is to determine the complexity of the summarization. If a significant amount of business rules must be applied to summarization, then the metadata for this process is useful. Therefore, the summarization should take place where the metadata is captured. For example, if a DW management tool is being used, summarization should take place on the platform where metadata is captured by the tool.

A historical conversion process is required when a historical basis is needed for a DW. The availability of the historical data and changes in data definition and format play key roles in determining the complexity of historical conversion. Some projects have been known to become so complex that the historical conversion was eliminated from the requirements.

A good test data set can reduce testing and corrections later in the project. This is the point at which developing the test data set can be leveraged the best.

A refined data model results if additional summarization of control table requirements is defined. A preliminary pass at summary table layout can be made at this point by creating tables to hold the key business measures and their dimensions (i.e., by month, by region, by SIC, etc.).

STEP: TRANSFORM DESIGN

	Project 1	Project 2
Transform specification	For this project, the transformations could be relatively simple for the granular credit card data, but do not overlook the potential complexity in the codes and parameters that may also be required.	In the case of this project, both CDC and snapshot approaches may be required, depending on the timing needs of the data and the source systems. Assuming some level of old legacy systems to be involved, this project could result in very complicated transformation processes.
Transform processes	The jobs to extract credit card activity are designed. In the case of this application, snapshots of card transactions would most likely be used.	The jobs to extract data for the uniform billing will cover, as stated previously, multiple subject areas. Transformation process may have dependencies and therefore timing problems. In a RAD environment, a complex project like this could even force proposal of scope change to stay within project time boxes.
Control design	Controls must be designed to ensure that all relevant card transactions are posted to the DW. There may also be a privacy requirement to ensure that individual spending habits are not made public.	Controls are vital to this project. The operational nature of ODS requires them. They would take the form of hash and batch totals for financial integrity and to ensure proper data transmission.
Summarization process	This project seems to require minimum summarization, so modest efforts would be appropriate here. Summarization could be limited to just one or two key measurements. Others would then evolve.	This project is summarization intensive by definition, so this would be a key effort. Future plans for this project call for on-line access to this data, so summarization processes design may want to attempt to position the transformation process to support this.
Historical conversion process	N/A (not applicable)	N/A
Test data	For Project 1, a representative set of card activity would make appropriate test data. Additionally, given potential volumes, a test data set of great size may also be necessary to verify performance during development and roll-out.	For Project 2, samples from the various subject areas that are related to the same customer accounts and financial periods would have to be developed.
Refined DW model	N/A—probably already done	N/A

PHYSICAL DATABASE DESIGN

This step features the DW database being physically specified and set up. This includes all control tables, granular tables, fact tables, and domain tables. If a star schema data structure is to be used, it is specified and set up here. The tables are created on whatever platform is so they will be available for DW development and end-user access development.

Domain tables are created in this step. Actual layout of domain, code, and transformation tables can take two routes. First, each domain, code, etc. is in a separate table. Alternatively, one common table can be defined. Any DBA can argue the merits of either approach, which depend entirely on the physical requirements. Creation and maintaining of physical tables during a DW project can consume a lot of DBA time.

Summarization tables are created to boost DW performance. Therefore, they should be created where it is known that access to the data will require a high level of performance. This tends to be the most popular dimension of business measurements (i.e., by month, by region, etc.).

Star join and fact tables (the design of the granular tables) is where controversy can arise. Traditional DBAs will have a hard time creating the redundancy they will perceive in these tables. It is best to utilize a DW-experienced DBA, or involve the DBA earlier in the development project so the concepts are not surprising to them. Also, the concept of star join has to be understood to make effective use of the technique.

Specifying and creating indexes is important for performance in both DW and ODS. Another area of potential culture shock for the DBAs is indexing. It is OK to use a lot of indexing in a DW.

To develop backup and recovery guidelines, a determination needs to made regarding how critical the DW is to the business. If a business does not use the DW in a mission-critical setting, then recovery may be as simple as reloading via retransforming. Other environments may require full roll forward, backward capabilities if DWT is used to implement an ODS.

STEP: PHYSICAL DATABASE DESIGN

	Project 1	Project 2
Domain tables	This project is typical, in that the amount of time to support even the limited amount of codes and domain tables could surprise the team.	Multiple DBAs would be required on a project such as this. Maintaining the control tables, codes, etc. will require full-time attention.
Summarization tables	Project 1 could create a table by SIC code, by month as a good start.	By definition, a lot of this project is summary tables.

(continued)

STEP: PHYSICAL DATA BASE DESIGN *(cont.)*

	Project 1	Project 2
Star join and fact tables	This project could really be one large star table with limited points.	N/A
Indexes	In Project 1, the ad hoc nature and the potential quantities of data would require significant indexing of the base tables.	Future query capability would require creative use of indexing on the tables that customers would be querying.
Backup and recovery guidelines	This project would qualify for a less intense approach to backup and recovery. The quantities of data here would preclude frequent full file backups. In the event of a total data loss, a traditional restore may take longer than a reload.	Project 2 would require traditional recovery mechanisms that would appear in any operational batch system.

END-USER ACCESS DESIGN, END-USER ACCESS DEFINITION, AND END-USER ACCESS DEVELOPMENT

As stated earlier, the end-user access steps are a discipline within a discipline. Some level of end-user access is always required against a DW. It can take many forms, as certain organizations may opt for using existing ad hoc tools, in which case very limited design and little or no development is required. Other projects may have the need to develop an end-user access application, or acquire new query tools, or both. This chapter chooses to emphasize the less obvious activities that may apply in developing DWT. If an ODS is part of the use of DWT, the following activities rarely apply.

During end-user access design, the types of end-user access to the DW are specified and laid out. If a prototype done earlier is available, it is refined. If developing some level of end-user access is required, determine how the data will be accessed from the external viewpoint. Dimensional analysis is performed as DW applications are often developed to support dimensional analysis decision support systems. Sometimes known as cube spinning, designing this type of access is more often a matter of configuring a purchased tool. Occasionally, an organization may want to develop their own, and this activity specifies the approach end users will use for viewing various business measurements. Metadata access is a unique aspect to be designed as well. It should be considered mandatory that access to transformation rules, data and measurement definitions, summarization calculations, and data change history be provided to users accessing data warehouse data. If it is not offered, it will be requested. It is also important to identify the "adhocracy" of users—that is, the types of users of the DW.

During end-user access definition, specific technical components, such as stored procedures, are designed and developed. For DWT, the one component that may be considered unique is preparing the environment for batch jobs. Canned reports within client/server environments are rare events, and existing facilities (such as CRON in UNIX) are crude at best when compared to more mature batch environments. Therefore, designing the facilities for scheduled report production should not be taken lightly.

End-user access development obviously features the development and unit test of end-user access panels and reports. The only unique feature is that when this step is complete, there is still a long way to go toward user acceptance of the DW. Using the data in conjunction with accessing it must still be verified. The goal here is to position end-user access to evolve along with use of the data.

WAREHOUSE DEVELOPMENT

At this point, the project team develops the mechanism to build and maintain the DW or ODS. The goal of this step is to produce the processes that build the DW and verify that the transformation rules and calculations are working accurately. Additionally, metadata is loaded to the DW repository, should it be available. Contrary to other types of software projects, user or subject matter expert involvement is key at this point. The first loading of the destination files takes place, with user verification of transformation. If a data warehouse tool is in use, the environment for the development team must be established beforehand.

Code is developed or generated during transformation development. This activity includes unit testing each module. Modules that create summaries are also developed, ideally after the granular transformations are developed. The only unusual item worth mentioning (face it, code is code) is that the domains, associations, and tables may not be mainstream, but will account for 60% to 80% of the number of modules generated and resources consumed.

Development and assembly of the transformation processes (e.g., batch Job Control Language, scripts, etc.) is done now. If a DW management tool is in use, the generated processes may or may not meet organizational standards. The team should get dispensation or be prepared to bring the jobs up to standards.

An atypical activity is the preliminary data load. After jobs are developed and some integration testing is complete, it is vital to load the destination files and allow users to access and verify the correctness of the process. They are not checking for usefulness or accepting the system. This approach accomplishes two purposes: (1) The end user stays involved during a portion of the project in which additional data problems will surface. (2) Integrity problems that have not surfaced by now are usually ugly. The user involvement aids in solving the data issues and softens the impact on the project.

Control and audit processes are completed and put into place. If automated, they are developed along with other DWT items. If manual, the new processes are documented, walked through, and tested on the data being generated by the developing system. Some of the warehouse management tools can support control routines; others cannot. Be certain of how the tool does this before committing to its use for controls.

The metadata load occurs as part of development to allow end users to view the quality of the metadata. It also is timely, because the team has the attention of the DBA support staff, and they are usually needed when it is time to load metadata from its various sources to the metadata repository.

System testing occurs after all the major subprocesses within the DW or ODS are constructed. The purpose is to verify that all recently developed components fit together. This is not done until after approval of the preliminary loading of granular data. System testing needs to occur when the chance for code changes is minimized.

STEP: DW DEVELOPMENT

	Project 1	Project 2
Transformation development	This project will be average; there will be the granular data, a few summary tables, and the domain tables. Given the classic 6-month approach, an ideal development time frame for this type of project would be around a month.	This project will have a large development effort. Given the complexities, it could benefit from a warehouse management tool.
Transformation processes	With one subject area, the processes (jobs) should not be too complicated. Domains and codes processes could be, depending on the amount of new domains and dimensions for ad hoc reporting.	Project 2 will feature a number of challenges. Given multiple subject areas and legacy systems, domain processes will be complicated. The processes for the granular data and the limited summary data will also be complicated. Batch windows may become a concern. In a mainframe environment, all of the efforts associated with implementing a new production system will be dealt with.
Preliminary data load	Once there is a module or job to grab the granular data, it should be loaded to the destination files and platform. Ad hoc queries can be used to verify the content of the DW with operational reports.	This project really makes the preliminary load become an early system test. Loading the multiple destination files will require team coordination and user attentiveness.
Control and audit processes	Develop any manual and/or automated processes to verify if all of the credit card transactions make it for the specified time period.	Develop any manual and or automated processes specified to verify integrity of the billing data.

(continued)

STEP: DW DEVELOPMENT *(cont.)*

	Project 1	Project 2
Metadata load	DWs with heavy ad hoc use invariably require metadata. If not provided, users ask for it. "Nonuser" metadata is also important, because ad hoc environments are more susceptible to data changes (i.e., data or business rules changes may go unnoticed without the operational flavor to rely on). Tried and true query results could become distorted over time.	Projects with the ODS flair like this one tend to deemphasize metadata. This is less than ideal, but until the on-line query part, metadata could be kept in a notebook. As more and more consolidation occurs, loading the metadata will become necessary. It is best, schedule permitting, to start loading and maintaining the metadata now.
System testing	Ideally, system testing will be a simple effort, that of ensuring that the pieces fit together and maintain data integrity.	Given the ODS nature, system testing will need to be as rigorous as it would be with a conventional OLTP system (test scripts, formal test teams, etc.).

DATA WAREHOUSE POPULATE AND IMPLEMENT

The final step in the framework includes the activities required to bring the DW on stream—fully converted, transformed, accepted, and operational. The various roll-out steps and training are complete, and the customer for the DWT will be contentedly utilizing the new application. Population run is the key activity at this time. This may include a historical conversion, or just the initial load and cut over to the new DW or ODS.

Software implementation happens in all projects, but the important aspect with DWT is to make sure it does happen, since many environments tend to end up with periodic updates to the DW being done per request, or from the desk of an analyst, rather than by the execution of a regularly scheduled job. Control and audit verification occurs at this point. The controls must be deemed effective enough to prevent data errors occurring without detection.

Data training and access training are often placed together under one label: "training." This inevitably leads to a class in mouse driving, but not on how to use the DW. Even though the data is freshly integrated, scrubbed, and ready to go, few DW efforts produce a database that is simple enough to navigate intuitively. But to be successful, the user must easily navigate through the DW data. Specific training regarding where the data is, how to use the tables, and the nature of query languages is required.

The user acceptance test is the result of combining final verification of data content (detail and summary) along with the access to that data. This is where the sign-off should occur. Then control and audit verification takes place to ensure that the internal controls built into the DW build process are adequate.

STEP: DATA WAREHOUSE POPULATE AND IMPLEMENT

	Project 1	Project 2
Population run	Relatively simple, with no historical conversion. Nothing really special. Do not overlook the need to run the domain and code jobs.	This task, too, is relatively simple. The ODS is starting from a point in time, so it will be difficult to start. Do not overlook the need to run the domain and code jobs.
Software implementation	Make sure ad hoc tools or software is implemented uniformly across the user's workstations. Ensure that the transformation jobs and processes are properly installed and documented.	The implementation of the jobs is fairly traditional. Until the user queries begin, you have a batch implementation.
Data training & access training	Developing good training for the ad hoc users can consume some time. Make sure that there is emphasis on finding a way through the data via solid training.	Not much needed here until the queries are completed.
User acceptance test	A formal set of tasks are executed to permit the user to indicate that the system meets expectations.	More elaborate for this project, this must be a formal sign-off to allow the system to print official billing statements.
Control and audit verification	Verify if all of the credit card transactions make it for the specified time period.	Verify the process with representatives from business (i.e., internal audit or its equivalent). The critical aspect of this project will require oversight from finance or audit.

SUMMARY

This chapter has provided some guidance toward developing a unique approach for a particular data warehouse project. It is obvious that the individual characteristics of a project create the need to develop a project plan that reflects the uniqueness of the project. Data warehouse–related projects are no different. Additionally, data warehouse projects require IT departments to adapt to different work flow, deliverables, and pace than offered by more traditional business application projects.

The essence of building the data warehouse project plan requires the following:

- Data warehouse projects must be iterative.
- Business needs must constantly be reflected.
- Specific deliverables enable the team to identify progress and keep focused while adhering to the "big picture."

PART THREE

DATA: THE CRITICAL ISSUE

"You may think that defining the meaning of data is simple... but it is not."

Dr. E. F. Codd
Seventh Annual Midwest DB/DC User
Group Meeting, September 1983

Although some vendors would like us to believe otherwise, technology is not the whole answer. Organizations that have simply moved data from existing operational systems into a data warehouse have been stunned by the impact of poor-quality data. Legacy systems contain a wealth of data, but much of it may be inconsistent, contaminated, and poorly defined. Inconsistent names and addresses, multiple names in a single field, multiple spellings for a single customer, multiple records for a customer who has moved, and data entry errors must be overcome before a warehouse is populated. Even if a legacy file contains high-quality, consistent data within an application, what will be the result of merging that file with one from another application?

If the warehouse is to be successful, it requires data that is well defined, integrated, and consistent. Chapter 10, "Data Quality," by Sid Adelman, addresses the issues surrounding the definition, creation, maintenance, and assessment of data quality within the organization. He describes key indicators for assessing data quality and the impact of poor data and suggests a process for its improvement.

In Chapter 11, "Metadata," Dave Gleason defines metadata and its role in the life cycle of the warehouse. He describes its collection, maintenance, and deployment and considers the role of metadata from the perspectives of the developers and end users. Since the integration of metadata with various end-user tools is a challenge, he describes the various levels of integration that are possible.

In Chapter 12, "The Role of a Directory/Catalog," Jack Sweeney discusses the role of directories/catalogs in an enterprise data warehouse. It appears that vendors are selling many pieces of the directory solution, but large organizations may need to integrate information from 15 to 20 different warehouse products. He presents a user experience in which a major bank has developed its own software called "The Active Directory/Catalog" to solve this problem.

In Chapter 13, "Data Transformation," Dave Gleason describes the process of extracting data from the operational systems and improving the quality and usability of data through cleansing, transformation, scrubbing, and integration. He discusses the use of manual and automated procedures for managing this complex task.

Data is of little value to end users if they do not know what data is available, where it is located, and how to access it. Furthermore, it is useless if it is incorrect. This section addresses the issues surrounding data in the warehouse.

CHAPTER

Data Quality

10

Sid Adelman
Sid Adelman and Associates
Sherman Oaks, California

"The quality of decisions by management is directly related
to the quality and availability of data."

GUIDE GRP-153 Repository Data Model Strategy Paper, September 1986

"Many organizations are going to find, unfortunately,
that their underlying data may not be sufficiently clean
to help the organization move forward."

John Murray

"Never underestimate the creativity of data entry."

Mark Atkins, President Vality Technology

In its 1994 annual report, Countrywide Credit Industries, a company that had the largest volume of loan originations in 1993, wrote, "Quality and accuracy of loan data shared between Countrywide and its business partners have always been a top priority." This attitude may have been a contributing factor to Countrywide's position in the industry. Most organizations give voice but not budget to the notion of quality data.

WHY IS DATA QUALITY IMPORTANT?

The quality of data will limit the ability of the end users to make informed decisions. The quality of data has a profound effect on the image of the enterprise. An example is a bank that consistently misspells addresses. In addition, poor-quality data will make it difficult to make major changes in an organization, such as a merger or a business process reengineering effort. The problems related to the quality of data are more severe and pervasive than is commonly believed.[1]

WHAT IS DATA QUALITY?

There are a number of indicators of quality data.

1. *The data is accurate.* This means that a customer's name is spelled correctly and the address is correct. If the marketing department does not have the correct profile for the customer, marketing will attempt to sell the customer the wrong products and present a disorganized image of the organization. When data on a company vehicle is entered into the system, it may be valid (a vehicle number that is in the database), but it may be inaccurate (the wrong vehicle number). See the data quality case at the end of this chapter (p. 131).

2. *The data is stored according to data type.* If a field is defined as a given data type (packed decimal, character, integer, etc.), all the instances of this field will be stored as packed decimal.

3. *The data has integrity.* Referential integrity rules will be properly defined in the logical data models and implemented in the physical data models. The data will not be accidentally destroyed or altered. Updates will not be lost due to conflicts among concurrent users. Much of this is the responsibility of the DBMS, but proper implementation of the DBMS should not be assumed. Robust backup and recovery procedures as implemented by the installation are needed to maintain integrity. In addition, operational procedures that restrict a batch update from being run twice are also necessary.

4. *The data is consistent.* The form and content of the data should be consistent. This allows for data to be integrated and shared by multiple departments across multiple applications and multiple platforms.

5. *The databases are well designed.* A well-designed database will perform satisfactorily for its intended applications, it is extendible, and it exploits the integrity capabilities of its DBMS.

6. *The data is not redundant.* In actual practice, no organization has ever totally eliminated redundant data. In most data warehouse implementations, the data warehouse data is partially redundant with operational data. For certain performance reasons, and in some distributed environments, an organization may correctly choose to maintain data in more than one place and also maintain the data in more than one form.

The redundant data to be minimized is the data that has been duplicated for none of the reasons stated previously but because

- The creator of the redundant data was unaware of the existence of available data.
- The redundant data was created because the availability or performance characteristics of the primary data were unacceptable to the new system. This may be a legitimate reason or it may be that the performance problem could have been successfully addressed with a new index or a minor tuning effort and that availability could have been improved by better operating procedures.
- The owner of the primary data would not allow the new developer to view or update the data.
- The lack of control mechanisms for data update indicated the need for a new version of the data.
- The lack of security controls dictated the need for a redundant subset of the primary data.

In these cases, redundant data is only the symptom and not the cause of the problem. Only managerial vision, direction, and a robust data architecture would lead to an environment with less redundant data.

7. *The data follow business rules.* For example, a loan balance may never be a negative number. This rule comes from the business side, and IT is required to establish the edits to be sure the rule is not violated.

8. *The data corresponds to established domains.* These domains are specified by the owners or users of the data. The domain would be the set of allowable values or a specified range of values. In a human resource system, the domain of sex is limited to "male" and "female." "Biyearly" may be accurate but still not an allowable value.

9. *The data is timely.* Timeliness is subjective and can only be determined by the users of the data. The users will specify that monthly, weekly, daily, or real-time data is required. Real-time data is often a requirement of production systems with OLTP. If monthly is all that is required and monthly is delivered, the data is timely.

10. *The data is well understood.* It does no good to have accurate and timely data if the users do not know what they mean. Naming standards are a necessary (but not sufficient) condition for well-understood data.

Data can be documented in the data dictionary/repository, but the creation and validation of the definitions is a time-consuming and tedious process. This is, however, time and effort well spent. Without clear definitions and understanding, the organization will exhaust countless hours trying to determine the meaning of its reports or draw incorrect conclusions from the data displayed on the screens.

11. *The data is integrated.* An insurance company needs both agent data and policyholder data. These are typically two files, databases, or tables that may have no IT connection. If the data is integrated, meaningful business information can be readily generated from a combination of both the agent and policyholder data.

Database integration generally requires the use of a common DBMS. There is an expectation (often unfulfilled) that all applications using the DBMS will be able to easily access any data residing on the DBMS. An integrated database would be accessible from a number of applications. Many different programs in multiple systems could access and, in a controlled manner, update the database.

Database integration requires the knowledge of the characteristics of the data, what the data means, and where the data resides. This information would be kept in the data dictionary/repository.

An integrated database would have the following potential benefits:

- Less redundant data
- Fewer possibilities for data inconsistency
- Fewer interface programs (a major resource consumer)
- Fewer problems with timing discrepancies
- More timely data.

12. *The data satisfies the needs of the business.* The data has value to the enterprise. High-quality data is useless if it is not the data needed to run the business. Marketing needs data on customers and demographic data, whereas accounts payable needs data on vendors and product information.

13. *The user is satisfied with the quality of the data and the information derived from that data.* While this is a subjective measure, it is arguably the most important indicator of all. If the data is of high quality but the user is still dissatisfied, you or your boss will be out of a job. A sample user satisfaction questionnaire can help determine just how satisfied the user is with the quality of the data. This questionnaire can be found at the end of this chapter and should be tailored to each installation.

14. *The data is complete.* All the line items for an invoice have been captured so that the bill states the full amount that is owed. All the dependents are listed for an employee so that invoices from medical providers can be properly administered.

15. *There are no duplicate records.* A mailing list would carry a subscriber, potential buyer, or charity benefactor only once. You will only receive one letter that gives you the good news that "You may already be a winner!"

16. *Data anomalies.* From the perspective of IT, this may be the worst type of data contamination. A data anomaly occurs when a data field defined for one purpose is used for another. For example, a currently unused but defined field is used for some purpose totally unrelated to its original intent. A clever programmer may put a negative value in this field (which is always supposed to be positive) as a switch.

DESIGN REVIEWS

An important set of information to be included in design reviews is the requisite quality of the data under consideration and the actual state of the data. The basic question to be asked is, "How clean, timely, etc. must the data be?" In the design review, the team members would consider the data source, the process of update and delete, and the quality controls imposed on those accessing the data.

The design review would review and validate that standards are being followed. The review process may make recommendations to clean up the data, establish strict controls on shared updating, and assure sufficient training for users who would query the data.

ASSESSMENT OF EXISTING DATA QUALITY

Organizations often overestimate the quality of their own data. A reality check is generally needed. Poor-quality data can be detected in a number of ways:

- Programs that abnormally terminate with data exceptions
- Clients who experience errors or anomalies in their reports and transactions and/or do not trust their reports or do not trust the data displayed on their screens
- Clients who do not know or are confused about what the data actually means
- On-line inquiry transactions and reports that are useless because the data is old
- Data that cannot be shared across departments due to lack of data integration
- Difficulty for clients to get consolidated reports because the data is not integrated
- Programs that do not balance
- The merged data that causes the system to fail (this occurs in the consolidation of two systems).

Quality may be free, but data quality does require an initial investment. It takes people and resources to bring data to the desired pristine state. If data is allowed to remain in its current (dirty) state, there may be a substantial cost and disruption to the organization. Very few organizations understand the costs and exposures of poor-quality data. A section at the end of this chapter (p. 133) lists these costs and provides a process to assess the costs.

IMPACT OF POOR-QUALITY DATA

Data has often been referred to as an asset. It can be an asset only if the data is of high quality. Data can also be a liability if it is inaccurate, untimely, improperly defined, etc. An organization may be better off not having certain data than having inaccurate data, especially if those relying on the data do not know of its inaccuracy. A hospital would be better off not knowing a patient's blood type than believing it to be O+.

The cost of bad data is related to the type of data and how it would be used. A large bank in California intends to prompt tellers with recommendations on products and services to market to customers based on their profiles and previous relationship with the bank.[2] If the data on the customers is wrong, customers will get a bad impression of the bank, the tellers, or both as the teller recommends a student loan to a childless couple. A minor misspelling of the street address, on the other hand, would not carry the same negative impression with the customer. In addition, if the data would never be accessed, there is no quality cost to having bad data.

WHICH DATA SHOULD BE IMPROVED?

It should be obvious that it is impossible to improve the quality of all the data in an installation. The prioritization is much like triage. The energy should be spent on data where the quality improvement will bring an important benefit to the business. Other criteria that would suggest data improvement are data that can be fixed and kept clean. Unimportant data can be ignored. Data that will become obsolete can also be bypassed. For example,

1. The business will be bought.
2. The data will be converted because of a new application.
3. A reengineering of the business will cause the certain data to be retired.

If the marketing department is reviewing the demographics of its customers, the zip code (as part of the address) is important, while the rest of the address is less critical.

There will be wide variations in the costs to clean different files and databases. This will enter into any decision about which data to purify. The cost of perfectly accurate data may be prohibitive and may not be cost effective. Based on the source of the data, accuracy may also be an impossibility.

Users of data may be willing to settle for less than totally accurate data. Even so, it is important that the users know the level of quality they are getting. A greeting card company asked retailers to measure the number of linear feet devoted to that company's card products. Those who analyzed the data knew the data to be inaccurate but preferred inaccurate data to no data at all. A large computer manufacturer asked their marketing representatives and technical engineers to report on how they spent their time. It was well known that the respondents were not keeping very good records themselves, and their reports reflected the lack of their concern

for accuracy. Those who analyzed the data knew of the inaccuracies but were looking for trends and significant changes to indicate shifts in how jobs were being
performed. The inaccurate data, in both of these cases, was acceptable.

PURIFICATION PROCESS

To clean up the data, the following steps should be followed:

- Determine the importance of data quality to the organization.
- Assign responsibility for data quality.
- Identify the enterprise's most important data.
- Evaluate the quality of the enterprise's most important data.
- Determine users' and owners' perception of data quality. Users will convey
  their understanding of the data's quality and will often indicate why the data
  has problems.
- Prioritize which data to purify first.
- Assemble and train a team to clean the data.
- Select tools to aid in the purification process.
- Review data standards.
- Incorporate standards in the application development process to ensure that
  new systems deliver high-quality data.
- Provide feedback and promote the concept of data quality throughout the
  organization.

ROLES AND RESPONSIBILITIES

The creation and maintenance of quality data is not the sole province of any one
department. The responsibility touches application developers, database administrators, data administrators, quality assurance, internal auditors, project managers,
and, most important, senior management. The importance of quality data must be
understood by senior management and expressly communicated throughout the
organization. Words are not as important as deeds. When quality measures appear
in performance plans, reviews, and bonuses, people finally believe that quality is
important. It is equally important that time and resources be allocated to development schedules to support management's commitment to quality.

In some organizations, the responsibility for cleaning up data rests with the
owners of the data. It is felt that they have the ultimate responsibility for the data
since they enter the data originally, are responsible for defining domains, and are
responsible for data standards for the data they own. Other organizations assign IT
to clean up the data. Unfortunately, in most organizations, there is no clear assignment of data quality responsibility. As data processing becomes more distributed,

on PCs, LANs, and on larger distributed machines, the responsibility for the quality of the data becomes even more clouded.

DATA QUALITY TOOLS

Data quality tools fall into the following categories:

1. Reconciling inconsistent data and determining the completeness of the data.
2. Identifying data that does not correspond to domains.
3. Reconciling problems of referential integrity. Most DBMSs have the ability to check referential integrity, the relationship among tables based on the definitions of primary and foreign keys.
4. Assessing the quality of existing data. The tools can validate for allowable values and perform range checking. Unfortunately, no tools will identify an incorrect address.
5. Data reengineering. Data can be reengineered to improve performance, to improve data integrity, to better support production applications, and to provide for decision support systems. Many of the CASE tools can reverse engineer from existing Data Definition Language (DDL).
6. Providing measurements of quality.
7. Data dictionary/repository. A data dictionary/repository can provide a critical component of quality: an understanding of the meaning of the data, its source, complete definition, and even an indication of the quality of the data.
8. The DBMS itself. The DBMS can control update security, referential integrity checking, domain integrity, and database recovery.

Software tools are often useful to automate the process of purifying data. They assist in the analysis of the quality of existing data so that management better understands the enormity of the problem, they help identify which data should be addressed first, and they identify exposures when the quality of the data is poor.

Most of the migration tools have a limited cleansing capability. In addition, the following companies have tools that perform some or all of the cleansing function that evaluates legacy data to identify dirty data and to filter, clean, and transform the data:

- Vality
- Gladstone
- Innovative Systems
- QDB
- Apertus
- Unitech

- Platinum
- Postalsoft
- Group 1 Software
- Harte-Hanks.

IMPACT OF DATA QUALITY ON OPERATIONAL SYSTEMS

Poor-quality data can have a devastating effect on both OLTP and batch systems. An incorrect checking balance could result in a loss to the bank or a rejected request for funds. A hospital with incorrect or incomplete patient information could allow a drug to be administered that could cause the death of a patient. An airline with the wrong seat inventory will either overbook or send out empty planes. Incorrect data types can cause operational systems to terminate abnormally, causing a batch run to fail and an OLTP system to falter.

IMPACT OF DATA QUALITY ON THE DATA WAREHOUSE

Bad data should never be allowed into the data warehouse unless the problems are recognized and acknowledged by those who will use the data. Whenever possible, the data should be validated and purified prior to extraction. If bad data enters the data warehouse, it may have the effect of undermining the confidence of those who access the data. Clients and IT must be able to rely on the data, regardless of whether it is detailed, summarized, or derived.

The effort to clean up data once it is in the data warehouse becomes a major and never-ending task. It should not be the responsibility of those administering the data warehouse to clean up bad data. The cleanliness standard puts an additional burden on the owners and the custodians of the data to perform validations of the source data.

DATA QUALITY FEEDBACK TO SENIOR MANAGEMENT

Unlike measurements of performance and availability, the quality of data will not be changing daily. Quality can, however, be quickly compromised by operating procedures that cause improper batch updates. Those responsible for data will want to make periodic checks to determine trends and progress in improving data quality. The results should be reported to IT management and to the departments that own the data.

The quality of data can be measured, but before any measurement takes place, the following questions should be answered:

1. Why is the quality of the data being measured? The classic answer is that without measurement, management of the data is impossible.

2. What is being measured? Some possibilities include (1) trends (e.g., Is the data getting cleaner or dirtier? and (2) user satisfaction with the quality of the data.
3. What will be done with the measurements? Some possibilities include (1) focus on the data that needs to be purified, (2) provide a basis for cost justifying the purification effort, and (3) give information for prioritizing the cleanup process.

Whenever possible, feedback should be quantified. Management can receive an abbreviated report showing the major categories of data quality. The report would show the major systems as well as the overall organization measurements. By comparing with historical data, trends will become apparent. The report would also briefly describe the quality improvement efforts completed as well as those in progress.

DATA QUALITY CASE

The following is a true example of data quality problems. A transportation company maintained its own buses and had a bus maintenance system (BMS) that supported this effort. The system depended on the mechanics entering the code of the activity they performed, the number of hours on this activity, as well as the unique bus number. This number was clearly displayed on the top, front, and back of each bus.

The BMS was producing reports that showed that certain buses had not had their transmissions serviced in the last 50,000 miles, while other buses were getting the transmission overhauled every 5000 miles. Further investigation revealed that the bus numbers were not being logged accurately, so the transmission maintenance was being recorded for the wrong bus.

Why was this occurring? The mechanics felt that the BMS gave management the ability to maintain excessively tight controls over them, and they resisted this control. They were also encouraged by their fellow mechanics to enter certain data incorrectly. There was no checking on the data entry process, no follow-up, and no penalties for entering the wrong bus number. The data became useless.

In addition, there were certain functions that were not highly valued by management, such as keeping the work area clean. This activity did have a work code, but it was rarely used. The mechanics' supervisors encouraged using more highly valued codes than the code for sweeping and cleaning up. The work reports did not accurately reflect how the workers spent their time.

Lesson 1: If those entering the data have a stake in the data being incorrect, the data will be incorrect.

Lesson 2: Reports may show desired results, but the reports may be highly inaccurate.

Assessing the costs of poor-quality data can help justify the budget and people resources needed to improve data quality.

End-User Satisfaction Questionnaire: Data and Information

The End-user Satisfaction Questionnaire can help an organization understand the impact of data quality where it counts, on the end user. It can help determine the level of user satisfaction and identify any dissatisfaction as a result of poor-quality data.

1. Do you receive reports from IT?
   ___ Yes   ___ No
2. Do you request information from IT?
   ___ Yes   ___ No
3. Do the reports contain accurate information?
   ___ Always accurate   ___ Accurate   ___ Usually accurate
   ___ Rarely accurate   ___ Never accurate
4. Is the information you receive consistent with other reports in the organization?
   ___ Always consistent   ___ Consistent   ___ Usually consistent
   ___ Rarely consistent   ___ Never consistent
5. Is the information timely?
   ___ Always   ___ Sometimes   ___ Rarely
6. Do you understand the meaning of all the data on the reports you receive?
   ___ Always   ___ Sometimes   ___ Rarely
7. Is the terminology on the reports clear and well defined?
   ___ Always   ___ Sometimes   ___ Rarely
8. Does IT respond in a timely manner?
   ___ Always   ___ Sometimes   ___ Rarely
9. Do IT personnel demonstrate the skills necessary to satisfy your business requirements?
   ___ Always   ___ Sometimes   ___ Rarely
10. Does IT keep you informed of changes that will affect your business?
    ___ Always   ___ Sometimes   ___ Rarely
11. Does IT deliver effective solutions that meet your expectations?
    ___ Always   ___ Sometimes   ___ Rarely
12. Does IT understand your business needs?
    ___ Always   ___ Sometimes   ___ Rarely
13. Does IT provide effective resolution to your problems?
    ___ Always   ___ Sometimes   ___ Rarely
14. Is the response time
    ___ Excellent   ___ Satisfactory   ___ Unsatisfactory

15. Are the interfaces
___ Excellent   ___ Satisfactory   ___ Unsatisfactory

16. How would you rate the development methodology?
___ Efficient and well organized   ___ Acceptable   ___ Poorly organized

ASSESSING THE COSTS OF POOR-QUALITY DATA

It will be difficult to assign real dollars to most of these categories. If estimates in real dollars are possible, conservative numbers should always be used. When an organization has experience with any of the following problems and if the costs of fixing those problems have been calculated, those figures can be assigned.

1. Bad decisions are due to incorrect data.

2. Opportunities are lost because the required data was either unavailable or was not credible.

3. Time and effort are required to restart and rerun jobs that abnormally terminated due to bad data.

4. In a buyout situation, you accept too low a price for your business because you cannot properly demonstrate your business potential, or your business seems to be in disarray because your reports are inconsistent.

5. Fines are imposed by regulating authorities for noncompliance or violating a governmental regulation as a result of bad data.

6. Time and resources are needed to fix a problem identified in an audit.

7. Hardware, software, and programmer/analyst costs are incurred as a result of redundant data.

8. The costs and repercussions of bad public relations are due to bad or inconsistent data (e.g., a public agency not being able to answer questions from the press or from the board of directors).

9. Time is wasted by managers arguing and discussing inconsistent reports that are the result of bad data.

10. Poor relations with business partners, suppliers, customers, etc. are due to overcharging, underpayment, incorrect correspondence, shipping the wrong product, etc.

11. Time is spent correcting inaccurate data. These corrections may be performed by line personnel or by IT.

12. The costs of lost business in operational systems are due to poor-quality data (data was wrong or nonexistent). An example is the lost marketing opportunity for an insurance company that does not have accurate information about a client and thus loses the opportunity to market an appropriate insurance product.

SUMMARY

This chapter identified various categories of data quality and discussed how to identify quality data problems and how to address those problems. It gave suggestions for incorporating data quality topics in design reviews. Roles and responsibilities were discussed, as were the tools that can assist in automating understanding data quality problems and in purifying the data. Also addressed was data quality as it affects both operational systems and the data warehouse and the necessity of bringing senior management into the picture.

Data is a critical asset for every enterprise. The quality of the data must be maintained if the enterprise is to make effective use of this most important asset. Improvements in data quality do not just happen, they are the result of a diligent and ongoing process of improvement.

REFERENCES

[1] HANSEN, Dr. MARK D., "Data Quality: What Data Base Managers Need to Know," *Data Base Management,* October 1992.

[2] MITCHELL, RUSSELL, "The Banking Industry's Best-Kept Secret," *Business Week,* August 8, 1994.

[3] MURRAY, JOHN, "The Issue of Clean Data," *Data Management Review,* April 1993.

[4] REDMAN, THOMAS C., *Data Quality,* New York, Bantam Books, 1992.

[5] WATSON, HUGH J., RAINER, R. KELLY, AND FROLICK, MARK N., "Executive Information Systems: An Ongoing Study of Current Practices," *International Information Systems,* April 1992.

11

Metadata

Dave Gleason

Information Management Consulting
PLATINUM Technology
Vienna, Virginia

"We shall not cease from exploration

And the end off all our exploring

Will be to arrive where we started

And know the place for the first time."

T. S. Eliot, "Little Gidding", Four Quartets

It is a commonly accepted belief today that metadata is an important component of a successful data warehouse. But how many people really understand what metadata is and why it is such an important part of a data warehouse? Let's examine some real-life scenarios in which metadata would prove essential to a data warehouse environment.

Scenario 1

The data warehouse team is preparing to launch a new portion of the data warehouse. For their pilot effort, they choose a relatively simple subject, with only one primary source of data. Now, however, they must add a very complex subject to their data warehouse. This subject includes several primary sources of data, including internal systems and some external, purchased data. Worse yet, the team does not have any members who understand the physical layout of all of the data sources. They need help in understanding the structure and meaning of the operational data that will feed the new portion of the data warehouse.

What this team requires is a clear and comprehensive understanding of the metadata for their potential data sources. If this metadata was collected and maintained, it could tell them

- The layout of all of the physical data structures in the sources, including all of the data elements and their data types
- The business definitions for all of the data elements
- How often each data element gets updated, and by what person or process
- Who in the company can be contacted for more information about each data element
- A list of the other data elements in other systems that have the same business meaning (even with different names or data types)
- The valid values for each data element.

Using this information, the team would be able to complete the analysis and data mappings required to implement the next phase of the warehouse.

Scenario 2

The database administrator has noticed that one set of attributes of a data warehouse table is very volatile, changing almost every time new information is added to the warehouse. Another set of columns on the same table is much more stable, often only changing one time each year. Therefore, the DBA wants to split the existing warehouse table into two tables, so that he can save DASD space for the attributes that are not frequently updated. However, he needs to figure out what the impact on the data warehouse will be and whom he should contact to request permission or notify of changes.

With a complete catalog of metadata, the DBA could easily establish:

- The business rules relevant to the table he wants to change
- Who on the data warehouse team is responsible for that table and its data
- The sources of the data on the table, and exactly which data movement and transformation entities would be affected by the change
- Which data marts are generated from the affected table, and which data mart creation routines would have to be modified
- Which stored queries access the table, and which users run those queries, so that proper assistance can be provided to rewrite the queries and retrain the users.

Obviously, having access to this kind of metadata would enable the DBA to research and fully understand the potential impacts of his change to the data structures before he makes any changes.

Scenario 3

A user of the data warehouse wants to research some claims data, a part of the warehouse that she does not frequently access. While she understands database fundamentals and has a good working knowledge of the data access tool she is using, she does not know what exists in the claims data subject and how to use that information.

If this end user had access to metadata about the data warehouse in an easy-to-use and understand form, she could learn the following information to guide her in her exploration of a new subject area of the data warehouse:

- What entities were defined in the warehouse relevant to the subject of claims, and what business rules were implemented for those entities?
- What attributes are populated for claims, and what are the definitions and valid values of those attributes?
- What are the sources of data for each entity, including major application systems and external data sources?
- What data marts have been created for easier access to subsets of the claims data?
- Who should be contacted to get business-knowledge assistance with each entity?
- What queries have already been written that access claims data, and who are the primary users of those queries?

Indeed, if the end user had this powerful road map to the data warehouse, she would be able to use the information in the warehouse much more effectively. This user also would require significantly less assistance and instruction from the data warehouse team each time she chooses to explore a new area of the warehouse.

INDUSTRY TRENDS

As previously mentioned, metadata is now widely considered to be an integral part of the data warehouse. Most early attempts to build data warehouses, however, did not include significant amounts of metadata collection and use. In fact, these attempts were largely successful despite the lack of metadata. This success can be attributed to the fact that most companies selected a small subset of their enterprise data for their initial data warehouse efforts. It was relatively easy to understand the content, organization, ownership, and meaning of this small cross section of data, even without formal metadata. Also benefiting these attempts was the fact that they chose to roll out their initial data warehouse capabilities to a very small number of end users. In many cases, they even selected end users who were more technically inclined than the average user.

These choices made sense at the time, since they helped to ensure that initial warehouse attempts would be successful. However, they may also have unwittingly stacked the deck against future, broader-scale data warehouse initiatives: The teams responsible for designing and implementing the data warehouse were not fully exposed to the difficulties of "maintaining" large amounts of metadata without formal processes or tools to assist them.

Today, the demand for data warehousing and high-level decision support has increased dramatically. Organizations are being challenged to roll out ever-increasing functionality in their data warehouses to an expanding audience of end users. Understanding the data in the warehouse and where it comes from once seemed a manageable job. A small handful of subject area experts could be relied on to maintain the knowledge of the data in the warehouse and its related business rules. As the scope of data warehouses grows dramatically, however, that small handful of experts has grown into a crowd. This crowd of business knowledge owners requires a better, more standardized way to document and communicate their knowledge of the warehouse, it rules, and its data sources.

Early data warehouse initiatives had the luxury of focusing on "early adopter" end users, who were more self-sufficient and required less training than the average end user. On the other hand, today data warehouse teams must roll expanded data content out to a very large user community. This new user community includes people of widely varying technical skills and with varying degrees of knowledge of the business information in the warehouse. Better end-user data access and analysis tools can help users figure out how to get information they need out of the warehouse, but only good, easily accessible metadata can help them figure out what is available in the data warehouse and how to ask for it. No data warehouse team can possibly rise to the challenge of providing more information faster to a knowledge-hungry organization if that team is spending exorbitant amounts of time helping end users understand what information is in the warehouse and what it means.

Fortunately for those faced with the task of building data warehouses on an ever-increasing scale, help is on the way. Actually, one could argue that help has been available for some time but was not widely recognized. This help, of course, is the metadata repository. Repositories are specialized databases designed to maintain metadata, together with the tools and interfaces that allow a company to collect and distribute its metadata. Until recently, however, repositories were not positioned specifically to help data warehouse efforts track their metadata. Rather, they were aimed at overall information systems management, promising to aid maintenance of legacy systems through impact analysis and to promote efficiency in designing new applications through the proper identification and selective reuse of legacy data structures. Today, however, repository vendors are working to position their products to help manage data warehouse metadata.

THE LIFE CYCLE OF METADATA

There are three fundamental stages in the life cycle of metadata. These three stages come together synergistically to make metadata useful in the data warehouse environment. Without all three, there can be very little benefit from metadata.

METADATA LIFE CYCLE

1 Collection   Identify metadata and capture it into central repository.

2 Maintenance   Put in place processes to synchronize metadata automatically with the changing data architecture.

3 Deployment   Provide metadata to users in the right form and with the right tools.

The first life-cycle stage of metadata is collection. In other words, you must find metadata and collect it into a central place, often a repository. To ensure a high level of accuracy, it is essential that this metadata collection be as automated as possible. For instance, envision collecting metadata about the file structure of a legacy application that uses a hierarchical database. Which would be more accurate: an analyst examining each structure and keying detailed descriptive information into a metadata store, or an automated scanner that parses the data structures and populates that metadata store? Obviously, the scanner would be far more accurate and would be less of a drain on human resources. Wherever feasible, the collection of metadata should be automated.

The second stage in the life cycle of metadata is maintenance. In this phase, metadata must be kept up to date with reality. For instance, if the structure of a relational table changes, the metadata stored about that table must also be updated to reflect the change. Like metadata collection, automation is critical to this step. The only way to ensure that metadata is accurately and faithfully maintained is to automate as much of the maintenance process as possible. One need look no further than more application system documentation to see the results of relying on procedures alone to maintain metadata. Most system modifications that take place after the initial release of the software are documented poorly, if at all, even in those systems where complete documentation was faithfully prepared during design and construction. Therefore, to keep good metadata for the data warehouse environment, it is mandatory to automate as much of the metadata maintenance as possible.

The third life-cycle stage of metadata is deployment. This is where the pains taken to collect and maintain good-quality metadata come to fruition. For metadata is only valuable to an organization when it is deployed and used. Simply keeping metadata, no matter how accurate, does not offer any tangible benefits. In the data warehouse environment, metadata can be deployed in different fashions to different groups of recipients, including data warehouse developers, warehouse maintainers, and end users. One of the keys to successful metadata deployment is correctly matching the metadata offered to the specific needs of each audience. The requirements of these different audiences will be covered in detail in the following discussion of metadata deployment.

METADATA COLLECTION

Collecting the right metadata at the right time is the basis for a successful metadata-driven data warehouse implementation. Occasionally, people think that collecting metadata will significantly add to the amount of work that they have to do when they design and build a data warehouse. Actually, the exact opposite is true. The fundamental thing to remember is that all of the metadata that should be collected is actually generated and processed by the team anyway, regardless of whether they understand metadata and try to collect it in a coordinated fashion. For example, one common form of metadata is that which describes the physical data structures used in a legacy application. In designing a data warehouse, the analysts must examine the physical structure for each system that might provide a data source for the warehouse. Since they are already examining that structure, there is very little additional work involved in preserving the analysis that they perform. In fact, if they use specialized tools such as a repository, they may even be able to perform this analysis faster. Later, when they need to refer back to some analysis previously done or they need to reexamine a data structure, having this metadata preserved in a central place will yield great efficiencies.

The metadata that can be useful for a data warehouse spans a wide variety of domains, from physical structure data, to logical model data, to business usage and rules. Each of these types requires its own strategy to collect. Some can be automated to a great degree, while others will involve more manual effort. Four distinct categories of metadata will be presented next, in roughly the order in which they would be available during the design and development process of a data warehouse.

Warehouse Data Sources

One of the most fundamental types of metadata that can be collected is information about the potential sources of data for a data warehouse. This can include existing operational systems, external data that is available, and information that is currently maintained manually. For example, an organization might identify among its potential sources of warehouse data several legacy applications, a PC-based spreadsheet maintained by the finance department, some purchased sales data acquired from a vendor, and some customer contact logs that are currently maintained on paper by the customer service department.

Even though these data sources are on different platforms and are stored in very different formats, we have a consistent need to understand both the physical structure of the data and the meaning of the data. The physical structure is usually the easier type to collect. We need to document what the record structures and discrete data elements are, including specific data types. For data structures that are stored on large-scale databases, this can be a highly automated process if a repository toolset is available. Scanners are usually available for common data storage mechanisms, which can scan or parse the data structures and document in the repository all of the physical metadata that is required.

If a repository is not available, or for data sources for which no scanner exists, there are two choices: Create a semiautomated scanning or parsing process, or manually collect and document metadata. For those sources that are relatively high volume, it makes sense to create a metadata parser. For example, if an organization has a great many databases deployed on a relatively unknown database technology, it would be well worth the effort to write programs that parse the database structures and produce standardized, readable documentation, rather than manually analyzing a large number of data structures. On the other hand, for small-volume data sources, manual analysis may be preferable. A single accounting department spreadsheet can be documented manually in considerably less time than it would take to develop an automated routine that parses the spreadsheet structure and data types used. Data that is not maintained electronically is usually analyzed by hand. For instance, a customer contact logging system that relies on paper forms filled out by customer service representatives can be analyzed by hand, and the information about what fields are maintained can be documented easily.

Data Models

The second category of metadata that plays an important role in data warehousing is information about data models. In designing the warehouse, it is important to understand the logical model that defines the business entities, relationships, and rules that exist in the operational environment. In many organizations, this information is formally documented in the guise of an enterprise data model. Often, this model is documented in some sort of CASE tool or model diagramming tool, although it is occasionally maintained manually. In either case, it is important to capture this information and bring it into the data warehouse metadata domain so that it can be correlated with the data models that reflect the data warehouse.

As the warehouse is designed, its data models evolve. Usually, the enterprise data model is used as a starting point for creating the warehouse data model, and then modifications and transformations are applied to that model. It is critical to be able to trace the connections from the enterprise data model to the warehouse model, so that we can understand how specific logical entities are implemented in the warehouse. The inherent relationships are not always obvious after numerous iterations of warehouse modeling techniques have been applied to the original model. Things can be made even more confusing when specialized modeling techniques, such as star-shaped schema modeling, are applied.

To capture this information, we must first capture the starting state, the enterprise data model. If this is documented in a CASE tool, it is essentially already captured. However, there are additional benefits that can be derived by combining all warehouse-related metadata in a central storage facility (i.e., a repository). If a repository is going to be used, the easiest route to moving the data model into the repository is to use an interface between the repository and the chosen CASE tool. Most repository toolsets include interfaces with numerous CASE tools that can quickly import a model into the repository.

After the data warehouse data model has been designed, it too should be captured with the rest of the warehouse metadata. If the same CASE tool was used to design the warehouse as was used for the enterprise data model, then the same method of capturing the metadata can be used. However, many people are finding that some of the CASE tools on the market today are not especially well suited for designing data warehouse structures. They enforce design criteria that are desirable for operational systems and facilitate the generation of source code from CASE tools, but these criteria are not applicable in a warehouse. Therefore, many projects use a different CASE tool to design the warehouse model, or even use a simple drawing tool to document the warehouse model. This provides a strong argument for the use of repository, since it provides a "neutral" place to which both the enterprise data model and the warehouse model can be ported, independent of any specific CASE or modeling tools.

Once you have collected metadata about your enterprise model and about the warehouse model, you must correlate them. That is, you should map the entities in the enterprise model to their representations in the warehouse model. This is very important, since it can provide the basis for future change impact analysis and end-user content analysis, as explained later. In most cases, this mapping will be a manual task, since there is no automated way to discern reliably which warehouse data structures were derived from which enterprise model entities. Only careful and thorough notes and documentation during the warehouse modeling process will provide a sufficient "audit trail" to allow you to populate these links once the warehouse is designed.

Finally, you must ensure that the entity and element definitions, business rules, valid values, and usage guidelines are transposed properly from the enterprise model to the warehouse model. This is a simple, mostly clerical, procedure that can readily be accomplished manually or with repository tools. Having this information stored with the warehouse model ensures that users of the warehouse will be able to access easily information that will help them write better queries and interpret the data in the warehouse.

Warehouse Mappings

The third category of metadata that must be captured in designing the warehouse is the mapping of operational data into the warehouse data structures. As analysis on the warehouse progresses and elements from operational systems, external data, or other sources are mapped to the warehouse structures, this mapping should be collected and maintained as metadata.

Each time a data element from one of these sources is mapped to the warehouse, you should record the logical connection between these data elements, as well as any transformation or alteration that takes place. That is, not only should you be able to tell that an element in the warehouse is populated from specific sources of data, you should also be able to discern exactly what happens to those elements as they are extracted from the data sources, moved, transformed, and loaded into the warehouse.

In cases where this mapping is done manually and code will be written to affect transformations of the data, the design specifications for the mappings will act as the source for this metadata. These mappings can be recorded in a form that is easy to understand for the developers who will implement the mapping, and will also be easy to integrate into the metadata store. Often, a spreadsheet or simple PC-based relational database can be used to record these mappings.

If specialized data warehouse development tools are being used, the mapping process is often indistinguishable from the process of implementing the mappings and transformations. In these cases, the mappings are specified directly to a tool, which then generates the necessary routines to move and transform the data. This eliminates the need for a separate step to document the mappings. However, this can also have the effect of "locking up" this metadata in the tool being used, unless that tool can export or communicate this metadata to your central metadata store. If you are using a repository, it may be as simple as using a vendor-supplied interface that extracts mapping information from your warehouse tool and ports it to the repository. Otherwise, it may be necessary to construct routines that extract this knowledge from your warehouse tool, assuming the information is stored in a manner that is readily accessible.

Warehouse Usage Information

The final component of metadata that should be captured in the process of creating a data warehouse is information about the usage of the information in the warehouse. This information can be captured only after the warehouse has been rolled out to users. It is very important, though, to understand who is using the warehouse and how they are using it. There are several reasons why this information is important. These reasons include better performance tuning of the warehouse, greater reuse of existing queries, and understanding of how information in the warehouse is being used to solve business problems.

Understanding what tables are being accessed, by whom, and how often can help us tune the physical structures of the data warehouse to better meet end-user needs. For example, if we find that a very large table containing daily sales figures is frequently being rolled up in user queries to show weekly sales, we have the opportunity to create a data mart or summarized table that contains presummarized weekly sales data. This could simplify end-user queries against that data and yield a significant performance improvement. Conversely, you would want to identify summary or aggregate data that is rarely used so that you can reclaim the disk space it occupies.

Collecting this information is not easy, however. To understand every query executed against the warehouse, you would have to depend on a database monitoring tool to intercept and interpret each query executed. The data from this tool would then need to be fed into a central metadata store so that it can be analyzed and tracked. At the time of this writing, the only option available to most sites is to create their own interface from a database analyzer to their metadata store.

Identifying what queries have already been written can also be valuable since it can promote the reuse of queries. Rather than spending time figuring out how to write a new query, an end user can simply retrieve an existing query that meets his or her needs and execute it. They can even make simple changes to the query without having the ability to write the query on their own from scratch. To collect this information, you need to catalog a description of the query in addition to information about what tables it accesses. This requires an interface from the query tool itself to the metadata store so that the technical and the descriptive characteristics of each saved query can be recorded centrally. Repository vendors are offering such interfaces for several widely used query tools, and more should be available soon.

The most sophisticated form of usage tracking is to understand how information from the warehouse is being used to solve business problems. This goes beyond simply cataloging who wrote queries, what those queries do, and how they are described by their authors. Instead, it involves capturing the nature of the business problem or question that the user sought to answer when he or she wrote the query in the first place. Obviously, such metadata cannot be captured automatically. But if standards are put in place to allow the creation and maintenance of this information, the power of the data warehouse can be increased dramatically. Imagine, for instance, that a user, or potential user, of the data warehouse has a business question that he or she needs to answer, but is unsure if the warehouse can help answer it. Without this information about why queries are written, the user will have to search the warehouse metadata to see what data exists that might be pertinent to the question at hand. Then, if the user finds relevant data, he or she will have to figure out what question to ask (i.e., what query to write). The catch is, if the user does not already have an idea about what information would answer the question, he or she probably will not find anything helpful in the warehouse.

On the other hand, imagine if this same end user had access to metadata that described the business problems that had been previously addressed through queries against the warehouse. Then the user would be able to search through several levels of hierarchically organized business issues and finally be presented with a list of queries that other people in the organization had written to address problems or questions similar to the user's. The user can execute one of these existing queries, or use it as the baseline for a new query. In effect, this approach has opened up the collective problem-solving capabilities of the organization to this user. No longer must the user already know what question he or she wants to ask before using the warehouse. Instead, the user has access to the problem-solving techniques developed by others in the organization and can reuse those methods where appropriate. Although the effort involved in manually maintaining this type of metadata can be heavy, the potential benefits are even more significant.

MAINTAINING METADATA

Once all of this metadata has been captured initially, it must be maintained. As with any maintenance process, automation is the key to maintaining current, high-quality information. The best approach for maintaining each specific type of metadata depends on how it was originally collected, how often it changes, and the volume of metadata generated.

For physical metadata that reflects the structures of the data sources and of the warehouse itself, a high degree of automation can be achieved. If a repository is used, the ability to maintain database structure information automatically is a common feature. If a repository is not being used, you can either implement an automated set of routines to detect changes in physical structures and update metadata accordingly, or you can put in place procedures that ensure that metadata will be updated when database structure changes are made. Because most IT shops already exert a fair degree of control over structure changes to production databases, it is feasible to augment these procedures to include updating metadata. Most proposed database changes already go through several levels of verification and authorization, so adding the metadata maintenance requirement would not be a significant additional burden. Because this type of metadata is usually very large, it is most practical to capture only the incremental changes, rather than periodically refreshing the entire set of physical data structure metadata.

For business rule information and data models, the metadata will probably have to be maintained manually. Even with an interface between a CASE tool and a metadata repository, it is probably not desirable to have model changes propagated to the repository automatically. This is because the model may go through several cycles of iterative modification and evaluation before you wish to "commit" these changes to the metadata store. Instead, it is probably best to rely on manual initiation of an automated refresh process to update data model information in the metadata store. Because the models are relatively small, a full refresh is possible and is much less complicated than detecting incremental changes.

Data warehouse mapping and transformation information should also be maintained. In cases where the mapping is done with a data warehouse construction tool and there is an interface between the tool and the metadata store, the maintenance of this information is inherent and automatic. If a warehouse tool is being used but there is not an automated interface, then you must rely on manual initiation of the process to update the mapping information.

Data warehouse usage information is the final type of information that must be maintained. Since information about the usage of specific tables and data structures by warehouse queries is dynamic, it should be periodically appended, rather than changing existing information. This periodic addition of information is usually inherent in the tool used to capture database access information. For higher-level usage information that specifies the description and business purpose of each query stored in the warehouse environment, a purely manual approach must be taken. Procedures should state that every time a query is created or significantly modified, a corresponding description should be created or updated, and the query should be categorized according to the type of business problem or question to which it pertains. Periodic audits can be run against the metadata to uncover stored queries for which this information does not exist, and users can be contacted and urged to supply this information.

METADATA DEPLOYMENT

Once metadata has been collected and appropriate maintenance procedures are in place, attention can be directed toward deployment of metadata to its audiences in the data warehouse environment. Supplying the right metadata to the right audience is critical to the success of a data warehouse initiative. It is vital to realize that there are several distinct groups of people who will use metadata, and their needs are different. A well-designed solution will present the right metadata in the right format and medium to each of these groups.

Warehouse Developers

Warehouse developers require sophisticated access to detailed metadata. The primary forms of metadata that they will use are the physical structure information for data sources, the enterprise data model, and the warehouse data models. They will use information about the data sources to perform analysis and to map those sources to the warehouse. This metadata can be used first to help them identify potential sources, by searching for elements whose names contain forms of a significant business term. Once candidates are identified, they can then use the element definitions combined with the enterprise data model to determine whether they should actually be mapped to the warehouse. Then, comparing the current physical structure and business definition (the "as is") with the warehouse target model (the "to be"), the developers can generate the data mappings from source to warehouse. These mappings are a form of metadata themselves, since they specify how data flows from sources into the warehouse and what transformations are applied to it. Developers are primarily concerned with the accuracy and completeness of the metadata that they use. Because of their need for completeness and flexibility, the warehouse developers will often directly access the metadata store, using the repository tool if it is available, or another query tool if repository is not used.

Maintaining the Warehouse

Once a portion of the warehouse has been developed and rolled out, someone must be responsible for operating and maintaining it. The requirements of this function can vary widely, but metadata can help in all of these situations.

One use that the data warehouse team has for metadata is in understanding the impact of proposed operational system changes on the data warehouse. If the structure of an application database, or of external purchased data, is being changed, the warehouse team needs to respond to that change. Warehouse data movement and scrubbing routines may have to be modified. Warehouse data structures may have to be changed. Data marts may need to be altered. End-user queries may have to be rewritten, and users may require additional training. Therefore, it is essential that the data warehouse team have access to comprehensive impact analysis capabilities so that they can understand the ramifications of changing one or more elements in the data sources that feed the warehouse. Using the metadata described previously, the maintenance team could assess the following information when an operational data element is scheduled to be changed:

- What data extraction, movement, and transformation routines may have to be modified
- What table structures in the data warehouse should be changed
- What data mart and summary data structures may need to be altered
- What stored user queries will be affected and should be examined to determine if they need to be modified
- Which end users use those queries, so that additional training may be provided if necessary
- What business questions or problems are addressed in part using the element that is changing, so that the team can understand the significance of the change and how it will affect decision making.

Of course, the modification to the warehouse may also be triggered by the warehouse team itself. This could happen when they are adding new types of data to the warehouse, or when they are changing the physical structure to improve performance and ease user access. For example, the warehouse team has identified that a table in the warehouse contains some columns that change every time new information is added to the warehouse; this table also contains a roughly equal number of columns that change very infrequently. The database administrator suggests splitting this table into two separate physical tables to conserve disk space taken up by the columns that rarely change. Before implementing such a change, the warehouse team would need to understand most of the aforementioned impact analysis so the change can be effected with minimal disruption to users.

A unique challenge faced by the developers and maintainers of a data warehouse is the task of defending the warehouse to those who raise doubts about its integrity or accuracy. This often happens when a user receives information from the warehouse that seems to contradict information he or she has been getting from another source. In this situation, there are three possible outcomes. The warehouse is correct, and the other system has been giving the user bad information that has gone unchallenged and undetected because there was no readily available basis for comparison. Another option is that the warehouse contains some incorrect data, possibly due to an error in the data movement and transformation layer or a business rule that was not correctly implemented. The third and final option is that neither system is wrong; they merely reflect two different sets of business rules, which dictate different methods for deriving the same answer. In this case, you may want to settle on one accepted method, or there may be a reason to continue using both. In any of the aforementioned situations, however, it is critical for the warehouse team to come up with a prompt, definitive response when the content of the warehouse is challenged. Only by maintaining detailed metadata can the warehouse team quickly trace an element in the warehouse to its origins in the operational world and quickly identify exactly what types of transformation are taking place en route to the warehouse. Even if this analysis shows that the warehouse contains some incorrect data, being able to pinpoint the precise cause of the inaccuracy and fix it in a reasonable amount of time preserves valuable credibility for the data warehouse.

Because of the breadth and scope of this impact analysis and tracing capability, the warehouse maintenance team usually requires access to all of the metadata, like the developers. When a repository is present, they would access it directly.

End Users

Perhaps the most important audience for metadata is the end user. Without proper metadata in an easy-to-access format, end users cannot explore the warehouse, create queries, and correctly interpret the data they find in the warehouse. An end user's metadata needs are simple compared to the previous categories. The real challenge, however, lies in providing the data to end users in a format that is easy to access and easy to understand. Too much detail may prove overwhelming, and a complicated access method will discourage its use.

Users of the warehouse are primarily concerned with two types of metadata. The first type tells them what is in the warehouse and where it came from. In other words, they want to be able to see an inventory of the warehouse by subject area or high-level topic. Then they want to select a table or an element and be presented with its full definition, business meaning, valid values, and usage rules. They also want to be able to see, at a high level, the sources of the data. For example, an end user would probably want to know that the weekly sales data was collected from the accounts receivable (AR) system, the billing system, and the order entry system. On the other hand, the user would probably not want to be presented with all of the details of how each element was moved and transformed on its journey from the operational environment into the data warehouse. All of this should be accomplished without burdening the user with technical names or cryptic commands.

The second type of metadata that is critical to end users is information about what queries already exist that they might reuse. If users identify a table that they wish to query, they should be able to view a list of queries that access that table, along with descriptions of those queries. If a query meets their needs or is similar to what they wish to do, they can reuse that query instead of starting from scratch. In a more advanced environment, users would also be able to access existing queries by selecting the type of business question they want to ask. They could navigate through a hierarchical menu of business topics until they are presented with the list of queries relevant to the issue at hand.

For both of these types of metadata, presentation must be easy to understand and easy to access. For example, many warehouse projects have been successful in publishing a printed data dictionary document that serves as the users' handbook to the data warehouse. This solution is simple, cost effective, and easily accessed. A more sophisticated solution to this problem is being promoted by vendors in the data warehouse arena. This includes repository vendors as well as vendors of other warehouse-oriented tools. Their offerings involve a specialized warehouse end-user metadata presentation tool, which presents specific types of metadata, geared to end users, in a very intuitive, user-friendly software tool. These tools can be accessed alongside the users' data access and analysis tools and are working to provide tight integration with those tools.

Providing the proper metadata to end users is often overlooked in warehouse projects, yet it can readily mean the difference between a warehouse with which end users feel comfortable and a warehouse that users view as yet another overly complicated database.

INTEGRATION WITH DATA ACCESS TOOLS

One of the most significant trends in data warehousing today is the integration of metadata into data access and analysis tools. The goal is to make as seamless as possible the movement from metadata to querying actual data in the warehouse environment. There are four levels of integration that can be accomplished with current technology.

The first level of integration is simply to have side-by-side access to metadata and to real data. On a desktop computer, this means being able to display end-user metadata in one tool concurrently with actual warehouse queries and data in another tool. This way, users can browse metadata, and then write queries against that data in the query tool. They can also use the metadata tool to help them understand what they are seeing in the query tool.

The second level of integration is to populate query tool help text with metadata exported from a central metadata store. In this way, the query tool can provide context-sensitive help when a user wants to know the meaning of a particular table or column. The major drawback to this approach is that the query tool's help data needs to be refreshed each time the metadata changes. If the query tool software is installed locally on client workstation computers, this can be a daunting task.

The next step in integrating data access tools with metadata is to provide query tools that are truly metadata aware. In this scenario, the query tools can be instructed to directly, dynamically access metadata in order to provide context-sensitive help for end users. This eliminates the problems of having to refresh help data, and it ensures that users always see timely metadata.

The fourth level of integration, and one that is being achieved today, is to have full interconnectivity between the metadata tool and the query tool. With this level of integration, users could start browsing metadata in the metadata tool and directly connect to the query tool of choice when they find a table they wish to access or a stored query they wish to execute. The metadata browser would activate the query tool that the user selects and bring up the selected table or selected stored query. Conversely, a user could be in a query tool and could transparently move into the metadata browser to view metadata pertinent to the data that is being queried. One of the benefits of this approach is that the metadata tool and the query tool remain separate. Each tool is free to focus on its specific mission, and the user can choose from many query tools. In the warehouse environment, where one data access tool seldom fits all needs, this is a major benefit.

SUMMARY

As data warehouses grow larger and more complex and stretch to deliver high-quality information to broader audiences, metadata plays a key role in enabling warehouse teams to meet these challenges. Because of the complexities involved in collecting, maintaining, and deploying metadata for the data warehouse, an organization should have a solid metadata plan in place before it begins building its data warehouse. What seemed easy enough on a small scale without the benefit of carefully controlled metadata will quickly prove to be unmanageable on a larger scale.

CHAPTER 12

The Role
of a Directory/Catalog

Jack Sweeney

Intellidex Systems
Winthrop, Massachusetts

"Don't be afraid to take a big step if one is indicated,
you can't cross a chasm in two small jumps."

David Lloyd George
British Statesman, 1863-1945

The focus of this chapter is the enterprisewide data warehouse and how critical it is to have the infrastructure, tools, technology and mind-set to position data warehousing as more of an environment for decision support rather than a point solution database application. Contained in an enterprisewide data warehouse environment is a plethora of data and information. We tend to look at a warehouse implementation as merely a collection of horizontally structured business data but, it is much more. It is the foundation for total business understanding and a leveraged framework for those decisions surrounding competitiveness in our business activities. For a warehouse implementation to be successful, it needs to be well architected—that is, it must have a framework and technical structure encompassing the data that supports the main objective of the warehouse implementation, which is delivering decision support data to the decision makers. However, the simplicity of the objective tends to get muddled in the complexity of the solution.

Another title for this chapter could have been "Lessons Learned while Building an Enterprisewide Data Warehouse" since most of the insights articulated were gained in a real-life environment by implementing the concepts put forth in this chapter. The environment that I mention is a large bank. I was fortunate to have a talented and dedicated staff to implement the data warehouse architecture, visionary leaders to sponsor the initial pilot project, and sophisticated business users whose involvement was critical in the success of the bank's implementation of the aforementioned architecture.

THE CHALLENGE

It is important to note that there are as many definitions and terms in the world of data warehousing as there are warehouse implementations. We as information professionals often get conflicting messages regarding the nature of our mission. Support the business user and decision makers' immediate needs or invest in a longer-term solution that is architected to handle the changes in the business environment. Change is the one constant in the world we live in, and this certainly holds true for us as information professionals. We need to keep up with the competition, contribute positively to the bottom line, deal with corporate edicts, and, in general, manage the various stress points in our environment by making the right decisions at the right time with the best information possible. It is a constant struggle to keep the decision makers informed, and we often compromise a longer-term, consistent view of information with quick-hit solutions that may or may not fit as we take the broader view of putting all the pieces of the corporate information puzzle together. The challenge is providing short-term benefit without disabling broader long-term flexibility with change enabled solutions.

Based on the latest vendor advertising campaigns and trade journal emphasis, the data warehouse is becoming the universally accepted decision support solution and will answer all questions posed by management about changing information needs. Our view is that the data warehouse does not contain information, it contains data (hence the name *data warehouse*). As one of our colleagues puts it, the data warehouse contains "data in formation" and is the foundation for information. Because as solution professionals we provide expertise in these areas and we follow the rules for building data warehouses, all that is needed is for someone to pull it all together. We believe that with the right perspective that encompasses the enterprise environmental view, with tools, technology, and business insight, the warehouse implementation becomes a formidable competitive advantage for the business.

This environment is often described using the library and card catalog analogy. Although appropriate, this analogy does not do justice to the enterprisewide nature of the data warehouse environment and the inherent complexities involved in connecting it to the decision makers. A more appropriate analogy, capturing the sophistication and complexity of the enterprisewide warehouse, may be something like a retail specialty store mail order catalog.

In this analogy, the catalog you receive in the mail represents the company's standardized approved offering of products for the consumer. The catalog is the front end to a very complex infrastructure maintained by the company to provide you, the consumer, with exciting lines of quality products that are available to satisfy your every need. The company's buyers have selected from a multitude of vendors those products that they have deemed suitable to fit into their company's offering. The products have been screened for quality, functionality, durability, and, most important, usability. This process is similar to determining which data will be warehoused based on the requirements and screening of the multiple sources available in your company's operational and legacy support systems.

The vendors ship the wide array of products to the catalog warehouse based on what was ordered; then the dock receivers log in the merchandise, check quantity and quality against what was ordered, and move it to a predetermined location in the consolidation facility. This process can be equated to extracting, transforming, and scrubbing legacy data and then incorporating it into the warehouse data structure. All along the way, data about the merchandise is collected and stored in a system that allows for the management and distribution of the merchandise. An example of this is how many were received versus how many ordered, the description of each item, when it was received, the location(s) where it is stored, the cost, the price, etc. This is data about each item that is collected and stored in a control system to manage the merchandise. In data warehouse terminology, we would call this metadata, or data about the data in the warehouse.

We have now come to the crossroads of traditional warehouse thinking. Getting the data into the warehouse is only half of the equation (Figure 12.1). Picture the thousands and thousands of merchandise items spread across acres of warehouse space. All the items are in different colors, sizes, shapes, locations, etc. Some of these items may be familiar, like tents or ski parkas, and some not so familiar, like fly-fishing accessories. Imagine yourself as a shopper walking in the front door of a 13-acre warehouse with floor to ceiling shelves full of interesting merchandise. Based on your catalog selection, you walk up to the sales counter and ask for a size XL teal colored sweatshirt and the response you get from the clerk is, "It's in there somewhere! You can take all the time you want to go and find it!" This is not an exciting prospect. You have now put yourself into a similar situation as most warehouse end users find themselves in today. There may be a knowledgeable clerk around to point you in the right direction, but the shear magnitude and size of the environment may prevent you from finding what you want when you need it.

"Getting data into a warehouse is only half of the equation"

Figure 12.1 Data Movement.

Continuing the catalog analogy, the retail specialty store has solved the problem of getting you what you want through maintaining a sophisticated infrastructure. The infrastructure supports the activities of acquiring, consolidating, storing, and ultimately delivering to you the merchandise that interests you the most. The retailer accomplished this by investing in the processes of acquisition, consolidation, storage, and delivery and then linking you, the consumer, to this infrastructure through the merchandise catalog. The catalog is the front end and entry point that connects you to what is available in that warehouse.

You, as a consumer using the catalog, can now browse through the well-structured pages searching for merchandise represented as groups of related items like outerwear, footwear, camping equipment, fishing equipment, etc. Each grouping represented in the catalog contains individual products that are described in terms that you understand. It is easy to describe merchandise in terms like color, size, cost, construction material, and shape, usually with a picture that helps you put each product in the context of how it may be used. Following this example a bit further, you can look in the index, narrow down the page, and browse through the clothing section to zero in on the teal colored size XL sweatshirt. Making note of the catalog number, you dial the toll free telephone number and request that your sweatshirt and a few other interesting items be sent to your doorstep via the most efficient package delivery service as soon as possible. Your package arrives the next day.

The data warehouse should be so accessible. Data consumers should not have to wade through gigabytes or terabytes of data searching for the bits and bytes you need to answer a question or make a decision. Not unlike the retail catalog process, the data warehouse environment narrows down all of the data possibilities and provides the infrastructure to acquire, consolidate, standardize, understand, define, describe, represent, and deliver to you, the consumer, the data needed to meet your needs.

As this catalog analogy illustrates, a robust infrastructure and the total enterprisewide data warehouse environment are critical success factors in constructing a well-architected enterprisewide data warehouse. Building an effective enterprisewide data warehouse entails designing and connecting the acquisition, storage, and delivery processes into a comprehensive information architecture. This is the fundamental point of this chapter—that you cannot buy a data warehouse; indeed, you must build it. The foundation of this architecture is the creation of a metadata catalog.

It seems like every vendor of hardware, software, and service is jumping on the data warehouse bandwagon. To the well informed, it also appears that most are selling pieces of the total solution. It is not inconceivable that we as information professionals need to tie or integrate 15 to 20 different products to implement an enterprisewide data warehouse solution. What does this all mean? It means that building an enterprise data warehouse solution is a monumental undertaking and, in reality, building the data warehouse means managing a very large, very expensive systems integration project. Just sorting through the marketing hype and the multitude of warehouse vendors is an arduous task. The trick is having a well-architected blueprint, like the retail merchandise catalog environment, that encompasses the total experience to maximize the time and money needed to complete the mission.

This chapter expands on and offers a plausible methodology based on experience that ties together all the various component pieces and functions of an enterprise data warehouse through the use of a concept called the active directory/catalog. The active directory/catalog is based on the management and integration of three fundamentally different types of data within an enterprisewide data warehouse implementation: physical data, semantic data, and environmental data. Physical data seems to be best understood in its simplistic form as the data moved from source or legacy systems to the data warehouse. Semantic data, including metadata, on the other hand, is commonly referred to as the data about the data in the warehouse. Even this definition needs to be expanded to address not only metadata but other contextual aspects of the warehouse and environmental data needs within an enterprise data warehouse implementation. As we become more experienced in data warehousing, these definitions become more and more important to the basic understanding of the contents and operation of the data warehouse environment.

The expansion and redefinition of a concept called the semantic layer within the context of an enterprisewide data warehouse implementation (Figure 12.2) is a way to make sense of the multitude of metadata that is generated or flows from the use and management of the data warehouse. In principle, the semantic layer is comprised of the metadata that originates from, or is needed by, the various components of an enterprisewide warehouse implementation. It can be represented as a three-tiered model that contains six distinct categories of data combined in the physical and semantic layers of an enterprise data warehouse architecture.

With few exceptions, most vendor product focus to date has been on the physical layer: moving legacy data with some specific tools to a relational database product that, by default, becomes your physical data warehouse. We see database,

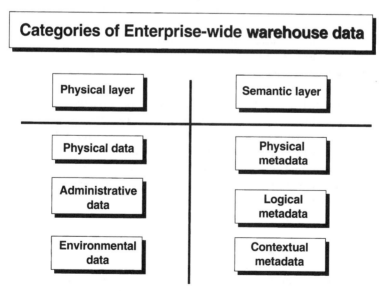

Figure 12.2 Data Categories.

extract tool, middleware, connectivity, query/reporting, and OLAP vendors concentrating in this space. Some have started to dabble in the metadata space, which
starts to address some of the semantic layers of the enterprise data warehouse
through the use of a directory product. We also see this in two areas: (1) in the
extract from legacy system space, and (2) in the query and reporting tool space.
These efforts are an important first step but need to be taken further to act as the
glue that ties all semantic and physical data layers together.

As we gain more and more experience with data warehousing, we will find that
it becomes increasingly important to understand and implement the concepts surrounding the semantic layer of data associated with an enterprisewide data
warehouse as well as to integrate the semantic layer into a tool specifically designed
to enable the management of such an environment. The incorporation and use of a
warehouse semantic data layer in conjunction with the physical data stored in a data
warehouse is increasingly important when the scope of the data warehouse is truly an
enterprisewide view that is "horizontal" in nature. The horizontal view cuts across
multiple vertical business units, and data used across the enterprise is prone to misunderstanding, misconception, misinterpretation, and often sets up definitional
dynamics within the organization if it is not well understood. Commonly lumped into
a category called metadata, the semantic layer of data is more comprehensive in that
it is not just data about data in the warehouse but is data about the warehouse data
and the environment that puts the data in context within the horizontal organization.

The semantic layer consists of metadata that is pulled from the entire data
warehouse architecture and includes physical metadata like data sources, transformation rules, target database, subject area, structure, definition, owners, and
periodicity. It also contains logical metadata, such as business descriptions of entities, elements, attributes, subject areas, and views, as well as contextual metadata
like cleanup rules and archive structure.

The physical layer consists of data that is utilized from the entire data warehouse
implementation and includes physical data stored in databases, tables, and columns
(including table codes and precision). Also included is environmental data like data
mart server hardware options, disk space, network, usage patterns, run logs, and performance metrics. Last but not least is administrative data, like who can access the data, user profiles, conversion formats, preferences, and subscription data movement.

The concept of directories or catalogs must migrate from the perception of
passive (library card catalog) to active (mail order catalog), managing both the
semantic and physical data layers of your warehouse. Positioning data within the
context of how it was created and delivering it to the decision makers as "information enabled" is the next challenge.

COMPONENTS OF AN ACTIVE DIRECTORY/CATALOG

The active metadata catalog monitors the flow of metadata through the enterprisewide data warehouse environment. It begins by capturing and storing the
business metadata or logical metadata. This is the metadata that describes ware-

house data in business terminology, with any associated business rules governing the context of the data. Business metadata is created in the logical design process and then moved within context to the active directory/catalog. Technical metadata is also captured. This includes data source and transformations and the description of the physical target or warehouse database environment. It is also very important to note that the mapping between logical and physical is also captured, and the relationship structure is maintained in the active directory/catalog.

Environmental data is also captured in the active directory/catalog. This data includes user profiles, security and access information, and data about the physical environment—such as data marts, hardware server capacity, server network location, and performance data. The consolidation of all the metadata and environmental data within the active directory/catalog allows it to be the "control center" of the enterprise data warehouse implementation. In this role, it ties the components and pieces of the warehouse environment together. Its objective is to provide ease of navigation through the enterprisewide data warehouse environment with a set of integrated tools and services geared to both decision makers and administrators. The tools and services facilitate searching for specifics to understand, access, order, and analyze pieces of data within the warehouse. By tying together the various components of the architecture, users and warehouse administrators alike are able to function in a controlled, efficient, and secure environment. The active directory/catalog is the front end that links the end users to the warehouse.

As noted in the conceptual architecture diagram (Figure 12.3), the active director/catalog is made up of component functions and services that fall into five or more basic categories:

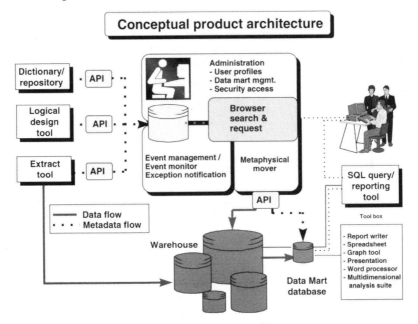

Figure 12.3 Conceptual Architecture.

1. Administration

Administration functions allow for user profiles to be established for warehouse users. End-user profiles might allow specific functions like browse, search, or request, along with some elementary reporting functions. Administrator profiles might allow for all active directory/catalog functions, including creation, approval, and scheduling of subscription and data mart–related data movement activities, as well as the basic functions. Security and access profiles are also managed through administration. User groups are maintained with specific authorities granted to participants of each group.

Warehouse environmental information is also provided through profiles contained in administration. Included are data specific to network servers, log-on parameters, and conversion preferences. Administration reports include usage and performance statistics, histograms, monitoring, server-related feedback, and other environment related data.

2. Browser, Search, and Request

This function is the looking glass to the metadata of the warehouse. The structure is both logical and physical, meaning that browsing is facilitated at the database, table, and column level, as well as the subject area, entity, element, and attribute level. This structure enables the end user or administrator to browse using business terminology or view metadata at the physical database level. Search allows the end user or administrator to zero in on a specific set of warehouse metadata based on a search string. The search string can be requested and filtered by logical structure, physical structure, or textual description. After the data is located, a request function, or subset data selection process, facilitates the building of a SQL-based request to move the selected subset of both physical warehouse data and business definitional metadata from the main warehouse to a data mart for local access and decision support. The requests and associated scheduling information are stored as a subscription and can be run as part of an ongoing subset request or data mart population process.

3. Metadata and Physical Data Movement

The metadata and physical data mover manages the launching of subscriptions from the warehouse to the data marts by monitoring scheduling data managed in the active directory/catalog. This mover provides seamless connectivity and data pumping between the warehouse database and the data mart for physical subset data movement. It also passes the corresponding semantic layer metadata between the active directory/catalog and the data mart query and reporting tool's abstract layer (or internal catalog).

4. Event Management

Event management contains features and functions that act as the "traffic cop" that monitors events throughout the warehouse environment. Notification is sent to the active directory/catalog upon completion of warehouse extract jobs via event monitors. Subscription completions are monitored as well. Subscriptions are not executed unless dependent warehouse extract jobs have completed successfully. Event management facilitates managing the delicate check and balance dependencies within the enterprisewide data warehouse environment.

5. Application Programming Interfaces

Application program interfaces (APIs) are the intelligent links to the metadata and warehouse environmental data sources. The APIs populate the active directory/catalog database with the appropriate and corresponding metadata from the individual sources like extract, repository, and case tools. The API can be a direct link to the individual product, or it can be a standardized import function. APIs also load semantic layer active directory/catalog definitions to the various query and reporting tools that contain an abstract layer.

SUMMARY

We have noted the function and importance of an active directory/catalog as the fundamental vehicle to connect end users to the enterprise warehouse. Without the tools and processes to link the physical and semantic layers of the warehouse architecture, the decision makers are at a disadvantage in understanding the context of the gigabytes or terabytes of warehouse data available to them for decision support, and administrators have only their instinct for managing the warehouse environment.

By allocating the time and resource necessary to implement an active directory/catalog in your warehouse environment, you will be able to understand the data in the warehouse, know where the data was sourced from and who owns it, track changes to the warehouse environment, track usage trends, facilitate and authorize end-user access, integrate business and technical data, and provide for efficient warehouse administration.

Data becomes information when someone is able to use it. The continuing challenge in the evolution of data warehousing is not getting data into the warehouse, but using the appropriate data to make better business decisions. With the data warehouse as an environment, not just an application, the active directory/catalog is prerequisite to converting legacy and warehouse data into meaningful and profitable information.

CHAPTER 13

Data Transformation

Dave Gleason
Platinum Technology, Inc.
Vienna, Virginia

"The more things change, the more they remain the same."

Alphonse Karr

One of the fundamental concepts of data warehousing is that as data is extracted from operational systems and other sources, it is transformed or "scrubbed" before being loaded into the data warehouse. This much is generally agreed on by those who have built data warehouses. Beyond that, however, there lies much confusion about the purpose of data transformation and the best ways to accomplish it. The goals of data transformation in the warehouse environment should be twofold: first, to improve the quality of data in the data warehouse, and second, to improve the usability of data in the warehouse.

Even the name given to this process of changing the structure and content of data as it moves from the operational environment into the data warehouse is subject to confusion and debate. In some circles, this process is called transformation; in others, it is called data scrubbing. Some companies refer to the whole process as S/T/I (scrubbing, transformation, and integration). Regardless of what name you give it, this process is crucial to the success and quality of the data warehouse. For the purposes of this discussion, I will refer to the overall process of changing the structure and content of operational data before loading into the data warehouse as data transformation. I will introduce other terms to define specific types of data transformation throughout the discussion.

Regardless of the name you assign to this process, data transformation is an absolutely crucial step in the process of building a data warehouse. There are many ways to implement good data transformation, ranging from custom-coded programs to specialized tools devoted to transforming data in a warehouse environment. No matter what method you use, though, there are certain fundamental aspects of transformation that must be implemented.

160

Transformation is significantly more than just changing the data structures of your data as you move it into the warehouse. Good transformation actually verifies and improves the quality and usability of the data as it goes into the warehouse. Many organizations underestimate the effort involved in establishing good data transformation in their initial warehouse projects and soon realize that what seems at first like a simple piece of the warehouse puzzle is sometimes quite challenging. This is an easy mistake to make, since many people focus their first data warehouse efforts on operational data that is readily available and easily understood. While that data may not require a large amount of complex transformation to place it in the warehouse, the same cannot be said for the remainder of the operational and external data, which will go into the warehouse in later stages of the effort. Often, the relative simplicity of these early transformations causes us to underestimate dramatically the difficulties we will face later when we must transform and reconcile data from poorly documented legacy systems. So it is crucial that warehouse teams understand that their early experiences in implementing data transformations are not necessarily representative of all of the transformations they will have to perform in building a data warehouse.

FUNDAMENTAL TYPES OF DATA TRANSFORMATION

To have a meaningful discussion of the intricacies of data transformation, we must define some basic types of transformation. Each of these types will have its own characteristics and scenarios. For the purposes of this discussion, consider the following four types of transformations:

- *Simple transformation.* Simple transformations are the fundamental building blocks of all data transformations. This category includes manipulations of data that is focused solely on one field at a time, without taking into account the values in related fields. Examples include changing the data type of a field or replacing an encoded field value with a decoded value.
- *Cleansing and scrubbing.* Cleansing, or scrubbing, is concerned with ensuring consistent formatting and usage of a field or of related groups of fields. This can include proper formatting of address information, for example. Cleansing also checks for valid values in a particular field, usually by doing range checking or choosing from an enumerated list.
- *Integration.* Integration is the process of taking operational data from one or more sources and mapping it, field by field, onto a new data structure in the data warehouse. There are numerous complex shades of integration, which will be discussed in detail in this chapter.
- *Aggregation and summarization.* Aggregation and summarization are methods of condensing instances of data found in the operational environment into fewer instances in the warehouse environment. In some cases, aggregation is done so that the warehouse does not store data at a level of detail as low as the

operational environment; in other cases, aggregation is performed to create data marts that contain aggregated or summarized versions of detail data found in the warehouse.

Completeness of Data Transformation

In most data warehouse implementations, all of the aforementioned forms of data transformation are required to ensure that the information in the warehouse is of the highest quality and is extremely usable. Unfortunately, many organizations that are new to data warehousing focus only on simple transformations and moving data elements to the new warehouse structures. In doing so, they neglect to pay attention to enhancing the quality of data. Another pitfall many companies face is that they are led to believe that data transformation is almost trivial, because they pilot their warehouse using data that has only a single operational source. By doing this, they eliminate the need to integrate and reconcile multiple sources of overlapping or conflicting information. While this may make it easier to create the first section of the data warehouse, it poses the danger of causing the company to underestimate severely the effort that will be required for data transformation in subsequent warehouse efforts. For these reasons, a solid understanding of the logical components of data warehouse transformation is essential to creating a sound, reasonable implementation plan.

Simple Transformation

As its name implies, simple transformation embodies the easiest forms of data transformation. These transformations are primarily concerned with changing the content of one data attribute at a time, without regard for the context of that attribute or the other information related to it.

Data Type Conversions. The most common form of simple transformation is the conversion of a data element from one data type to another. A simple data type conversion such as this is usually done without changing the semantic value of the data element, except in the case of changing a null value to blanks or zero, or vice versa. Most often this type of transformation is required when a legacy application stores data in a data type that makes sense within the context of the application, but not at the enterprise level. For example, a billing system might have been designed to accommodate dollar amounts up to $99,999.99, on the basis that no single statement amount would ever approach or exceed that limit. In the data warehouse, however, you might choose to use a consistent data type for all dollar amounts; this would probably be a significantly larger field than what is appropriate for a single billing system. Some older legacy applications reuse existing data elements for new meanings rather than expanding the current data structures; this is especially true of legacy applications built on older hierarchical databases. In this case, the fields should be moved to data elements of the correct data type in the warehouse. Of course, simple transformations, like all data transformations, may also rename elements to the standardized names chosen for the data warehouse data structures. The following table illustrates some examples of simple data type conversions.

Data Source		Data Warehouse
AMT-BILL DECIMAL(7,2)	→	AMT-BILL DECIMAL(13,2)
D-SALES-AMOUNT DECIMAL (13,2)	→	AMT-SALES DECIMAL(13,2)
ACCOUNT-STAT-CODE CHAR(1) NULLS ALLOWED	→	CD-ACCT-STATUS CHAR(1) NO NULLS

Transformations of this type can be accomplished through simple program logic in coded programs, or using data warehouse data transformation tools. Every transformation tool has the capacity to perform this simple transformation easily and quickly. In addition, many simple transformations can be accomplished through a database unloading or loading facility, which allows simple data type conversions as data is taken from a flat file and loaded into a database, or vice versa.

Date/Time Format Conversions.   Typically, when operational applications are designed and constructed, there is very little uniform handling of date and time formats across applications. Frequently, application designers choose to represent date and time information in a format that works the best with the DBMS that will contain the operational data. In some cases, though, date and time fields are not even handled consistently within an application. Designers of program modules are free to design date and time fields in the way they see fit, with little attention paid to consistency. Perhaps one of the most visible examples of date problems is the "Year 2000" problem that we face as the end of the century approaches.

Whatever the reasons behind the differences in handling date and time in operational systems, one thing remains clear: The data warehouse must have a single scheme for identifying date and time information. As the Year 2000 situation has shown us, we must store dates in a robust fashion, including the full year. The choice for the actual physical representation of dates and times is dependent on many factors, but whatever representation is chosen, it should store four digits for years, and it must be applied consistently throughout the data warehouse.

Because most operational environments have many different types of dates and times, almost every data warehouse implementation will have to transform dates and times into the standard warehouse formats. This can be done through manual program coding, which breaks a date or time field into its subcomponents and then reassembles them into the desired field. However, most data transformation tools on the market offer facilities to convert between date and time formats quickly and easily, with significantly less effort than is involved in manual coding.

Field Decoding. The final type of simple transformation that will be discussed here is the decoding of encoded fields. Simply put, there are very few cases in which data should be stored in the data warehouse in an encoded format. We create codes in our operational databases to conserve database storage space. Though these codes are not understandable by humans, that is not a major problem since all of our interaction with those codes is regulated through application programs, which decode those values for us when necessary. In some cases, our on-line screens or batch reports show users the encoded values, but their familiarity with the system allows them to deal directly with those codes.

In the data warehouse environment, the situation is very different. While some query tools can decode database values, there is no guarantee that there will always be application logic that can insulate users from the encoded values in the data warehouse database. This is especially true when you consider the proliferation of query tools and user-written queries that most data warehouses experience. When they run or write ad hoc queries, users will see information presented as it is stored in the database. Since the users can be from any part of the company, it is not likely that all users of the warehouse will have the background and training to understand the encoded values that are used in the operational database.

Therefore, encoded values in operational systems and external data should be converted to their decoded, easily understandable values before they are stored in the data warehouse. Of course, there is a fine line that must be followed in doing this. On one hand, we want to expand the encoded values sufficiently to make them easily understood by the largest number of users. On the other hand, expanding a value too much requires additional storage space and makes it very awkward to use that value as a search criteria in a query. Also, the users' familiarity with the business meaning of the data element must be considered. For instance, it would probably be overkill to represent a gender code in the warehouse database as "MALE" or "FEMALE." This is a universally understood business element, and the vast majority of users would find "M" or "F" to be readily understandable. On the other hand, a customer status code is not universally understood and would need to be expanded to a meaningful and understandable value so that warehouse users could identify it. So for instance, account status codes of "A," "I," and "S" might be decoded to "ACTV," "INACT," and "SUSP," respectively. Note that you are able to understand the meaning of these decoded values, even though they are not fully spelled out. The guideline used here is that they should be just long enough to be understood readily by the majority of the warehouse users, bearing in mind that this audience includes people who are not intimately familiar with this aspect of the company's systems. To assist people who need further explanation, metadata should be made available that identifies the business meaning of these terms in full, with context and examples.

Field decoding is a very simple process to implement from a technical perspective. It can be easily incorporated into transformation programs, and it is readily performed in data transformation tools. However, deciding exactly how much decoding should be introduced can be tricky. But a good solution is often to provide enough decoding so that a normal user can reasonably be expected to understand the meaning of the value and to augment that with metadata that more fully explains the data element values and their proper usage.

Cleansing and Scrubbing

Cleansing and *scrubbing* are used here as interchangeable terms. They refer to a level of data transformation that is more complex than simple transformations, in which the actual content of field or groups of fields is examined rather than just the storage format. One type of cleansing is checking for valid values in a data field. This can be done through ranges, enumerated lists, or dependency checking. Examples of each are given here.

Valid Values. Range checking is the easiest form of data scrubbing. It involves examining data in a field to ensure that it falls within the expected range, usually a numeric or date range. For example, an invoice number can be checked to see that it is between 1000 and 99999, the valid range for invoice numbers. Or an invoice date can be checked to see that it falls between April 1, 1965 (the date the company began operations) and the current date; any invoice with a date outside that range should be kicked out.

Enumerated lists are also relatively easy to implement. In this method, the value in a data field is checked against the list of acceptable values for that field. For example, an order delivery type code could be checked to see that it contained one of the valid values "express," "FOB," or "customer pickup." Any value that does not match this list would be kicked out for further investigation.

Dependency checking is slightly more involved since it requires comparing the value in a field to the values in another field. For example, we might check the purchase order number field on invoice records to make sure that it refers to a purchase order that exists in our system. Any invoice record that contains a purchase order number with no corresponding purchase order should be investigated further.

Of course, often our data scrubbing rules are a combination of these different methods. For example, another rule might state that the order delivery type code should be "express" only when the order date is on or after January 31, 1985. This would be used to ensure data quality when our company began using "express" shipping on January 31, 1985. Any order created prior to that date that specifies express shipping is probably an error in the operational application, since it violates the business rules as we know them. Valid value checking does not usually require complex logic, and it can be implemented easily in manually coded programs, as well as in the data transformation tools available today.

Complex Reformatting. The other major type of data scrubbing is the formatting of specific types of data. This is used for information that can be stored in many different ways in different data sources and must be converted to a uniform representation in the data warehouse. One of the most common formatting needs is for address information. There is no one standardized way to capture addresses, and the same address can be represented in many different ways. Of course, when humans read those addresses, they are able to recognize that they refer to the same location. But in a database, the addresses would be stored differently, and that correspondence would be lost. Therefore, we need to translate addresses into a common format so that we can establish in the database which addresses are really the same.

For instance, observe the following two addresses. By looking at them, you can tell that they refer to the same location. But if you asked an SQL query to test them for equality, the result would certainly be negative. Therefore, from a technical point of view, these addresses are different.

Mr. John M. Smith
Suite 1335
N. Main St.
Washington, DC
20006

John Smith
North Main Street, #1335
Washington, D.C. 20006

A data scrubbing tool, however, could reformat these addresses and make them the same so that an SQL query could detect them as identical. This would be achieved by parsing each address to determine its essential components and then changing some of the components to standardize wording and abbreviations. For example, the data scrubbing tool would recognize that "St." and "Street" meant the same thing and would make appropriate substitutions.

Since this requires parsing an address into its component parts and then translating and rearranging those component parts into a consistent format, it can be very difficult to do. It is usually not practical to write custom programs to accomplish this task. Fortunately, there are software packages available that are designed to perform specialized data scrubbing such as this. Most of these packages are designed to do very specific forms of scrubbing, such as address reformatting, proper name formatting, or telephone number formatting. These packages have been available for some time, and they are often not marketed as data warehousing tools but as general system utilities.

Integration

The real challenge in combining operational data from disparate sources is in integrating it into one cohesive data model. This is because data must be taken from multiple sources and combined into a new entity. Often, those data sources do not adhere to the same set of business rules, and these differences must be accommodated as the new data is created. While it is not possible to identify every possible type of integration that might have to take place, some of the more common ones are discussed here.

Simple Field-Level Mappings.   Simple field-level mappings account for the majority of data integration that must be performed. In a typical data warehouse, as many as 80% to 90% of the transformations specified are simple field-level mappings. These are defined as cases in which a field in a data source (such as a record from an operational database) is moved to a field in a database target (usually a data warehouse data structure). Along the way, it can be transformed using any of the types of simple transformations discussed previously. The field can also be scrubbed and reformatted. These field-level mappings are easy to implement and account for the majority of the data integration that takes place.

Complex Integration.   In a typical data warehouse, 10% to 20% of the data movement and integration is more complex than simple source-field to target-field moves. In these scenarios, more analysis must be done to transform source data into target data. The scenarios can vary greatly, but some of the more common ones are discussed here.

Common Identifier Problem.   The common identifier problem is one of the most difficult integration issues that many companies face in building a data warehouse. Essentially, this situation occurs when there are multiple system sources for the same business entities and there is no clear way to identify those entities that are the same. Most frequently, this takes the form of customer entities or vendor entities. Consider, for example, a company that has customer master files in several different application systems. In some cases, the same customer may exist in different systems, but with a unique identifier within each of those systems. Therefore, there is no way to determine in the system that it is really the same customer. In the warehouse, we want to have this customer uniquely identified, with only one customer master record.

This is a challenging problem, and in many cases it cannot be solved in an automated fashion. It frequently requires sophisticated algorithms to pair up probable matches. In some cases, the risk of storing probable matches in the warehouse may be acceptable, but in other cases these probable matches must be verified by humans before they can be stored in the data warehouse. Because of this complexity, many companies choose to implement a two-stage strategy for dealing with their unique identifier issues. The first stage is isolation, in which we attempt to ensure that every occurrence of the entity in question is assigned a unique identifier. Then, in the second stage, reconciliation, we begin the process of identifying which entities are really the same and merge the occurrences together. This two-stage process allows us to continue to populate the warehouse without having to reconcile all occurrences of the entity before loading can be completed.

Multiple Sources for the Target Element.   Another complex data integration scenario occurs when there are multiple sources for the same target data element. Rarely can you ensure that the sources for that element will always agree. In fact, it is much more common for there to be contradictory values for such a data element than for the values from different sources to agree. In this case, you must determine how to resolve this conflict. Frequently, this is done by simply designating which system will prevail in the event of a conflict. However, there are cases in which resolving the conflict is less straightforward. For instance, you have to check the effective dates on the records containing the conflicting values and choose the value with the more recent effective date. Or you may have to compare other related fields to determine the prevailing element. In some cases, you might even have to summarize or average the conflicting values to arrive at the value that should be stored in the data warehouse.

       Missing Data Problem.   Just as difficult as having conflicting values for a data element is having no value for a data element. In some cases, it is acceptable to put blanks or null values into the warehouse for a missing element. In other cases, however, there must be some value in the element so that queries against the table will be valid. For example, if there are flaws in a data collection system and you do not have sales figures for some regions for some months, you may need to put some estimated figures into the data. If this were an operational system, it would not do to have data that was known to be inaccurate in the database. But for a data warehouse, there may be cases in which it is far better to have estimated data than to have no data at all. For example, if a user writes a query that produces a graph of sales data, having a zero or null value in an occurrence of the data element would cause an unnatural valley in the graph, indicating a sudden drop in sales when that is not necessarily the case. So for each type of data in the warehouse, the designers must weigh the inherent risk of storing estimated data against the risk of misinterpretation that can be caused by missing data.

       Therefore, it is often necessary to create data to fill in missing data. Probably the most common technique used for this is to create data that will smooth the curve. In other words, a data element is created that falls halfway between the previous and subsequent data elements, so that a graph of the data would show a smooth curve. Some businesses, however, have very complex data estimation methods, which can accommodate many variables to produce a very realistic value for the missing data. Most data transformation tools include only rudimentary abilities to perform complex estimation, since obtaining the variables that are needed for the estimating algorithm can be very complicated.

       Derived/Calculated Data.   One of the most common forms of data integration is the calculation and creation of derived or calculated data elements. These can include averages, sums, or statistical calculations. They can also include complex business calculations, such as stock turn or gross margin. Usually, the derived data field is redundant, in that the components that go into the calculation are also stored in the warehouse. However, it can greatly simplify queries and ensure accuracy and consistency to store these derived values in the warehouse so that they can be selected in queries rather than having to be calculated each time a user needs them. This is an area in which data transformation tools can be useful since they can perform a broad range of calculations quickly and easily, without having to be concerned about whether a programmer has coded the calculation logic correctly.

Aggregation and Summarization

Most data warehouses employ at least some aggregation and summarization of data. Often, this is useful to reduce the number of instances of a certain entity to a manageable number, or to precalculate widely used summary figures so that each query does not have to calculate them. Although the terms *aggregation* and *summarization* are often used interchangeably, they do have slightly different meanings in the data warehouse context. Summarization is the addition of like values along one of more business dimensions, such as adding up daily sales by store to produce monthly sales by region. *Aggregation* refers to the addition of different business elements into a common total. An example of aggregation is the calculation of total sales by adding daily product sales and monthly consulting sales to get a monthly combined sales figure. For the purposes of this discussion, however, we do not need to distinguish between aggregation and summarization; they are both accomplished the same way in the data warehouse.

In some cases, the lowest level of detail stored in the data warehouse is still not as low as the detailed data stored in operational systems. In these cases, it is necessary to build some data aggregation functionality into the process that transforms the operational data. This will result in a reduced number of rows being stored in the data warehouse. For example, a credit card processing company using a data warehouse to analyze purchasing patterns to make strategic sales and marketing decisions would not necessarily want to store every single credit card transaction in the warehouse. Instead, it might summarize transactions, perhaps by account number by day, and store summary information in the data warehouse.

In other cases, aggregation is used to create data marts, which are derived from more detailed data stored in the data warehouse. Suppose, for instance, that a group of users frequently performs analysis comparing sales across geographic regions, broken down by product line. To execute a query for this information against a data warehouse containing very detailed transaction data, they would have to summarize individual transactions to the region and product line level each time they execute a query. This would make their queries unnecessarily complex, and it would result in poor query performance. If a data mart were created that stores the sales data already aggregated to the desired level, the users' queries could be simpler and would perform better against fewer rows of data.

A third use for aggregation is to remove aged detail from a data warehouse. In many cases, data is stored at a very detailed level for a certain period of time. Once the data reaches a certain age, though, the need for all of the details may diminish greatly. At this point, the very detailed data can be transferred to off-line or near-line storage, and a summarized version of the data can be stored in the data warehouse.

Of course, for any detailed data, there are numerous ways to summarize it. Each summarization or aggregation can be along one or more dimensions. For example, a retail organization might maintain transaction data for each individual sales transaction. From this detailed data, summaries can be created along many dimensions, including product category, sales transaction type, geographic area, customer, and time period. Each summary created can be the result of aggregating on one or more of these dimensions. Therefore, it is extremely important that users be able to access metadata that tells them exactly how each type of summarized data was derived, so that they understand which dimensions have been summarized and to what level.

Many of the data scrubbing tools available today have summarization capabilities built into them, especially in the area of aggregation along the time dimension. Of course, often this can be achieved just as readily through the use of sorting utilities, which often include sophisticated summary logic capabilities. Regardless of how it is accomplished, it is essential that the criteria used for creating the summary be readily available to end users in the form of easily accessible metadata.

IMPLEMENTING TRANSFORMATION

There are, of course, many ways to implement data transformation in a warehouse environment. The most significant choice, though, is between using a dedicated data transformation tool to supply data to the warehouse and creating manually coded programs to implement transformation logic. The best choice depends on many factors, including the following:

- *Time frames.* Although using a data transformation tool can dramatically streamline the process of building and maintaining a data warehouse, it does take time to acquire, configure, and learn. Projects under very tight time constraints to produce their first warehouse deliverables often choose to use manual coding and then to migrate to data transformation tools once the warehouse is more established and the warehouse team has built credibility.
- *Budgets.* Data warehouse tools can be expensive, but so can programmer time to create transformation programs. So the best choice depends on which type of budget is more readily available in the immediate future in your organization. In the long run, though, investing in a transformation tool can save significant money over the cost of painstaking manual coding and maintenance of transformation programs.
- *Size of the warehouse.* A data warehouse with a very small scope (i.e., few sources of data, few transformations to implement) may not justify the cost and effort of using a data transformation tool. However, as the warehouse expands in scope it will become more and more difficult to maintain the manually written transformation programs, and a tool will begin to make more sense. But for a small initial data warehouse effort, a transformation tool is certainly not required.
- *Size and skills of the warehouse team.* If the warehouse team is large enough and has the appropriate programming skills, it is easier to manage the task of creating and maintaining transformation logic. Most warehouse teams, though, are constrained for resources and cannot get adequate developer time to maintain all of the transformation code. Therefore, they find transformation tools

to be especially helpful since the warehouse analysts can create and maintain most of the transformations with no assistance from programmers.

Of course, one of the most compelling reasons to use a data transformation tool has nothing to do with time savings or cost efficiencies. It is the simple fact that a good transformation tool will automatically generate and maintain valuable metadata. This aspect of data transformation is discussed in the following subsections.

Manual Methods

Until a few years ago, all data transformation that was done in a data warehouse environment had to be implemented manually. Usually, this meant writing programs in a programming language such as COBOL, combined with the use of Syncsort™ or other sorting and summarizing utilities. Today, some warehouses are still built in this fashion. This approach has the distinct advantage of drawing on skills that already exist in most shops, and it requires no additional expenditures for specialized software.

Unfortunately, there are some drawbacks to manual coding of data transformations. First, it does require significant personnel effort. The data analysts who determine what transformations are necessary must clearly document these requirements, in a form that is clear enough and detailed enough for developers to create data transformation programs. Then there is the actual effort involved in coding and testing the potentially large number of transformation programs required. Finally, the programs must be maintained. As questions arise about data in the warehouse or as operational data sources change, the programs will have to be examined and modified. Doing this manually can be a very time consuming and expensive task.

Perhaps the bigger drawback with manual transformations is the lack of metadata. The metadata involved in transformations is the information that documents clearly and precisely exactly what transformation rules have been implemented. If the transformations are created manually, then this valuable metadata must be maintained manually as well. Anyone familiar with systems development knows how much rigor and reliability usually go into documentation. Suffice it to say that relying on manual creation and maintenance of metadata is risky at best.

Automated Tools

As data warehousing began to grow rapidly several years ago, vendors recognized a need for tools to assist in the process of defining and implementing data transformations. One of the goals of these tools was to eliminate the need to code manual programs for data transformations, especially since the majority of transformations implemented are relatively simple. By eliminating the need for custom programs, these tools can save on the overhead that is required to code and test any program, even if it contains only simple logic.

Data transformation tools also have the advantage of removing a difficult communications link from the transformation process. That is, they enable the data analyst, who does the research and analysis, to determine what transformations should be performed (to define the transformations). In doing this, they consolidate the process of documenting the transformation rules with the process of implementing the transformations. This removes the step of having the analyst try to communicate the transformation requirements to a developer who would write the actual transformation code. This communication requires detailed and tedious documentation, which takes time and introduces a possibility for errors or miscommunications.

Above and beyond the efficiency and accuracy benefits that can be gained from data transformation tools, these tools also provide the potential for superior metadata handling. By allowing data analysts to specify directly the rules for data transformations to the tool, these tools are capturing metadata. They store this metadata internally and use it to generate the code or modules that perform the data transformations. If this metadata can be extracted from the data transformation tool and stored in a central location with other warehouse-related metadata, it becomes a powerful tool. In this scenario, metadata is generated when the data analyst uses the transformation tool to specify the data transformation that should be produced. Because this process is automated, there is a high assurance that the metadata corresponds to the transformation rules actually implemented. Only when a complicated transformation requires a manually coded exit routine is the metadata not automatically generated to describe the transformation.

During the warehouse operation, as adjustments and changes to the data transformation are required, these are accomplished by having the data analyst use the transformation tool to specify the changes. This again captures revised metadata describing the new transformation rules. Of course, to be the most useful, this data transformation metadata needs to be combined with other warehouse-related metadata. This requires that the data transformation tool support some sort of open interface or export of metadata so that it can be combined with other metadata and delivered to end users in an appropriate, easy-to-use fashion. This robust handling of metadata can move the data transformation tool from an efficiency gain to being an integral, vital part of the warehouse architecture.

SUMMARY

This chapter has examined some of the business requirements that make up the process of transforming raw operational data into data warehouse data. We have examined some of the issues and types of transformations that must be performed and looked at the roles that data transformation tools can play in the process of transforming data. Although these tools can yield impressive efficiency benefits, their real value is that they can automatically capture the metadata that describes the data transformation rules so that this metadata can be leveraged in the warehouse environment. Although data transformation can be a difficult and complex undertaking, it is absolutely necessary to ensure that the data delivered to the data warehouse has high quality and high utility.

PART FOUR

DESIGN
AND IMPLEMENTATION

"The best laid schemes o' mice and men gang aft a-gley."

Robert Burns

Colin White laid the foundation for this section in his chapter entitled "A Technical Architecture for Data Warehousing" in Section II (Chapter 7). In any particular organization, the technical architecture may be tailored to meet specific needs. This section delves into the data architecture and various design options that may be considered in implementing a data warehouse.

This section begins with a chapter by Joyce Bischoff entitled "Physical Design" (Chapter 14). She describes the physical design process and design objectives, which must be clearly defined in terms of business requirements. She discusses the components of the data architecture and the types of structures that may be used to implement an effective data architecture. She then discusses the design of each physical structure that may be found within an architecture.

Multidimensional databases are an option that may be used in the physical implementation of a warehouse. Colin White discusses the controversy surrounding such databases in Chapter 15, "Multidimensional OLAP versus Relational OLAP." The author looks at OLAP and multidimensional data analysis from various perspectives and provides guidelines for choosing a multidimensional solution when desired.

Marie Buretta's chapter, "Data Replication in a Global Warehousing Environment" (Chapter 16), identifies the critical factors in maintaining data consistency across data marts and operational systems. It discusses the importance of integrating any and all replication alternatives and presents evaluation criteria for the selection of replication tools. Buretta also presents a real-world case study of a successful global warehousing implementation.

Very large databases (VLDB) are a fact of life in large organizations. In Chapter 17, "VLDBs and Parallelism," Richard Yevich discusses parallel solutions that may be used to implement large warehouses. He gives guidelines for using various parallel options and discusses future directions in using hierarchies of Symmetric Multi Processing (SMP) and Massively Parallel Processing (MPP) platforms.

Trina LaRue presents a real-world experience in "Implementing a Warehouse in a Multiserver Environment Using Parallel Technology" (Chapter 18). She discusses the issues surrounding the implementation of a very large warehouse in a heterogeneous environment for a major telecommunications company.

In "Middleware: Gluing the Warehouse Together" (Chapter 19), Susan Gausden and Terry Mason discuss the business issues that prompt the need for middleware and its use in populating the data warehouse. They also consider the connectivity issues that arise when setting up middleware, including the choice of communications protocols and choice of hardware and software, front-end tools, and applications and the need to position middleware for the future.

In "Design Reviews for the Data Warehouse" (Chapter 20), Joyce Bischoff discusses the differences between traditional production design reviews and those that are appropriate in a data warehouse in a client/server environment. This chapter considers design reviews to be a dynamic tool that can be used to uncover design flaws at the earliest opportunity and presents guidelines and leading questions for planning appropriate reviews.

In "The Virtual Data Warehouse" (Chapter 21), Ed Peters explores the role of information logistics in the information environment and introduces the concept of a virtual data warehouse that takes on the demand side of providing information. The traditional view of data warehousing emphasizes the supply side of data warehousing, which considers the warehouse to be a secondary database fed with operational data, often summarized and stated in the subject fashion. The author feels, however, that this overlooks the true role of the warehouse as one part of an overall logistics strategy that supplies information to the knowledge worker in an effective manner.

The ODS is an offshoot to the data warehouse phenomena. Although an ODS is built like a data warehouse, it is subject to the same sorts of demands placed on traditional transaction-based data stores. In "Operational Data Stores: Developing an Effective Strategy" (Chapter 22), John Ladley discusses the issues involved in implementing a successful ODS.

Data mining is defined as a process of analyzing large amounts of data to identify patterns, trends, activities, and data content relationships. It is one of the most exciting technologies in the world of information technology. There are many examples of the benefits of data mining. The process of market basket analysis can be used to determine which products are usually purchased at the same time, enabling retailers to position these products next to each other. Data mining can identify patterns likely to precede fraud and analyze medical practices and their related costs and benefits over large populations. Richard Yevich writes about all of this and more in Chapter 23, entitled "Data Mining."

14

Physical Design

Joyce Bischoff

Bischoff Consulting, Inc.
Hockessin, Delaware

"Form ever follows function."

Louis Henri Sullivan

I f computers were infinitely fast and database management software were perfectly efficient, all databases could be physically implemented in third normal form and achieve perfect performance. Unfortunately, this is the real world. Designers are forced to implement databases that may be denormalized, summarized, replicated, and placed in specialized data caches to achieve design objectives. This chapter contains a

- Description of the overall design process
- Discussion of how physical design fits into the overall design process
- Description of the components of a physical data architecture
- Discussion of physical design issues for each of the components of the data architecture.

DESIGN PROCESS

The process of designing a data warehouse is iterative and consists of the following steps:

1. Identify user requirements and project scope.
2. If not already available, develop subject area data model, including an entity-relationship diagram and associated metadata. A subject area usually covers a particular aspect of the business: for example, sales information, financial information, or customer information.

177

3. Develop a data warehouse logical data model from the subject area data model. Although the logical data model should be as complete as possible, a decision may be made to implement only part of the model. This will be represented in the data warehouse data model.

4. Develop a data warehouse architecture if a general warehouse architecture has not already been developed. See Colin White's chapter, "A Technical Architecture for Data Warehousing" (Chapter 7), for more information.

5. Design the physical database.

6. Populate an end-user-oriented repository/directory with metadata for the physical database. See Dave Gleason's chapter, "Metadata" (Chapter 11), and Jack Sweeney's chapter, "The Role of a Directory/Catalog" (Chapter 12), for more information.

7. Identify the source of data from operational systems or external sources for each target field in the data warehouse.

8. Develop or purchase programs to extract, cleanse, transform, integrate, and transport data from the legacy systems to the warehouse. See Dave Gleason's chapter, "Data Transformation" (Chapter 13), for details.

9. Populate the warehouse using these programs.

10. Test for user satisfaction with the data warehouse, including data quality, availability, and performance. See Sid Adelman's chapter, "Data Quality" (Chapter 10), for more information on the subject.

11. Rework the design as needed to achieve ongoing user satisfaction.

Design reviews should be conducted throughout the warehouse design and development process. See the chapter by this author entitled "Design Reviews for the Data Warehouse" (Chapter 20) for details on the planning and scheduling of reviews within the aforementioned framework.

THE FOUNDATION FOR DESIGN

This chapter assumes that user requirements have been identified and documented and a logical data model has been developed with appropriate metadata to serve as the foundation for the design of a data warehouse. It will not cover issues of metadata and end-user directories since they were covered in other chapters in this book. There are some people who skip the data modeling process with the claim that "Data will be denormalized. Why should I bother with a data model?" This seems to be especially common when a star schema is used and the designer is looking for an excuse to skip the traditional data modeling process. According to Ralph Kimball,[1] inventor of the concept, a star schema is "a specific organization of a database in which a fact table with a composite key is joined to a number of single-level dimension tables, each with a single, primary key." This author believes that data is not truly understood until it is properly analyzed. The result of this analysis should be a data model in third normal form (or higher) and associated metadata.

Although it is ideal to have an enterprisewide data model, it is not always possible to obtain management commitment to develop an enterprisewide data model, with a top-down approach, before beginning the development of a warehouse. If one waits for the corporate funding and time needed to develop a corporate-wide data model, the development of a warehouse of any size may take years, which is unacceptable in today's world. A bottom-up approach is more practical and may be used to build the model, one subject (business) area at a time. Over a period of time, the models can be integrated into a complete corporate model. Subject area or business area models tend to be more detailed than high-level corporate models, and the transformation of these models into physical structures is straightforward.

Although CASE tools may be used to develop the basic data model, they may not provide much help in creating the physical objects required for the data warehouse. Denormalization is common in the warehouse, and the denormalized structures should be well documented for the end users. A data directory/dictionary should be used to accomplish this task.

DESIGN OBJECTIVES

Design objectives for the data warehouse must be clearly defined in terms of business requirements. Design objectives usually include performance, future flexibility, scalability of servers, ease of administration, data integrity, data consistency, data availability, user satisfaction, and other issues. There are many trade-offs between these objectives. Everything that is done to enhance one of these objectives may have an offsetting trade-off in another area. There is no such thing as a free lunch in the database arena.

There are many examples of the trade-offs to be considered. If a database is denormalized for short-term performance benefits, there will be an offsetting loss of future flexibility. If there is a requirement for high availability, possibly approaching 24 hours a day, 7 days a week, the cost of designing and implementing the warehouse will be significantly increased. A decrease in administrative effort through minimizing the need for reorganization may be offset by a loss in performance.

Performance

Performance in the warehouse context is different from performance in the OLTP environment. Although response time in the OLTP environment usually ranges from a subsecond to a few seconds, response time in the data warehouse may range from a few seconds to a few minutes or possibly longer, depending on the amount of work to be done. User expectations must be managed in the area of performance. Do not lead users to believe that response time will be similar to that in the OLTP environment. Poor performance in the data warehouse may be the result of unrealistic user expectations, inadequate hardware, inflexible data architecture, poor physical design, or problems with query tools.

The processes must be in place to build, monitor, and tune for performance. As the warehouse is designed and built, design reviews can identify and address potential performance issues at the earliest opportunity. After the warehouse is in production, processes must be in place to solve query and performance problems and address underlying database design and maintenance issues.

A data architecture must be in place. Network and CPU utilization must be optimized. Dataset placement is critical if the best use is to be made of both network and CPU resources. In placing datasets for performance, a benefit of decreased network traffic may be offset by an increase in disk space and CPU utilization on another server. Dataset placement on available servers will be affected by many factors, including size, data volatility, replication, frequency of data access, and other factors.

Performance is built in several phases. The operating system and network issues are outside the scope of this chapter. It is assumed that there will be ongoing tuning in these areas. From a database perspective, performance starts with the DBMS installation and the selection of appropriate parameters for the warehouse environment. In many performance reviews, the author has found that poor selection of installation parameters is the reason for many performance problems. If the maximum number of concurrent users is set too low, bottlenecks may occur. If it is set too high, resources may be consumed unnecessarily. In DB2, if the checkpoint frequency is set too low, too many CPU cycles will be consumed. If it is set too high, it may adversely affect recovery. If too many traces are automatically turned on, it may be costly in terms of CPU. The same issues are present with other parameters. If the DBMS installation parameters are not optimized, it does not matter how well the database or application is designed. Performance will suffer.

Database design is the next step. If the database is not properly designed and optimized, application performance will suffer. Again, efficient queries depend on the quality of SQL coding and a well-designed database. The efficiency of queries will also depend on the SQL that has been generated by a query tool, which is outside the scope of the database designer's responsibility. Databases that are not properly maintained will perform poorly. In one warehouse, the author found a set of very large tables that were performing so badly that the users refused to use them. When the DBA was asked how often he reorganized the tables, he replied, "We don't reorganize until users complain. The tables are too large for regular reorganizations." If the DBA waits until users complain, it is too late. There will be considerable dissatisfaction because users may not lodge an official complaint until things are really out of hand.

As shown in Figure 14.1, performance builds from the bottom to the top. It starts with the installation and tuning of the operating system and proceeds through installation and maintenance of the DBMS, design, implementation, and maintenance of the database, application design, and query generation. Performance

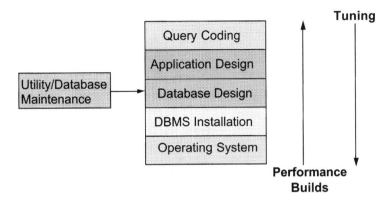

Figure 14.1   Building Good Performance.

problems may be first noticed during ad hoc queries or application use. Tuning usually starts with the offending query and works down through the application and
database in stages, as shown by reading Figure 14.1 from top to bottom. It is interesting to note that different people may be responsible for each block in Figure 14.1.
All of these blocks are interrelated, which points up the need for good communication between those whose responsibilities are shown in Figure 14.1.

Ease of Administration

It is possible to design tables so that the need for frequent reorganizations will be
minimized. In DB2, for example, the clustering sequence of rows can be designed so
that the natural sequence of adding new records occurs at the end of the dataset. In
this instance, if rows are of fixed length, no free space will be required and rows will
not be inserted out of clustering sequence. In this case, there may not be a need to
reorganize until the tablespace has grown to multiple extents. Although maintenance
has been simplified, the trade-off may be in terms of poorer query performance
because the clustering sequence has not been optimized for query performance.

Server Scalability

Server scalability, which means the ability to handle large increases in the number of
users, is vital in a growing warehouse. Older mainframes were well known for poor
scalability. As usage increases, response time degenerates, user satisfaction
decreases, and the impact on the mainframe production environment may be significant. Newer mainframes that allow upgrading in smaller increments are more
scaleable. Although many successful warehouses have been implemented in a main-
frame-only environment, many shops have found it necessary to expand eventually
into a multiserver environment to meet the mushrooming growth in the quantity of
data and the number of users. In the warehouse environment, the mainframe may

become the "great server in the sky" and be used as a source of data for other servers, which should be scaleable.

Flexibility

Flexibility to meet future requirements must be designed into the warehouse. This is managed by using the data model and associated metadata as a foundation for physical design. Flexibility may be provided by giving users the autonomy necessary to handle their own analysis, query, and reporting requirements. They also need the security and procedures to move data from the global warehouse into personal or work group databases. The warehouse must provide a flexible basis for "what if" processing and extensive reporting on subsets of data. Although change may be viewed as the enemy, it is a constant factor in a data warehouse. Design is an iterative procedure, and the organizational structure must be in place to respond to changing user requirements, which has been likened to trying to hit a moving target. (See Chapter 3 for more details.)

DESIGNING A DATA MART

Many shops have developed data marts. Data marts are warehouses that are developed to meet requirements specific to a department or community of users. Although some companies have developed data marts that are independent of the corporate IT department, care should be taken to ensure that data marts follow corporate standards relative to hardware and software selection, network standards, naming conventions, and database design. The physical design guidelines that are appropriate for a corporate warehouse are also appropriate for a data mart, since a data mart is simply a subset of a corporate warehouse. It may be large or small and may be built either before or after an enterprise warehouse is in place. It should be considered as part of the overall architecture of a data warehouse. Although many vendors have been promoting the concept of data marts that are developed without corporate IT, be careful. This may result in isolated islands of information that may not be easily accessed across the corporation and will not meet corporate design objectives.

COMPONENTS OF THE DATA ARCHITECTURE

The overall technical architecture of a data warehouse was described in Chapter 7. This chapter will focus on the data architecture, which is one aspect of the overall technical architecture of the data warehouse, and its physical implementation. Please note that this chapter does not deal with the full physical implementation of the IDSS, or super datastore, which may include data across multiple organizations. (Remember the questions: Where can I obtain the lowest mortgage rate with my credit rating? Where can I get the best price on a Mercedes within a 100-mile radius of my home? These types of questions will not be dealt with in the basic data architecture for a single organization.) Just as a builder requires a blueprint to build a house, a data warehouse designer must develop a basic data architecture to meet business requirements. At the highest level, the data architecture may consist of these pieces:

1. *Legacy systems.* These operational systems contain current data that may or may not be in a relational format, may or may not be based on a data model, and may or may not have associated metadata. Although there are products advertised that will access data from these legacy systems across all file and DBMS types and across application lines, they may be of little value because performance is often poor. Also, the lack of data consistency and integration across the environment may make query results meaningless.

2. *Data warehouse.* The data warehouse contains historical data, which should be designed with a logical data model as the foundation with associated metadata in a format that is easily understood by end users. It may contain detail data, summary data, external data, specialized data subsets, multidimensional data, and external data.

3. *Data marts.* Data marts are warehouses that are designed to meet the needs of a specific department or work group. They may contain the same types of data found in the warehouse. Although some organizations consider them to be outside the corporate framework, it is best if they are designed with corporatewide interests in mind. They should be considered as a component of an overall data warehouse architecture.

4. *Personal data warehouse.* These databases are not officially part of the warehouse but will draw data from the warehouse as needed. They may also contain purely personal data, which may be combined with data from the warehouse for query and reporting purposes.

5. *Operational data store.* This is an optional component that is shared between the operational and warehouse environments. It contains detail data only and will be updatable. It may or may not be fed by the legacy environment and may be used to feed the data warehouse. Some shops have used the operational data store as a transition mechanism during data integration and reengineering. This is a difficult area to design because it may require optimization of both on-line transaction processing and ad hoc queries.

Data flows from the legacy on-line transaction processing systems into the data warehouse. In the process, data will be cleansed, transformed, and integrated, as discussed in Chapter 13. It may, optionally, flow into an ODS, where detail data may be positioned to serve both the on-line transaction processing environment and the ad hoc requirements of the data warehouse.

The ODS is usually updatable, in contrast to the traditional data warehouse. In some cases, the ODS may serve as the source of detail data for the warehouse, which

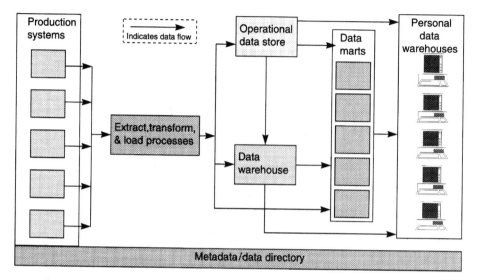

Figure 14.2   Data Flow across the Corporation.

may contain data at multiple levels of aggregation. Design of an ODS can be complex because it functions as a traditional transaction processing environment and as an ad hoc decision support environment. As shown in Figure 14.2, the two environments are quite different and techniques for optimizing the performance of these environments are directly contradictory. The design trade-offs are many. From an architectural perspective, users must be able to access the data directly, select, or extract data into personal or work group data warehouses as needed.

Data marts, which may contain historical data, summarized data, external data, and/or multidimensional data that is of interest to a particular department or work group, are usually placed on separate servers. They may be fed from legacy systems or from the data warehouse. At some point, data must be cleansed, transformed, and integrated before populating the data marts.

Types of Data Structures in the Warehouse

Now let's look more closely at the structure of a data warehouse or data mart. It may consist of any combination of the following types of data: detail data, summary data, external data, multidimensional data, data subsets, specialized data caches, replicated data, and archived data. The database designer must determine the types of data structures needed to meet design objectives. Physical design in the warehouse environment is an iterative process. The database designer will make a first cut at design based on expected data usage, which may not be well defined. The design may require modification to achieve desired performance when actual usage patterns become more apparent. The architecture shown in Figure 14.3 contains the basic structures that may be used in the construction of a data mart or data warehouse.

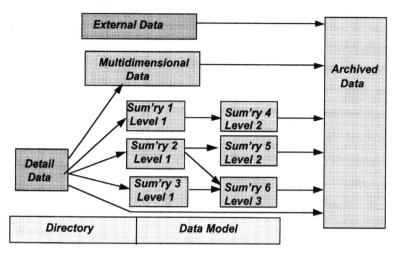

Figure 14.3 Data Warehouse Architecture.

Detail Data

The foundation of the warehouse consists of detail at its most basic level. Detail data is the basic source of subsets and summaries of data that are derived from it. The design of detail data should begin with the logical data model in third normal form.

Detail data in the warehouse will be different from production in that it will include only the data needed for decision support. It should also be well defined, consistent, and integrated. Counters, flags, and application-specific fields should not be included in the data warehouse. The element of time should be included in the warehouse data. This can be done in several ways:

1. A timestamp can be placed on each row. In a very large table, this may be costly in terms of disk utilization.
2. The time can be included in the table name (for example, Patient Records— 1994, Patient Records—1995, etc.).
3. The "as of" date can be captured in the data directory. For example, customer data may be refreshed on a nightly basis and will represent the status of customer information as of the previous midnight.

One of the most common mistakes made by end users is the misuse, aggregation, and comparison of data representing different points in time. Unless the point in time is well understood, users may be confused.

In theory, all queries and reports could be run against detail data. Since this is not a perfect world, with infinitely fast hardware and software, and it is not always easy to set up five-table joins, denormalization is expected. Derived data and summary data may be added as needed to obtain satisfactory performance. Fields such as LAST_ORDER_DATE or LAST_INVOICE_DATE may be included for convenience.

In some shops, warehouses have been built with summary data only. Although this may be attractive when large quantities of detail data would be required, it is often a mistake. Average companies manage by using averages. Companies with exceptional performance manage by exception. Which customers have buying patterns that are very different from the average? Why? Who is *not* buying our product? The last question will require additional data from external sources.

In some cases, the lowest level of detail data may not be stored. For example, in a credit card operation, it might not be necessary to store details on each charge to a customer account. A low level of summarization may be appropriate at the lowest level in the warehouse. Detail data is often stored for a specified period of time, and summarized data will be kept for a longer period. This should be noted in the metadata.

Normalization and Denormalization

Although the foundation for the data warehouse is a normalized data model, denormalization is expected in the warehouse environment. Users often feel that there are too many tables, too many joins that they do not understand, and too many cryptic names and data formats in a fully normalized environment. Views may be created to minimize the number of joins that will be required. Naming conventions should be meaningful and easy for the users to understand. Users should be part of the team that adopts naming conventions. Denormalization has many advantages:

- It promotes better performance by minimizing the need for joins.
- It may eliminate the need to write special decision support applications because data will be more accessible with ad hoc query tools.
- It recognizes a spreadsheet view of data, which is intuitive with most users.

However, be careful. Huge, wide tables are impractical and may have many null fields. Denormalize as needed, but do not go overboard.

Arrays of Data

The creation of arrays of data violates the relational model but is quite common in the data warehouse environment. An example might be a table that contains monthly sales figures for 24 months for each salesperson. Although this is a clear violation of third normal form, it will be easy to use and provide good performance when comparing sales figures. When the number of occurrences can be clearly defined with a practical limit, it works well.

Referential Integrity

Although it is desirable for operational systems to define referential constraints within the RDBMS, this may not be desirable in the warehouse. Data will be populated from the operational systems after cleansing, transformation, and integration. Its quality can be no higher than that found in the source. The RDBMS evaluation of constraints can add considerably to the load times for the warehouse and be of little value. Since the warehouse contains historical data, the valid domain for a particular field may change over time. An example would be the addition of new sales territories. From 1990 to 1992, there were 12 sales territories. In 1993, they were realigned and 20 sales territories were created. How should referential constraints be managed under these circumstances? Would it be worthwhile to rework old data in the light of the new territories? Some shops have solved this problem by adding a new field called `NEW_TERRITORY_ID` so that "what if" processing can occur against old and new data. Although this may work for a single realignment, how should it be handled after multiple realignments?

Some shops have turned on referential integrity in the early days of a particular data warehouse until such time as the cleansing processes have proven to be reliable. After these processes have proven themselves, referential integrity is turned off to minimize resource consumption.

Indexing for Performance

Warehouse tables will usually have many more indexes than those found in the OLTP environment. The maximum number of indexes that should be placed on a table will vary inversely with the size of the table. Smaller tables will accommodate a larger number of indexes than large tables. Since the warehouse is a read-only environment, indexes are very beneficial to performance. If a table has a large number of indexes, the load time may be unacceptable. In general, indexes may continue to be added until the load time or reorganization time becomes unacceptable.

Always place indexes on primary and most foreign keys as a starting point. It is usually best not to add many other indexes unless there is a reasonable certainty that they will be used. In one shop, the DBA tried to provide flexibility and performance by placing an average of 15 indexes on every table. After the warehouse went into production, users complained about performance. A usage analysis showed that a number of new indexes were needed, but the tables could not handle more indexes because of lengthy maintenance times. It was also learned that most of the existing indexes were not in use. It took much effort to determine which indexes were probably not in use. It would have been far better to start with primary and foreign key indexes and add additional indexes as needed.

Tables with hundreds of millions of rows may only support one index comfortably, which may or may not be acceptable. If a table is very large and additional indexes are needed, consider splitting the table. Some RDBMSs, such as DB2, will use index-only access if all requested columns are in the index. By designing indexes to contain all columns that may be needed, access to the table itself may be avoided and save input and output (I/O). If an index exists with three columns and consistent queries require the same five columns, the addition of two more columns to the index may be worthwhile.

Although some DBAs have tried to get around the question of which indexes to build by building many single-column indexes, this may be counterproductive in many RDBMSs. When multiple indexes are used in a single query, sorting of the eligible index entries may occur, which can be costly. Be sure to understand how your RDBMS handles multiple index access to the data. As a general rule, plan indexing carefully and build multicolumn indexes as needed. Critical indexes may also be cached to improve performance.

One last indexing issue: If a table is too large and incurs many lengthy scans, consider the possibility that the addition of a summary table may offload some of the scans. If the scans are caused by a requirement that data be summarized at a certain level, creation of an appropriate summary level may solve part of the problem.

Divide and Conquer

Detail data may be centralized on a mainframe or large server or partitioned across multiple servers by work group, department, subject area, or application. The partitioning of data by department or work group may be viewed as a data mart approach, in which data structures are specific to each user community. Although there is a legitimate need for departmental data, no department is totally isolated. At some point, it may be necessary to compare sales data from various departments. It is best to view data marts as part of the corporatewide architecture, and not as stand-alone data stores. Unfortunately, it is not always politically easy for a company to control independent user development of data marts.

For example, there may be servers in place for each department or subject area or special servers for particular applications. If it is understood that a large percentage of accesses to the data will be against a single department's data, partitioning by department on multiple servers may make sense. For the small percentage of times when data must be scanned across the corporation, it will be necessary to union the data across multiple servers. Data will be positioned across servers to provide optimal performance in the majority of cases. Data may be horizontally partitioned, with departmental subsets placed on departmental servers. If tables are designed with consistent keys and data names, data may be queried across servers. Obviously, the efficiency of a corporatewide scan of data would be better if it were all on a single platform. The performance trade-offs and expected data usage must be understood when making this design decision.

Vertical partitioning across multiple servers may also be beneficial to performance. In this case, a subset of columns from a normalized table will be physically implemented as a separate table. This approach may be considered when data from a single entity may be used by two different groups. For example, one group may need to look at payroll data and another group may be only interested in basic personnel information without payroll details. If these groups have their own servers, the entity may be split into two physical tables, which will share the same key. The two tables may be joined in a view to support end users who need the full picture.

Partitioning is a critical design decision because it may be complex or time consuming to change it after tables are in production. Partitioning may be accomplished through DBMS-controlled partitioning or user-managed partitioning. In DB2 or ORACLE, for example, partitioning may be managed at the dataset level while maintaining a single physical table. Although it is possible to reorganize a single partition of data and keep other partitions updatable (in DB2, for example), there may be a performance degradation. Since the user is unaware of the partitioning that has occurred "under the covers," this is a user friendly approach that can benefit performance and promote parallel processing if properly implemented.

User managed partitioning, which implies a set of look-alike tables, may be very effective in terms of performance. If partitioned so that most queries run against only one partition, tables will be smaller and large table scans will be minimized. It may also be convenient for reorganizing data on a partition basis. This means that the designer must have some understanding of the expected data usage. It is impossible to design for performance unless there is some knowledge of expected data use. Some shops seem to pride themselves on the fact that they know nothing about expected usage. They must either take advantage of any understanding of expected usage during initial design or rework the physical design later to respond to actual usage.

In data warehouses that serve multiple time zones, data may be partitioned by time zone. Since there will be more or less activity during certain periods of the day in the various time zones, this approach can facilitate data loading and maintenance. Partitioning by geographic area is also common, especially in sales tables.

Parallel Processing

The potential of parallel processing during large tablespace scans, loading, reorganizing, etc. is a key design issue. Partitioning schemes must consider how the data will be used and design to promote parallel processing. Partitioning schemes also depend on the type of parallel architecture. The strategies are very different. There are more shared systems, in which table partitioning is prevalent, versus shared-nothing systems, in which the entire database is partitioned. Dataset placement is critical. Would it make sense to place two partitions on the same device if there is a need to process them in parallel? Although parallel processing has provided the potential for improved performance, the designer must decide how and when to use it.

In general, SMP implementations are most appropriate in the OLTP environment for mission-critical applications. It is also appropriate if growth tends to be predictable and moderate in size and the number of users is reasonable. MPP is more appropriately used for more complex, analytical applications with very large amounts of data and rapid, unpredictable rates of growth. In the MPP environment, configurations may support thousands of users.

Another key design issue is the potential of using shared disk, shared memory, shared nothing, or shared everything architectures. Although this has become almost a religious issue with some people, there are advantages and disadvantages to the options. Although shared disk tends to be more flexible, there will be additional communication overhead. In the OLTP environment, load balancing will be more flexible In a shared nothing environment, there will be less flexibility but it will be more scaleable. (See Chapter 17 for more information.)

Summary Levels

When users consistently ask for data that is summarized at a certain level, summary levels may offload some of the processing against detail data. Summary levels may be implemented as separate summary tables or as part of a multidimensional database structure. The level of granularity in a summary should be selected to minimize I/O and provide access to the right data at the right time at a reasonable cost. If the level of granularity is too high, queries will continue to process detail data to provide answers. If it is too low, there will be a higher I/O rate than necessary. Select the proper level of granularity based on the probability of access. For example, sales data may be stored at the detail level and also at the monthly level. If users frequently require data at the weekly level, it would make sense to store data at the weekly level of granularity; otherwise, they must scan the detail data to summarize repeatedly at the weekly level. On the other hand, if data is only stored at the weekly level and detail data is unavailable, they will be unable to meet their requirements. The trade-off is between disk space and repeatedly summarizing the same information. Some multidimensional products are intelligent enough to use intermediate summary levels to create a higher-level summary. For example, if data is stored at the daily and monthly level and the user asked for yearly data, the engine is smart enough to use the monthly level as a basis for the summary rather than the daily level.

Do not try to build all possible summary levels during the initial building stage of the warehouse. In one shop, the DBA tried to anticipate all summary levels that might be needed. Although the initial detail data was rather small, his database would have required approximately 400 million rows to accommodate all planned summary levels. It is a good idea to build only the most critical summary levels during the first design iteration. Work closely with the users to determine which levels will actually be used and add them later. Try to track data usage to determine which data is actually being used and drop unused tables.

External Data

Many organizations purchase data from outside sources, including government bodies, industry sources, and other providers. There is a real need to merge external data, personal data, and "official" warehouse data in individual queries. Plan to document the external data with appropriate metadata. There are several different types of external data. A shop may purchase data to enhance customer information, such as demographic data, life-style data, attitudinal data, and data in response to questionnaires circulated by outside vendors. If it is nonvolatile in nature, it would make sense to include it with customer profiles.

Another type of external data comes from government regulatory bodies or industry data providers and tends to be dynamic and changing on a regularly scheduled basis. It is not usually a good idea to intermingle this type of external data and official corporate data in the same tables because the quality of the external data may be questionable. From a practical perspective, the format of external data can change on a frequent basis. A company may receive a file with 40 fields one month and receive another with 60 fields the next month, only 30 of which are the same on both files. The DBA must be prepared to document the data and deploy it quickly so as not to lose its timeliness. The easiest way to handle this is to separate it from the official data and label it as external data. It is not usually worthwhile to attempt to normalize the data before deployment because of the volatility of the data formats.

External data is becoming more important every day. When warehouses are initially implemented, it is not uncommon for companies to try to determine the demographics of their customers. After that step is taken, companies may then want to know who is *not* buying their products. At that point, data about prospective customers may be obtained from an outside source and used effectively. External data will be required for this step.

Data Replication

In the client/server environment, data replication can improve performance and availability. If a particular table is frequently joined with tables that are located on other servers and network traffic becomes a problem, replication of the table to other servers may reduce network traffic and improve performance. If a table has a requirement for high availability, it may be replicated so that the data will be available even if the primary server is down. For more information, see Chapter 16.

Placement of Data

Placement of data on particular disks or servers is a critical design consideration. The following guidelines are suggested:

- Do not place tables that are frequently joined on the same device.
- Place tables that are commonly joined on the same server.
- Consider replicating tables across servers if joins across servers will cause severe network traffic problems.
- Consider placing basic, detail data that is shared across the enterprise on a mainframe or other centralized server.
- Do not place indexes on the same devices as the tables on which they are built.

RAID Technology[2]

Redundant arrays of inexpensive disks (RAIDs) are frequently found on large servers. These arrays can recover from any single disk failure while the server remains on-line with a process that is transparent to the users. Data is broken into pieces and written to multiple disks in a "striping" process. When a disk fails, the data can be reconstructed by reviewing the data that remains. Although the server performance will degrade while the disk is reconstructed, the process is handled automatically by the server and is transparent to the user.

Such arrays may use techniques like the following:

- Disk mirroring, which uses two drives attached to the same controller
- Disk duplexing, in which each drive has its own controller
- Parity checking, in which an extra bit is added to the data to ensure that information has been correctly transmitted
- Disk striping, in which data is spread by sectors or bytes across multiple disks through an algorithm.

If fault tolerance is a requirement, RAID technology is a potential solution. There are six levels of RAID implementation:

RAID 0:   At this level, data records are sector interleaved across groups of drives without parity, which is called striping. No redundancy is provided.

RAID 1:   Called mirroring, this level involves data that is written redundantly to pairs of drives and can be read independently from each drive. The downside to this approach is that it requires twice the disk capacity since it maintains a full copy of the data.

RAID 2:   Data records are bit-interleaved across groups of drives, some of which store error correction codes.

RAID 3:   Data records are bit-interleaved across groups of drives, but only one drive stores parity information. This approach is best for applications that transmit large blocks of information and require high bandwidth.

RAID 4:   This approach includes one dedicated parity drive with data records sector-interleaved across groups of drives.

RAID 5:   If this level is used, data records are sector-interleaved across groups of drives, but all drives store parity information. If many small I/Os are needed, this approach is best for transaction processing.

Personal Data

The quality of personal data is not the responsibility of the DBA. Personal databases may contain extracts from departmental, warehouse, and operational data and data that has been aggregated or manipulated in some manner. In general, it is undocumented and should not be shared with other users without the caveat "Buyer beware." If personal data is allowed to flow into the warehouse, it should only be done with a DBA-sanctioned process. Although some people worry about the quality of personal data, this is not a new problem. When reports were produced manually without computers, they were viewed critically by users. Nothing has changed in this respect.

Archived Data

Although users will usually claim that they need "all of the data, all of the time," they must live in the real world. If a charge-back scheme is in place, their needs may become more realistic. In any case, a decision must be made regarding data retention for each table, and the information should be captured as part of the metadata. There are many issues associated with archived data. What if data is archived in its current format and the format of the table changes? How do we bring it back? What if we want to bring another year's worth of data back and there is no room in the current table? All of these issues must be addressed. Fortunately, there are vendors who have begun to address the problem through software products. In at least one case, data may be extracted and copied along with the table format in a baseline. If the data is brought back, the original format is known and can be restored by the software.

OLAP and Multidimensional Data

According to Dr. E. F. Codd and Associates,[4] OLAP tools must provide a multidimensional conceptual view of the data, with a client/server architecture, and meet 10 additional evaluation requirements, which will not be reiterated here. (For more information on this topic, see Chapter 15.) Although some vendors are promoting multidimensional products as the sole solution for data warehouses, the buyer should consider options carefully. OLAP is most useful when business problems involve substantial analysis, transformation, and aggregation of detail data, and it may not be the ideal solution for every warehouse. It is of greatest value if tables contain relatively static data and are not overly large. Multidimensional tables are often used in data marts.

In a multidimensional model, data is stored as facts and dimensions instead of rows and columns. A star schema uses major tables, called fact tables, that contain quantitative or factual data about a business. It also uses smaller tables, called dimension tables, that may be in third normal form and hold descriptive data. A dimension represents a single perspective on the data. It is a single measurement or one side of a cube. This type of model is often called cubic, star, facts and dimensions, or a dimensional model. It represents the business analyst's conceptual view of the data. In Figure 14.4, a sales fact cube is shown with dimensions of time,

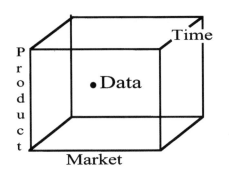

Figure 14.4 Sales Fact Cube.

product, and market. A single data point represents the intersection of time, product, and market information.

A dimension of a fact table represents the "by" criteria. For example, we may wish to see sales by region, shipments by shipper, or monthly sales by salesperson. Dimensions are the smaller tables surrounding the fact table in a star schema. They are reference tables and may be hierarchical in nature. A hierarchical dimension might include product group, product type, and product. The hierarchical time dimension might include day, month, and year.

The fact table is usually large and is highly denormalized. In fact, data for multiple time periods may appear in a single table. Since all of the data is in one table, there will be fewer joins. Numerous vendor products are designed to provide a user friendly front end that allows the user to pivot the table on any dimension and slice and dice the data to meet user requirements. These products also mask the underlying complexity of the basic fact tables. Small dimension tables may be stored in memory to improve performance. It is possible to implement a multidimensional model without an OLAP tool. Unfortunately, the storage of many different roll-ups of data in the same table may be confusing to end users without a specialized multidimensional engine. One major manufacturer developed a star schema and wrote a custom-designed front end that has been very successful. If there are many dimensions, there will be a large number of rows. Since all fields may not be appropriate at each roll-up level, there may be many null fields and performance may be affected. Many vendor products have been designed to handle null fields efficiently. To achieve good performance, keep the number of dimensions at a manageable level, probably less than five to seven dimensions. As the number of dimensions is increased, the number of rows in the fact table will increase. In some cases, dimension tables are combined with the main fact table.

Designing Multidimensional Tables.   The design process is slightly different if a multidimensional structure will be used. The requirements will not be at the atomic level of data but will represent the business analyst's view of the world. For example, we might have requirements such as the following:

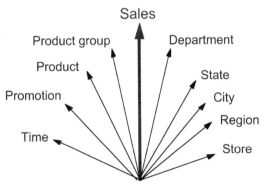

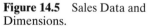

Figure 14.5 Sales Data and Dimensions.

- What is the sales trend in quantity and dollar amounts for each product sold by store, region, department, and state?
- Compare the quantities of products sold by store, region, city, and state for various periods of time.
- What is the impact of promotions on sales in various stores, regions, cities, and states?
- List the top 10 stores in terms of sales for the first quarter of 1996.

The steps involved in designing multidimensional tables are as follows:

1. Identify requirements. (See the preceding list for examples.)
2. Identify `facts` from the requirements. In the preceding example, all facts relate to `sales`.
3. Identify `dimensions` or the `by` criteria. In the preceding example, the dimensions include store, region, department, state, city, region, time, product, and product group. Sales data and dimensions might be viewed as shown in Figure 14.5.
4. Identify the roll-up levels (historical aggregation levels).
5. Design `fact` and `dimension` tables.
6. Determine data retention and sizing requirements.
7. Identify partitioning requirements.
8. Validate the design against the DBMS and end-user tools that will be used.
9. Modify the design as requirements change.

DESIGN EXAMPLE

Consider the partial entity-relationship diagram shown in Figure 14.6. You will notice the hierarchical relationships on the E-R diagram. The diagram must then be transformed into a multidimensional model. The product dimension includes

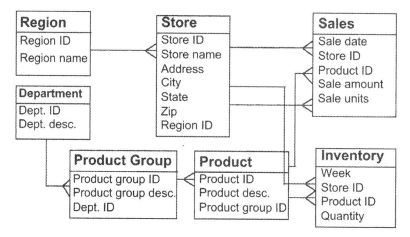

Figure 14.6   Partial Entity-Relationship (E-R) Diagram.

department, product, and group. The location dimension includes region and store. A time dimension, which is not usually present on an E-R diagram, is added because time is an important dimension from the analyst's perspective. The time dimension includes year, month, week, and date. At this point, a decision has been made to ignore inventory and concentrate on sales facts. The multidimensional model looks like Figure 14.7.

In the multidimensional model, entities have been mapped into the dimensions. Entities that belong to more than one dimension become `facts`. This is then translated into a star schema using generic dimension keys, as shown in Figure 14.8. Notice that the sales fact table shows a three-column key representing the concatenation of the single-column keys from each dimension table.

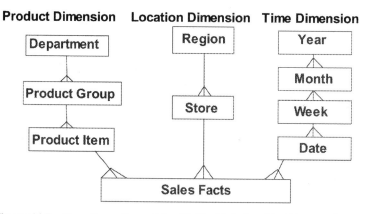

Figure 14.7   Transformation of the Entity-Relationship Diagram into a Multidimensional Model.

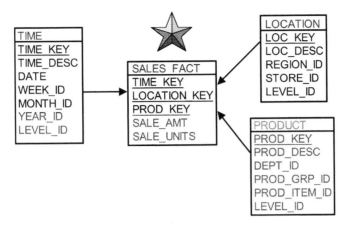

Figure 14.8   Star Schema Using Generic Dimension Keys.

Generic key lookup tables have inherent problems. The descriptions of department, product group, product item, region, and store and the time dimensions are missing. It will not be easy to provide descriptions of these fields for reports. Since the dimensions have multiple levels, a level number has been added to each of the dimension tables. The levels are numbered from the bottom to the top, where 1 represents the lowest level in the hierarchy. If the location level is at the store level, the LOC_KEY, LOC_DESC, REGION_ID, and STORE_ID will contain non-null values. If the location level is the region level, LOC_KEY, LOC_DESC, and REGION_ID will be filled in but STORE_ID will contain a null value. An example of a generic key lookup table appears in Figure 14.9.

The design may be modified to allow attribute descriptions to print on a report, as shown in Figure 14.10. Descriptions for region, store, department, product group, and product item have been added. This is an example of a typical star schema. The star schema has proven itself most useful at the data mart level since the technology has current limitations on table sizes. Vendor products may allow a great deal of query flexibility, including the ability to "pivot" data along different dimensions for a different perspective on the data. Since many of the products pre-summarize much of the data, load times may be lengthy, but queries may be extremely efficient. A multidimensional approach is most appropriate when queries require aggregation at many levels. For more details on designing a star schema, see

LOC_KEY	LOC_DESC	REGION_ID	STORE_ID	LEVEL
100	Northeast	1		2
105	Midwest	2		2
110	Southeast	3		2
115	Boston	1	2024	1
120	Chicago	2	2349	1
125	New York	1	2542	1
130	Atlanta	3	2211	1

Figure 14.9   Example of a Generic Key Lookup Table.

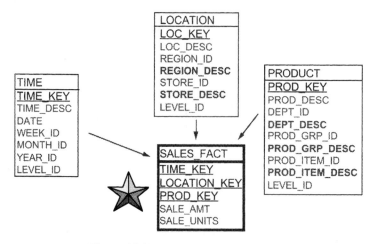

Figure 14.10 Modified Star Schema.

Ralph Kimball's book.[2] Designers must analyze the data and determine which rollup levels may be needed. Some designers skip the traditional data modeling process and create a multidimensional design as the initial design. This is a controversial approach, and it is still necessary to provide adequate metadata for the end users.

SUMMARY

This chapter has discussed issues involved in developing a data architecture and selecting the types of data structures that may be used in the warehouse implementation. It has discussed design issues for each of the structure types—detail data, summary data, external data, replicated data, multidimensional data, etc.—and made recommendations for the conditions under which it is appropriate to use each of them. Whether the design is implemented as a star schema or a more traditional multilevel architecture, you will still need to make decisions regarding summary levels to be physically stored. It is extremely important to be aware of the issues involved in using various design options.

REFERENCES

[1] KIMBALL, R., *The Data Warehouse Toolkit*, New York, John Wiley & Sons, 1996.

[2] DEWIRE, D., *Client/Server Computing*, New York, McGraw-Hill, 1993, pp. 120–122.

[3] BEDELL, J., *Data Modeling and Database Design for Data Warehouses*, 1996 Course Book, Bethesda, MD, The Data Warehousing Institute, 1996.

[4] CODD, E. F., CODD S., SALLEY C., "Providing OLAP (On-line Analytical Processing) to User-Analysts, an IT Mandate," E. F. Codd & Assoc., 1993.

Multidimensional OLAP versus Relational OLAP

15

Colin White

DataBase Associates International
Morgan Hill, California

"Nothing is good or bad but by comparison."

Thomas Fuller

A s the use of data warehousing grows within an organization, there will be many different kinds of users with differing skill levels and requirements accessing warehouse data. These users will range from so-called data farmers, who perform repetitive tasks using query and reporting tools on a routine basis, to data explorers, who carry out sophisticated data analysis with queries that are predominantly ad hoc in nature. These latter users will employ advanced techniques like OLAP to analyze known data patterns (such as monthly sales figures) and data mining to seek out unknown patterns in data (to analyze customer buying habits, for example). This chapter discusses the use of OLAP and reviews the different database technologies that support it. Chapter 23 looks at data mining.

OLAP OVERVIEW

The term *OLAP* first surfaced in a paper entitled "Providing On-Line Analytical Processing to User Analysts," by Dr. E. F. Codd. The original paper,[1] published in 1993, defined 12 rules, or features, of an OLAP system—an additional six rules were added in 1995.[2] A more succinct definition comes from the OLAP Council (which has the objective of promoting the use of OLAP):

> On-Line Analytical Processing (OLAP) is a category of software technology that enables analysts, managers and executives to gain insight into data through fast, consistent, interactive access to a wide variety of possible views of information that has been transformed from raw data to reflect the real *dimensionality* of the enterprise as understood by the user.

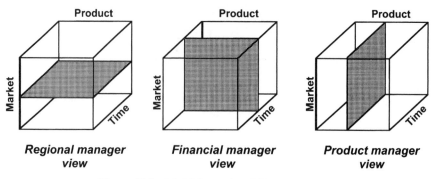

Figure 15.1 Multidimensional Data Analysis.

"A fancy term for multidimensional analysis" is an even simpler definition to be found in the April 1995 issue of *DBMS* magazine.

Examples of OLAP applications include sales and marketing analysis, product pricing, profitability analysis, and budgeting and forecasting. OLAP applications typically employ small- to medium-size databases (up to 100 gigabytes) containing summarized, historical, and derived data. Characteristics of this style of application are ad hoc and predefined analyses involving calculations and modeling across multiple dimensions, and the drilling down from high-level to lower-level summarized and possibly detailed data.

OLAP allows users to view and analyze data across multiple dimensions–hence the term *multidimensional analysis* (MDA). Figure 15.1 shows how MDA can be used to analyze sales data from a product, time, or market dimension or viewpoint. As the figure shows, MDA tools view data as though it were stored in an array or cube, with each side of the cube representing a dimension. The cells of the cube contain the actual data values of interest. These data values are called variables, measurements, or facts.

Dimensions consist of one or more members. For example, the market dimension could consist of the east, west, north, south, and central members, and nuts, bolts, and washers could be members of the product dimension. Members are roughly equivalent to fields in a file, while cells are roughly equivalent to the records of a file. The members of a dimension may be organized based on a parent-child relationship in a hierarchical manner, where a parent member represents the consolidation of the members that are its children. Examples of hierarchical dimensions are markets, product structure, and corporate structure

Surprisingly, MDA is not new—many MDA vendors originated in the early 1970s, when time-sharing products were used to do this analysis. APL from IBM was one of the first MDA tools. With the advent of the PC in the 1980s, MDA-style processing moved to packages such as spreadsheets. During the evolution of MDA tools, the growth in the use of database products increased exponentially, and today, as more companies build data warehousing systems, the amount of data being gathered in database systems is staggering. OLAP represents a merging of desktop

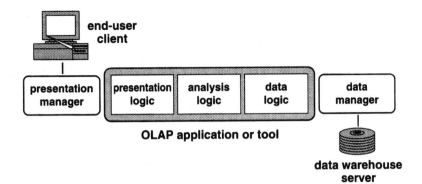

Figure 15.2 OLAP and Client/Server.

MDA tools and database products into an integrated client/server system (see Figure 15.2).

One major issue regarding OLAP usage and products centers on whether it is better to use MDA end-user tools in conjunction with a relational DBMS (so-called ROLAP), or a multidimensional database (hence the term *multidimensional OLAP*). Many of the discussions about OLAP lack clarity and confuse end-user processing issues with data management issues.

Any discussion of the OLAP capabilities of a product (see Figure 15.3) should be viewed from two perspectives: the client and the server. From the client viewpoint, the main focus should be on a product's external end-user MDA features—for example, in the areas of analytical processing (ratios, ranking, consolidation, trend analysis, statistics, comparisons, complex logic), time calculations and handling of time-series data, modeling, reporting, and support for alerts and event-driven agent processing.

From the server viewpoint, the key issue is the internal database technology used to manage the data. This latter discussion is almost entirely concerned with performance, scalability, and storage management issues.

MULTIDIMENSIONAL OLAP

The main multidimensional OLAP architecture is shown in Figure 15.4. Here, the MDBMS server does both data management and analytical processing, resulting in a "thin" MDA client architecture. An MDBMS can be thought of as a spreadsheet with two important extensions—support for many more dimensions, and the ability to handle multiple concurrent users.

Conceptually, data in an MDBMS is stored as a multidimensional array, where each cell in the array is formed by the intersection of all the dimensions. In such a design, not all cells have a value. For example, in a sales system not every product may be sold in every store or during any given time period. As the number of

END-USER PROCESSING

Platform Support
  Hardware and software
  Client/server architecture
  Stand-alone desktop version
OLAP Features
  Analytical functions (e.g., ratios, ranking, consolidation, trend analysis, statistics,
    comparisons, complex logic)
  Modeling capabilities
  Time-dimension awareness
  Exception and alert handling
  Event-driven agents
Logical View of Data
  Hypercube vs. multicube
  Cross-datacube access

DATA MANAGEMENT

Platform Support
  Hardware and software
  File server, MDBMS, or RDBMS
Scalability and Performance
  Database size
  Number of dimensions
  Number of levels within a dimension
  Number of cells
  Concurrent users
  Predefined vs. dynamic consolidation
Storage Management Capabilities
  Data types provided
  Sparse data handling (e.g., simple vs. compressed arrays)
  Indexing techniques
  Read-only vs. update mode of operation
  Incremental data refresh
Administration Tools
Data Import and Transformation
Data Export

OPEN ARCHITECTURE

Client API (e.g., support for DDE, OLE)
Documented Server API (e.g., SQL, ODBC)

Figure 15.3   OLAP Product Checklist.

dimensions in the data cube increases, so does sparsity (i.e., the number of empty cells). Breaking the logical design into multiple datacubes in a so-called multicube design can reduce the impact of sparsity. Some products, however, do not allow this and require all the data to be kept in a single hypercube. Special physical storage management techniques (such as data compression) and indexing schemes are also used by some MDBMS products to reduce the impact of sparse data and to provide

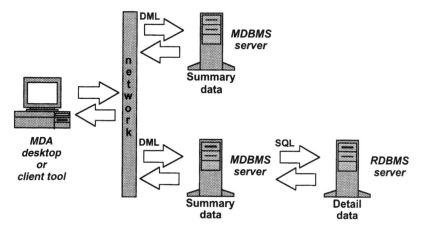

Figure 15.4   Multidimensional OLAP.

fast access to datacube cells. MDBMSs also typically provide the ability to consolidate input data during the loading process. Preconsolidated data provides fast
response times for users requiring high-level summarized data, but has the disadvantage of increased database size.

One key issue with MDBMSs is lack of standardization—each MDBMS has
its own proprietary client interface. These interfaces usually offer more powerful
data manipulation capabilities than the SQL in RDBMSs, but they suffer from the
problem that each client tool has to be tailored to each interface. The lack of a common interface or language for MDBMSs is being addressed through the OLAP
Council, which is attempting to design a common API for OLAP products. It will, of
course, take some time for this specification to be implemented by vendors, and
even then the API will have to use a lowest-common-denominator approach similar
to what Microsoft had to do when designing the ODBC SQL interface to RDBMSs.

Another issue with MDBMSs is scalability—they are good for handling summary data but are not always suited to handling large amounts of detailed data. This
issue is being addressed by vendors, who are gradually improving the performance
of products and adding dynamic consolidation facilities, and also by the provision
of a pass-through facility, which allows MDBMS users to access transparently data
stored in an RDBMS (see the bottom half of Figure 15.4). Here, detailed data is
stored in the relational server, and summary data in the MDBMS. One challenge
will be to keep data in the two servers synchronized.

MDBMS architectures are at present especially well suited for access to summarized data (typically less than 10 to 20 gigabytes) involving a small number of
dimensions (typically less than about 10) and where the data access paths are well
defined. Products do, however, vary in performance and scalability, and it is important to mention that significant development work is being done on many MDBMS
products in these areas.

ROLAP

ROLAP replaces the MDBMS server by an RDBMS, as shown in Figure 15.5. One key characteristic of MDA is the ability to drill down from highly summarized to detailed data, and so in this configuration the RDBMS server will typically contain both detailed and summary data. Where summaries do not exist, the client tool builds them dynamically. This offers more flexibility, but often at the cost of performance. The plus side of ROLAP is that relational products have robust administration tools and open SQL interfaces, which make it easier for vendors to build portable MDA tools, and they provide good database scalability via techniques such as parallel query processing. The down side is that the large number of relational tables required for MDA degrades performance because of the overheads of table join and index processing.

RDBMS processing overheads can be reduced by denormalizing the tables into a star schema design. (Note that certain ROLAP client tools require a star schema design.) Such a design has a central fact table and one or more related dimension tables.[3] The fact table contains the numerical measurements (for example, sales figures) at the intersection of all dimensions. A zero value is not stored in a star schema if a combination of dimensions does not yield a value. The dimension tables describe each dimension and are used to slice the data in the fact table along each dimension. RDBMS vendors are enhancing their products to optimize the performance of processing star schema databases.

Another disadvantage of ROLAP is that all the analytical processing is done on the client. Product direction here is to offload analytical processing into a separate server. The analytical engine's job is to retrieve data from the relational database and do the MDA processing. This reduces client overhead and allows the analytical server to be shared by multiple clients. This architecture is shown in the bottom half of Figure 15.5. ROLAP architectures are especially well suited for

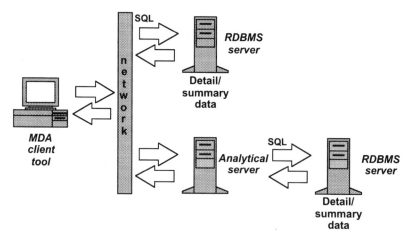

Figure 15.5   Relational OLAP.

dynamic access to summarized and detailed data, where the flexibility and scalability offered by a RDBMS is more important than the performance offered by an MDBMS for accessing databases containing summarized and preconsolidated data.

SUMMARY

What product you use for OLAP will depend largely on the type of processing being done and the amount and type of data to be processed. Multidimensional OLAP lends itself to the processing of derived and summarized data, where the data access paths are well defined, whereas ROLAP is more suited to the dynamic processing of both summarized and detailed data. Even within each OLAP category, the products are often designed for different types of application. Each of the OLAP approaches has its strengths and weaknesses, and users must match these to requirements.

REFERENCES

[1] E. F. CODD. "Providing OLAP (On-Line Analytical Processing) to User Analysts," E. F. Codd and Associates, 1993.

[2] NIGEL PENSE and RICHARD CREETH, *The OLAP Report, Volumes 1 and 2*. Business Intelligence, 1995.

[3] RALPH KIMBALL, *The Data Warehouse Toolkit*, New York, John Wiley & Sons, 1996.

Data Replication in a Global Warehousing Environment

16

Marie Buretta

Marie Buretta, Inc.
Princeton, New Jersey

"If a man empties his purse into his head, no man can take it away from him. An investment in knowledge always pays the best interest."

Benjamin Franklin

Maintaining data consistency between operational systems and decision support systems in a global warehousing environment presents many challenges. Multiple internal and external data sources must be merged, transformed, and distributed; data integrity is paramount and cannot be compromised; degrees of latency between consistency points must reflect the demands of the business users; schema designs are not identical even though data content may be redundant; techniques for reconciliation and recovery may have to be designed into the schema; network resources are finite and expensive; and various levels of administrative and support skills exist across locations.

This chapter identifies the critical factors that influence data consistency alternatives. Topics addressed include requirements for information integration across any workstation tool, technical approaches for attaining data consistency and their associated challenges, the importance of integrating any and all replication alternatives, evaluation criteria for replication tool selection, and a case study of a successful global warehousing implementation.

INTEGRATED INFORMATION ACCESS FROM ALL WORKSTATION SYSTEMS

Firms are becoming flatter and putting more control in the hands of the business user. This can be seen in the decentralization of business functions to a widening set of locations. These new information users have more complex and integrated applications at their disposal. These include transactional systems (OLTP), decision support systems (OLAP), business integration systems, and personal productivity/workgroup systems. Transactional systems are the core systems that capture and maintain detailed, accurate information about the business. Decision support systems are used to make critical decisions that ultimately control the enterprise's ability to compete in the marketplace. Business integration systems are a newer type of application that generally span multiple departments and cross organizational boundaries. They have been made possible by the availability of greater computer power and more sophisticated software, and they include rule-based management systems, complex trend analysis (i.e., data mining), and data visualization. The final type of workstation application is the personal productivity/work group systems. These are off-the-shelf, PC-based packages that make the individual more productive. They include such software as word processors, spreadsheets, graphical packages, mail-based applications, and document management and publishing systems. All four of these types of applications require data. From a user and application perspective, the line between current operational data and/or historical data has become blurred.

SEPARATE DATA STORES FOR OLTP AND OLAP ENVIRONMENTS

If the line between current operational data and/or historical data has become blurred, then is it possible to use the same physical data store(s) to support both OLTP and OLAP systems? The basic production RDBMS, when used for OLAP in a two-tier client/server architecture, falls short of being able to provide the data manipulation necessary to meet the user requirements for data analysis and information synthesis. Two major reasons for this are the limitations of the SQL and the restrictions of a two-dimensional relational model.

OLTP production data is often stored in normalized relational databases. These operational databases are designed by database administrators to provide efficient data access for rapid processing of transactional systems. However, these normalized structures are not designed to be comprehensible by end users; nor are they particularly suited for the complex query demands of OLAP users—thus the advent of MDDBs that store data in structures that offer an alternative way of organizing data. Through the use of optimizing, cross-indexed hierarchical structures, data is organized into dimensions and measures, by time. Other OLAP alternatives include adapting relational technology by using a specialized star schema, or using an OLAP tool that provides a middleware approach to accessing relational data.

But does the data still need to be stored redundantly? Currently, the answer is yes. Decision support systems require access to broad sets of data usually from multiple corporate sources. Most often, the data from these diverse operational systems requires data transformation and distribution to servers. Before arriving at a user's server, the data is repaired, merged, appended, rationalized, and summarized. However, as middleware becomes more robust, it will become easier to perform parallel access from heterogeneous data stores and to perform dynamic transformation and summarization. This will allow the amount of data redundancy to be reduced.

TRADE-OFFS BETWEEN DATA CENTRALIZATION AND DATA DISTRIBUTION

There are multiple ways of implementing a warehousing environment. There are approaches that advocate a top-down corporate centric information system and others that stress a more conservative, bottom-up, application-centric approach. The bottom-up approach uses application decision support systems as building blocks to achieve a global warehousing environment. Whichever approach is used, decisions must be made with respect to where the data should be physically stored. This can vary from a single central warehouse from which all users (both local and remote) access information, to many distributed data marts that are only accessed locally.

There are trade-offs associated with any data distribution decisions. The advantages of a centralized data source for warehousing are as follows:

- Data viewed by all decision support users is identical (i.e., totally consistent and at the same degree of latency, or timeliness).
- Maintenance and security are relatively simple and straightforward.

The disadvantages of this centralized data approach are the

- Existence of a single point of failure. When a failure does occur, all decision support systems are unavailable to users.
- Large network usage to meet the query requests of remote users. This can be very costly.

The advantages of a more distributed data environment for warehousing include

- Avoidance of a single point of failure in the OLAP environment. A failure at one node does not interfere with usage at other nodes.
- Better performance and availability of all decision support systems. Users access local data, thereby avoiding the time and cost associated with remote access.

The disadvantages are as follows:

- Data viewed by all decision support users is *not* identical. The amount of latency before data consistency is achieved with the designated primary sources is a factor of the replication service used for that location.
- Administration and security are more complex.

- Costs are associated with maintaining data consistency across all distributed locations.

The data distribution challenge for warehousing is to achieve the optimal mix of centralization and distribution, what I call judicious distribution. This mix should optimize for local use of data and yet centralize for ease of maintaining consistency.

OLAP AND THREE-TIER ARCHITECTURES

Information access tools have come a long way since the early report writers and spreadsheets. Originally, OLAP vendors supplied their users with databases. Some of these databases were based on their own proprietary resource managers, and others were based on relational DBMSs supplied by other vendors. Along with these underlying databases, OLAP vendors supplied tools to conduct analysis, and they supplied repositories for metadata and storage of user-defined calculations. This was a very limiting and closed environment. Therefore, the current trend is to decouple the tools from the other components. This allows vendors to present them as front-end tools to other vendors' DBMSs. This is extremely important because it pushes the OLAP environment into a multitier architecture. The tiers of this architecture include (1) industry standard database(s), usually relational DBMS, that act as the data stores; and (2) an application server layer, which performs the analytical processing functions and interacts directly with the database(s). This layer is truly the heart of OLAP. It maps the multidimensional business views to the physical databases. In addition, it contains a repository that holds the definitions of the dimensions, consolidation paths for data, formulas used in query calculations, and database access information. The final layer (3) is the client, which is the presentation layer and which may also perform some analysis and administration. Complimenting this multitier OLAP architecture is a technical service layer that prepares the data for the OLAP database engine. This layer performs such functionality as replication, transformation, and distribution. Implementing the replication, transformation, and distribution as part of a service-based environment keeps the environment very open. It also paves the way for more interoperability between the OLTP and OLAP environments.

DATA REPLICATION SOFTWARE IN OLAP ENVIRONMENTS

When E. F. Codd coined the OLAP acronym, he also identified 12 rules for evaluating OLAP products. These rules state that OLAP products should provide such capabilities as a multidimensional conceptual view, transparency and accessibility, consistent reporting performance, dynamic sparse matrix handling, unrestricted cross-dimensional operations, and unlimited dimensions and aggregation levels. The Gartner Group added nine guidelines to Codd's original list. These additional guidelines include support for database management tools, detail (row-level) drill-down, object storage, incremental database refresh, multiple arrays, OLAP joins, subset selection, local data support, and SQL interface.[1] For the purpose of this chapter, the critical guideline is the ability to perform incremental database refresh. This can easily be supplied by a replication service.

DEFINITION OF DATA REPLICATION

Data replication is much more than simply the copying of data between data stores. It encompasses the analysis, design, implementation, administration, and monitoring of a service that guarantees data consistency across multiple resource managers in a distributed environment. In essence, it is a reusable technical service that is used to support the distributed environment of the enterprise. It should be part of the middle tier of the architecture and be implemented with enterprisewide standards. This will permit both upward and downward scalability.

APPROACHES TO ACHIEVING DATA CONSISTENCY

Approaches used to maintain data consistency are either of the synchronous or asynchronous variety. This classification is based on the amount of latency that exists before data consistency is achieved across replicas.

Synchronous Data Replication

Synchronous data replication provides what is called tight consistency between data stores. This means that the latency before data consistency is achieved is 0 (zero). Data at all replicas is always identical no matter from which replica the update originated. This can only be accomplished through a two-phase commit protocol.

Synchronous replication can be provided by DBMS software or by a distributed transaction processing (TP) monitor/transaction manager. In either case, all updating within the synchronous replication process occurs as one logical unit of work. In other words, it is an all or nothing transaction. Transactions exhibit what is called the ACID properties. ACID is an acronym for atomic, consistent, isolated, and durable. A transaction is atomic because either all its actions happen or none of them happen. A transaction is consistent because the transaction as a whole represents a correct transformation of all the resource manager(s) involved. A transaction is isolated because each transaction executes as though there are no other concurrent transactions. A transaction is durable because the effects of a committed transaction survive failures.

Whenever the business requirement demands the data consistency that only a global commit protocol can supply, then synchronous replication must be used. Distributed transaction management is the only means of ensuring real-time data consistency across n number of homogeneous and/or heterogeneous resource managers. If this tight data consistency is not a business requirement, then an asynchronous replication technique that preserves the required level of transactional integrity and sequential consistency should be considered. This lowers the cost, improves concurrency within resource managers, and generally shortens the length of the originating database transaction.

Asynchronous Data Replication

Asynchronous data replication provides what is called loose consistency between data stores. This means that the latency before data consistency is achieved is always greater than 0 (zero). In other words, the replication process occurs asynchronous to the originating transaction. There is always some degree of lag between when the originating software transaction is committed and when the effects of the transaction are available at any replica(s). If the appropriate infrastructure resources are sufficient, the latency is usually measured in seconds.

There are multiple ways of implementing asynchronous data replication. A hierarchy of the approaches and a subsequent detailed discussion of each approach follows.

Asynchronous data replication:

- Via complete or incremental refresh
- Via delta propagation of events
  - Accomplished through database-to-database communication
  - Accomplished through process-to-process communication

Complete or incremental refresh.   When a complete refresh is used to maintain data consistency, extracts from what is considered the primary data source(s) are scheduled and executed. Any data merging and transformation that may be required occurs. Finally, the target replicas are loaded. For an incremental refresh, the same processing occurs, except instead of a complete extraction from the primary source(s), only the changes that have occurred from the last extraction are collected. The assumption for any type of refresh is that this processing is of a batch nature. In batch replication, the real-time transactional nature of the originating event is usually lost. This loss of transactional identity occurs when the updated data is written to persistent storage for the start of the merge and/or transformational processing. At this time, the transactional BEGIN and transactional COMMIT is discarded. A further assumption of refresh replication is that the target is available in a single writer mode during the loading process.

Delta propagation of events.   When delta propagation of events is used for asynchronous replication, the transactional nature of the originating event is not lost. Once a target has been initialized to bring it to a consistent state with the primary source(s), only the changing events that occur at each primary source are forwarded. The event can be a software transaction or a message that represents the software transaction itself or some sub- or superset of the software transactions. This event propagation can occur either through database-to-database communication or through process-to-process communication.

Database-to-database asynchronous replication. Many of the existing vendor-supplied solutions for asynchronous replication are of the database-to-database communication type. The major reason for this is that these packages are supplied by database vendors. This type of asynchronous data replication generally has three separate and distinct components. The first component is the collection process from the primary data source; the second is the distribution process; and the third is the apply process at the designated targets. An additional component, a monitoring process for all the other processes, is also usually present. There is not a standard way that these distinct processes should be implemented. Because the technology is still new, each vendor has implemented its own strategy; however, they all have the following characteristics:

- They are implemented as middleware (i.e., a technical service type of application, with a complete or at least extremely high degree of application transparency). Application transparency is important because it allows the data used by existing applications to become part of the asynchronous replication process without changing any lines of existing application code. Depending on the vendor implementation, database objects to a greater or lesser extent may have to be altered, but the actual existing user application code need not be changed. For example, some vendors require that triggers be installed at primary source databases. Application transparency preserves the investment in existing applications and shortens the entry time into the asynchronous replication arena.

- They may provide table-to-table event-based replication and/or the replication of stored procedures.

- They preserve the transactional nature of the originating event during the collection, distribution, and apply processes.

The importance of the aforementioned preservation totally reflects the business requirements for the replication process. For most OLTP environments, the preservation of transactional semantics is critical. For the OLAP environment, in which most updating occurs as part of a batch process (i.e., refresh technology), it is not that critical. However, the designers/architects for a replication environment must have full knowledge of the originating transactions and the data sources they use. Only then can an architect define what makes a consistent whole for each target.

If transactional semantics are preserved across the replication process, then the logical unit of work that was executed as the originating transaction is also executed at the replicas. The more near real time the asynchronous replication, the more important this concept becomes. Figure 16.1 illustrates the effect of preserving transactional semantics across the asynchronous replication process.

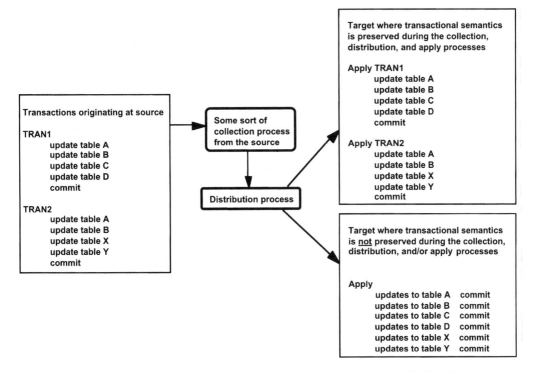

Figure 16.1   Preserving Transactional Semantics during Replication.

As can be seen in Figure 16.1, the target data where transactional semantics is preserved is always consistent transactionally with the source. No matter what cross section of tables is queried at the target, the data is always transactionally consistent. For example, if this was a banking application and a debit and a credit were part of the originating transaction, a user of the target data would always see a balanced account. Asynchronous replication, in which transactional semantics is preserved, is a must where near-real-time updating of a target occurs. It is usually used when the target site does not have the luxury of a batch window in which to apply all of the changes from the originating source(s).

It is important to note that if the originating transaction was the result of a distributed unit of work (i.e., one that updates multiple databases within the BEGIN and COMMIT scope) and the collection mechanism was a pull from the database log technique, transactional semantics will not be preserved across the replication process. For transactional semantics to be preserved across a distributed unit of work, the replication software must be able to remerge the information captured from multiple logs and then apply it at subscribing target(s) as a single unit of work. I know of no asynchronous replication product of the log pull variety that currently has this functionality. Therefore, if the business requirement is to subscribe to all the updated information from an originating distributed unit of work, then either synchronous replication or an asynchronous messaging type of replication should be used.

From a data integrity perspective, asynchronous replication, in which transactional semantics is not preserved, is only suitable for use when some sort of batch window exists for applying all the changes from all originating sources as a whole. With this type of replication, the onus for the integrity of the data at target sites falls totally on the scheduling of the updates for each target. Assume from Figure 16.1 that Tran1 and Tran2 share the same originating data source. If tables A, B, X, and Y are updated as one replication set at point in time M and tables C and D are updated later at point in time N, during the time between M and N, users see all of the results of Tran2 and one-half of the result of Tran1. This may or may not be acceptable from a business perspective.

Another variation with the same result occurs when the target subscribes to all updates from tables A, B, X, and Y, with the anticipation of receiving only the results from Tran2 updating. Since Tran1 and Tran2 share the same originating source data, their users view all of Tran2 updating plus one-half of Tran1 updating—an unexpected surprise for the target users. When transactional semantics is lost, there is no way of just applying the results of a single transaction.

The final characteristics of database-to-database asynchronous replication are as follows:

- They ensure that the distribution process provides guaranteed delivery (i.e., every database event will only be delivered once)
- They maintain some level of sequential integrity—in other words, ensures that the delivery sequence at a target matches to some extent that from the primary source(s).

Process-to-process asynchronous replication.   This type of asynchronous data replication is usually based on a publish/subscribe messaging model, which uses a store and forward mechanism. In this context, the processes involved in this asynchronous replication can be application programs or business or technical reusable services implemented within the middle tier of a multitier architecture. Process-to-process asynchronous replication has four separate and distinct components. The first component is the publish process, which is accomplished as part of the originating event. The second is the distribution process, which usually makes use of a store and forward paradigm. The third is the subscribe process, by which those other processes (i.e., applications or services) interested in the event receive the message. The fourth is the apply process, in which the receiving process performs tasks dictated by business rules defined for the receipt of that particular message. An additional component, a monitoring process for all of the other processes, is also usually present. As with database-to-database asynchronous replication, there is not a standard way that these distinct processes should be implemented. However, in general, they all have the following characteristics:

- They are implemented as middleware (i.e., a technical service type of application) and have simple APIs that are used to send and receive messages. Since APIs are used by sending and receiving processes, it is obvious that process-to-process asynchronous replication is not application transparent. The application code for new or legacy systems must contain calls to the put API to publish a message and to the get API to retrieve messages. In addition, the receiving process must contain code to handle the message it retrieves (i.e., the apply code, which reflects the business requirements for receipt of this particular message).

- They support multiple message formats such as fixed format (e.g., IBM COBOL records), delimited format (e.g., C null delimited strings), variable format, and self-describing messages.

- They provide publish/subscribe with transactional integrity (i.e., provide persistent storage for messages that are integrated with the transaction management of the sending and receiving processes).

The latter is extremely critical. It ensures that messages are not committed to the delivery systems until the sender commits a transaction, and that messages are not considered delivered until the receiver commits a transaction. This is called preserving transactional state. Since messages are committed by the message delivery system when a sender commits a transaction that includes one or more messages, the delivery system state matches the sender's transactional state. Likewise, since messages are considered delivered when a receiver obtains one or more messages and commits a transaction, the message delivery system matches the receiver's state. The ACID properties of transactions are preserved at both sending and receiving processes. See Figure 16.2 for an illustration of what could happen if transactional integrity was not preserved.

The final characteristics of process-to-process asynchronous replication are as follows:

- They ensure that the delivery process provides guaranteed delivery (i.e., every message will only be delivered once).

- They maintain some level of sequential integrity.

When to Use Each Approach

As stated earlier, whenever the tight data consistency of synchronous replication (i.e., two-phase commit processing) is not demanded by the business requirement, then an asynchronous replication technique is best. This lowers the cost, improves concurrency within resource managers, and generally shortens the length of the originating database transaction.

OLAP environments generally do not demand the tight data consistency provided by synchronous replication. Therefore, an asynchronous replication approach

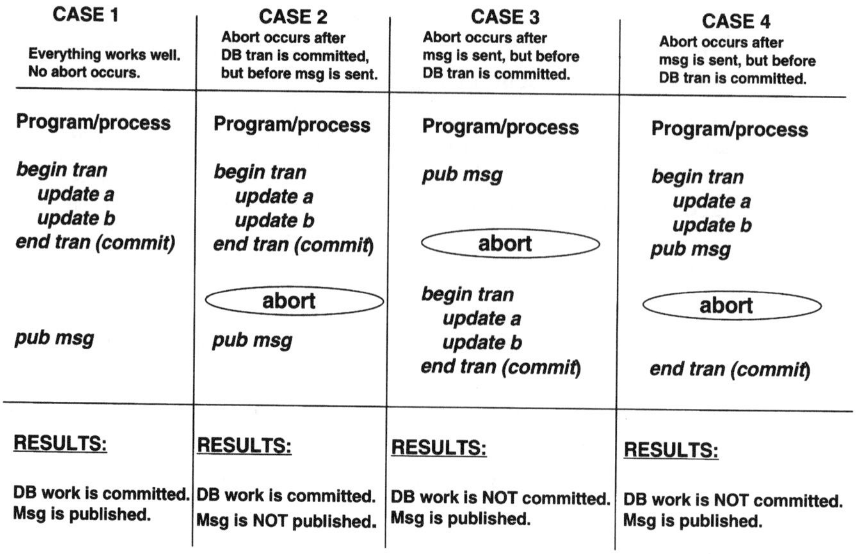

CASE 1	CASE 2	CASE 3	CASE 4
Everything works well. No abort occurs.	Abort occurs after DB tran is committed, but before msg is sent.	Abort occurs after msg is sent, but before DB tran is committed.	Abort occurs after msg is sent, but before DB tran is committed.
Program/process	**Program/process**	**Program/process**	**Program/process**
begin tran *update a* *update b* *end tran (commit)*	*begin tran* *update a* *update b* *end tran (commit)*	*pub msg*	*begin tran* *update a* *update b* *pub msg*
		‹abort›	
	‹abort›	*begin tran* *update a* *update b* *end tran (commit)*	‹abort›
pub msg	*pub msg*		*end tran (commit)*
<u>RESULTS:</u>	<u>RESULTS:</u>	<u>RESULTS:</u>	<u>RESULTS:</u>
DB work is committed. Msg is published.	DB work is committed. Msg is NOT published.	DB work is NOT committed. Msg is published.	DB work is NOT committed. Msg is published.

Figure 16.2   Undesirable Outcomes Associated with Lack of Transactional Integrity between Database Updates and Message Infrastructure.

is the best choice. When deciding between the various asynchronous approaches, the following rules apply:

- The more near real time the requirement for data consistency, the more an event propagation type of asynchronous replication is appropriate.
- The more batch oriented the environment with a relaxed data consistency requirement, the more a refresh type of asynchronous replication is appropriate.

Important Issues to Consider when Using Asynchronous Replication

1. The asynchronous replication solution that is chosen must support the appropriate level of transactional semantics or transactional integrity. With a refresh type of asynchronous replication, all transaction demarcation is lost. With database-to-database event propagation, full transactional integrity is usually preserved across the collection, distribution, and apply portions of the asynchronous replication. However, an open issue is the handling of distributed units of work at a replica. With process-to-process event propagation, information about the originating event, which is either a software transaction or a sub- or superset of software transactions, is received and applied by a subscribing replica. The critical issue here is that transactional integrity exists between the message queues and the sending and receiving processes.

2. The asynchronous replication solution that is chosen must support the appropriate level of sequential integrity. Since all transaction demarcation is lost with the refresh type of asynchronous replication, all sequencing of originating events is also lost. The refresh occurs in batch and brings the replica to a more current point in time (i.e., a more current snapshot). With both database-to-database event propagation and process-to process event propagation, sequencing is an issue. There are multiple publishers of events with numerous entry points into the queuing and distribution systems of the replication process. Distribution occurs asynchronously and is composed of many distributed components. Networks may be slower at some publishers versus others, and individual collection or distribution components may be in a failed state or just simply slow due to lack of sufficient CPU resources. However, the assumption with event propagation is that the apply process is always executing at each replica. Once an event is applied, it cannot be unapplied to alter its sequence with respect to other events. Therefore, the sequencing that is generally maintained is the originating sequence for all events published from within each individual publisher. They are applied in a first-in, first-out queue at a replica. There is no simple way to ensure sequential integrity across all publishing sites for a given replica in an asynchronous environment.

    3. Conflict detection and resolution mechanisms are used. There are two ways to distribute data and assign ownership when data is stored redundantly. The first is a master/slave model, and the second is an update anywhere model sometimes referred to as peer-to-peer replication or symmetric replication. For OLAP replication, the model most often used is the master/slave model in which the OLTP environment is the master and the OLAP environment is the slave. However, it is important to note that if the OLTP environment permits an update anywhere model and then uses those replicas as input into asynchronous replication to the OLAP environment, some sort of conflict detection and resolution mechanism might be necessary.

    In a master/slave model, each individual piece of data has only one designated master (i.e., updatable replica) at any given point in time. Therefore, all update activity occurs at that designated master, and all update conflicts for that data element are avoided. With peer-to-peer replication, there is no designated master for any individual data element. Any replica can be used as the updatable source at any point in time. When asynchronous replication is used, the conflicts are determined after the fact and are resolved at the target replica(s). Rules are applied at a target to aid with the resolution. A rule might be to apply updates in a fashion in which the target always reflects the most current data based on the timestamp of the originating changes. Another rule might be to apply updates so that the target reflects the update that occurred at the prioritized replica. Whichever rules are used, the fact is that users of the data are not seeing a globally consistent state. Yes, compensating transactions can be issued to resynchronize all replicas, but other updating transactions were entered based on these earlier data values. This may or may not present a problem for a firm. It totally depends on the business requirements and associated risks for that firm. If it was an airlines reservation system and flights were overbooked, the airline need only issue free tickets for future flights. If it was an investment banking system managing global risk, the firm could be in jeopardy. The critical issue is that resolution schemes are complex and present integrity risks to users. Weigh the alternatives carefully before peer-to-peer asynchronous replication is implemented.

TOOLS THAT AID WITH MAINTAINING DATA CONSISTENCY

Many vendor products are available that supply replication services. The objective is to solve the business problem for achieving data consistency with the best available tool. The following evaluation criteria should help in the decision process.

Evaluation Criteria for Replication Software Selection

The following list is a good starting point for the evaluation process. The list is not completely exhaustive since every firm is unique and will have specialized requirements. Each firm should modify this list and assign weights to reflect their specific requirements.

Architectural Criteria

1. Is the replication solution architected as middleware whose purpose is to provide data replication services? In other words, does the solution integrate well into a multitier architecture?
2. Is distribution transparency supported? Do applications need to know the location of an object?
3. How transparent are the interface(s) to the resource managers involved in the replication process? Do resource managers have to be altered in order to participate in the replication process? If yes, how easy is it to do and to undo?
4. How transparent are the interface(s) to the application code that use the resource managers involved in the replication process? Does application code have to be altered in order to participate in the replication process? If yes, how easy is it to do and to undo?
5. How industry compliant is the replication solution? For example, does it use DCE security, DCE naming services, and the like? DCE is the Distributed Computing Environment as defined by the Open Software Foundation (OSF). It is a set of integrated services that works across multiple systems and yet remains independent of any single system. Does it support both XA and non-XA compliant resource managers? XA is a component of X/Open Distributed Transaction Processing (DTP) standards as they relate to the interfaces between a resource manager and a transaction manager.
6. How robust are the security implementations? Who can use the functionality of the replication software? What IDs and passwords are stored? Where are they stored? Are they encrypted? What IDs and passwords are used on the

resource managers to alter the data? How is network security integrated with the replication software?

7. Does the product fail in a manner that protects other components in the environment?

8. Are there centralized facilities that represent bottlenecks in a distributed environment?

Functionality Criteria

1. Is the product scalable? With respect to replication, scalability means the ability to replicate both small and large volumes of data across heterogeneous resource managers. What resource managers can be used as primary sources and/or targets?

2. What functionality is available to handle data transformation and mapping so that source and target data schemata need not match?

3. For asynchronous data replication, is there a scheduling mechanism? This is most applicable for targets but may also be applicable for primary sources depending on what mechanism is used to capture the changes.

4. How friendly is the provided mechanism to describe the data and/or objects that are to be replicated?

5. How friendly is the provided mechanism to subscribe to the data and/or objects that are available for replication?

6. How easy is it to implement transformation and mapping services?

7. How easy is it to initialize a target (i.e., initially get a target in synchronized with its primary source[s])?

8. What quality of service is provided? For example, is data delivery guaranteed? Are precautions taken to ensure that data is not corrupted during the replication process?

9. Is there a log mechanism that records any failed replication effort(s)?

10. For refresh type of asynchronous replication, is any concurrent access available during the refresh process? What locking granularity is used (i.e., page, table, or row)? How fast is the load process? Can the load process be restarted in cases of failure?

11. For the database-to-database event type of asynchronous replication, is the appropriate level of transactional integrity preserved throughout the replication process? Does it support the apply of a distributed unit of work as a single transaction (i.e., the merging of extractions from multiple logs)? Does it support transaction nesting?

12. For the process-to-process event type of asynchronous replication, is transactional integrity preserved between the update of the resource manager and the insert/removal of the message from the persistent storage used for queuing?

13. For the event type of asynchronous replication, what type of sequential integrity is preserved throughout the replication process?

14. What metadata with respect to the replication process is available to designated users? For example, for each target, identify each data element's primary source and data latency level.

Administration Criteria

SYSTEMS MANAGEMENT

1. *Configuration:* How simple is the replication software configuration process? Can the system be dynamically reconfigured?

2. *Monitoring:* Is there a GUI (graphical user interface) monitoring tool for the entire replication environment? How does the replication monitoring tool integrate with the existing monitoring infrastructure of the firm?

3. *Performance monitoring:* Is there performance reporting?

4. *Error management:* Is there an error log?

5. *Shutdown:* How is emergency shutdown handled? Can the replication system be quiesced?

RESOURCE MANAGEMENT

1. *Space management:* How efficient is the queuing mechanism for the replication process?

2. *CPU:* How efficient is the subscription resolution engine for the replication process?

3. *Network:* Is the replication process well behaved with respect to network utilization?

4. *Access management:* What are the supported access protocols?

CHANGE MANAGEMENT FOR REPLICATION SOFTWARE

1. How easy is it to apply upgrades and fixes to the replication system software?

2. For new release migrations, must all components migrate to the new release level at the same time? Can multiple release levels coexist within the same replication environment?

CHANGE MANAGEMENT FOR RESOURCE MANAGERS INVOLVED IN THE REPLICATION PROCESS

1. What tasks must be executed when the DDL of a primary source is altered? Are utilities provided that aid with the change process?

2. What tasks must be executed when the DDL of a target is altered? Are utilities provided that aid with the change process?

RECOVERY

1. Is there an automatic recovery mechanism that provides recovery after specific types of failures?

2. Do components fail safely (i.e., do not affect other components when they fail)?

3. What type of data reconciliation facility is available? This can be used to validate the replication process and to resynchronize source and target sites after a failure.

Vendor/Market Forces

1. How viable is the vendor? What is the financial health of the company? What is the size of the company? Is it public or privately held?

2. What is the market share?

3. What do industry analysts such as Gartner, Forrester, and Seybold say with respect to this vendor?

Implementing Replication as an Enterprise Service

As defined earlier, a replication service provides a complete copy management facility in a distributed heterogeneous environment. This is not an easy task. It demands an architectural effort and the necessary support infrastructure. This can be accomplished from either a top-down or a bottom-up approach, but it does require strategic planning. If an enterprise service perspective is not used, a firm might successfully implement replication for a small number of isolated applications but fail when it attempts to implement replication on an enterprisewide scale.

Using a service approach for replication, even on the first small replication effort, ensures that the following are addressed:

- Replication will remain open. By *open*, it means that the service be architected to allow multiple vendor products and home-grown applications to be part of the total solution.
- Replication will be scalable (i.e., be able to support a heterogeneous database environment with small and large volumes of data transfer across a heterogeneous network environment, with minimal impact on any of the resources involved).
- Replication will be easily and consistently administered.

CASE STUDY OF A SUCCESSFUL GLOBAL IMPLEMENTATION

A global investment banking institution needed to implement a decision support system that would allow users to query the results of the international trading environment and support leading-edge technologies, such as data mining and data visualization.

Assumptions and requirements regarding the environment are as follows:

- All read-only reference data needed to validate and complete trades is maintained by legacy systems on a mainframe in New York. This reference data is replicated to all locations where trade information is stored locally.

- Decisions on whether to store OLTP trade data locally at any particular trading branch are made on an individual basis. Factors that influenced the decision are regulatory issues specific to the country of that branch, number of traders and trade volume generated from that branch, and administrative support level and skill set available for that branch. As other branches are added to the organization or as trade volumes grow, the data distribution issue is readdressed.

- All back-office trade processing occurs in one of three international hubs. The locations of these hubs are New York, which services both North and South America; London, which services all of Europe; and Tokyo, which services the Far East and Australia.

- Results of all trades are forwarded to the appropriate regional center for back-office processing and subsequently forwarded to the headquarters in New York. All global positions and risk are maintained in near real time in New York and adjusted after back-office processing at each regional center.

- The OLAP environment stores all details and appropriate summary information to meet performance requirements. It is centrally stored in New York, with appropriate slices replicated to the hubs in London and Tokyo. The OLAP environment is used not only for decision support but also for data mining, data visualization, and other leading-edge analysis.

- Data distribution and replication services for OLTP and OLAP must be scalable and flexible to support future directions with respect to mobile computing.

Architecture

Both OLTP and OLAP client/server environments are migrating away from a two-tier architecture into a three- or more-tier architecture. In a two-tier architecture, both the presentation and application logic reside on the client. The server only runs the database system. The database systems used throughout the firm are RDBMSs supplied by IBM and Sybase. The existing two-tier applications do not scale well. The maximum number of users that can be supported is around 100 simultaneous users.

As a result, a three-tier architecture is being used for all new development. This architecture partitions an application into three distinct segments. These include the GUI, presentation logic, application business logic, and data access layer. In this model, the application business logic resides in the middle tier, sometimes called the application server layer. It is possible to have some of this business logic span multiple servers and/or clients. The presentation tier still resides on the client, and the data access layer still resides on the data server. This multi-tier architecture improves application scalability and encourages reuse of the middle logic tier. The reuse of code applies to both application business services and technical services. Reuse is planned for the technical services of data replication and data transformation.

Building the Infrastructure

Placement of components. Figure 16.3 shows the OLTP environment. Replication components—for example, LTMs (log transfer managers), which pull committed transaction information from data server logs—were placed on the same LAN as the data server logs that they use as input. Replication servers were placed at WAN hubs. Since the quantity of data being transferred to and from Frankfurt was small, its replication server connection was to a replication server in London. This also simplified administration. Figure 16.4 represents the OLAP environment. The replication infrastructure developed for use in the OLAP environment was architected to reuse the existing components already used for OLTP environments. Data hubs for OLAP were placed in New York, London, and Tokyo. Since the number of OLAP users in Frankfurt is small, they do remote data access to data stored in London.

Replication Data Flows. Read-only reference data is replicated near real time from the DB2 mainframe in New York to all front offices, where trade data is permanently stored. After a trade is entered, trade data is replicated to the appro-

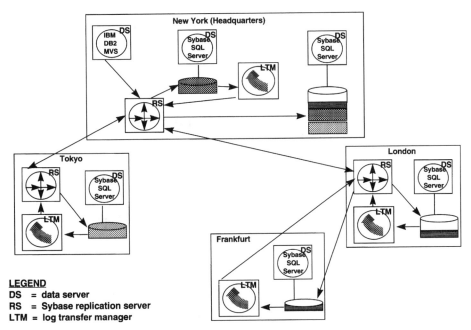

Figure 16.3 OLTP Environment.

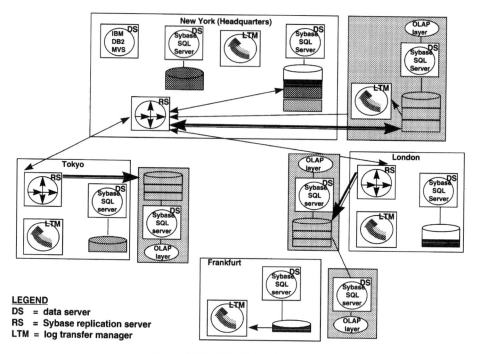

Figure 16.4   OLAP Environment.

priate back office, where further validations and back-office processing occurs. In addition, position and risk data is replicated to New York for day-in-progress analysis and alerts. Final end-of-day positions and risk data are forwarded to New York after each region finishes its end-of-day back-office processing. Use of an asynchronous approach for replication from judiciously distributed data stores ensures a high degree of performance and availability.

Data Transformation and Mapping Services.   A high degree of data transformation and mapping services was integrated into the replication process for the OLAP environment. The transformational services included

- The altering of data types for situations in which the data types between primary and target types did not match.
- The altering of data content to ensure that all data marts represented code values identically. For example, in human resource data the gender code was stored as a single character, with "F" representing female and "M" representing male.
- The denormalization to improve query performance. Summary totals were created, and the replication service updated these new data elements in addition to the raw detail fields. For example, financial balances were created that stored monthly and quarterly totals.

Vendor Products Utilized for Replication

The vendor selected to supply the replication service for OLAP was Sybase's Replication Server™. It was already in use for data replication in the OLTP environment; therefore, the physical and administrative support infrastructure was already established. Sybase offers replication services to IBM's DB2™ and Sybase's SQL Server™ and SQL Anywhere™ DBMSs. These are the existing and strategic platforms identified for the firm. In addition the replication software is architected so that function requests are separate from how the requests are implemented. This allows extensibility. We used this extensibility to incorporate extensive data transformation and mapping services. The replication server function strings were altered to invoke stored procedures that performed the necessary data transformation and mappings.

REFERENCES

[1] GARTNER GROUP, *On-Line Analytic Processing: Getting the Most from the Data Warehouse*, Vol. XI, No. 4, M. Light, January 25, 1995.

VLDBs and Parallelism

17

Richard Yevich
RYC, Inc.
Key Biscayne, Florida

"Any sufficiently advanced technology is indistinguishable from magic."

Arthur C. Clarke, The Lost Worlds of 2001

Data warehouses in support of information processing are in the forefront of the movement toward massive data stores (VLDBs are very large databases). Warehouses measured in the terabytes (1 terabyte = 1000 gigabytes) are in production systems that will be dwarfed by the amount of data in warehouse systems. One warehouse being constructed for data mining will be in the range of 300 to 400 terabytes. Another system will be adding over 150 gigabytes per month to its warehouse. Information data stores, as warehouses, by their very nature require vast amounts of storage. Planning for growth to over 1 petabyte (1 petabyte = 1,000,000 gigabytes) is under way, though that size is difficult to comprehend.

To keep growth size in perspective, in 1990 a 50-GB (gigabytes) database with relational tables holding 1 million rows was considered a VLDB (note: 5 GB was considered a VLDB on the open systems market). By 1992, single operational databases were approaching 300 gigabytes and 50 million rows, and shortly thereafter 100 million rows appeared followed by the famous VLDB installation at UPS (United Parcel Service) of 3.6 TB (terabytes). Warehouse data for detail analysis stores information over time, not just for the operational cycle data. The aforementioned data stores contain operational cycle data. Multiply these numbers by the number of cycles to be maintained plus the added information and redundancy necessary, and VLDBs of 100 TB are short term, with petabyte VLDBs becoming more common before the millennium changes. These VLDBs are the basis for data mining—the ability over time to look at all the details to find trends and patterns that allow a business to adjust its practices to become more profitable. (Refer to Chapter 23 for more details on data mining.)

The industry has progressed from gigabytes to terabytes in operational systems with relational databases in five years. Detail warehouses are a factor larger than operational. It is therefore conceivable that an exabyte warehouse (1000 petabytes or 1,000,000 terabytes or 1,000,000,000 gigabytes) will be in existence before the year 2000. IBM has modified its DB2 relational database to support a 1-TB relational table.

A major impact of this sizing is constantly overlooked: the object data stores that will become warehoused, and object data that is already measured in single columns of up to 2 GB, for both textual and binary data. This could affect the size of warehouses by a factor of hundreds of millions (terabyte to petabyte to exabyte to zettabyte to yottabyte). Data mining is in its infancy, as are VLDBs to support the mines. Handling growth, developing new design strategies, and improving performance become more complex, not less.

THE PROCESSING

Data mining applications using these large warehouses are leading the movement toward parallel processing. Through the early 1990s, machines with many processors were used for simple multiprocessing and not true parallelism. Parallel processing was limited to very specific machines used in niche environments. With the advent of generally available SMP and MPP platforms (see the subsequent section on parallel solution), the processing requirements of the VLDBs for data mining and other complex queries could be achieved.

Data mining for pattern analysis and trend analysis requires significant processing power. With the very large data stores, the need exists to search through huge amounts of data to produce the desired results. The ability to solve complex queries by putting multiple engines to work is a mandatory requirement. The parallel technology, while critical for the complex queries, is required for loading the large VLDBs, performing backups, repartitioning data across the nodes, and handling all the normal database utility requirements. (These strategies will be examined in detail in the subsequent section on parallel solution.)

THE DATABASE MANAGEMENT SYSTEM

RDBMSs are being used to integrate the user and the information through both internal parallelism in their respective engines and through tight integration with parallel hardware platforms. Until recently, these trends toward large databases and parallelism outpaced existing technology in terms of storage and processor power. Even the largest single mainframe computers do not have the power and the I/O bandwidth necessary for the very complex warehouse databases and the complex queries associated with data mining. (The section entitled "DBMS Parallel Strategies," which appears later in this chapter, focuses on this.)

THE PARALLEL SOLUTION

Parallel systems available today offer the advantage of the wider I/O bandwidth and more processing power by integrating multiple processors to focus on a single task. There are two basic types of parallelism: SMP and MPP. SMP covers everything from dual-processor PC servers to large servers with any number of processors, with each server sharing all other components (memory, disk). MPP systems basically are interconnected independent nodes (computers), with each having processor(s), memory, and disk.

Parallel systems are built today using primarily three different approaches with two different methods of hardware architecture. These approaches have many different names, but Figure 17.1 shows the most common and relates many of the common terms to the appropriate architecture.

There are only two approaches to solving the application problems. The first, in which all the servers share all the data, is called shared memory architecture. The second, in which each server has its own portion, or partition, of the data, is called shared nothing architecture. The primary difference in approaches is the power required and scalability. Shared memory has been implemented using many different architectures based on SMP and shared memory clusters. Shared nothing has been implemented with many proprietary approaches, ranging from special proprietary hardware to connection of standard processors, normally using a UNIX-type interface.

SMP has limitations today due to the sharing of other components, including the database, while MPP can use hundreds of nodes, each owning a partition of the entire database. The trend today is moving away from strictly SMP, in which the concern is the number of CPUs, to architecture approaches involving the connection of multiple machines/servers into a "single" solution. In this architecture, the individual nodes, or machines/servers, could each be an SMP server or a cluster of SMP servers appearing as a single SMP server. The terms lose meaning, but the important approach is utilizing individual components, interconnected to solve a problem. It is not of primary importance what comprises an individual component, node, or server. Each individual component, in reality, could be a large interconnection of nodes.

Formal Term	Also Called	Structure	Architecture	Details
Shared memory	Shared everything	Tightly coupled	SMP	Many processors, shared memory, shared data
Shared disk	Shared data	Loosely coupled	SMP	Many processor nodes, global shared memory, shared data
Shared nothing	Partitioned data	Noncoupled	MPP	Many individual processors each with owned memory and owned data

Figure 17.1   The Most Common Parallel Systems.

229

Most DBMSs have been enhanced to use available machine parallelism. Parallelism has been implemented as an internal process with some DBMSs, and others have been integrated using the SMP/MPP platforms. These new DBMS engines are necessary to implement the very large databases (VLDBs) and handle the complex queries, often called OLCP for on-line complex processing. The parallel processing is used to decompose large complex queries and run the separate components simultaneously, reassembling the results at the end of the process. (Note: Parallelism has many other applications other than warehouse, but the focus here is complex queries and data mining for warehouses.)

The parallel DBMSs today can be used for both parallel OLTP (on-line teleprocessing) systems and parallel DSS, but the prime use of parallel DBMSs is for DSS and warehouse application processing. DBMSs have been built focusing on a particular style of parallel processing, actually targeting different segments of the industry. There are DBMSs implemented solely for the SMP platforms, while others have been designed for the MPP platforms. The difficulty arises in that warehouse processing differs in requirements, just as the scope of warehouse ranges from enterprisewide to departmental (enterprise servers to smaller local servers). The physical design of the database, especially the enterprisewide VLDBs, is completely different, depending on whether the design is for an SMP implementation or an MPP implementation.

MPP architectures represent the highest end of parallelism. To get a proper focus on this, the others need to be examined because MPPs of the future will be based on a combination of clusters of SMP machines. Each node might be an SMP parallel machine, with all of the nodes working as a higher-level SMP or MPP "machine," until the point at which names are meaningless.

SMP Defined

SMP is an architecture that involves a limited number of processors sharing common memory. More processors can be added to a configuration until contention either on the shared memory or on the path to the shared memory prevents any further benefit. Most of the SMP servers available today are built with four to eight processors. Increased scalability and performance are achieved by special proprietary software or hardware or optimization algorithms. Gains may be realized by replacing older processors with newer, more powerful processors, but there are always limits between balancing the processing power and the shared memory access.

SMP is the easiest to use. Since the scalability involves approaches that deal with the configuration internally on the server, applications are not affected and databases do not require redesigning. This is critical in warehouses. Any requirement to change the physical structure of the database involves large volumes of data and consumes unacceptable amounts of time. In SMP, the parallelism is achieved by the operating system and the DBMS in thread management, having no impact on either the design of the application or the database. The database design in this environment is built strictly on the requirements of the particular warehouse or mining application. While there is no theoretical limit to the number of processors in an SMP environment, there are real-world limitations. SMP has a basic theoretical limit to its usefulness, and a limit can be reached when adding more processors has no advantage. However, SMP machines exist with up to 96 processors, but most in use are built around 12 to 16 processors.

MPP

MPP is an architecture that generally refers to the shared nothing approach, in which each processor has its own memory and its own data—basically an independent processor with a privately owned partition of the data. The only component shared in this environment is the communication network, which connects all the independent processors. There are two areas of complexity in this approach. First is the problem of the DBMS vendor, and second is the problem of the physical database designer.

The DBMS vendor must develop entirely different strategies to accommodate the partitioning of the database. The relational access language, SQL, must have its queries broken up (rewritten) into discrete subsets and then sent to the different nodes in the system, where the data that satisfies the subset request exists, and then merge all the data from the subsets into a final solution. The DBMS must also support distributed deadlock detection and multiphase commit protocol.

The user difficulty with the MPP approach is effective physical database design that can be continually scaled without a major redesign effort and still satisfy the performance requirements. The designs for warehouses are considerably different from designs for operational systems, and warehouse physical design can be considerably different between SMP and MPP systems. In an MPP system, the entire database structure is split into discrete partitions, with each partition on an independent node.

SMP and MPP Combinations

The second generation of SMP is based on shared memory clusters. Shared memory clusters are single-processor complexes built by interconnecting multiple logical SMP machines. This is simply a hierarchical structuring of hardware platforms. The lower-end approach is to build SMP superservers out of an interconnection of four clusters, with each cluster containing four processors sharing memory. This is the approach some vendors have taken with the Intel Pentium Pro™ four-processor SMP board (1996).

On the high end is the sysplex approach, using an interconnection of cluster-based machines, with each cluster employing multiple processors, and then using another cluster as the shared memory. It is logical to believe that someday we may see each large sysplex as nothing more than a single node in a multinode shared nothing environment. For example, this type of SMP structuring at the high end is the IBM sysplex environment. Currently up to 32 machines can be interconnected, with each of the machines built around a shared memory cluster of 10 CPUs. This structure is integrated with DBMSs that can split a query to run on any of the processors. In this example, 320 processors across 32 machines are working on a single query against a single database. Other examples of combined structuring of SMP/MPP occur when each node in a shared nothing environment (MPP) is an SMP machine—perhaps an unlimited architecture, always upward scalable.

Each of the three architectures with two variations can be diagrammed as shown in Figures 17.2 through 17.5. Each of the architectures has distinct advantages and disadvantages.

This structure supports large shared VLDBs, where each computer is an SMP processor using a global shared memory between all the individual computers. An example of this is the IBM sysplex using DB2 data sharing to support the VLDB. This parallel structure is technically referred to as NUMA (non-uniform memory architecture).

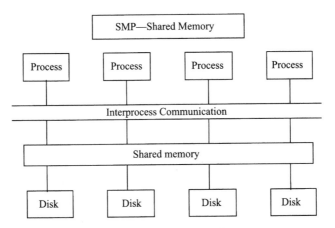

Figure 17.2   Shared Memory Structure.

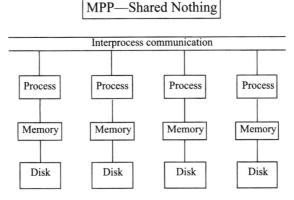

Figure 17.3   Shared Nothing Structure.

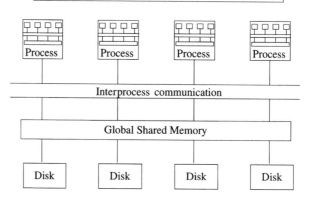

Figure 17.4 Shared Memory Structure in which Each Processor is a Shared Memory Structure.

MPP Parallel System of SMP Processors

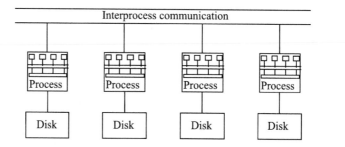

Figure 17.5 MPP Shared Nothing Systems Also Use SMP Processors in Place of Single CPU Processors.

SHARED MEMORY SYSTEMS

Advantages

- Easier to administer
- Standard systems management tools
- Easier DBMS implementations
- Standard database design strategies

Disadvantages

- Interprocess communication problems

- Limited scalability
- Interprocess lock contention

SHARED NOTHING SYSTEMS

Advantages

- Can linearly scale up to hundreds of processors
- No shared memory access bottleneck
- No processor interconnection bottleneck
- No shared disk access bottleneck

Disadvantages

- Difficult to administer
- Systems management tools more complex
- Relational DBMS query access optimization
- Distributed deadlock detection
- Multiphase commit protocol

DBMS PARALLEL STRATEGIES

Most DBMSs have full support for the basic SMP architecture of multiple processors and shared memory. Incorporating support for shared memory clusters and shared nothing approaches requires additional architecting of the internal engines. Some DBMSs are based solely on the shared disk architecture, and others are built on the shared nothing architecture. It is difficult to get a DBMS built for a shared disk architecture to function on a shared nothing hardware platform without additional specialized code. The performance and scalability would be limited.

Warehouse use should determine what platform and DBMS is best suited for the application. Enterprisewide warehouses for data mining have different metrics from data marts or distributed warehouses (subsets of enterprisewide systems). A major factor often overlooked in building warehouses is the additional access required for legacy systems. If the criteria for trend analysis for a corporatewide strategy involves access to legacy data by any of the accepted practices, then a logical approach could be a large SMP approach built on shared memory clusters, such as a high-end CMOS mainframe (technically a larger server). If the criterion was for geographical areas with distinct business patterns, then the design could be for separate and distinct servers. If the criterion was for analyzing all the data over 10 years to locate associate buying patterns based on demographic conditions, a large shared nothing approach would probably be the best choice. In all these cases there are simply "best choice" and "second best choice," as any platform can work on just about any type of application, with the major dependency being performance criteria.

The decision for DBMS and database design for VLDBs using parallelism requires difficult decisions on at least the following criteria:

1. Enterprisewide or distributed
2. Data mining or decision support
3. Large number of concurrent users or light use
4. Time frame requirements for data storage
5. Support staff
6. Value to business
7. Data source
8. Legacy data access
9. Data mining methods.

None of these criteria determine which platform to use, and in many cases any of the platforms can work. However, enterprisewide VLDBs for intensive complex queries (data mining) probably will function best on either the modified SMP using connected memory clusters (sysplex) or the shared nothing approach. Simple SMP quickly fades as the size of the database increases and as the queries become more frequent or more complex. The basic SMP machines are adequate for the regional or distributed warehouses, as long as the data size that the machine and DBMS can support is understood. There are many cases of an SMP approach being quickly surpassed by the system requirements and having to be completely restructured for a shared nothing environment.

MPP SHARED NOTHING DATABASE

For unlimited growth and scalability, the MPP architecture and the DBMSs that support the shared nothing approach appear to be the best choice for large VLDBs of details that need to be mined. The bottlenecks of shared memory and shared data are avoided. The shared nothing approach offers the potential of infinite scalability. In reality, however, this is a very difficult issue. The generally accepted criteria for MPP direction is query complexity, warehouse database size, and growth potential. Major impacts are also the number of concurrent users, frequency of queries, support staff, and knowledge. Shared nothing databases cannot be designed simply, and data sourcing and loading are difficult problems. The big benefit occurs if the database is designed properly and clusters and processors can be added as needed without sacrificing the existing hardware and software (something done too often in the past with operational systems).

Database Partitioning

Most relational DBMSs are being rearchitected to support the shared nothing environment, providing extensions to the SQL language necessary to allow users to control the placement of the database across the machines, "the partitioning definition." The data placement design is separate from the physical database design in support of the application. First, there is database design to support the warehouse (which has been covered in detail elsewhere in this book). Second there is database design as it relates to database partitioning, data row assignment, and individual table distribution.

Individual table distribution has been referred to as the opposite of clustering, declustering. In a relational system, we cluster data based on range retrieval. In a shared nothing environment, we will decluster the data, across either all the nodes or some of the nodes. The most common design mistake is the assumption that all data must be partitioned across all the nodes. This simply is not true or necessary. Flexibility in designing for performance is most often achieved by not fully partitioning a table. Maximum flexibility in design is achieved by partially partitioning tables and related tables across nodes, without interfering with other tables and table sets partitioned across the other nodes. (The number of nodes that a table is spread over is called the degree of parallelism.) The determination of the degree of parallelism on a table or set of related tables is the most difficult design decision.

The degree of parallelism is selected first, followed by the method of partitioning data over the number of degrees selected. For example, if we selected 10 nodes to support the table set, we have to determine the method to distribute the data over 10 nodes. The most common method for partitioning the data is either by selecting physical ranges based on column(s) from the table, or by using a hash algorithm again based on column(s) from the table. Hashing would be required to get a predictable distribution of data when ranges would not be evenly distributed. Range partitioning is difficult to design and implement, particularly since the values of the column supporting the ranges tend to change as new data is added and old data is archived. Hash partitioning should not have that problem. The only difficulty with the hash methods involves the database designer determining the data to be used by the hash algorithm.

The goal in partitioning for the shared nothing environment is to have the appropriate amounts of data in the proper number of partitions. In a warehouse that is being mined, an equal amount of data could be on each partition to achieve the best performance and growth. In a warehouse for decision support, often the queries go mostly against current and near current data, while older data requires a less frequent access. In these cases, larger data partitions might be assigned for the older data while smaller partitions are designed for the new and near-term data. Most DBMSs allow control of the percentage of rows based on the partitioning method to be placed on specific partitions. The minor difficulty in a warehouse is to ensure that it is logically designed for the type of application (see other chapters in this book for details on warehouse design). Once there is a solid logical design, the physical design can be done with great planning and understanding. In many information data stores, there is redundancy of data, which can affect the partitioning schemes. The choice of the data for the partitioning methods should be based on both distribution and collocating joins between related data.

Data Loading

For VLDBs that are built on shared nothing platforms, it is advisable to design the database so that DBMS-supplied utilities can load in parallel. It is extremely difficult to write application load processes that can effectively load in parallel. Inserts from an application proceed at a single step; therefore, applications would have to be developed to build and load the warehouse data, in parallel, by discrete ranges. If the method was hashing, then this is a very difficult strategy, as the hash must first be determined, requiring passing all the data first to determine the hash value and node number in order to split the input by nodes. Also, the insert mechanisms of the DBMS are used, and most DBMSs or vendor-supplied utilities can preformat the data into the internal format required and lay them onto the storage medium.

Database Maintenance

All the normal database maintenance functions are still required in a shared nothing environment along with some new functions. Repartitioning utilities are specific for this environment and are necessary if the selected method of partitioning or the number of degrees change. Data is often loaded in what appears to be an evenly selected database, only to find after loading that the data is heavily skewed. Normally, this can be predetermined for initial loading of the warehouse, but as data is added, as new information columns are added, the distribution of data can change. Redistribution is then required and vendor-supplied utilities should be used to control this function. Initially, redistribution seems like a simple strategy. However, in a relational warehouse there are many related tables, each table participating in the redistribution. Vendor utilities can also take into consideration the related set problem.

PUTTING IT TOGETHER

VLDBs and parallelism are the direction for the future. Warehouses today that support detail information and tomorrow subject areas, and those that support object information, will all result in VLDBs. The accessing of these VLDBs will require parallelism. Today this appears to be MPP, but in the future parallelism will be based on SMP clusters in a hierarchy of SMP or MPP platforms. Operational systems will also require parallelism, as the normal path is the growth cycle. It is not of primary importance to know how parallelism works, but to understand the two different styles of sharing or not sharing data.

The massive VLDBs will probably require the new 1-terabyte tables that are being implemented in the DBMS engines at this time. The limits of 32 and 64 across all vendors, those magic numbers, will begin to become 128 and 1024—number of processors, clusters, connections—whatever. To implement the VLDB warehouse, do nothing different from what we have always done: risk analysis,

Future: MPP Parallel System of SMP Sytems Comprised of SMP Processors

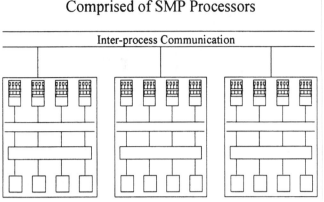

Figure 17.6

planning, understanding the business requirements, and then picking the architecture and the platform.

Figure 17.6 shows the potential for massive parallel systems processing very large amounts of data and handling unlimited numbers of users. It is probable that in the future, large SMP structures using SMP processors will act as a single node in large MPP shared nothing environments. There is no theoretical upper limit to scalability in this structure.

SUMMARY

Nothing is stand-alone. All this data needs to be integrated at some level, even if it is simply through access tools. Look at the Internet today, in which a single user goes wandering off into a vast empire of information, all unrelated and yet all related. The Internet is a VLDB of information that allows us to access it either directly or though searches of connections provided by sophisticated indexes. No one has yet performed an Internet scan, or database sweep, accidentally of all the information stored in the entire Net. Individual nodes can be restructured or rebuilt at any time without taking the whole system down. As a client, I have an acceptable interface into the world of information. It is that same strategy that we must build on in our in-house VLDB warehouses: simple, thin client interfaces to servers that are not locked forever to a static structure.

Implementing a Warehouse in a Multiserver Environment Using Parallel Technology

18

Trina LaRue
AT&T

"Implementation: One day at a time."

Trina LaRue

This chapter describes the implementation of a data warehouse for a large telecommunications company with a heterogeneous hardware and software environment. The main objective of the warehouse is to consolidate customer data into one centralized datastore that will support both operational and decision support requirements. All applications using and manipulating customer data will work from the same copy of data. In an effort of this size, there are a number of stakeholders involved in decisions about the information contained in the warehouse, and decisions about the data are time consuming. When the project is complete, it will contain more than 15 terabytes of data for the billing applications and more data to support other customer service applications. The implementation of the data warehouse in a multiserver environment is a complex task that is being achieved using a phased approach.

In the data warehouse architecture, the mainframe maintains the master copy of the operational data in DB2/MVS.™ The decision support data warehouse and the application-specific processes use UNIX with ORACLE,™ SYBASE,™ and Teradata.™ Users access the warehouse through X-Windows in a client/server environment. This varied platform implementation takes advantage of the new software and hardware technologies. The architecture uses transaction-driven message processing to access the detail data and supports both the MVS and UNIX environments. This chapter will also discuss how CPU parallelism and I/O parallelism can address needs of the users while taking advantage of both loosely associated MVS systems and tightly coupled UNIX multiprocessors. Implementation of this technology makes a heterogeneous environment a viable option for meeting user requirements in the data warehouse architecture.

There is an ongoing effort to separate the data from processes. This approach has allowed the implementation of new technologies in the architecture where it is appropriate and has created a true heterogeneous environment for both hardware and software.

Building a warehouse is a very large task, and we have received ongoing support from our management in this effort. This is essential since there are many risks involved in moving to this new architecture. Currently, we are investigating the design of a billing data warehouse that would work in conjunction with the customer data warehouse.

THE LEGACY ENVIRONMENT

In the legacy environment (Figure 18.1), customer data for different systems is logically and physically divided between many large MVS system images to meet the throughput requirements for processing large quantities of data. This means that each physical image needs to provide maintenance of data that logically belongs in one data store. The duplication of effort has added to the size of the system. In working with data that is physically partitioned across machines and devices, there is duplication of data, requiring redundant maintenance of customer information. The data is not only logically and physically partitioned because of size, but is also divided across different geographic locations.

In this example, the customer data for a specific product/service in a geographic location is physically located in separate databases. The application and data

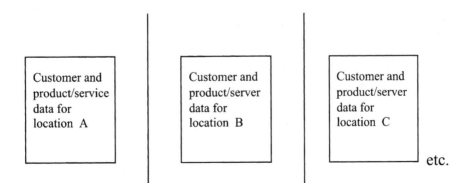

Separate databases in multiple physical locations

Figure 18.1 Legacy Architecture.

239

reside on the same server, and each copy of the system provides full functionality. The problem occurs when data analysis requires access across all databases, which requires considerable effort on behalf of the application.

In moving to the warehouse, we have identified the roles of different servers in a client/server-based architecture. They will be discussed next.

THE ROLE OF THE MAINFRAME SERVER

The mainframe server stores the operational detail data of the warehouse. The detail data has been provided by all applications that have participated in the data definition process. This part of the design brings together the data from 10 or more new and existing applications. These applications reside today in both IMS and DB2. The single largest of these applications is approaching the 15 terabytes in size. This includes all parts of the application. Since the mainframe server will only be storing customer-related data, application and data separation needed to take place. This process of separating data from the application was started a number of years ago to prepare it to move forward to the warehouse. These applications will migrate to the warehouse with a long-range plan. Since the movement of large production applications to the warehouse could be a risk to the business, a detailed plan was created to avoid possibly large revenue losses to the company.

PHYSICALLY ACCOMMODATING VLDBs

The mainframe server must accommodate very large databases and a high transaction throughput. Because of the volume of data that is to be migrated, the IBM Sysplex was selected. The initial implementation includes an S/390 microprocessor configuration that can become part of a large data sharing Sysplex environment. The Sysplex will couple a number of database servers together. The data is spread across the servers, and data requests are directed through the request broker. This allows for a set of tables to be brought up on one server and the same set to be brought up on another server to partition the data physically by ranges. This allows for full scale and accommodates today's database limits.

WHY THE SYSPLEX?

This environment offers a large-scale solution for the data warehouse. It allows loosely associated MVS systems using parallel Sysplex to share data concurrently among multiple systems in the Sysplex. It will serve as a high-capacity superserver using data sharing groups. Data sharing is a necessary option across multiple MVSs for this warehouse.

IMPLEMENTATION AND DESCRIPTION
OF A DATA SHARING ENVIRONMENT

This DB2 data sharing environment is made up of an S/390 microprocessor cluster, which consists of one or more S/390 microprocessors, a 9021 711-based Central Processor Complex (CPC), a 9121 511-based CPC, and, for parallelism, a 9672 parallel transaction server linked together with a coupling facility microprocessor unit along with coupling technology (which includes a coupling facility channel comprised of a high-bandwidth fiber-optic link). A Sysplex timer, which is an external clock used to keep the system clocks synchronized, is used along with data sharing via connection of the Enterprise Systems Connections (ESCON) channels, as shown in Figure 18.2.[1]

WHY WE NEED PARALLEL PROCESSING

In working with databases in the terabyte range with approximately 6000 on-line users and a high batch volume, parallel processing was a necessary criterion for selection of the hardware and software for both the MVS and UNIX servers in the warehouse.

Parallel processing allows simultaneous processing of a workload distributed among many central processors. Parallel processing permits multiple central processor complexes to work on a common workload, resulting in reduced elapsed time for processing. Each central processor complex can be configured individually to provide maximum processing power.

Each processor complex can have multiple processors; for example, a machine that is configured with a complex of 12 to 16 central processors with 8 central

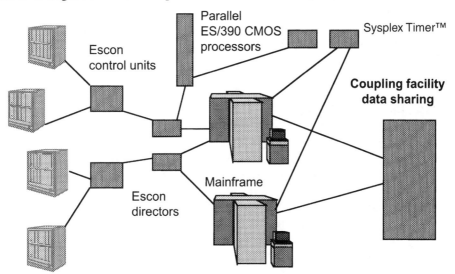

Figure 18.2   DB2 Data Sharing Environment.

processors per system will give a total of 96 to 128 central processors that can process a workload in parallel. This provides a high margin of processing power when designing applications that need to process large volumes of data in a specific amount of time. Configuration of a physical environment depends on things such as the number of users, transactions, expected response time, run schedule, networking, location, and many other variables.

The ability of this environment to handle both batch and on-line/transaction processing with data sharing has enabled many legacy systems that pass data from one very large system to another via files to access the data directly. With this process independence, each process uses up-to-date changed data instead of receiving a file. The MVS parallel transaction server with data sharing allows the warehouse to process large volumes of transactions and queries. In an application of this size, it will be necessary to take advantage of the parallelism that DB2 and the Sysplex have to offer.

THE DB2 PARALLEL TRANSACTION SERVER

The DB2 parallel transaction server, as previously discussed regarding the Sysplex environment, uses the S/390 parallel microprocessors, along with parallel coupling facility, to achieve high throughput. Each processor works independently of the other processor and has a copy of the operating system. A large query can then be split among multiple processors, access the shared data, and return a consolidated result set. When more transactions are added to the system, more processors can be configured, which will continue to reduce end-user response time by splitting the work. This can also be achieved in the UNIX environment with the ORACLE parallel query option.

In using the architectures discussed, full data sharing is available in the warehouse and can provide high availability and throughput utilizing parallel technologies.

INITIAL IMPLEMENTATION

The initial implementation/configuration is an S/390, configured to be scalable to a data sharing environment as the legacy systems migrations occur. Adding additional central electronic complexes (similar to a CPC) will add capacity for more work and makes the S/390 scalable to the S/390 parallel Sysplex by design. This will allow us to learn to use the parallelism as the data grows.

In planning for utilization of a parallel Sysplex, it is suggested that data be physically partitioned to take advantage of the parallel processing power. Dataset placement is just as important as it has always been. The DB2 parallel Sysplex with the multiple processors can process large-scale work in parallel if the data is partitioned and the programs have the capability to run more than one copy, with each one working on its own range of data. Maximum processing and application throughput will occur. Batch applications can continue to be designed in this manner, with partitions on devices with separate I/O paths to avoid contention.

Physical implementation is important when working with parallel processors. This type of configuration allows for the design to take advantage of the type of transactions and how those transactions will be used in the warehouse. With the implementation of data sharing being so new to MVS, it may be beneficial, as recommended earlier, to start with a single DB2 member utilizing the data sharing group. As migrations occur, begin adding new members to the group to become familiar with the new functionality of the database parallel processing.

Transaction/Message-Based Architecture

In accessing the warehouse in a transactional-type mode, message processing allows for different types of access to share the same data and stored procedures. Using transactions as part of a queue, not a stack, allows for new messages to be added to the queue in either a first-in, first-out fashion or a last-in, first-out mode. The queue can then be read in different orders. A message-based architecture allows for a set of transactions to be provided to the users/applications of the warehouse. This allows the maintainer of the warehouse to enforce a message standard across all users and access that will be invoked via message/transaction processing.

USING A REQUEST BROKER SERVER FOR TRIGGERING AND COMMON ACCESS

The message/ transaction process can be an OLTP message or a batch message that is triggered from the user platform. This triggering will be performed from the user application or a common platform and invokes a stored procedure in the warehouse. If it is to return data via a message in an OLTP situation, the message will be sent back to the user. If it is a batch-type function that is to retrieve data and format a file, a completion message can be returned. This message processing architecture can be implemented by using a request broker server, which will allow for the legacy systems to begin the data transition to the warehouse.

Customer data is separated from application-specific data. The customer data is stored in a common warehouse accessed via the request broker, and then the data is returned to the application engines. These boxes can represent one or more servers. This type of architecture allows the applications to perform application processing only, and a common view of the customer is available to all applications.

NEW ARCHITECTURE AND LEGACY SYSTEM TRANSITION

The legacy systems are being transitioned to the warehouse in a phased approach. Each legacy system refers to a customer in a different way. The warehouse will refer to a customer with its own identifier; therefore, it will be necessary to translate the legacy system ID to the new warehouse ID during the phased migration. This data is kept external to the warehouse since it does not have a logical relationship to the data in the warehouse and may be transitional data.

It has been determined that this type of cross reference is necessary for both batch and OLTP. This cross reference can be stored on the request broker. The request broker server is responsible for receiving the request from the legacy systems and new systems and translates the request via the cross reference tables to an access path known by the warehouse. The transaction/message processing will ensure that the return result message request is linked up with the original message. This can be done with different types of software. Implementation in this type of architecture allows the warehouse to grow from one to any number of copies of the tables needed to satisfy the users. This is where it is vital to the project that the request standards be set and the initial design be tested in a prototype.

The architecture is made up of a number of UNIX servers that exploit the technology of UNIX and the capability of the physical hardware. The request broker is used as the "traffic cop" of the warehouse and allows for a common form of identification to access the warehouse with a seamless interface. This will continue to aid while the legacy systems transition data from the legacy databases to the warehouse.

Each application server will concentrate its efforts on processing for that specific application. This new architecture, in which the application processes are separate from the warehouse data, has allowed us to choose the best hardware and software solution for the business process, providing a true choice of heterogeneous application servers (Figure 18.3).

New Architecture

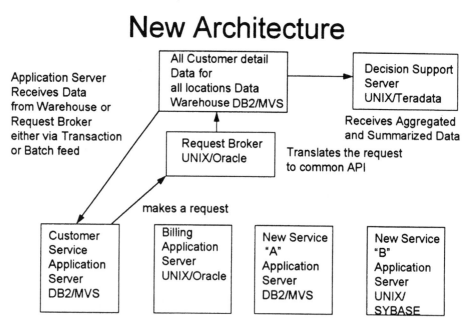

Figure 18.3   Data Warehouse and Server Architecture.

In taking advantage of many leading-edge software and hardware tools, the architecture has a wide variety of software. In the decision making for these software products, as mentioned earlier, the selection is based on what products solve the business problem best. In such a true heterogeneous database environment, we have found specific specialties of each database. Today's solutions cannot be solved using a "one size fits all" theory. Some applications even use a mixture of databases in one application. We have found that for specific performance reasons we should utilize an in-house main memory database manager. This main memory database adheres to all data persistency and is fully recoverable using logging. In utilizing the relational manager of the main memory database, we can take advantage of relational algorithms, such as referential integrity and binary searches, while exploiting the speed of the CPUs and internal memory.

Using such a solution enables the specific process to achieve a very high level of performance. This is important to large applications that require scalability. Many will say that memory is expensive and limited on each machine. This is where the hardware configuration will enter the picture. We are currently working on workload balancing for the servers in this application. Some of the workload distribution will depend on a number of factors, such as location of data and the scope of the full unit of work or commit frequency. Some common tables used for application processing are brought into main memory to allow efficient processing of the amount of data required to process a full unit of work for n number of customers. The n can be related directly to the number of customers that can fit into main memory with all related processing data for a full unit of work. Using such controls on the process will make it easier to configure the amount of main memory needed for processes. It will also allow new processes to be added to an existing server or a new server to be added to the architecture without interfering with existing processing.

Other applications may require some sort of replication of data across multiple servers. This can be done with a number of software solutions. If end users, such as marketing, accounting, and high-level management, need data summarized and aggregated from the detail data in the operational warehouse, the data can be gathered and transmitted to the decision support platform(s). This data has the capability of being replicated across many local servers automatically when the detail data changes so that the users have the latest up-to-date changes. These changes usually occur on different parts of the customer account data and can be used to aid the business in promotions and target markets.

As noted previously, all applications in the warehouse need to be analyzed for characteristics to determine the correct application category. This will then drive the selection of the software and hardware solutions.

BENEFITS OF USING UNIX PARALLEL PROCESSORS

With the roll-out of the new parallel processors in both an SMP and MPP, the UNIX alternative is becoming an option for large systems processing. Placing the request broker on a UNIX platform allows for high availability of the warehouse data and a high rate of transaction processing while protecting the integrity of the warehouse data. It does, however, add a level of complexity to the design and obviously to the networking architecture.

Using a high-availability data center quality processor that can address both an SMP and MPP architecture would be a desirable option. Vendors are currently working on creating this type of box, and many of them are beginning to produce them. In a multinode environment or a cluster, the use of RAID technology with fault tolerance minimizes downtime in transaction processing in the data warehouse environment.

USING PARALLEL CPU AND PARALLEL DATABASE TECHNOLOGY

Today's configurations of multiple CPUs allow for scalability of the server to service many users and for the introduction of new and better chip technology. The chip technology does not automatically induce parallelism. Parallel CPU processing along with a parallel database ensures the best of both worlds. With multiple nodes in the same box, it is desirable to have a high-speed bus between the nodes for the data transfer and data sharing. The first high-speed bus, which is patented by AT&T (which is now NCR), is referred to as a BYNET. Other hardware implementations, such as Sun's centerplane/gigaplane technology, with a high-speed interconnect between servers are in the same technology realm.

Using this type of highly configured UNIX platform with a high-speed interconnect will allow high-volume processing with a single operational view. The newest release of machines from the major UNIX hardware vendors can support SMP and MPP. These systems are also able to provide features such as complete fault isolation, automatic fault recovery, automatic system configuration, and node self-diagnosis. These features provide the high level of availability needed to use a UNIX solution for mission-critical applications.

UNIX implementations were selected for the decision support datastore, and the application-specific processes are on different platforms, thus utilizing different operating systems. The UNIX environments will provide high availability data services for enterprise computing utilizing high-availability servers. The SPARCcluster high-availability server allows for 24 × 7 operations and is generally used for systems that need high availability and can be provided for by a single environment. The high-availability servers provide automatic fault detection and recovery and have the ability to restore data and provide access within a short period of time. These servers will utilize the ORACLE 7 RDBMS in a single-node solution. The additional node would be to provide high availability.

Another option in the UNIX world is the use of SPARCcluster parallel database servers that would provide a scalable solution across nodes. This option provides a single view of the database using the ORACLE 7 RDBMS and the ORACLE parallel server option. These options are required for this type of configuration. The ORACLE parallel server will spread the database image across multiple nodes and manage the concurrency of the data with the distributed lock manager. In case of a failure of a node, the database will still remain up and users can access the database through another node. In working with parallel server options, different degrees of parallelism can be supported. To achieve the optimal scalability across nodes in the ORACLE parallel server, the data must be partitioned to eliminate possible disk contention.

In using these solutions, it is necessary to look at the application requirements to determine the best hardware and software solutions for the application. The UNIX environment is not a "one size fits all" solution. Each solution has to be carefully configured.[2]

HIGH-SPEED CONNECTIVITY

This high-speed interconnect technology is available from most hardware vendors. It is called a BYNET by AT&T, which is now NCR, and is similar to a telephone network in which many persons can establish connections. These connections work like a bidirectional network that allows multiple SMP nodes to communicate at high speed in a loosely coupled fashion. The initial release will interconnect a maximum of 16 to 128 nodes and will accommodate 4096 nodes in the future. With the total bandwidth of 10 MB/s for each link to a process, it is said to be linearly scalable. In this configuration, there are two network links per node that provide a total throughput availability of 20 MB/s. The BYNET performs load balancing dynamically for a uniform flow of traffic throughout the network no matter the size or configuration.[3]

In an environment made up of multiple platforms spanning long distances, external networking is a critical issue. The model for such an environment will need to consider all the network traffic in the warehouse. Common statements can be made such as, "It doesn't matter how fast the data can be processed, if it takes too much time to get the answer back to the originating server, we have failed."

In determining the network model, the locations of the servers need to be considered. If a process server is driven by customer data, analysis of the location of its detail data will be required. For a bulk data transfer to service a batch-oriented server, the lines to carry the data to the server must transmit the data in the time required by the business process.

Utilizing external high-speed connectivity, such as T1 technology, will provide substantial throughput. The T1 transfers data at approximately 400 MB per hour on a fully open and dedicated line. It is strongly recommended that large volumes of data (e.g., greater than 50 gigabytes) be analyzed to determine the need for compression before transmission. Home-grown compression routines have enabled us to compress data anywhere from 7 to 10 times. This provides substantial shrinkage of the data. When using such a model, the decompression time needs to be added to the time to process the data on the receiving server.

This brings us to the issue of very large data transfers. Double-digit gigabytes of data must be transferred daily. It may be necessary to configure a T3 line, which is an equivalent of approximately 28 T1's. This is a network configuration that will enable an MPP process to load the data in parallel. However, we must remember that there is no benefit in sending the data across high-speed data lines to a database that cannot load it in a reasonable amount of time for the business process.

Our network configuration utilizes Transmission Control Protocol/Internet Protocol (TCP/IP) based software as the connectivity software package. This is used for both bulk transfers and for single-user transaction access. It is recommended that the compression routine that is delivered with the software not perform the compression. The compression ratio is approximately 2 to 1, which does not compare to the aforementioned ratios.

Defining all areas of capacity prior to hardware purchase is highly recommended, and a small-scale prototype could be used to prove the network capability. With this type of high capacity, the UNIX platforms provide flexibility and high performance for a transaction/message-based process, which is discussed next.

SUPPORTING A MULTITIERED APPLICATION ENVIRONMENT

The implementation of a request broker is important in moving the legacy systems forward to a message-based architecture. The task of separating the data from the process is very time consuming. In the large systems that have evolved over the past 20 years, which are utilizing structured programming techniques, this will launch an effort that will take a substantial amount of time. In a message-based architecture, a decision can be made to purchase software that will coordinate the transaction ID to transaction ID functions along with matching the returning data from the warehouse to the legacy system via the transaction ID. This can also be handled with a batch file that is downloaded utilizing large data movement software to transmit the data to the appropriate platform. To implement a message-based architecture, it will be necessary to design the message formats and lengths and tie them to the process or stored procedure that is invoked in the warehouse. If the transactions will be returning data to an on-line user, it will be necessary to place those high-service transactions on their own nodes so that they can be serviced by a high configuration of available CPUs.

Flow of a Transaction-Based Multitiered Application Architecture

For batch-type processing, the transaction in the legacy system can kick off a transaction/message to the warehouse that will initiate the process and create a file to be transferred. The point is that all access to the warehouse is to be via transactions that will be serviced by software, possibly sockets coded by the developers, along with a transaction manager piece of software. Then data will be received either for

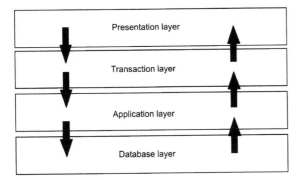

Figure 18.4 Multitiered Application Architecture.

an on-line request back through the transaction server or a batch request download. Using a message-based architecture, as shown in Figure 18.4, will enforce the application/users to begin moving the application code toward a multitiered application architecture. In a multitiered application architecture, the designer has the ability to decide what type of server would service the specific part of the application. In this type of design, there is a tremendous amount of flexibility in both the physical and logical designs.

In Figure 18.3, a request would come in via a presentation layer (for example, an x-terminal with local code running on a local server). This request would then connect across the network to a transaction processor; it could be Customer Information Control System (CICS) or Tuxedo that determines the location of the application and the code of the application. The application code would then execute based on a transaction, and a request would then be made to the database layer, where the data is stored in the warehouse. The database layer would contain the stored procedures and views of the data needed by the application.

In moving to the multitiered architecture, the task of separating these layers will involve a significant amount of time. This will allow for a plug-and-play type of architecture. If the database manager needs to be changed, it can be changed and the new stored procedures coded for access. The application layer will not need to be aware of this change since it communicates via transaction/message processing software. The message will be the same on the application layer and received on the database layer, and then the translation for execution would occur.

The creation of a common presentation layer across all systems that would be using the warehouse is usually desirable. In creating a presentation layer that uses up-to-date technology, the presentation layer will begin to present to the users a common touch-and-feel front end no matter what application they are accessing. This can be done and the legacy systems can be accessed via an emulation package. When they are moved to the new architecture, users will require minimum training. They will already have learned how to access the application via the new presentation layer and will just need to learn how to navigate the new screens for the specific application.

USING MESSAGE PROCESSING BETWEEN APPLICATION LAYERS

In designing this type of architecture that uses message-type processing, a tool for such processing will need to be selected. The message processing can be designed to use different types of queuing methods if available in the product. A message-based architecture allows for a set of transactions to be provided to the users of the warehouse. Decisions of how the data is accessed will be determined by the groups providing the data access. However, this type of architecture has to be looked at on a transaction-by-transaction basis.

Utilizing a message and queuing product allows for different types of queuing and message processing. Message queuing, with several programs putting messages on the same queue in a client/server architecture, can be set up as follows. Applications A and B put messages on queue manager 1, and it talks to queue manager 2, which could be the database access layer and server to the application layer. The messages would then be received in the queue, and processed on the server, and then returned to the queue to be passed back to the original queue and the transaction. Local applications like a transaction server can put messages on the queue on the server side, demonstrated by C in Figure 18.5.[4]

This is a true client/server transaction processing example. In using a message-based transaction architecture, there are a number of possibilities for processing the data via queue-to-queue methodology. This allows for heterogeneous servers to communicate and process data no matter where the data resides.

When the message processing did not reach our performance threshold in the UNIX side, we chose to use Tuxedo for the UNIX-to-UNIX communications.

TESTING THE ARCHITECTURE USING A PROTOTYPE

It is highly recommended that a prototype warehouse structure be implemented. This will provide some insight to users regarding the type of data that can be

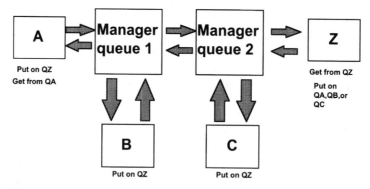

Figure 18.5 Message Processing in the Client/Server Environment.

requested and how the designer will implement the access. One of the most important aspects of the prototype is performance and testing of the network connection. It is important to get timings of how long it will take for a transaction to reach the database server from the presentation layer and return. Networking overhead is critical to the success of the project. This prototype will also help with getting all the products in the warehouse to work together. If the performance is undesirable, it may be necessary to implement replication, as described earlier, and test the prototype.

Creating a prototype as a proof of concept allows identification of the data movement in the organization as the information warehouse evolves. This will allow other organizations to begin working on the migration plan for moving to the warehouse and for understanding how the other legacy systems will begin to migrate. Prototyping is a way to achieve short-term success that can be capitalized on to yield long-term success.

SUMMARY

Movement to the data warehouse will introduce a sufficient amount of work to an organization and will require a detail plan. When implementing a transaction/message-based architecture, it will be necessary to identify the transactions along with the data flow through the multitiered architecture to the database server. The data integrity/data flow is protected by specific access only and by the transaction server. It is essential that all pieces of the warehouse are tested via a prototype from the client to the servers to determine the rate of access via the network. Prototyping provides a solid foundation for movement to the information warehouse architecture, in which a heterogeneous database and physical implementation can provide success.

REFERENCES

[1] System/390 MVS Sysplex Application Migration, 1994. System/390 MVS Sysplex Overview, "Introducing Data Sharing and Parallelism in a Sysplex," 1994.

[2] Sun Microsystems, 1996, SPARCcluster HA Server, "Just the Facts" technical document.

[3] AT&T/NCR, 1996, BYNET technical document.

[4] IBM, "Message Queue Interface Technical Reference," SC33-0850-02, November 1994.

Middleware: Gluing the Warehouse Together

19

Susan Gausden

Director
Brooklands Technology Limited
Weybridge, Surrey, UK

Terry Mason

Director
Brooklands Technology Limited
Weybridge, Surrey, UK

"The best way to get connected is to have connections."

Sue Gausden adapted from: "The best way to get clients is to have clients"
from The Secrets of Consulting *by Gerald M. Weinberg*

This chapter addresses the involvement of middleware as it pertains to data warehousing. The following aspects are covered:

- Why middleware: business issues
- Using middleware to populate the data warehouse
- Connectivity and interoperability issues
- Proof of concept
- Front-end tools and middleware
- Using middleware to access data warehouse databases
- Planning for the future

WHY MIDDLEWARE: BUSINESS ISSUES

Data warehouses are more than simply another series of databases used for decision support. They also encompass such functions as data analysis and data modeling of existing operational databases, data extracts, data transformation, database replication, and business tools for accessing and actually using the warehouse to make informed business decisions.

Figure 19.1 depicts the components of a data warehouse architecture:

1. Operational data includes relational and nonrelational (legacy) data from operational applications.
2. Data extraction and transformation include data extracts, data conversions and enhancements, summarizations, aggregations, replication, and synchronization.
3. Data warehouse databases (DBMSs) can take a variety of forms, including RDBMSs, object-oriented databases (OODBMSs), and multidimensional databases (MDBMSs). The implementation can be as an enterprise data warehouse or a data mart or both.
4. End-user data access tools include business intelligence tools such as ad hoc query and reporting tools, decision support systems, and executive information systems.

The various components that must work together to create and maintain a coherent business data warehouse do not magically integrate themselves into a coherent business warehouse. In addition to the obvious building blocks of hardware and software, the warehouse needs a software component called middleware to provide the "glue" to hold the warehouse together.

What Is Middleware?

Middleware is a generic term that refers to system software that shields end users and developers from differences in the services and resources used by applications. In a multivendor computing environment, these differences may be due to differences between vendors' products or between application requirements. The goal of middleware is to simplify user interfaces by providing a uniform and consistent view of the services and resources that exist in a heterogeneous computing environment.

Middleware provides a level of seamless connectivity for end users or developers using products from different vendors on the same or on different platforms, and hence middleware is "transparent." It is, more accurately, invisible because it is not actually seen by developers or by business users of the data warehouse.

Business Rationale

If middleware cannot even be seen in the data warehouse, how is it possible to justify the cost of its purchase? This must be viewed in the light of the business

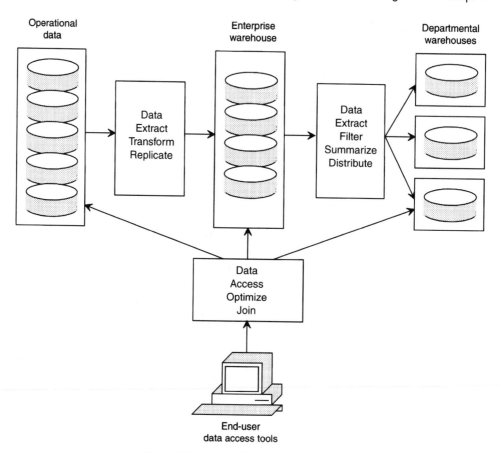

Figure 19.1 Data Warehouse Architecture.

rationale driving the creation, enhancement, or deployment of the data warehouse. Two examples illustrate the types of business problems that may be addressed by a data warehouse implementation.

1. A major airline has recently entered into a code sharing agreement with a partner airline. In the analysis of potential new routes, the business analysts need information that is housed in the partner airline's operational systems. To integrate this new aspect of its business effectively, the airline decides to build a passenger marketing data warehouse. The relevant data for the two airlines is on different platforms with different database types. The partner airline's data sources must be accessed and the new data warehouse must be populated. Middleware components can be called on to assist in the creation of the airline's data warehouse.

2. The people in the marketing department of a major airline are planning a promotion aimed at passengers in their frequent flyer program. The information

needed to develop a successful promotion is in data warehouses residing on two different platforms. To connect the business users' front-end tools to the back-end warehouse databases requires middleware. Without middleware, the software components in the airline's marketing department are not integrated and data cannot easily be consolidated.

Hence, the acquisition of middleware in a data warehouse environment is cost justi- fied within the context of

- Business decisions that need to be made
- Competitive advantage that these informed business decisions bring to an organization.

Middleware Categories

Middleware can be categorized as follows:

1. Copy management: data extraction, data transformation, replication, propagation
2. Gateways: database and independent gateways
3. Program-to-program middleware: remote procedure calls (RPCs), transaction monitors (TP monitors), and object request brokers
4. Message-oriented middleware.

While distributed function middleware and message-oriented middleware typically reside in OLTP applications, such functions as remote procedure calls also reside within decision support applications. Most of the middleware components in a data warehouse implementation fall into the copy management or the gateway cate- gories, and these two main categories are covered in this chapter.

USING MIDDLEWARE TO POPULATE THE DATA WAREHOUSE

In a data warehouse environment, the role of middleware is twofold:

1. To assist the developer in the data extraction, data transformation, and popu- lation of the data warehouse database
2. To assist the business end user in accessing the warehouse DBMS itself.

Hence, middleware is needed at different points throughout the life cycle of a data warehouse. Its initial use is often to assist in the creation and ongoing population of the first data warehouse. Products employed in this middleware area include Plat- inum InfoPump™, HP™ AllBase/Replicate, Praxis OmniReplicator™, and IBM Data Propagator™.

Warehouse Data Sources

Middleware plays a role in the data warehouse creation and replication arenas since there are many heterogeneous software and hardware environments in existence today. The source of data to create a data warehouse is often found in operational databases. While these databases may be relational and use SQL to access their data, often the operational or legacy data resides in nonrelational databases such as IMS or CA-IDMS, where proprietary data manipulation language (DML) is used to access the data.

Therefore, when choosing a product or products to provide data extract, data transformation, and data cleansing capabilities (see Chapter 13), it is important to consider how the tool(s) will access the legacy database or databases. Two issues arise when examining access to operational data:

1. How to connect the data extract or data transformation tool to the hardware platform housing the operational database (i.e., the type of networking or communications protocol involved).
2. How to provide access to the operational (especially nonrelational) databases themselves. In other words, what type of access method (e.g., in CA-IDMS: using a CALC key or DBKEY, doing an area sweep, walking a set, etc.) is used to access each different data source?

Middleware plays a role in addressing both of these issues (see connections A and C in Figure 19.2). It provides connectivity, using a particular communications protocol, between an extract tool on one platform and the source data that may be on another platform. In addition, middleware that supports data drivers or database interfaces to different types of data sources allows SQL tools to access nonrelational data.

Populating Warehouse Databases

In addition to the access that is required to all the data sources, there is the requirement to connect to all the data targets (the data warehouse databases) in order to populate them. The warehouse database may be a relational database on MVS, Windows NT, or on UNIX (or distributed across both platforms), or it may be a specialized database, such as a multidimensional database.

Two issues arise when examining access to target warehouse databases:

1. How to connect the data extract or data transformation tool to the hardware platform housing the warehouse data (i.e., what type of networking or communications protocol is involved)
2. How to provide access to the warehouse databases themselves (i.e., what type of access method is used to connect to and update each different data source).

Again, middleware plays a role in addressing both of these issues (see connections B and D in Figure 19.2). It provides connectivity, using a particular communications protocol, between an extract tool on one platform and the target warehouse data-

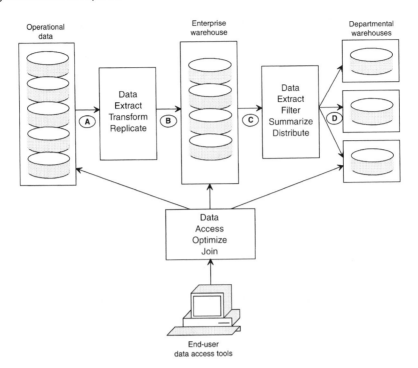

Figure 19.2 Populating the Data Warehouse.

base(s) that may be on another platform. In addition, middleware that supports data drivers or database interfaces to different data stores enables those data stores to be populated.

The Role of Middleware in Maintaining the Data Warehouse

The ongoing maintenance of data warehouse information leads into the area of data replication. Replication involves the management of copies of data. Replication is required either on a scheduled or on-request basis, in order to provide timely information to the business users of the data warehouse. This timeliness does not have to be instantaneous, however.

Replication in a data warehouse environment differs from replication in an operational environment in that the currency of the data is less critical. In operational applications, as the source data changes, it is often imperative that updates to copies of data be propagated in a real-time or near-real-time mode. In informational applications, such as a data warehouse, it is more important that the copies of data be stable and consistent as of a given point in time. (Chapter 16 covers data replication in detail.)

Middleware has a role to play in the replication arena since replication may be carried out in different heterogeneous computing environments. Many replication tools on the market today are limited in terms of sources they can replicate from and targets they can replicate to. Hence, a data extract tool from one vendor may be combined with connectivity components from a middleware vendor to access all the source data on multiple platforms.

On the target data side, a middleware component may be required to provide support for

- A particular network protocol, or
- An update capability for a given DBMS.

Figure 19.3 illustrates the use of middleware to create and maintain the data warehouse.

- Suppose there is a requirement to replicate data from MVS and VMS to a warehouse database on UNIX. For this site, there is operational data contained in VSAM and in CA-IDMS on MVS (platform A) and in Informix and Sybase on Digital Equipment Corporation's VMS (platform B). The target warehouse database is ORACLE on a UNIX platform (platform D).

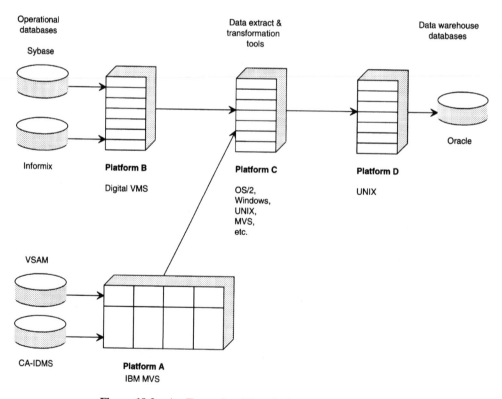

Figure 19.3   An Example of Populating the Data Warehouse.

- An extract tool on platform C must be connected to the platforms where the operational data resides. Also, a data driver must exist for each individual DBMS on the source platforms (platforms A and B). Middleware components may be required to provide connectivity between platform C and platforms A and B, or to provide support for access to one or more of the source DBMSs.

- Once extracted, the data may need to be transformed in some way, such as summarization or aggregation. Finally, the integrated view of the transformed data must be populated or replicated into the warehouse database. To populate the warehouse database, connectivity must exist between the data extract or data transformation tool and the target warehouse. Middleware components may be required to provide connectivity between platforms C and D, or to provide an update capability for the target warehouse data on platform D.

CONNECTIVITY AND INTEROPERABILITY ISSUES

A data warehouse may exist in a relatively homogeneous environment. The source data, the target data, all the tools, and the end users may exist in a single UNIX environment with a single type of DBMS. In this case, middleware may not be required. In many instances, however, disparate hardware and software platforms exist, even in the data warehouse. Middleware is then required to help glue all the pieces together.

This middleware glue often takes the form of a gateway. A gateway allows networks running on totally incompatible protocols to communicate. In PC-based networks, for example, gateways typically link PCs to host machines, such as IBM mainframes.

Communications Protocols

The realm of middleware includes such areas as communications protocols and internetworking. Communications protocols and APIs come in a variety of flavors, ranging from TCP/IP, DECnet, NetBIOS, ODBC, SPX/IPX, Async, OBDC, and DRDA through LU0, LU2, and LU6.2. Each of these protocols has its own particular setup and its own particular way of behaving. In addition, there is no one protocol that has become a de jure or de facto industry standard at this time.

Many companies have networking environments containing multiple communications protocols. This has occurred largely due to the proliferation of PCs and LANs. Decentralized decision making has resulted in individual departments making their own decisions regarding the purchase of network operating software (NOS). Multiple NOSs within an organization are not necessarily connected to the enterprise network (often SNA) (see Figure 19.4). When building a data warehouse, the issue can be how to integrate heterogeneous networks to provide interoperability.

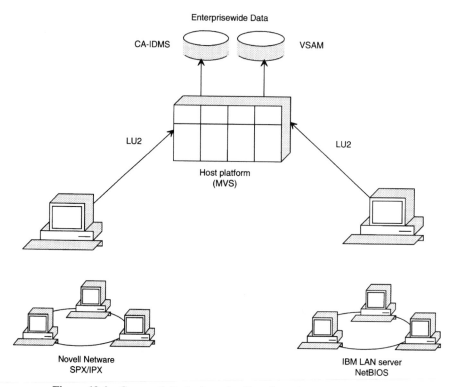

Figure 19.4   Connectivity before the Creation of a Data Warehouse.

One approach is to try to consolidate multiple protocols into a single protocol. This means that an organization standardizes on one (and only one) network protocol (TCP/IP, for example). However, given the existing installed base of applications in other operating environments (SNA networks, for example), this is often not practical. A great deal of effort would probably be involved in migrating from one configuration to another. Therefore, techniques must be found for linking disparate network environments. Middleware has a role to play in this regard; middleware, in the form of a network gateway, can be used to connect a TCP/IP LAN to an SNA network.

An existing architecture may acquire more platforms and connections with the creation of a data warehouse. A company may previously have had stand-alone departmental LANs and an MVS machine accessed in 3270 emulation mode (see Figure 19.4).

In Figure 19.5, a data warehouse has been implemented consisting of the following:

- Warehouse data in the form of DB2 for MVS
- A third tier in the form of a UNIX machine

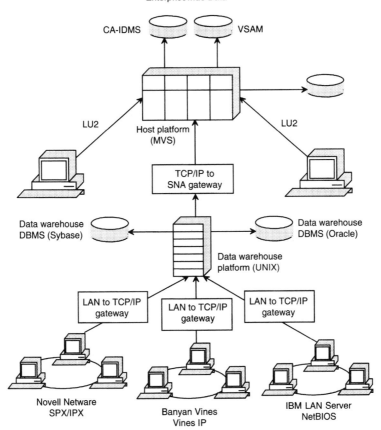

Figure 19.5 Connectivity after the Creation a Data Warehouse.

- Warehouse data in the form of both Sybase and ORACLE for UNIX
- A LAN with a new NOS in the form of Banyan Vines.

The LANs (Novell Netware, Banyan Vines, IBM OS/2 LAN server) must now be integrated into the enterprise. The issue arises of how to connect

- The LANs to the UNIX platform
- The UNIX box to the MVS host.

Middleware may be called on to provide a gateway to translate from one communications protocol to another:

- In the bottom half of Figure 19.5, the LAN to TCP/IP gateway connects the LAN PCs to the TCP/IP network. One machine acts as a gateway to the

TCP/IP network. The PCs communicate within each LAN using the specific PC-to-PC communications protocol that each network provides. PC applications needing to communicate outside the LAN, and requiring TCP/IP services, send requests through the gateway. The gateway translates the PC's network-protocol environment to the TCP/IP environment.

- In the middle of Figure 19.5, the TCP/IP to SNA gateway connects the TCP/IP network to the SNA network. The TCP/IP protocol that comes off the network goes through a gateway, where it is converted to SNA before it reaches the mainframe. The VTAM environment on the mainframe remains untouched. This functionality lets users run MVS applications, which normally require an SNA network, from a TCP/IP network.

Architecture Feasibility

In a multiplatform, multivendor computing environment, and in spite of the vendors' best intentions, it can still be a nontrivial exercise to install and then to integrate different software and hardware components. Vendors produce lists of environments that their products support (client platforms, local and remote relational and nonrelational data sources, communications protocols). However, even with a list of supported environments, it is important to look in detail at each component. For example, in the area of TCP/IP support, one UNIX-networking vendor's flavor of TCP/IP may be supported, whereas another vendor's flavor may not be. Hence, each organization must compare the software components in its own configuration to the list of the vendors' supported products.

Versions

It is important to verify exact versions of workstation and server operating systems, front-end tools, network communications protocols, and back-end databases. Suppose the end-user access tool runs under Microsoft Windows. In this case, software compatibility and support must exist for a given flavor of Windows (Windows 3.1, Windows 95, or Windows NT). It may be the case that OS/2 is the operating system of choice for some end users. Each version of OS/2 has a slightly different set of features; for example, if TCP/IP support is needed, then a particular version of OS/2 is required. The issue of versioning extends to the versions of DBMSs and to the middleware components.

Upgrades

It is essential that the data warehouse computing environment be stable, both during the pilot project and in production. Upgrades of middleware components may be required periodically; this may trigger the need to upgrade other software components in the configuration. Likewise, the upgrade of nonmiddleware components may trigger the need to upgrade middleware components. These upgrades may also dictate the need for hardware upgrades. The frequency of upgrades may have an impact on the evaluation of the technology for the data warehouse.

Single-Vendor Solutions

Verifying configurations can involve more or less work depending on the degree of integration provided by the middleware vendor. With middleware components all provided by a single vendor, it would seem that integration would be a simple matter. There are middleware vendors that provide an entire range of products, from accessing operational and external data through to end-user data analysis. Some vendors have developed their products in-house and other vendors have acquired products through the purchase of other software companies. In other words, some middleware solutions have been architected with an integrated product design from the outset, whereas other solutions are a series of components bolted together, which may or may not integrate seamlessly.

Hence, there are varying degrees of product integration that exist in the marketplace. There are also varying degrees of optimization among middleware products, with some products designed from the beginning with optimization in mind, and other vendors adding optimization and performance tuning facilities later. In all cases, it is important for the data warehouse architect to verify the degree of integration that exists among middleware products.

Multivendor Solutions

On the other hand, there are many niche vendors, who provide products in one or more areas, but not in all areas. They may rely on partnerships with other vendors to provide a complete solution. There may be varying degrees of partnerships that exist; even with a close partnership, the degree of cross-vendor testing may vary considerably from partnership to partnership. Also, some companies who partner on some product lines may compete on other product lines, which may affect the level of vendor support or of product integration. Again, it is important for the data warehouse architect to verify the integration of middleware products across multiple vendors.

DBMS-Independent Vendors

Organizations with heterogeneous computing environments tend to find themselves evaluating products from a variety of different vendors to integrate disparate components. Many DBMS vendors do not find it in their best interests to provide access to their competitors' products. Hence, there is DBMS-independent middleware, which provides the hooks that are not provided by each proprietary DBMS vendor. These middleware products integrate heterogeneous, multiplatform environments (DB2/6000 to CA-IDMS, for example).

With more than one DBMS middleware vendor participating in a data ware-house implementation, each providing a piece of the connectivity, a patchwork quilt of multivendor components and connections may result. A true independent mid-dleware implementation may only require a single connection, instead of multiple point-to-point connections, to integrate a heterogeneous environment.

Architecture Standards

There are few architecture standards from the standards bodies to assist the data warehouse architect in configuring middleware components to connect different databases, tools, and operating systems. The standards are largely vendor driven (Microsoft's Open Database Connectivity [ODBC], IBM's Distributed Relational Database Architecture [DRDA]). Independent bodies have proposed standards. These include X/Open's call-level interface (CLI) and Open Software Foundation's (OSF's) Distributed Computing Environment (DCE). However, no single standard has been universally adopted by the middleware vendors, so organizations are dependent to a certain extent on these vendors for success.

Technical Skills Required

The technical skills required to verify the proposed configuration may demand the intervention of more than one person. If an existing LAN is to be connected to a TCP/IP network and to an MVS environment, the expertise of the LAN adminis-trator(s), the UNIX systems administrator(s), and the MVS and VTAM systems programmer(s) may all be required.

The same persons may then be involved in the installation of the middleware components. People such as DBAs from the UNIX and MVS DBMS sides of the shop may also be required. The DBAs are needed to set up the initial catalogs and database views and may be involved in granting access to data. The security people (for RACF, ACF2, Top Secret, for example), will provide access to software and operating environments. As the warehouse matures, other people, such as capacity planners and performance specialists, will be called on to monitor growth and response times within components of the middleware itself.

PROOF OF CONCEPT

When introducing middleware, it is highly recommended to start with a pilot pro-ject or proof of concept, wherein a representative small- to medium-sized application is chosen to try out the new technology. For a successful introduction, this application should satisfy a business need and be supported by the proposed technical environment. For instance, requirements may include a GUI on the client presentation side and access via middleware to a new UNIX DBMS as the back-end warehouse database.

Staffing a Pilot Project

To set up and evaluate a data warehouse pilot project, certain skill sets are required. In addition to technical expertise, end users with business knowledge of the front-end tools are required. In the marketplace today, there is an increasing proliferation of products, and expertise in certain technologies, both leading-edge and legacy technology, must be found. Ideally, people with expertise in more than one area should be found, such that they can understand and deal with more than one specialized area of technology. The ability of people to be able to cross over from PC to UNIX to MVS is extremely valuable.

It is possible, though, that not all the required skill sets will be found immediately within an organization. This may be because new front-end tools are being introduced, or an existing tool is to be deployed in a new way. It may be because an organization is looking at UNIX databases or at an LU6.2 connection for the first time. Perhaps an organization was a UNIX shop that has been acquired by another corporation, and now its people must learn a technology, such as MVS™, VTAM™, or CICS™.

One option is to look for outside help; it is important to understand the availability of particular skill sets in the marketplace before embarking on the pilot project. Another option is to train the in-house people. The education may include middleware training such as installation, systems administration, database administration, capacity planning, or performance monitoring. The costs of training must be factored into the data warehouse plans, and the training should be carried out before the pilot project begins.

Vendor Support

An essential player in the data warehouse and middleware scenario is the vendor. The middleware vendor often has the responsibility for ensuring that all the components of hardware and software integrate. So, while a particular front-end tool such as Microsoft Access™, Powerbuilder™, or LOTUS 1-2-3™ may support ODBC™, it is the middleware components that must connect to a back-end warehouse database. To ensure a successful pilot project, the support of the middleware vendor is extremely important.

Installation Verification

Each individual company's configuration is unique. With the large number of permutations and combinations of hardware and software that potentially exist, each company must check its particular configuration against what is supported by the middleware vendor(s). Even with vendor testing, it is not necessarily true that the components that exist in a company's real-world environment will behave exactly as they did in the vendor's lab. One option is to have the data warehouse architect define the configuration as it is envisioned and ask the middleware vendor to demonstrate it at their site prior to introducing the products in-house. This provides assurance that the configuration is supported.

Before embarking on the proof of concept, it is important to create an installation verification plan. This is a checklist of items that must be verified with project team members and with the participating vendors. The plan helps ensure a successful pilot project.

INSTALLATION VERIFICATION PLAN

- Define the customer's business problem and verify the scope of the project.
  - Define the business problem.
  - Identify the personnel involved in the implementation and pilot project roll-out.
  - Verify the scope of the project, including functionality and performance expected (e.g., number of users, volume of data accessed, response time expected, etc.).
  - Verify the data stores to be accessed to create the data warehouse, the frequency of the download, and the volume of data to be downloaded.
  - Verify the target data stores, and ensure that the target data stores can handle the types of data transformations being proposed (e.g., aggregations, outer joins, denormalizations, etc.).
- Verify technical feasibility and prerequisite products.
  - Draw a configuration diagram showing all the proposed components, including network connectivity.
  - Identify all the data stores to be used as source data (and their versions).
  - Identify all the data stores to be used as target warehouse databases (and their versions).
  - Identify the front-end tools to be used (and their versions).
  - For each platform (e.g., PC workstation, OS/2 server, UNIX server, MVS source, etc.), identify all the hardware, including CPU, memory, hard-disk space (DASD), and model numbers.
  - For each platform, identify all the relevant software (and the version of each), including operating system, data stores, data access tools, etc. For example, MVS operating system (MVS/XA™ or MVS/ESA™), release and version number, fix level; VTAM network version and fix level; system security package (RACF™, ACF2™, Top Secret™).
  - For each connection between platforms, identify the communications protocol to be used, including vendor, version, and underlying physical connection (e.g., Token Ring or Ethernet™ card).
- Install and customize the components required on the source server, where the legacy data resides.
- Install and customize the components required on the target server (e.g., UNIX), where the data warehouse will reside.
- Set up required security (e.g., user IDs, database authorizations).

- Install and customize required components on the client platforms.
- Define data sources and data targets to the middleware global catalog.
- Identify and set up predefined joins, views of the data, and remote procedure calls.
- Test the access to the source data, the creation of the targets, and the access to the warehouse database(s).

FRONT-END TOOLS AND MIDDLEWARE

For the deployment of the data warehouse to be effective, business end users need front-end tools. The actual deployment of these tools falls into two categories of warehouse use:

1. Production applications and queries
2. Ad hoc access in the decision support environment.

Production Queries

There may be an existing base of data access tools (query and reporting, EIS tools) and canned queries. The data warehouse issue is how to leverage existing investments in these tools and their queries. If a new data warehouse has been created, the architect and designer of the warehouse must ensure that existing tools can access the new data. Middleware components, such as a communications subsystem to forward requests from a client to a remote server and to return answer sets from the server to the client, may be required. For instance, such components may be needed to provide connectivity between a Microsoft Windows tool and a remote UNIX warehouse database, where previously the tool may only have accessed LAN data.

Ad Hoc Queries

Ad hoc queries may also involve existing tools, which must be integrated into the data warehouse in a similar fashion to the canned queries. Ad hoc queries, by their nature, are unpredictable. They range in complexity from very simple to extremely complex and may scan and return only a few rows or may scan millions of rows. These queries may have a major impact on the overall system resources, such as CPU, I/O, memory, buffer pools, etc. Since ad hoc queries have the potential to become runaway queries that execute for a very long time, performance becomes a major consideration. Middleware has a role to play in the performance arena:

- The area of "intelligent" global optimization is one aspect of performance, and this functionality may be provided by some middleware products.
- The use of query governors may facilitate the capacity planning and performance tuning of queries in the data warehouse environment. Query governors

may be provided by the vendor of a particular RDBMS. These governors typically let the queries run until they hit the predetermined limit set for them, and then they are stopped by the governor.

- A predictive governor determines the estimated cost in terms of factors such as CPU utilization and I/O usage before running the query. It will then either allow or disallow the query to be run. In a particular scenario of a front-end tool connected to a warehouse database, it may be neither the front-end tool nor the database that provides a query governor function. It may be the middleware that provides such functionality.

All Tools to All Databases

Many front-end tools are PC or LAN based and operate within the data warehouse in a client/server mode, with the workstation being the client and the server being the warehouse database. However, there may be front-end tools running on other platforms (QMF™ on MVS, for example). These tools may also need to access the data warehouse databases, and middleware components may be required to provide connectivity from MVS to UNIX.

Front-end tools need to be able to access not only relational databases that participate in the data warehouse, but also the specialized warehouse databases (e.g., multidimensional or parallel databases) and operational databases. If the connectivity is not provided by the database vendor or the front-end tool vendor, then middleware components may be needed to provide the required connectivity. Suppose that IBM's QMF needs to access alternately Teradata and DB2 data. TS/API, a form of middleware supplied by Teradata, may be used to provide such access. In another scenario, QMF needs to join data in Teradata and CA-IDMS. Here, middleware supplied by an independent vendor such as IBI's EDA/SQL™ may be used.

New end-user tools may need to be added to the existing data warehouse. The choice of new tools or application packages must take into consideration the connections, and hence the middleware components, needed to function within the existing warehouse infrastructure.

USING MIDDLEWARE TO ACCESS DATA WAREHOUSE DATABASES

A data warehouse can range in size and scope from relatively small departmental warehouses or data marts to enterprisewide warehouse databases that typically store large volumes of data. The actual implementation of the data warehouse may take a top-down or a bottom-up approach. In the top-down approach, a corporation may decide to create an enterprisewide data model that will be the basis of its global warehouse. The global warehouse may then be the basis for extractions of subsets of data to be populated onto the data marts (see Figure 19.1). Alternatively, a corporation may decide to implement a department or work group data warehouse to satisfy a particular immediate business need. These data marts could then be integrated into the enterprise data warehouse at some later point in time.

Data Warehouse Data Stores

In the world of operational (OLTP) applications, the satisfying of specific business needs has often produced heterogeneous database environments. In the world of DSS applications, fiscal decentralization has often resulted in heterogeneous database environments.

The data stores that are used for data warehouses are often RDBMSs. However, even in the RDBMS world, access may be needed to more than one type of RDBMS and on more than one platform. An organization may have data warehouse databases on DB2 for MVS, and on Oracle UNIX and on Sybase UNIX database platforms.

Some of the data stores that need to be accessed in a data warehouse scenario may be nonrelational (IMS™, CA-IDMS™, Adabas™, VSAM™, CA-Datacom™). This may occur if budget constraints within an organization prevent the creation of an ideal global data warehouse and access is still required to legacy data. This situation may be temporary or it may persist for a long time. Access may also be needed to other midrange and large-scale platforms (AS/400, Digital, VM/CMS, UNIX). Multidimensional databases are becoming increasingly popular as a way to store time-series data, and access may also be needed to these types of databases.

As the data warehouse grows, say because of increased business activity or historical data archiving, performance may degrade in a traditional uniprocessor environment. Databases based on MPP and SMP hardware configurations provide the necessary speed and scalability to manage such situations. Selected middleware needs to be engineered to connect to such environments—do not assume that they are already enabled. Additionally, the middleware itself may eventually take advantage of parallel processing for better performance—verify the vendor's plans in this regard.

Role of Middleware

The role of middleware in accessing warehouse databases is to provide software components that facilitate access in a multivendor, multiplatform computing environment. Middleware can take the form of

1. A database gateway, which provides access from a database application developed using one vendor's DBMS to a DBMS of a different vendor on the same or different platform. It shields the application developer from some of the differences between the products. A database gateway is usually provided by an RDBMS vendor and requires its own DBMS. It typically only accesses its own database and possibly some other relational databases. IBM DataJoiner™ and Sybase/MDI Database Gateway™ fall into this category.

2. An independent gateway, which also provides access to different databases provided by different DBMS vendors, but without the need for a DBMS as part of the connectivity. It is DBMS-independent data access middleware that accesses different vendors' RDBMSs and often accesses nonrelational data sources as well. IBI EDA/SQL and Cross Access™ fall into this category.

Some gateways provide point-to-point connectivity to one remote data source at a time. Hence, multiple, distinct connections are required when an application needs data from multiple sources. Other gateways provide a point-to-many-points connectivity to several remote data sources at the same time.

Data Location Transparency

Database and independent gateways vary with respect to the levels of location transparency they provide. Some gateways provide little or no location transparency (i.e., users must know the physical location of each data source on the network). Other gateways provide a single-location image of the DBMSs on the network. One way to implement location transparency is through a global catalog of metadata, which stores information about the remote data objects that participate in the globally integrated database. Entries in the global catalog indicate the locations of their respective data sources on the network. This is usually accomplished via the use of three-part names, which consist of a server name, table owner authorization ID, and the data source table or view name. Once the catalog entries have been defined for tables and views, the users may then formulate requests in a single version of SQL as though all the data resides in a single local database. It is the role of the middleware to handle differences, such as in SQL dialects, networking protocols, data types, and operating systems.

Distributed Databases versus Centralized Databases

One of the design considerations in the data warehouse is whether to have distributed databases or centralized databases. If the databases are centralized, the middleware may simply have to provide access to a single point of control. However, if the databases are distributed, it may be the responsibility of the middleware to provide access to the distributed data stored in MVS databases and UNIX databases.

Database Integration in a Heterogeneous Environment

Business requirements drive the need to access information from more than one platform, and access to distributed data may require the use of cross-platform (heterogeneous) joins. The capability of doing cross-platform joins falls into the realm of middleware. Key to data warehouse integration is the ability to produce query results by combining data from different tables into a new result table. Heterogeneous joins enable both end users and application developers to join tables that are located in multiple data sources. These data sources can be multivendor, multiplatform and can be relational or nonrelational. Suppose some of the enterprise data resides on DB2 for MVS and some of the data resides on a UNIX database. The business application may dictate that information is required from both platforms. To accomplish this, a heterogeneous join is required.

Various options exist for performing this heterogeneous join function. The middleware may provide a capability for bringing down the tables from two separate servers and joining the information on the platform, where the middleware resides. Other middleware provides a global optimizer for performing an intelligent optimization; the optimizer will determine the least-cost strategy for moving and materializing tables. It may not be necessary to bring down the entire tables onto the middleware server to satisfy the request. Alternate strategies, such as moving a smaller table to the location of a larger table, may be employed.

Many factors will likely be used by a middleware product's global optimizer. These factors may include such items as the location of the data, the indexes on the data, the relative CPU speed, relative I/O speed, and relative network bandwidth. A global optimizer may gather statistics about each of the data sources and store them in a global catalog. It then uses this information to determine the least expensive, most efficient method for performing a query.

The use of SMP may also have implications for global optimizers. As middleware matures, it may well employ SMP. In a multiplatform environment, a heterogeneous join may be able to take advantage of a database such as IBM's DB2 Parallel Edition (DB2 PE). In such a situation, a global optimizer may attempt to perform aggregations, sorts, unions, and other operations on each individual node whenever possible. Its goal is to maximize the use of each node such that as much work as possible is performed in parallel. Hence, increased performance and reduced costs can be achieved by minimizing the amount of information that must be moved from node to node.

It is ultimately with an integrated view of the data in a data warehouse that the best business benefits can be achieved.

PLANNING FOR THE FUTURE

While a data warehouse project may start at a departmental level, it is important to plan for ongoing enhancements. This may occur both within the middleware components themselves and within the business environment. The marketing department may start out with its department's view of the warehouse on UNIX and subsequently be joined by the engineering and human resources departments. In this case, the choice of middleware must allow for expansion and incorporation of ongoing business requirements into the warehouse. If the engineering department has standardized on Digital Equipment Corporation hardware and software, its requirements to integrate information with other departments on different platforms must be planned in advance.

Scalability

Another issue that must be planned into the data warehouse at the outset is that of scaling to large volumes of data and users. This may involve migrating to a larger platform. An organization may start out with a departmental data warehouse on a uniprocessor UNIX platform and later need to scale up to a data warehouse on a large-scale SMP or MPP platform. The middleware solution chosen must be able to support the connectivity to the new platforms. It must also provide the required performance to support an increased volume of data and a larger number of users, on all data warehouse platforms.

Middleware Software Maintenance

The area of middleware enhancements must be explored as well. This includes upgrades to new versions of middleware components and application of program temporary fixes (PTFs) to existing versions. Installing and testing middleware components across two or more platforms, irrespective of what vendors sometimes claim, tends to be a complex process. Many companies plan months in advance for upgrades and are not in a position to download from the Internet and regression test, on a weekly basis, every new patch. Hence, the stability of the product lines and the smooth progression to new versions or releases becomes a primary consideration when evaluating middleware.

Changing Business Environment

The other area of consideration for middleware enhancements is the area of the changing business environments. A company may merge with another company or acquire another company and then be faced with having to integrate new hardware and software components into its existing data warehouse. The role of middleware is to add new components that integrate the new business realities into the existing warehouse. The integrated data warehouse can then continue to deliver business benefits to the organization.

SUMMARY

Many organizations today operate in a heterogeneous software and hardware computing environment and are trying to implement data warehouses. These warehouses have to be integrated into distributed environments with heterogeneous data sources, data targets, platforms, operating systems, and communications protocols. Middleware has an important role to play in heterogeneous environments. It provides the connectivity for the developer to access legacy data and populate data warehouse databases, and for the business user it provides the connectivity between data access tools and the multivendor, multiplatform data warehouse. Middleware is rarely seen since it operates behind the scenes, but it is the glue that holds the data warehouse together.

CHAPTER

Design Reviews
for the Data Warehouse

20

Joyce Bischoff
Bischoff Consulting, Inc.
Hockessin, Delaware

"It is much easier to be critical than to be correct."

Benjamin Disraeli

T he design review process provides a structured approach for reviewing design decisions objectively. Design reviews have been used for many years in the traditional, transaction environment; however, there are significant differences between design reviews in a traditional transaction-driven environment and those that are appropriate in a warehouse environment. This chapter covers the need for design reviews, the differences between traditional production reviews and those that are needed in a warehouse environment, and the planning process. It also provides guidelines for conducting various types of reviews.

WHY DESIGN REVIEW?

The popularity of design reviews has waxed and waned over the years as new technologies have been introduced. As people become more familiar with new technologies, the need for design reviews is lessened. In the early days of hierarchical databases, design reviews were very popular. There was a resurgence of interest as relational technology took hold, and the advent of the warehouse has increased the need for a well-planned set of design reviews to minimize the errors that are frequently made by less experienced users of new technology.

The primary business objectives in warehouse design are in the areas of data integrity, flexibility to meet future unknown requirements, user satisfaction, performance, data currency, and system availability. The old adage that "there is no such thing as a free lunch" applies to the data warehouse. Everything that is done to enhance one of these areas will probably have an offsetting effect in another area. It is well known that short-term performance gains that may result from denormalization may have an impact on future flexibility. If data currency is improved, there may be an impact on system availability or performance in the source production system, depending on how the improved data currency is achieved.

LIFE CYCLE OF THE DATA WAREHOUSE

The life cycle of the typical data warehouse is different from the life cycle found in the typical transaction processing environment. In a traditional environment, requirements are gathered, the application and database are designed, and programs are coded, tested, and moved into production. Although the system may be modified after it is placed in production, requirements are (or should be) well understood up front. In sharp contrast, the design of the data warehouse is based on a set of general requirements that may identify the subject area and provide few hints on the expected usage of the data. One or more subject databases will be designed using the enterprise data model as a foundation. If processors were infinitely fast and database management systems were perfectly efficient, the design could stop there. It would be possible to answer every query by accessing the databases containing detail data. There would be no need for summary tables, multidimensional databases, or specialized subsets of data. Unfortunately, warehouses that have been implemented with this approach have usually failed due to poor performance.

The real world has not yet produced infinitely fast processors. Physical design must consider performance. It is important that the design of the detail data be correct before adding summary levels and other types of structures to the data warehouse. The warehouse may be accessed through specialized decision support applications, ad hoc queries, or both. The warehouse is usually implemented, tested by users (who provide feedback to developers on their level of satisfaction), and optimized for performance. There will be frequent modifications to meet constantly changing user requirements. Depending on feedback from users, there will be a need to cycle back through design, coding, and performance optimization in an iterative procedure. Requirements are constantly changing, and meeting them is like trying to hit a moving target.

OPERATIONAL VERSUS WAREHOUSE DEVELOPMENT

There are significant differences in the way operational systems and data warehouses are designed and used. Design reviews must reflect these differences in the way they are scheduled and conducted. The design review process must reflect the major differences between the two environments. In a warehouse, there should be more emphasis on data than programs that process the data. The warehouse design process is iterative in nature, and the review process must also be iterative in nature. Although there is some similarity to production reviews, the emphasis in each review and the sequence in which they will be held will be different. Since users will determine warehouse requirements and be the ultimate judges of the relative success of the warehouse, there will be more emphasis on users in various reviews.

MULTILEVEL DATA ARCHITECTURE

A typical multilevel physical data architecture may consist of detail data, various summary levels, external data, multidimensional data, and specialized data subsets. Data warehouses may be global in nature or may consist of one or more data marts, which provide additional challenges for developers. Although early warehouses were not usually updatable in the on-line environment, many warehouses now include an operational data store that may be continuously updated.

In most warehouses, legacy data in the production environment feeds the warehouse with data that has been cleaned up, validated, integrated, and summarized. Various elements of the data architecture may be placed on the mainframe or spread across other platforms in a client/server environment. The design review process must be flexible enough to support any and all options.

DESIGN REVIEW DIFFERENCES

Although the basic design review approach is similar to production, there are major differences. The review process needs to reflect the iterative nature of development, and more emphasis must be placed on the data and flexible access to the data. The sequence of reviews may be slightly different. For example, there may be more than one physical design review. Reviews of detail data may be separate from the reviews of summary levels or multidimensional objects. Because the movement of data between production and the warehouse may be resource intensive, a special review may be scheduled to deal with it.

Because users are the end-all and be-all of the warehouse, there will be more emphasis on users and organizational issues in every phase. In the first review, it will be important to determine if an official alliance has been created with users and what their role will be in each successive phase of development.

A combination of design reviews and design workshops may be cost effective in identifying design flaws at the earliest opportunity and providing an opportunity to manage the transition from logical design to physical design in a methodical manner. *It is important to note that every type of review will not be necessary for every project.* Typical design reviews may include any or all of the following: logical design review, physical design review, architectural review, copy management review, code review, utility usage review, application design review, and performance reviews, as needed. To ease the transition from logical to physical design across multiple hardware platforms, a logical/physical conversion workshop may be held. If there are difficult programming challenges, a programming approach workshop may be held. If only one review is held, it will probably be a physical design review.

PLANNING ISSUES

Planning for design reviews and workshops should be built into the project plan. Design reviews may take from a few hours to a few days depending on the size of the project, the level of technical skills available for the project, and familiarity with warehouse development. If multiple reviews are held, each individual review will take less time. The time required for reviews may range from one to three days. It may be counterproductive to spend more than three days on a single review. For large implementations, it may be advisable to divide the review into multiple subsystems to ease the review process.

Since it is important to identify design flaws early in the development of a warehouse, it is best not to skip the logical design review. Database design flaws that are not picked up until the physical design review may require the team to reconsider the logical data model. If management support is to be obtained, reviews must be perceived as cost beneficial. Many companies have been forced to make major design changes during performance reviews because the basic architecture and design were not properly reviewed early in the project. This can be truly expensive.

DESIGN REVIEW TEAM

As the warehouse development progresses, the participants and their roles in review will change. The participants in a design review will include a team leader and someone assigned to take notes and document points of consensus. For the logical design review, the data modeler and business analyst will present the model and answer business questions. Users should also be present. The DBA will be preparing to convert the logical design to a physical design that will provide adequate performance. Developers might be involved so that they will understand business objectives.

For the physical design review, the DBA will present the design, the data modeler and business analyst will answer business questions, and developers and network specialists will consider data access and network requirements. Users may or may not be present, depending on the situation. The code review will involve DBAs and programmers. A performance review may involve DBAs, developers, systems programmers, and network specialists. The composition of the team will vary with the phase of development and must be tailored to fit the specific project. The size of the team usually ranges from 6 to 10 people, although some government shops have been known to hold reviews with 30 to 40 people. The author considers this to be unnecessary and often reduces a review to a formal presentation with little or no discussion of issues. For many reasons, participants may be reluctant to raise issues in such a large forum.

Management must understand that participants should not be evaluated on the number of weaknesses found in the design. They should be evaluated on their willingness to cooperate with the design review process and work toward the best possible solution.

AGENDA

An agenda should be developed and circulated to all attendees before the review. The agenda depends on the stage of development and the experience level of the team. A typical agenda might include

- Introduction to design review (if the team is new to design reviews)
- Discussion of objectives
- Overview of the warehouse application
- Review of the data model (logical or physical, depending on the stage of development)
- Review data movement and copy management requirements
- Review business processes
- Summary, findings, and an action list.

LEADING QUESTIONS

Leading questions may be used as a convenient starting point in the review. Many shops publish lists of leading questions as part of their design review procedure. This can be helpful for participants who are concerned about what questions may be raised about their design. When they know what might be asked, they are usually well prepared for the review and the process is more efficient. It is important to understand that leading questions do not cover every issue that could be raised but are only a starting point that will trigger questions and discussion from other team members.

FIRST REVIEW

During the first review, which may or may not be a logical design review, key user issues must be addressed. Questions such as the following should be answered:

- Has an official alliance been developed between users and the project team?
- How will users be involved in each stage of the project?
- How will users be trained and supported?
- How will the technical staff track changing user requirements?
- Will a process be in place to handle change requests?
- What process is in place to manage performance complaints?
- Is the organization ready for the warehouse? (See Chapter 3 for details on this topic.)

Leading questions are an important tool in the review process and serve to bring critical issues to the table. They may also trigger other questions as discussions take place. Communication with users is critical, and this step raises critical concerns.

LOGICAL DESIGN REVIEW

In a logical design review, the data model is analyzed for correctness and completeness and to ensure that it accurately represents the users' environment. During this review, the business and technical issues will be thoroughly examined, but the emphasis will be on preparing for the next step of development, which is physical design. Data relationships must be reviewed, whether or not they will be physically implemented with the DBMS. Constraints, business rules, data or structural redundancy, and the life history of each entity may be reviewed.

Philosophically, a review is not held to "grade" the data modeler. It is part of a team approach to developing an effective data warehouse in which the goal is to work together to achieve the best possible design. During the review, potential physical design challenges or complex processes may become apparent. These should be noted for consideration during the logical/physical design workshop that follows.

Input for the logical design review should be prepared in advance and should include descriptions of data in third normal form or higher, definitions of data entities and attributes, data volumes, and an E-R diagram. A description of business processes should also be available. The results of a successful review include an evaluation of the data model, an action list of required changes to the data model, an understanding of the data model, and a list of issues to be addressed during the logical/physical conversion workshop, if one is to take place.

Sample leading questions for the logical design review include the following:

- Is the data model complete?
- Does it accurately represent the users' environment?
- Is data in third normal form (or higher)?
- Is data displayed in tables?
- Have repeating groups been eliminated?
- If there are multiple candidates for the primary key, has the best one been selected?
- Does the primary key contain the minimum number of columns needed to guarantee uniqueness?
- Are all attributes dependent on the key, the whole key, and nothing but the key?

After the data model has been completely reviewed, plans should begin for the process of converting the logical design to a physical design. The following questions will help prepare for the transition:

- Which front-end tools will be available to the users?
- Are user expectations realistic in view of available hardware and software?
- What summary levels are being considered at this time?
- How will the need for additional summary tables be evaluated?

- Is a multidimensional design under consideration?
- What processes will be in place for extracting data from the global warehouse or data mart for personal use?

LOGICAL/PHYSICAL CONVERSION WORKSHOP

Organizations that are new to the warehouse, the database management system, or client/server technology would do well to use this workshop. The warehouse design process is different, and the issues associated with data movement in and out of the warehouse may not be fully appreciated. The logical/physical conversion workshop is a working session, and only those who are potential contributors should participate in it. This workshop is an appropriate place to consider the data cleanup and validation processes and their efficiency.

The emphasis in this workshop, which can be held as often as needed, will initially be on the detail data. It should consider dataset placement, possible data replication, optimization of design parameters, all aspects of denormalizing for performance, if necessary, and indexing for performance. When issues of this type are considered in a working session, plans may be made before processes are developed. The cost benefits of not having to rework processes after development can be significant. It is amazing how there is always time to do it over but never time to do it right the first time. This workshop is dedicated to doing it as close to right as possible the first time. When the workshop has been completed, the DBA will be ready to code the data definition language to create warehouse objects.

PHYSICAL DESIGN REVIEW

A physical design review should be held after DDL has been created and before programming, data movement processes, or utility job streams have been created. Known or suspected data access requirements will be reviewed against the proposed physical objects, and a performance judgment will be made. The purpose is to identify design weaknesses and ensure optimization of physical design alternatives. Critical design issues, such as denormalization, partitioning, clustering, and others that will be difficult or time consuming to change later, will be considered. Simple processes should receive little or no attention.

Although there may be only limited information about expected data usage, all available information should be used to evaluate the model. Although some shops seem proud to state that they have no idea how data will be used, this is not usually correct. In some cases, they seem to prefer to ignore what is known about expected data usage. If the warehouse project was built with business objectives in mind, there should be some idea as to how the data will be used. If available information is ignored, performance reviews will be intensive.

There may be one or more physical design reviews, which must reflect the iterative nature of development. Initially, the emphasis in most traditional warehouses will be on detail data, which may reside on one or more platforms. After implementation and a "shake-out" period, other levels may be developed. Consideration of other objects will depend on the size and complexity of the warehouse and the phases of development. In many cases, later reviews will consider summaries, multidimensional databases, etc. For warehouses that are distributed across a client/server environment, data movement and its implications must be carefully considered. However, this will be entirely dependent upon the type of project.

Input to the physical design review consists of the data definition language for all objects, the install parameters for the DBMS, descriptions of on-line and batch processes, expected data usage, to the degree that it is known, data and transaction volumes, estimated growth rates, and documentation from the logical design review, if it was held. The results of the review will include an evaluation of the physical model and its ability to meet requirements in terms of flexibility, performance, data integrity, system availability, data currency, and user satisfaction. There will also be an understanding of design alternatives and trade-offs.

Leading questions will include review of physical design options for all structures.

TABLESPACE ISSUES

- Are there tablespaces larger than 1 gigabyte that are not partitioned? If so, are time estimates available for loads, reorgs, etc.?
- If there are multiple tables in one tablespace, will there be contention when tables are joined?

PARTITIONING ISSUES

- Which tables are partitioned, and why was the partitioning scheme chosen?
- Will tables use DBMS managed partitioning or user managed partitioning (i.e., lookalike tables)?
- If partitions will be reused as part of the archiving process, how will this be managed?
- How many partitions have been selected, and how was this number chosen?
- Was parallel processing considered in partitioning?
- What are data retention requirements? Are they the same for all partitions?

FREE SPACE

- What is the pattern of inserting and deleting rows?
- Will the free space allocation support this pattern?

LOCKING STRATEGY

- Has a locking strategy been developed that will optimize the trade-off between the cost of locking versus concurrency requirements? (Note: Row-level locking may provide the greatest concurrency but is also the most expensive. If it will support the concurrency requirements, tablespace locks or partition locks should be used.) Will cross-platform locking be an issue? Since data warehouses are not usually updated in the on-line environment, this is usually not an issue. In an operational data store, it may be a serious concern.

TABLES

- If denormalization has occurred, explain the expected performance benefits and the trade-offs.
- Are data types and lengths flexible enough to support future requirements?
- Which columns allow null values? In these columns, is there a need to distinguish between zeros or spaces and the absence of data?
- Have corresponding data elements (primary/foreign key related columns) been specified with the same data type and length? If not, what is the impact of joining these tables?

DATA COMPRESSION

- How much disk space will be saved?
- How often will data be read/updated?
- How much CPU consumption will be expected?

CONTROL AND REFERENCE TABLES

- Are there possible performance bottlenecks?
- Will these tables contain data other than keys?
- Has referential integrity been specified? What will be the impact on recovery processes? Are recovery processes being planned?

INDEXING

- Have indexes been placed on all primary and most foreign keys? If not, why not?
- Has the primary key been specified with the minimum number of columns to guarantee uniqueness?
- Are frequently used access paths supported by an index?
- Is there a known requirement for each index?
- Are there candidates for index-only access?

DATA VOLUMES

- What data volumes are expected?
- Are lengthy load, unloads, or reorgs expected?
- Will it be difficult to add additional indexes to large tables? If so, consider partitioning or adding additional summary levels to offload some of the expected usage.
- Are there plans to move heavy ad hoc processing to smaller platforms with less resource contention?

DATA DISTRIBUTION

- On which platforms will detail and summary data be placed?
- How will data be distributed? (Horizontal or vertical partitioning? Shared versus ad hoc personal extracts? Timestamp extracts? Replication? Propagation?)
- Has the impact of joining tables on separate servers been considered?

REPLICATION

- If there are plans to replicate tables, evaluate the replication strategy.
- Will replication be asynchronous or synchronous?
- Is it possible that users may obtain different answers to the same query by using different copies of the same table?

LINE TRAFFIC

For each user or group of users, consider

- How much line traffic will be generated?
- Is the major usage at a local or remote site?
- Is remote availability critical?
- Will answer sets be small or large?
- What priority will remote users have?

UPDATING WAREHOUSE DATA

- How will warehouse data be updated? (extraction, propagation, examination of audit trails or the log, merging before and after images, etc.)
- If data propagation or replication will be used, will it be real-time or delayed? What will be the impact on the source data?
- Are there potential bottlenecks with full volumes of data?
- Who is responsible for the updating process?
- How will the process of cleanup and integration be handled?

FEEDING WAREHOUSE SUMMARIES

- How will summary tables be created/maintained? Rebuild tables from scratch with each load? Modify summary tables with new data?
- How will data integrity be assured?
- What point in time is represented by each table? Where is this documented?
- If incorrect data is sent to a summary table, how will it be corrected?
- Will summary tables be updated during peak processing times?

ANTICIPATING CHANGES

- What is the probability that data will require restructuring to meet user requirements?

- How flexible is the database design?
- Is the data architecture scalable?
- If large numbers of users are added to the system, will it be possible to migrate easily to a larger platform? Will the operating system, end-user tools, and RDBMS operate on larger hardware platforms?

DATA DOCUMENTATION

- Are data definitions available to all users? End-user directory available?
- Will information about data ownership, the source of data, and data transformation be available?
- Who will maintain definitions and guarantee consistency across platforms?
- How will archived data be documented?

There are no right or wrong answers in a design review. As more than one guru has said, "It depends on the unique situation at hand."

PROGRAMMING APPROACH WORKSHOP

A programming approach workshop may be held to consider lengthy or complex processes, such as data movement processes, and their alternatives. It may range from a simple meeting between a programmer and a DBA to a more formal workshop with a full team. As with the logical/physical conversion workshop, it will only be held if needed. As the staff becomes more experienced with the technical issues of warehouse, the need for this workshop will be reduced.

CODE REVIEWS, COPY MANAGEMENT REVIEWS, AND UTILITY REVIEWS

These reviews are designed for programs and processes whose efficiencies might be improved. They will be most prevalent with large tables and complex processes. It may be cost effective to review processes of extracting, cleaning up, and integrating data that must be moved into the warehouse.

Input to the review will consist of program code, SQL statements, or plans for copy management or utility usage. Material will be reviewed, and others may be called in as needed to provide technical assistance. The results of the review should be improved code, copy management, etc. Lack of space prevents the publication of sample leading questions for these reviews.

PERFORMANCE REVIEWS

Performance reviews may be held when problems are noted during routine monitoring or are reported by users. Performance problems in the data warehouse usually fall into at least four categories: problems transferring data into the warehouse, problems transferring data from a global warehouse or data mart to a personal or work group database, problems with data maintenance, utilities, etc., or query problems. Problems in the first three categories will be solved in the same manner as production. Query problems may be caused by

- Poorly stated, resource-intensive queries
- Problems with query tools and their handling of queries
- Database design that does not support current usage
- Unsuitable installation parameters
- Other issues.

Staffing must be adequate so that problems may be solved quickly. In some cases, poor handling of query problems has killed the warehouse idea. Because of changing user requirements, performance problems may require indexing modification, addition of summary tables, or other design changes.

SUMMARY

Design reviews are a dynamic tool that can be used to review design decisions in an objective manner. In the warehouse environment, they must reflect the iterative nature of development. The right technical people, with the right questions, at the right time, in a cooperative environment can be used to uncover design flaws at the earliest opportunity. Properly conducted design reviews will improve the probability of developing a successful warehouse.

CHAPTER 21

The Virtual Data Warehouse

Edward M. Peters

DataDirect Division, INTERSOLV, Inc.
Rockville, Maryland

"Technology ... the knack of so arranging the world that we don't have to experience it."

Max Frisch, quoted in Daniel J. Boorstin, The Image

Data warehousing has become the de facto information systems strategy for supporting the analytical/decision-making functions in most organizations. As with many IT-led initiatives, data warehouses are often costly, require a high level of maintenance, and are lengthy to deploy. Recently, the concept of the virtual data warehouse has emerged in response to this situation. By combining a demand- rather than a supply-driven view of the information resources, with a logistics-focused deployment method that leverages middleware rather than database storage technology, the virtual data warehouse can be a value-added complement to more traditional methods. This chapter discusses the rationale for the virtual data warehouse as well as the associated methods and technologies for its realization.

Today, most organizations face a new and more complex set of business challenges than ever before. The boundaries among nations, markets, and business relationships shift and blur almost daily. Product life cycles continue to shrink. In organizations intent on thriving, the focus is expanding from simply managing operations to understanding individual customer needs and promptly meeting them.

This new focus, in turn, propels organizations to demand new kinds of support from their information systems groups. Corporate decision makers know that a better understanding of customer buying patterns enables the organization to build better products and provide better services that result in competitive advantage, and they know that the information they need is buried somewhere in the organization's computer systems. As a result, many IT executives now encounter enormous pressure to furnish the tools necessary for truly easy access and manipulation of the information required for better-quality decision making.

Given the vast amounts of data shoveled into most organization's computers, the uninitiated might think it is comparatively simple to get the right information back out again. But many IT groups simply do not have the ready ability to respond to such demands. Stored in various locations and structures, the information essential to making the right decision at the right time is often difficult to access and, in its raw form, carries little meaning from a broad business perspective. Typically, the assorted, discrete databases housing narrow streams of raw operational data are hopelessly incapable of responding to demands for timely, consolidated information about an organization's customers, products, and service competencies.

Data warehousing offers one of the best ways to translate this raw data and present it in ways that are useful to decision makers. As a database that provides end users with data extracted from OLTP and production systems, a data warehouse can support the business analysis activities that are so critical to staying competitive in these volatile times.

By establishing a data warehouse, IT managers can ensure that end users get access to the information they need while preserving the integrity of the organization's business production systems.

Traditional approaches to data warehousing require laborious construction and maintenance of separate databases specifically designed to handle the business-oriented questions of corporate decision makers. Such supply-driven data warehouses are often IT oriented and built to contain highly summarized, subject-oriented data structured for general use across the organization.

Typically, an IT manager attempts to determine the overall organizational need for decision-oriented data, develops a generalized model, chooses a physical database management system, and then loads a database containing all the data he or she believes anyone will want. The IT department must then maintain a large, generalized inventory of summarized data, as well as warehouse maintenance routines. This traditional process consists of the following steps and issues.

IDENTIFYING SOURCE DATA

This requires careful analysis of existing data and, often, development of an enterprise data model. Because this step is so complex and time consuming, it has on more than one occasion brought down entire projects before they could get on their operational feet. The problem revolves around ensuring that all the data in the enterprise data model is clarified in terms of corporate semantics, meaning that all terminology is consistent (i.e., everyone refers to "customer number" as "cust_num" or in some other immutably consistent fashion). This metadata—or data about data—is critically important to successful implementations. It ensures that the end-user view of data remains consistent no matter what semantics are in use. Another example of this uniform semantics challenge is agreeing on a definition for aggregate demand.

EXTRACTING DATA FROM OPERATIONAL SYSTEMS

Typically, data must be moved from source systems to the data warehouse, which raises such issues as refresh rates, replication methods, maintenance, and adapting data to business needs. In a typical data warehouse implementation, a batch program is written that takes data out of the OLTP system and moves it into a transformation routine and then places it in a data warehouse.

TRANSFORMING DATA FOR USE BY CORPORATE
DECISION MAKERS

Data must make sense to those using it, different data representations used in different operational databases must be resolved, and data must be cleansed to eliminate anomalies. Additionally, data may need to be combined in order to create a new data instance (such as a worldwide product code) that supports new analytical demands. This, in effect, turns the original data items into intermediate products that must be quality audited, cleansed, and transformed before further repackaging and usage.

STORING THE DATA

It must be determined whether an existing database can be used, or if there is need for a new one. Another issue is the question of whether or not there is a need for a high-speed query environment to keep up with end-user demand.

ACCESSING THE DATA

There are several issues to assess here. It must be determined if end-user tools can be used, or whether or not there is a need to develop proprietary tools. Other questions to be answered include the following: Does the warehouse really provide answers to important business questions? Is it designed to be used by all of an organizations knowledge workers, or only some?

Experience has shown that the traditional supply-driven approach to data warehousing has resulted in a number of problems and limitations. While IT departments undertake the intensive data extraction, transformation, and loading processes necessary in traditional data warehousing, end users are being told to hang on and wait for the information they need to do their jobs. IT departments need to reduce, not lengthen, lead times to access enterprise information. It has been argued that this cannot be done using a supply-side approach to data warehousing.

Other key considerations IT departments must deal with include the many constantly changing end-user information requirements. These requirements change day to day and department by department. As more information becomes available, it triggers new questions that spawn demands for still more information. Too often, inflexible, traditional data warehouses simply cannot produce the new information decision makers need.

The inability to use current desktop tools, as well as high ongoing maintenance costs associated with traditional data warehousing approaches, compound these problems. Corporate decision makers need to spend their time analyzing information, not struggling with the proprietary interfaces of traditional data warehouses. As new data sources are established, end users need flexible and open tools to enable immediate access to key information. The initial hardware and software expenses of traditional data warehousing constitute only a small part of the total cost, which is largely shaped by maintenance demands, particularly those incurred when data requirements change. These costs inevitably overburden understaffed IT groups.

THE DEMAND-DRIVEN, VIRTUAL DATA WAREHOUSE

The demand-driven, virtual data warehouse has been developed as an alternative to its supply-driven, physical data warehouse predecessor. According to advocates of this technology, in a demand-driven data warehousing process, an organization focuses on determining the data needs of individuals, departments, or work groups, concentrating on providing them with the data they need as expeditiously as possible. The concept of the virtual data warehouse was designed to address the issues discussed next.

Faster Time to Market

Delivering information to knowledge workers leads to better business practices and customer satisfaction. Understanding customer buying patterns enables organizations to build better products and services that lead to a competitive advantage. While traditional data warehousing approaches can take months (or even years) to implement, the virtual data warehouse approach focuses on understanding the end user's requirements and, wherever possible, enabling immediate access.

Complementary to Physical Data Warehouse Implementations

Data warehouses are designed to provide a storage mechanism for historical data (often summarized) that is needed for decision support or other management-oriented applications. As organizations decide how best to build and locate data warehouses in their environments, virtual warehouses can be used either as a prototype or to provide a view into operational data for real-time/operational decision making that is outside the bounds of the historically based/highly summarized warehouse data. Whether the final implementation is a centralized data warehouse, a data mart, or an operational data store, a virtual data warehouse provides a way of accessing the data from whatever storage location it resides in and also provides a semantic map that allows the end user to view it as "virtual-ized" as to its specific physical location.

Open and Flexible Architecture

Today, the average organization has implemented somewhere between four and seven distinct database platforms and a plethora of business intelligence tools. As new data sources are established, flexible and open environments are required that can provide for immediate access. Industry standards such as ODBC (and the future JDBC for Java applications) provide a widely accepted means of establishing interoperability among applications and databases. A virtual data warehouse leverages these standards and seeks to provide the widest possible range of access capabilities. Also, an open environment allows both the end users and the IT groups to focus on tools that provide "best in class" functionality, rather than becoming victims of vendor lock-out due to the implementation of proprietary technologies.

Reduced Maintenance

Initial hardware and software acquisition costs are only a small part of the entire cost of a traditional data warehouse. Indeed, the overall maintenance costs will grow exponentially as data warehouses increase in both size and scope. Highly focused data marts and virtual data warehouses allow for the overall warehouse size and complexity to be managed in a scalable fashion. This approach allows organizations to either "ramp up" to larger implementations or "ramp down" to lighter technologies as required.

The virtual data warehouse is like your office telephone PBX system. When you dial someone overseas, you have no idea how your voice is transmitted. The technical transfer mechanism may be wireless or utilize underwater fiber-optic cabling. The public carrier company provides infrastructure transparency for your telephone call. In a similar manner, a virtual data warehouse provides a "dial tone" to the data without burdening the end user with where or how the data is stored, whether it be in a data warehouse, a data mart, or an operational data store. Also, by providing a transparency layer, the warehouse/data access coordinator has the option to change the infrastructure in relation to network demands, as is the case in the telephone analogy. Overall customer service and fulfillment of customer demand in the shortest time frame is the predominant issue.

By using virtual data warehouses in addition to structured query data, end users are also able to access unstructured data—in the form of images or audio clips—whether from the Internet or via an Intranet server connected to a multimedia database. This kind of flexibility is essential as the Internet threatens to become the dominant computing paradigm and as information systems are increasing with multimedia requirements.

To build a demand-driven data warehouse, an IT group minimizes the processes needed to produce and store information. Such a just-in-time approach is designed to ensure availability of the right information to end users at the right time, allowing them to determine quickly which data is most often required. This insight can then be used to establish patterns for storing data where and when it is needed.

On the highest level, the goal is to let organizations decide what data should be stored, what data should be staged, and when. On a lower, operational level, the goal is to provide unprecedented flexibility to desktop-based end users who want to be able to access transparently any kind of data from any corporate repository without having to worry about how the process works.

By empowering these end users with their personal virtual data warehouses, they are able to access unstructured data—whether it be from the Internet or in the form of images or audio clips—as though it were a more conventional data type. This can be accomplished by providing access to multimedia databases (BLOB storage and management systems) that are either independent or coupled with a more traditional database management system. This kind of flexibility is essential as the Internet threatens to become the dominant computing paradigm and as information systems are increasingly integrated with multimedia requirements.

In this advanced environment, where the data warehouse becomes more than just a distribution center, the warehouse administrator is granted the freedom to supply the most optimized information distribution network design possible. This means that all the various data types can exist in repositories that make them the most easily accessible. This kind of logistical network engineering can only exist in a true virtual data warehouse environment.

There are striking similarities between virtual data warehouse techniques and the underpinnings of consumer goods storage and distribution. In the case of the "efficient consumer response cycle" paradigm, the idea is to shorten the path from the plant to the warehouse and from the warehouse to the consumer. This approach is based on assessing access demand patterns and then working backward, determining the best methods for meeting the demand. In the case of virtual data warehousing, this process involves deciding whether it is better to build a storage facility that provides fast data access, or to allow the data to go directly against the operational system or a shadow file of the operational system.

In addition to the aforementioned examples, other examples of virtual data warehouses include the use of an intelligent front-end query tool on a COLD (computer output to laser disk) application in the banking environment. This application starts from the assumption that all the data that appear on the report image are scrubbed and transformed and are, in essence, ready for use. By creating an indexing scheme on top of the data and allowing access via an SQL query and reporting tool, the application created a virtual warehouse out of the information stored in the reports. This information can be combined with other data that is relevant to the user/department in question independent of where the data is stored.

DATA MARTS AND THE FUNCTIONAL WAREHOUSE

As the data warehouse environment has grown more sophisticated, spin-off technologies have evolved. The data mart is one such technology. Widely viewed as a departmental warehouse, it encompasses all the operational data required by a department to perform its daily functions. Data marts are highly compatible with data warehouses because departmental users who access warehouse data download what they need to work with their internal data stores and then upload the corporate data back to the warehouse when they are finished with it. That way, their internal data mart is not contaminated with incompatible, exterior data.

Well-organized and maintained data marts based on demand-driven philosophies allow administrators to add enhanced tools such as server-based intelligent agents. Intelligent agents are capable of prompting helpful extracts and transformations (e.g., if an administrator wanted to see certain data every Friday at 4:00 P.M., the intelligent agent would make it happen). These tools can also be used in conjunction with a utilization monitor to notify the administrator that, for example, the 4:00 P.M. Friday data is being extracted daily and loaded into the data warehouse even though it is only viewed once a week. As an alternative, the intelligent agent could point out, an abstract could be run off a shadow file at noon the day before.

Data marts are integral to functional data warehouses, the latest trend in data warehouse technology. Functional data warehouse users construct data marts employing information from leading client/server or database software companies. The word *functional* is linked to these warehouses because they focus on a single corporate discipline, such as human resource planning or marketing. These glorified data marts are easy to justify because they need only gain the approval of a single department.

End users benefit because they are able to analyze better and gain enhanced access to data hidden in the databases and archives maintained by their application packages. For their part, vendors come out ahead by building seamless links between their products and the applications packages and providing semantic layers that are able to translate arcane table names into common business terms.

INFORMATION LOGISTICS

To support warehousing and the movement of information from source to target user environments, the concepts of logistics can provide some useful insights. In this case, however, the key is to view information as the product being moved. Information logistics applies modern concepts of distribution and logistics to the data management environment. It requires an organization to examine its processes for producing and distributing information as if it were an actual product. It looks to minimize both the actual processes for producing information as well as the data (parts) and storage mechanisms. It accomplishes this by using a value-chain approach following information through a life cycle from collection to distribution

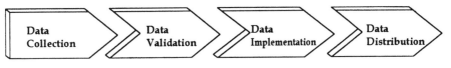

Figure 21.1   Information Value Chain.

(see Figure 21.1). Organizational activities are mapped to each life cycle/value chain stage to determine both if and where value is being added. Each phase can be defined as follows:

1. *Data collection.* This activity focuses on when, where, how, and by whom data is collected across the organization. Usually, the scope of the activity is limited to a business process (e.g., marketing) or a data subject that is shared across multiple functions (e.g., customer data). Each data attribute within the process must be classified as to whether it is data that will be commonly used across units or if it will pertain to only one specific group. Once the common data is established, an analysis is performed to determine its exact definition and range of possible values. All multiple acquisition points are eliminated yielding a single source for each attribute. This semantic map ensures that interoperability regarding the exchange of information can be accomplished. If the organization has a current repository and/or data dictionary, it can be a great source of value in this exercise.

2. *Data validation.* Most organizations spend an inordinate amount of time validating data after it has been collected. In some companies, entire units exist to simply check the work of other groups. With information logistics, validation activities for all data are implemented as part of the data collection process. Business rules for the validation of each attribute are documented during data analysis. These rules are then implemented directly in the collection technologies. If this is not possible, validation routines that check the data can be implemented before a transaction is allowed to update databases or other files. If data is being submitted on separate media (e.g., disks), special data quality software can be used to prescreen the data. If errors are present, the disks can be returned to the submitting party to be rectified.

3. *Data implementation.* This activity is concerned with the maintenance and storage of data prior to distribution. The implementation of each attribute is assigned to a specific maintenance system. It is then the responsibility of each system to ensure that the data is properly implemented so that all information demand can be sourced from that storage mechanism. This concept is analogous to a factory that is designated the single-source manufacturing location for a given product component. This allows for maximum flexibility in the information production process.

4. *Data distribution.* Data distribution is concerned with ensuring that data is available for using processes when and where needed. Information logistics utilizes the concept of cross docking. Cross docking is a modern logistics concept that promotes the idea of placing product in a staging area rather than in a warehouse to avoid the costs associated with physical storage and distribution. Cross docking assumes that the product will spend a minimal time in the staging area and will be picked up at the customer's (or customer agent's) earliest convenience. In terms of the hierarchy of distribution alternatives, it is not as preferable as direct factory shipments but is more desirable than warehousing for the previously given reasons. Additionally, data placed in the cross-docking facility will have the following characteristics:

- *Short-term inventory.* Data will reside in the staging area for a maximum of one day. This will require each user and/or application process to pick up fresh data daily and move it to its own warehouse or storage location if it is required.

- *Populated at the lowest level of detail.* While some derived data will necessarily be placed in the cross-docking facility, no summary data will be located there. Summarized data is rightfully stored in application-specific (e.g., sales history) data warehouses, which can be created from data found in the staging area.

- *No backward migration.* A cross-docking facility does not permit goods to be transferred back to the source location. All maintenance to source data can only be performed via designated collection and validation processes.

- *Not responsible for data quality.* Quality is the responsibility of the data collection and validation processes. The staging area is a distribution mechanism and has no role in the production process. Therefore, it has no role ensuring the quality of the data received; this is the domain of the data creation and validation programs.

A second supporting factor in the information logistics and virtual data warehouse environment is the subject of middleware. Despite the warehousing approach or combinations thereof (e.g., virtual data warehouses combined with data marts), middleware is the piece that connects the end user with the desired source data. To provide data access effectively, any middleware solution must have the following capabilities:

1. *Ability to access multiple databases simultaneously.* Multiple databases are the norm in most organizations. Middleware solutions that provide access to all data sources contained in heterogeneous databases are critical for any decision support or data warehousing implementation.

2. *Ability to access mainframe and client/server data warehouses without performance bottlenecks.* While much attention has been placed on the legacy data that resides on the mainframe (often MVS) environment, little attention has been focused on the legacy applications that exist in the client/server environment. These applications are often storehouses of source data that are required for the decision support environment. Often, these databases can only be accessed via gateways that provide an unacceptable performance bottleneck. The best solution would be for the middleware to provide an open systems network connection (such as TCP/IP) that allows organizations to leverage existing network protocols.

3. *Flexible and scalable architecture for data warehousing.* As organizational needs for data access change, middleware solutions need to manage connections efficiently and maintain context information between databases without impact to the desktop analytical applications.

4. *Ability to use best-of-breed desktop tools.* In addition to using multiple database management systems, most end users have a combination of analytical tools ranging from spreadsheets to OLAP engines on their desktops. A true middleware solution needs to provide users access to all their tools by supporting industry standards, such as ODBC and JDBC.

On the highest level, the goal is to provide unprecedented flexibility to desktop-based end users who want transparent access to any kind of data from any corporate repository, from anywhere, at any time without having to worry about how the process works. On an operational level, the goal is to let organizations decide what data should be stored, what data should be staged, and what data should be accessed directly.

In such an environment, the data warehousing and middleware connectivity strategy allows the IT group to provide the most optimized information distribution network design possible. All the various data types can exist in repositories that make them the most easily accessible, thereby providing the maximum value to the end user. This level of value, so necessary in today's competitive environment, can only be delivered where the focus is squarely on solving the data accessibility problem—with the virtual warehouse, physical warehouse, and middleware all working in concert to a common end.

SUMMARY

Virtual data warehouses can be extremely useful to organizations that wish to shorten their technology implementation cycles. By focusing on the overall demand for information and working backward through the information logistics cycle, faster implementation times can be achieved by leveraging the middleware/data access technology. This approach complements the physical data warehouse by permitting faster implementation of pilot projects and helping to clarify both the type of information and the access requirements that the warehouse efforts will need to support. Additionally, it provides an insulation layer between the business intelligence tools and the physical databases, allowing the warehouse administrator to make performance changes to the physical structures without disturbing the end users' ability to access their critical data consistently.

CHAPTER

Operational Data Stores:
Developing
an Effective Strategy

22

John Ladley
META Group
St. Louis, Missouri

"What we need is a long-term quick fix."

caption from a Wall Street Journal *cartoon, March 17, 1992*

The data warehousing concept has, in most cases, proven to be an effective application of information technology to business needs. Organizations swept up in the fervor and potential benefits of data warehouse invariably run into the operational problem, however. This occurs when the integrated data begins to appeal to others than decision makers in the organization. For example, the controller function sees the data warehouse cranking out information that could be used to generate adjusting journal entries as well as financial reports. The data warehouse manager receives the request and cries "Infidel, you can't make a data warehouse operational!" While resident data warehouse experts are correct in this statement, they will also find themselves challenging the data warehouse gurus. You cannot combine operational behavior and data warehouse, but why not apply elements of the data warehouse approach to operational and legacy software problems? Shouldn't there be a way?

THE ODS

Enter the ODS. In the last few years, this other vehicle for storing data has surfaced. The ODS is an off-shoot to the data warehouse phenomenon. An operational data store is built like a data warehouse, yet it is subject to the same sorts of demands placed on traditional transaction-based data stores. An ODS is an architectural construct that is

- Subject oriented
- Integrated (i.e., collectively integrated)
- Volatile
- Currently valued
- Comprised of only corporate detailed data.[1]

The ODS is organized by subject, vis à vis a specific application or business function. The data in the ODS is organized around a consistent model. It is updated on a frequent, regular basis—that is, specific columns in tables are updated. No historical data is kept. Finally, the data is kept at a detailed level with little or no summarization.

A data warehouse can be contrasted with an operational data store as follows:

DATA WAREHOUSE	OPERATIONAL DATA STORE
Nonvolatile	Volatile
Time variant	Current, or near current
Integrated	Integrated
Subject oriented	Subject oriented

For example, if an organization was developing a data warehouse, the following scenario would usually occur:

- *Legacy data is inadequate.* All DW projects start with a business's need for integrated data and an infrastructure to support it. For example, a business is having trouble making effective decisions because data is contradictory and incomplete. One decision support system is based on financial data, and it shows that two product lines are not performing adequately; while another, based on manufacturing data, shows performance in excess of forecast. Meetings between the finance and manufacturing executives have been very intense.
- *Model the desirable data.* The next fundamental step in DW is the creation or use of a data model. Over the years, an organization has had to adapt legacy systems to business changes, and you are now to the point where the operational environment does not reflect the current business environment model. A model representing a benchmark view of your industry is developed. This model reconciles the difference between the financial view and the manufacturing view.
- *Source and transform the data.* A system of record is analyzed and defined to provide data to the data warehouse, and then the old data is mapped to the new model. One or two crucial subject areas are sourced and transformed into the new business model. Consensus is developed for business measurement because the same business rules for transformation apply to the data that finance and manufacturing will be viewing.
- *Use it.* A data warehouse environment also provides a means to access the new data. Ad hoc tools are used by power users to access the new integrated data

stores. The uniform presentation of data allows manufacturing and finance to work from a common reference point.

Applying the same process to developing an operational data store would result in the following example:

- *Legacy data is inadequate.* A business organization is growing via acquisition, and the new subsidiaries are marketing products also produced by the parent. It is impossible to tell if the new subsidiaries are cannibalizing the market for the similar products. It is also possible that products could be shipped interchangeably, thus improving delivery time.
- *Model the desirable data.* New operating divisions run disparate software, but results must be merged for responding to business needs. A model representing a uniform view of products and product lines is developed.
- *Source and transform the data.* A system of record is identified in each subsidiary to provide data to a mapping process. The mapping process restates the various product data into a uniform set of daily activity. The appropriate transactions are identified and mapped to the new model. New product activity is added to the ODS on a daily basis.
- *Use it.* New operational reports are produced from the operational data store. New reports show that products can be interchanged to speed up delivery. Once the product activity data is too old for operational use, it is summarized to a data warehouse.

Updating a column or field in a data warehouse is usually not smart; doing the same in an operational data store is OK. Asking a data warehouse to create an operational transaction for a downstream system is not smart. Asking the operational data store to do this should be encouraged. If a data warehouse is like a public library, an ODS is the magazine stand on the corner.

An ODS is *not* OLTP, however. Like DW, ODS is a way to work around a legacy environment that does not present data uniformly or in an integrated fashion. Little is done in the way of defining specific business processes (for example, update order, deny credit) when an ODS or a data warehouse is developed. When an OLTP system is developed, business process definition is extremely important.

This chapter assumes that an ODS is another aspect, or flavor, of data warehouse–based decision support technology. The ODS and data warehouse are branches on the same tree. They may perform different functions, but both are capable of bearing fruit. Once this is accepted, determining if an ODS or data warehouse is called for becomes part of the overall strategy of using this type of technology. ODS can be leveraged as much as classic data warehouse to provide value to an enterprise.

The remainder of this chapter will discuss the following:

- The architectural advantage of ODS.
- Development of a strategy to recognize the need for ODS by examining the various business drivers that can be involved.

- Examination of the business drivers in light of tactical and strategic use of ODS. Within each approach, key data and architectural considerations affecting the ODS design and development will be examined.
- Review of considerations common to strategic and tactical uses of ODS.

One attendee at a conference for ODS and DW recently summed it up in a conference evaluation: "I understand what one is, but I still don't know if I need an operational data store." At the end of this chapter, you should be able to answer this question.

WHAT IS THE ADVANTAGE OF ODS?

The best way to answer this question is to understand what kind of technology data warehouse technology (DWT) really is. First, it is a leveraging technology. Data warehouse technology refers to a set of methods, techniques, and tools that are leveraged together and used to produce a vehicle that delivers data to end users on an integrated platform. Data warehouse technology *is not* a data warehouse. You apply data warehouse technology to create a data warehouse. Data warehouse technology can also be applied to build an ODS. Data from applying data warehouse technology can be used to supply managers and executives with data to form decisions, trigger business events, or assist in day-to-day operations. Most applications of data warehouse technology are accomplished without radical new types of hardware or software. Most are developed with existing hardware and RDBMS technology. The focus is on approach.

Data warehouse technology is not the end in itself. Too many advances in information technology have met with an untimely fate by focusing entirely on the technology as an end, not the means to solve a business problem. Data warehouse technology must therefore be applied to business problems. By understanding the business problem, the application of DWT becomes simplified. Creation of an ODS versus a data warehouse becomes a decision driven by business reasons, not technology.

Both ODS and data warehouse offer a layer between the operational, legacy world and the access to the data produced by that world. Note that there is no real difference in paradigm, or even primary architecture (refer to Figure 22.1). I can have an ODS in place in my enterprise. Several old systems are feeding data through a data transformation. An old system can be replaced. The new data may replace the old data, but there is no apparent change to the user of the ODS or DW.

Figure 22.1 pertains to ODS, but the picture could just as easily apply to DW. There is source data, extract, transformation, and placement on an accessible database. One of the old data sources is replaced by a shiny new application, which produces new data to be transformed. To the user of the ODS, there is no visible change in the report content. The user of the data is protected from the vagaries of the operational data by the integrated model on which the operational data store or data warehouse is built. This last fact is what opens up both tactical and strategic possibilities for use of data warehouse technology, particularly ODS.

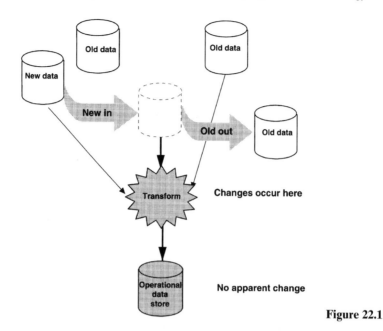

Figure 22.1

There are many times when an organization would like not to interrupt usage of a system while it is undergoing major overhaul. Transitioning to new hardware or replacing large legacy systems can be made simpler by continuing to pull data from the ODS, even while the new operational system is built. Refer again to Figure 22.1. A new system could be built upstream from the data transformation process, and in theory, it would be transparent to the users. Data warehouse technology offers a consistent data layer while the operating environment is in transition.

Another possibility for use of ODS is reference data. Uniform codes and core subject areas can be placed in an ODS or data warehouse and act as a transition agent. Developing the model produces consistent definition of codes and reference subject areas (like customer or product). A bonus benefit from a data warehouse project can be a uniform set of enterprisewide allowable code values (domains) as well as an integrated customer or product master file. Not only are they used by data warehouse technology applications, but new operational application development teams benefit immensely from this level of work that is already accomplished.

Although the popular perception of ODS is that it is operational or tactical only, the ODS can also be used strategically. The roots of ODS lay in the desire for organizations that do not have integrated operational systems to act as if they have one.

UNDERSTANDING THE BUSINESS DRIVERS

Classifying the Problem

Determining the need for an operational data store is harder than asking if a data warehouse is needed. Many organizations have slipped up here while applying data warehouse technology. Take the controller's request in the early paragraphs of this chapter. It is easy for the pragmatic person to say, "Why not? How often do I get a chance to really impress the controller?" But implementing a data warehouse when operational data store was called for, or vice versa, has created widespread problems for users of this technology. Imagine the uproar when operational performance constraints are demanded from a data store containing a star schema structure or when an analysis of seven years of data is requested from a data structure that is updated hourly. To apply and determine the efficacy of data warehouse technology, there must be a process to classify the business problem at hand. If not, you risk a technical project failing for technical reasons, and this is a great way to ruin the credibility of any development effort. The starting point for this process, like many other information technology projects, is defining the types of events that are driving the business. The business needs can be used to determine the mix of ODS/DW.

Like other business decisions, the application of information technology is directed by strategic or tactical factors. Strategic projects have long-term benefits and tend to take a bit longer to develop. They may profoundly alter business processes and are usually internally inspired. For example, the replacement of a core business system is strategic in nature. Tactical efforts focus on earlier benefits and rarely alter basic business features drastically. They may be instigated externally or internally. For example, tactically, an organization may reorganize business units, acquire a company, or be forced into meeting a regulatory requirement.

Strategic Drivers

Strategic events can take place in an enterprise that affect the application of data warehouse technology. These events can be classified into generic groups. There may be overlap perceived between the groups, but that is OK. We need to define a starting point in order to understand the process of determining the type and flavor of data warehouse technology and the use of ODS. The following approach has proven to be effective. What are listed are strategic events that can be enhanced by the application of data warehouse technology. It is understood that other strategic events that are not listed here can take place in an organization, such as buying a competitor or opening a new factory.

- *Technology transition:* A company decides to replace core mainframe systems with client/server technology.
- *Competitive use of data:* A retailer decides to control inventory level closely by looking at point-of-sale transactions many times a day.
- *Trend performance:* An insurance company monitors profitability of a financial insurance product over a period of five years.
- *"Influencing" reporting:* Another insurance company uses its data warehouse to disclose proof of higher losses and qualify for a rate increase.
- *Merger/reorganization:* An international financial organization needs a way to consolidate its lending and investment subsidiaries into one database for executive decision making.

Tactical Drivers

Tactical events can also be identified that influence the application of data warehouse technology. These events are also classified into generic groups. There may also be overlap, and our purpose is still to get a starting point for sorting out the nature of the requirements presented by business problems at hand. Certainly, there are tactical events an enterprise can initiate that do not appear here. Once again, we are only looking for those that affect the application of data warehouse technology.

- *Integrated reporting:* Multiple operating units have developed software too independently. It is impossible to get a consistent view of product data.
- *Feedback/triggers:* A health plan wants to alert physicians to possible drug interactions by monitoring patient prescription activity.
- *Transaction generation:* Accumulation of frequent flier miles needs to trigger issuance of a free travel voucher.
- *Consolidated reporting:* An organization needs a way to consolidate its subsidiaries into uniform financial statements.

When these general classifications are mapped into a matrix, we can see how ODS or data warehouse can be leveraged to satisfy these business drivers.

Examine the ODS column in Figure 22.2. (Since this is a chapter about ODS, the data warehouse column will be ignored—or else the title of the chapter has to change.) Our drivers have been classified by strategic and tactical and have been placed where it is felt that data warehouse technology can appropriately be applied.

As each business driver is discussed, refer to Figure 22.3, which shows, in a generic sense, a fairly typical arrangement of old and new information systems. Some of the systems are single functions at one location, while others are spread across several locations. One system is external, originating from a subsidiary. It does not matter what particular function the systems perform. All of them are planned, according to this chart, to be fed into an ODS. After some period, another process will populate the data warehouse.

	ODS	DW
Strategic	• Technology transition • Merger/reorganization	• Competitive use of data • Influencing reporting
Tactical	• Integrated reporting • Consolidation and migration • Transaction generation	• Feedback/triggers

Figure 22.2

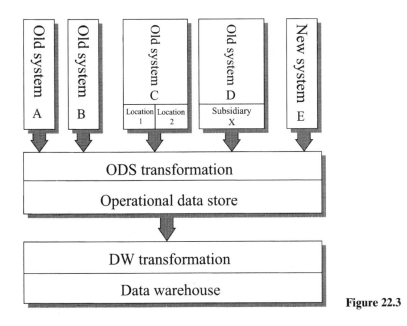

Figure 22.3

ODS AS A STRATEGIC TOOL

Strategic applications are usually thought to be an unlikely use of ODS. This happens for several reasons. First, ODS and data warehouse are relatively new concepts. New approaches to problem solving are usually applied tactically at first. Second, the entire data warehouse technology approach is very iterative and rapid. Tactical speed is therefore implied, with frequent iterations and short-term deliverables. Finally, a robust market of software products exists that also address some of the problems addressed by data warehouse technology, such as coordinating reference data or reproducing data in new formats. There is a tendency in the information technology disciplines to seize on the most robust items and overlook simpler approaches (like ODS).

How, then, does operational data store accommodate this long view?

Strategic Business Drivers

The first driver to examine is technology transition: a prominent IT strategy is to implement client/server applications to replace traditional mainframe applications. The average IT organization is presented with a problem: How do we report operational results and provide data to operate the business while the technology transition is taking place and new technology is coming onstream? At some point there will be new software on one platform producing operational data alongside the old software. There will most likely be multiple data models, with limited commonality between them. The objective is to convert from an old environment to a new one with as little disruption as possible. The transparent flexibility offered by ODS becomes valuable. (Remember Figure 22.1.)

The strategic use of ODS here is to combine operational results from old and new systems into the ODS and generate reports based on the new data model. In Figure 22.3, assume that new system E is a shiny new client/server application. Several benefits accrue:

- Progress in replacing systems B and C can be made transparent. Old systems functions can be moved to the new system E, making migration less difficult.
- The data model produced for the ODS forms a solid foundation for an enterprise-level data model.
- Reference data and domain tables are available to the old systems that are not slated for replacement. If B and C are from different business lines, the reference data provides excellent benchmarks for business changes.

If the business solution is to support merger/reorganization strategies, a new data model is also generated, but one that is common to the various enterprises being viewed as one. Holding companies with many similar businesses or large multinational organizations would find strategic ODS appropriate for this driver. Again refer to Figure 22.3. A pro-forma set of reports could be developed to determine effects from merging Subsidiary X into the business line in System C, or reengineering common processes into both C and Subsidiary X. The benefits are as follows:

- Up-to-date business events translated into common terms are available.
- Possible currency and timing differences are factored out.

Data Considerations

The technology transition presents interesting challenges for the data warehouse technology implementor. Due to the operational nature of ODS, the data model and ODS physical structures will be much more normalized than the traditional data warehouse. Many business events will be stored as transactions. Data within this operational data store will be synchronized across multiple systems, functions, or operating units. If there is a requirement for frequent updating of the ODS (i.e., several times a day), then these efforts can incur relatively high expenses in middleware to maintain data consistency.

If Systems A, B, and D are extremely different in the data relationships contained, mapping to the ODS can get very difficult. Serious consideration may be given to restricting this type of strategic activity to single subject areas. Once the success of the single subject area proves the concept, funding for the remainder of the subject areas can be obtained.

The merger/reorganization scenario offers a simpler challenge—that of defining a level of measurement and summarization that still reflects business events (remember, it is an ODS) and presents an "apples-to-apples" picture. The data considerations also should include security of critical nearly real-time business events.

Architectural Considerations

The technology transition ODS will most likely feature a mix of platforms and topologies. Mixed source systems and the combining of data residing in new and old networks can complicate the development of transformation processes and the use of a data warehouse management tool.

During client/server migration projects, several other technologies may enter the picture. Data replication and synchronization tools can be used in conjunction with data warehouse technology tools to create an ODS. Combined with the mix of source systems, there can be a substantial investment in tools. A more likely scenario is the use of ODS instead of synchronization and replication tools. Change data capture technology is critical to successful use of ODS in a technology migration project, as is the metadata capture that any data warehouse technology tools may offer.

The migration/reorganization scenario can be handled on any topology that supports data warehouse technology. Given the possible global nature of one of these, communications and transferring data create the largest technical challenges. In addition, communications security requires serious consideration, given the sensitive nature of the data being transmitted.

In summary, ODS does have strategic usefulness. Organizations may have to evaluate costs of development versus the advantages presented by an integrated source of operational data. ODS does offer a simple, proven alternative to coordination and synchronization challenges that arise from strategic projects.

ODS AS A TACTICAL TOOL

Developing and using ODS tactically is nearly the same as using data warehouse. The leveraging aspect of the technology shines. Iterations of development are used to bring integrated data into an operational arena. Tactical operational data stores should be developed in a Rapid Application Development (RAD) environment, with six months being the average duration between value-added deliverables. Refer to Figure 22.3 once again as the business drivers supporting tactical operational data store are reviewed.

Understanding the Business Drivers

Integrated reporting is one of the more common tactics associated with ODS. Due to historical changes to legacy systems, organizations may find it impossible to get a consistent view of data across common business lines or physical locations. Subsidiary X manufacturing results and data from old System C locations can be combined to give uniform, near-current updates of all locations under the control of the enterprise. The business value of ODS becomes obvious when this information is needed to keep an enterprise competitive.

- Information that is integrated in a near-current fashion allows greater responsiveness.
- New domain or reference data can be integrated and made available; for example, to prevent duplicate servicing of customers and allow for a central data store of membership.

Transaction generation has received a great deal of attention from data warehouse technology experts. The tactical approach is to use the integrated aspects to make decisions and generate business events. Besides the aforementioned frequent flier example, other examples are contacting customers after long periods of inactivity, generating rewards and premiums, or alerting management when predetermined measurements are exceeded. In Figure 22.3, assume that Systems A, B, and C would represent activity captured from multiple credit card transaction sources. Unusual buying patterns could trigger an intervention to ensure a credit card has not been stolen. The business benefits derived from transaction generation via operational data store are as follows:

- There is responsiveness, even when there are multiple factors influencing business events.
- Transactions can be provided to multiple downstream systems to synchronize triggering events and present integrated information.

Consolidation and migration is different from integrated reporting. The integrated ODS is used not only to provide a uniform view, but detailed data is also uniformly consolidated for roll-up and analysis. Consolidation of detail to uniform financial statements is a common use for this tactic. Collection of external data to do operational reports and then migrate or roll up the data from the ODS to the data warehouse is another common use. For example, suppose Systems A, B, and C are work-order-type systems that provide data on vehicle maintenance. System E collects data from an external service that monitors overhaul trends in major machinery components. The ODS is used to provide operational reports and do predictive maintenance. Data is then migrated to the data warehouse for analysis and feedback into future preventative and predictive maintenance programs.

This business driver appears frequently with the other drivers. The primary benefits are as follows:

- Provides an architecture to leverage both the ODS and the DW.
- Offers the benefits of synchronization and responsiveness that were presented earlier.

Data Considerations

None of the drivers for tactical operational data store demand anything unusual from a data modeling aspect. There may be somewhat of a challenge if the consolidation requires producing summarized tables for reporting. Designing frequently updated summary tables requires consideration and management of expectations, given that a report produced from the summarized data one day may look different the next. There is an argument to be made that an ODS used to meet the aforementioned business drivers can be based on more narrowly defined or less abstract models. This will not contribute much to an enterprise model, however.

Architectural Considerations

ODSs developed for consolidation and migration and integrated reporting tend to be small and may contain limited types of summarization for the production of near-current reports. ODS for transaction generation can get large, especially in financial environments. Tactical ODSs are developed as any other data warehouse technology. Considerations have to be made for the fact that you may be updating columns. The amounts of storage can rival DW and get expensive due to the dynamic nature of operational data store. If transaction generation is occurring, OLTP issues enter the picture, such as rapid database recovery, file locking, etc.

COMMON CONSIDERATIONS

The ODS approach to strategic and tactical business problems requires certain considerations.

Accuracy, Integrity, and Controls

Mapping legacy data to another data model changes the appearance of that data. This means that credibility must be developed with those that have spent time using the old data. As data is transformed, appropriate controls must be in place to ensure consistent and accurate transformation. Controls must also be in place to ensure that data integrity is maintained as data moves between platforms and across networks. Eventual users of the ODS or data warehouse must also approve of the controls in place to generate assurances of accuracy as soon as possible.

Domain Tables and Reference Data

The new model will produce requirements for new domain tables (code values) and reference data (product, customer, etc.) Developing and populating these tables can generate a large portion of the project budget, and subsequent maintenance of these can provide incremental costs for the IT organization. Never underestimate how difficult it is to have an organization define what a customer is.

Migration Rules

The rules for when and how to migrate the ODS data to data warehouse are crucial when the operational data store supports tactical business drivers and provides data to populate the DW. These migration rules are, in essence, transformation-type business rules. They state when data in an organization is no longer required at a detail level.

Role of Metadata

Metadata is important. There is a tendency to allow metadata to take a back seat to accessing the data and using it. The bad taste left by experiences with CASE tools promotes this tendency. Metadata is the crucial documentation for data warehouse technology. Implementing data warehouse technology without it is like building a 70-story office building and not saving the blueprints.

Support and Maintenance

The ODS is like any other piece of business application software: It will require administration, user support, and maintenance. ODS using data synchronization will require expertise to maintain the middleware. Additionally, communication of changes to upstream systems is crucial, and many organizations do not have change management processes that are tight enough to prevent miscommunication. Integration of data will not occur if the groups maintaining the legacy applications fail to inform the ODS team of changes to file structures. ODS does tend to be more expensive—staff familiar with DWT must be retained, as well as talent that can work in an environment of multiple architectures. These ongoing costs are overlooked by many organizations.

SUMMARY

The ODS and data warehouse are members of the same technology family. Both are delivered by a common approach, and both add value to businesses. When dealing with the possibility of ODS as a solution, it is most important to evaluate the nature of the business situation (i.e., is it strategic or tactical?). Then it is important to understand what kind of driver, or result, the business requires from the application of data warehouse technology. Several examples were provided to show that understanding the business needs can simplify any confusion that may arise while deciding if an operational data store is required.

REFERENCES

[1] INMON, W. H., *Building the Operational Data Store,* New York, John Wiley & Sons, 1996.

Data Mining

Richard Yevich
RYC, Inc.
Key Biscayne, Florida

"True genius resides in the capacity for evaluation of uncertain, hazardous, and conflicting information."

Sir Winston Churchill

Data warehouses today encompass all forms of informational processing, with data mining being a major part of this trend. Data mining cannot be easily defined; in the past it has been referred to as knowledge management or knowledge engineering. Data mining has, until recently, been an obscure and exotic technology, discussed more in the theoretical realms and the artificial intelligent arenas. The generally accepted definition is that data mining is the process of searching through details of data for unknown patterns or trends. Past methods of searching through mounds of data for a specific fact, or facts that match certain criteria, is not what data mining is today. Data mining is more comparable to a forensic pathologist and a detective, examining everything in their domain, looking for related patterns to solve a crime. They do not ask a query language to look for specific facts, but rather to look at all the facts to ascertain if there is a pattern or relationship that has meaning. This involves a method of searching until a sequence of patterns emerge or not, whether complete or only within an allowable probability. This also involves software extensions to query languages and new software tools. Data mining software products are specialized query tools, or extensions to SQL, that allow users to perform mining processes.

WHAT IS DATA MINING?

Large databases are searched for relationships, patterns, and trends, which prior to the search were not known to exist or were not visible. Sometimes these relationships might be assumed by knowledge engineers or marketers but need to be proven or refined. The result of data mining is new information or knowledge that will allow the user community to be better at what it does. The difficulty with data mining is that very large databases need to be processed for what is often just a few related facts. The algorithm and search criteria that was used will probably not be used in the exact same way again. The search criteria, once used to gain insight into some particular pattern or trend, will tend to be modified before the next execution, and the data that is being examined tends to cover years of details or terabytes of storage.

In simpler terms, data mining is asking a processing engine to show answers to questions we do not know how to ask. Rather than saying in normal query language to a relational database, "Go find me all the people who bought windows shades this year that also bought linens sometime later," it is asking the process to "find related buying patterns" and getting a response: "There is a pattern that occurs x% of the time that when someone buys window coverings (not shades, or blinds, or other specifics), and within 1 to 3 months buys linens, within the next 4 months buys furniture." When asking for specific relationships, more important relationships might be missed. Asking to find relationships that we do not know exist will yield more meaningful data or business knowledge.

There are several technologies that have to come together to allow data mining to function. First, and one of the most important, is enterprise data warehouse implementation. Data mining should be able to examine all the data in some cohesive storage format. Databases implemented as data warehouses are only the beginning of that format. Second, there should be a repository or directory of enterprise information. This is necessary to allow users or tools to locate the appropriate information sources. To allow information analysts to search the data mines, it is critically important for them to be aware of all the information that is stored in these systems. Information mined from only part of a business's data store yields potentially worthless information. Data mining tools actually need to be able to search the warehouse data, the operational data, the legacy data, and any distributed data on any number of servers. To effectively mine data, all data must be known and available. Third, there must be tools available that implement mining technology. Several tools are available, and they fall into very different categories. Mining technology has been developed using tested algorithmic processes such as nearest-neighbor algorithms, decision trees, and data visualization. Newer methods are being discovered, and some are extensions to SQL through standard use by means of user-defined functions, or UDFs. Others are stand-alone products built on the framework of research or software developed for artificial intelligence, such as neural networks. Some tools are specific for particular areas of the industry, such as finance or insurance. These tools result from research conducted in those specific market areas, and they use defined relationships in the particular business model. General data mining tools are also beginning to appear, without a specific business market but relying on defined relationships in the data model. The neural network tools have had a tremendous impact on businesses when searching for information to solve problems that human analyses could not find. What has happened with data mining is that technology has finally leaped into an information processing arena from the older daily data processing paradigm. The result of the research is that data mining methods are falling into standard categories, and the result of these methods is specific groups of information that have similar properties.

DATA MINING WAREHOUSES

Data mining can be done most easily on data that has been moved or processed into a data warehouse. Mining does not mean analyzing details of data alone. Pattern analysis is also critical when performed on lightly summarized data, especially for trends and patterns in financial analysis. What is different with data mining is the dominant need for enterprisewide data warehouses, or at least access to enterprisewide data. This data may or may not be in an enterprise warehouse, but it could be stored in multiple heterogeneous systems scattered throughout the enterprise. Many businesses are using data warehouses built from operational data housing all the details of the business. The simple reason for this is ease of construction. Operational data is available for any business cycle. Capturing it and storing it in a historical set of tables allows easy data mining for both trend and pattern analysis. The other extreme is being able to mine all the data, within a distributed enterprise, when the data is in a number of formats stored on different platforms, not even related. The ultimate warehouse is all the data in the enterprise available through the network, appearing as a single warehouse store, accessible through the use of an information catalog. The larger problem with this approach today is not the accessing of that data, but whether the data is clean. This adds a layer of complexity to the data mining warehouse: the validation of the data being searched. Many redundancies will exist in the data. These will not be easily identified because nonrelated application areas use the same data but call it differently. This is especially true where legacy systems are involved or where their data is accessible.

Non-enterprisewide data is also used for data mining, where information is required for an individual business function or divisional area. These warehouses tend to be extractions of relational databases propagated to smaller servers used with powerful workstations. The data mining in these instances tends to be very industry or function specific. For example, why are so many insurance claims of a particular type occurring in a geographical area? The dilution of the data over the entire enterprise may not yield any patterns; however, the region-specific data may yield a frequent pattern of associations.

Within financial analysis, the data tends to be summarized or grouped with value-added data. This data, propagated and processed on the regional server, will allow an industry- or processing-specific analysis. These smaller sets of data warehouses tend to be called data marts. Data marts participate in data mining, possibly to a higher degree than enterprise warehouses, depending on the type of mining and the intended results.

Within both the enterprise data warehouses and the server-sized data marts, the added value issue is the difference between the historical storage of operational data and the requirements for data mining. This is best demonstrated with a simple diagram (Figure 23.1) of mining patient and diagnosis data.

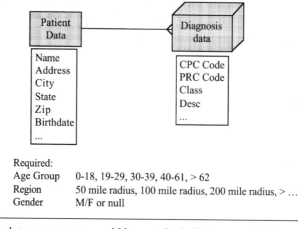

Required:
Age Group   0-18, 19-29, 30-39, 40-61, > 62
Region   50 mile radius, 100 mile radius, 200 mile radius, > ...
Gender   M/F or null

1 – From birth date, age groups would have to be built, but would change with queries
2 – Region could be done by zip code, but not radius – additional data required
3 – Gender was stored in operational data but not certified leading to 17 different types
    of gender. Required an operational deviation based on percentage of dirty gender.

Figure 23.1

Value-added data, such as age group, would have to be calculated and verified. The patient's age in some of these systems is different among tables or data stores and is in disagreement with the age maintained on historical records. The age groupings would be different depending on the reason for the mining. The data mining could be for a very specific assumed relationship between age, gender, and diagnosis. It could be completely unknown, with the mining tool having to define and relate differing age groupings.

The same difficulty holds true for the retail market. The analysis for buying patterns and the relationship between sequential buying events is dependent on some common identifier, which may not have been captured during the purchase transaction. The common identifier might have to be derived by querying other systems. The purchaser might have used a store credit card, a bank credit card, a check, or cash. If a system is going to mine data coming from purchases, it will need that common identifier. The accuracy of the results that could be driving marketing campaigns could end up severely damaged. For example, one large electronics chain always asks for phone numbers when any purchase is made. From an analysis made, some individuals use different phone numbers or phony numbers each time they purchase, without any apparent devious reason. If this is a common practice, the data should not even be considered as a target for the mine, and if this information was contained in the warehouse, it should not be made available for mining processes.

Some business operational data immediately lends itself to a data warehouse that satisfies all categories of queries. In the transportation industry, for example, with railroads, a warehouse of cars and customers would be very accurate and could easily be mined for patterns. A large railroad, crossing many geographic boundaries, would easily provide justification for regional data marts for marketing and projection mining.

As we continually move into processing information, data stores in data warehouses, data marts, and even object-oriented databases will continually change in structure and use. With each new query and information result, new data or value-added data might be required. Competitiveness in business will rewrite the standards for data warehouse construction for data mines.

VERIFICATION VERSUS DISCOVERY

Decision support methods utilized for many years are, in many instances, a form of data mining. These are verification systems that assume that a lot of knowledge already exists prior to the data mining. In the early 1980s, with the advent of relational databases, it was possible to ask a database for answers dynamically. This was a new technique in data processing previously done by hand. In casinos, there were casino hosts, who employed a unique set of classification systems. As knowledge engineers, they could observe a new customer and immediately categorize that customer into either a high roller of value or one of many other categories. When a casino stages an event, hosts could select from their customer base a group that fits a particular classification pattern. As the casinos started to computerize customer play and store this data over time, sequencing patterns, as well as classifications, began to emerge. A casino could now effectively target a specific market (a classification group) based on a similar sequence, with the knowledge rules from the hosts affecting the bottom line of the business. In these systems, a decision maker forms an SQL query, using predicates based on the hosts' rules, and submits it against the required tables in the relational database. The resulting data could then be turned over to the marketers. This is verification data mining.

This was data mining of relational databases in its infancy. While it has high impact business value, it can only assist or automate known processes. The information desired must fit into a set of definable rules or logic. The resulting data only has value if the query is accurate. A business could be doing the wrong thing if the query is not constructed correctly or if the rules are not correct for the percentage of the set being examined. Basic decision-making systems rely on this type of data mining, and for ordinary simple decisions, it may be accurate. However, it is totally inaccurate for competitive advantage that must change with each business cycle. Today, these older approaches can make use of new tools and processes to add discovery data mining systems to the decision-making process.

DATA MINING TECHNIQUES

Relational databases are the best store of data for data mining. Data mining depends in part on existing relationships, which are easily built into the design of relational databases for warehouses. The information that is to be retrieved from these databases is not necessarily result sets from the databases, but information derived from an analysis of the relational data. The derivation of data comes from two different techniques, which have always been identified with any logical approach to information. These two different methods are deduction and induction.

Deductive methods are available in all relational DBMSs through the application of simple operators. A relational join between a parent and child table matched on a defined equality defined in predicate logic is an example of deductive logic use to provide information.

Inductive methods are not directly available in relational DBMSs. This is because inductive methods refer to the ability to infer results from information that is contained in the database. Using the parent/child induction example, it can be stated that all children have parents. This might be a solid fact or probability. This is the process that is being used in data mining. Deduction always yields information that can be proven to be factual, whereas induction always yields information that is assumed to be true for some probability but cannot necessarily be proven or is not necessarily true.

The computer is required to use inductive methods in data mining. Terabytes of data need to be examined to yield results in a timely fashion. This can only be accomplished by application of new technologies in relational databases. These new technologies are supplied as additional tools or extensions to the relational DBMSs. Depending on the types and classes of data, there are different methods and classes of information to be derived. The major difficulty is that traditional query methods cannot be used due to the current limitations of SQL and the complex constructs required to do this processing. These areas are being addressed with extensions to DBMSs combined with the availability of MPP.

Methods Used (Algorithm Classes or Rules)

Data mining query requirements have been classified into four major types of processing algorithms or rule methods: associations, clustering, classification, and sequential patterns.

Associations or Link Analysis. Mining associations usually refer to searching all details or transactions from the operational systems for patterns that have a high probability of repetition. These are based on a large database of transactions, with a transaction being defined as a set of items with a relationship. This type of query requires an associative algorithm to find all the rules that will correlate one set of events or items with another set of events or items. Typical results of this type of process are shown in using retail examples. Of all the people who buy desktop computers, 78% will also purchase additional add-on products. This type of processing can be used on relational sets of data that have been defined using standard SQL predicate logic. The goal of associate algorithms is to be an extension of SQL, so that the algorithm can be applied to restrictive relational sets through normal query technology. The algorithms must be highly adaptive and dynamic. As a rule, to find an associative pattern, the set of data being examined may change, minimum percentage rules for association occurrence may change, and a different percentage of customers might be required to participate in the set to have any business value. These rules may then be adjusted on repetitive executions to find the best possible occurrence for marketing strategies or product placement. A good example of this is in grocery stores, when an item from one part of the store is used as an end-aisle display in another part of the store (such as a 10-foot-high stack of pretzels on the aisle where beverages are displayed). These stores have determined that a large percentage of beverage buyers will also buy pretzels if they see them on the way to get the beverages. As the industry moves forward, there will be multiple associative algorithms and process tools available, specific not only by industry type but by business process. Generalized algorithms are good for generalized results but will not offer the precision required for competitive business practices.

Sequential Patterns.   Sequential patterns use the same basic data as associative except that the data must be stored over a period of time. This is a historical data store of all the details or transactions from the operational systems, to be searched for patterns that have a high probability of repetition. Sequential patterns are primarily used in the business world for pattern analysis. This is the most common example used to describe the impact in the business world of data mining. Typical results of this type of process can be shown using the retail example from associative with sequential modifications. Of all the people who purchase laptop computers, 78% will also buy a parallel tape backup device within seven months. Purchasers who buy window coverings and then buy linens within three months will purchase furniture within the next 12 months (pattern identified: new residence furnishings buying pattern). This type of processing can be used on relational sets of data and can also benefit from extensions to SQL. These sequential algorithms must be highly adaptive and dynamic. In the window covering example, there was a rule to find an associative pattern that exceeded some minimum percentage occurrence and stayed within some minimum time period. These rules may then be adjusted on repetitive executions to find the best possible event occurrence for target marketing for high-profit furniture items. Again, the difficulty in these mining technologies is very easy to minimize. In a sequencing of events, there is a high probability that an elongation of time between the first and second event will show a pattern where the third event never occurs. This can be seen more clearly in Figure 23.2. Refinement of rules through repetitive execution, adjusting the minimum and maximums, is the domain of the business analyst using this technology.

There is another approach to sequential that has an important impact on business. This technique is called similar sequences. In normal sequential, the result is a sequence of events over time. With similar sequential, the database of time events, in time order, is examined to find a timed sequence of events similar to another sequence. Once a sequence is found, are there any other sequences that are similar (based on similarity and probability rules)? The most common example in the retail market is finding another department with similar sales streams. Finding stocks with similar price movements is another example. Data mining is not

	Item 1 and item 2 within 1 month	Item 1 and item 2 within 2 months	Item 1 and item 2 within 2 months	Item 1 and item 2 within 3 months	...
	Item 3 within 1 month of item 2	Item 3 within 1 month of item 2	Item 3 within 2 months of item 2	Item 3 within 1 month of item 2	...
Bought item 1 followed by item 2	21%	37%	15%	7%	...
Bought item 1 followed by item 2 followed by item 3	18%	7%	2%	3%	...

Figure 23.2

limited to the business world. With the advent of the Internet in every home, a large database of information is available to the average user. With data mining technology available to process against that information, any user can apply it in many different areas of interest.

Clustering.   In some cases, there is no known way to define a class of data to be analyzed. In these cases, clustering algorithms must be applied to discover a previously unknown or suspected class of data. Clustering examples are defect analysis or affinity group analysis. There is a process to find a group that shares some common classification. Clustering processes could be based on some particular event, such as a good customer canceling his own credit card. In this case, the rules for defining a class of this type of customer are unknown, and clustering might be able to define rules that will allow the company to prevent the next cancellation. Clustering in knowledge systems is referred to as unsupervised learning.

Classification.   Classification identifies the process and must discover rules that define whether an item or event belongs to a particular subset of data (class). In this case, the business is defining the class. Classification in a relational database can become a very complex process because often many tables and thousands of attributes must be examined to identify the class. These classes of data are rarely defined in a relational database because they have no place in the normal data model. As such, they have no given name or attribute class. The most common business example of classification is the credit card approval process. Does the cost of the item, and many other criteria, put the purchaser in a class that allows charging? Classification in knowledge systems is referred to as supervised learning.

The Searching Process

The types of methods for mining have been identified, but what about a search engine? While an exhaustive search could always be done, it is generally impractical due to the size of the warehouse. Efficient search algorithms are required, and most mining implementations use some basic operation and then modify through iterative operations. The strategies used in these approaches are of several different types. There is no best approach to any search, but a dependency on what is desired to select the best operation.

As stated, the basic approach is to begin a search with an initial description and then iteratively modify it based on user or business thresholds. In the implementation of the initial approach in the search, the process can be either bottom-up or top-down.

The bottom-up approach is also referred to as a data-driven approach. This starts with the set of data and the initial rule and begins a process of refinement until only the result set remains that meets or exceeds the user thresholds and contains no data that violates the rule. In simpler terms, it examines the data, finding all the individual elements that individually meet the rules, and then builds a final set from those elements.

The top-down approach begins by applying some initial operations to the description and initiates a process of set selection that contains all items that could match. Through a process of refinement operations, it will eventually cast out those elements that do not match the rules until the set meets or exceeds the desired thresholds.

The bottom-up approach can be thought of as examining all the good and bad in the entire world of details and working inward one detail at a time, keeping only the good, to find the pattern or sequence of events. Top-down can be thought of as starting with the large set and throwing out the bad guys.

In both approaches, a series of refinements or operations is performed, resulting in a new set or description of the set. Then the process can begin again, applying the same operations to the new set. This process is actually building a search graph through the data, trying to find a rule or construct a rule that meets or exceeds the thresholds. It is easier to understand when dealing with real data. To demonstrate this rule creation and refinement, try to visualize the following set of operations:

1. Examine every purchase made in a grocery store, and select any two items from that individual purchase.
2. Examine all other purchases made to see if the two initial items picked were purchased together. If these exceed the thresholds, start building a result set.
3. Keep one of the first items and pair it with another from the first purchase and start over.

The ability in the search engines is to perform the preceding set of operations without doing a complete exhaustive search. These engines use different approaches and strategies to prevent an exhaustive search and arrive at a conclusion rapidly. There are search graph strategies, exhaustive strategies, irrevocable searches, tentative searches, hill climbing strategies, and many others.

DATA MINING WAREHOUSES

Using any of the aforementioned techniques to implement discovery data mining requires some basic operations on relational databases. Of primary importance is the segmenting of the databases into clusters that can be effectively mined. While easy to say, it is difficult to implement. It is one thing to cluster the data effectively. It is another to have the ability to mine this cluster with any acceptable degree of resource consumption. This is because most databases are designed for operational purposes. It is the movement of operational data into data warehouses that will allow data mining. These data warehouses must be constructed for data mining or be able to be segmented for the mining process. A retail business might have a year's worth of operational sales detail in a warehouse, but very rarely is it categorized into categories such as summer sales or Christmas sales. Before associate or link analysis can work, proper segmenting of the database should occur. This can occur either by implicit physical design or logical accessing of the database. Each approach of class and scope definition has its advantages and drawbacks. For example, physical segmentation of existing data would hurt processes that do not require the segmentation. Logical segmentation would consume significant resources each time it was performed. This segmentation is required to limit the scope of the mining, as well as to define the classes of data being examined. The design of the data warehouse for data mining becomes a critical event. Unfortunately, most of the data warehouses built today are built without the knowledge or impact analysis of data mining. Data mining warehouses built separately have the added burden of being kept up to date with the source data.

There is no set of rules for aiding in this definition process. It is unique to each business, and unique to each application process already in place. To mine data effectively in an insurance company may require building a data mining store that uses extract and summarized data, from any number of existing applications that were never intended to be integrated. For example, to look for individuals and families with patterns of insurance coverage might mean looking into an IDMS administration system, a DB2 life system, an IMS health system, and a VSAM casualty property system, extracting this data into a temporary relational database, and applying the mining strategies.

The proper approach to building a warehouse for data mining is to identify, through data modeling, the detail items required for analysis by each business unit that would benefit from data mining. Data mining databases should be built from operational details forming a dynamic subject area. There would normally be a collapsing from a third normal form relational database into some denormalized tables depicting information about a subject. The same identifiers are to be used, but inside the data, look for correlational attributes that can define relationships between the tables. The mining tools must be able to infer the proper relationships from a definition of the database in order to work. A pure third normal form operational database can be used, but it is not the best form. It is more important to adopt some methodology that builds a value-added informational structure that can either be permanently maintained or dynamically built. It is this second option that will become a critical factor in the data mines in the near future. The structure of information is not static. The overall goal of data mining is competitive business strategies that translate into better marketing efforts, better product development, better customer service, and truly understanding one's customers.

PUTTING IT ALL TOGETHER

Your company has decided to move into some data mining applications. For this exercise, we will assume that this is an insurance company offering many products. There is currently no data warehouse in place to support the types of enterprisewide queries necessary. The first problem occurs in the structure of the enterprise data warehouse that will be required. There will be other chapters in this book to assist in all the areas of data warehouse, but for data mining we have that big difference of design to support data mining processes efficiently.

The initial application is to find unknown information of any type, across the enterprise (unrealistic perhaps, but easier for demonstration purposes). To make it more specific, we wish to find associations only at this level. Assume that we have only four major product categories: life insurance, medical insurance, auto insurance, and disability insurance. In the real world, each of these are application areas never designed to be integrated. Even the same attribute, like name, can be called many different names in each application. More difficulty is presented by life insurance, the oldest application, which was implemented in an indexed flat file system. The medical insurance is very new and is in a relational database. The auto insurance is in an older hierarchical database structure, and the disability insurance is in regional relational databases. The solution to these problems is not unique to data mining, but pertains to any enterprisewide information technology. Some kind of high-level repository or directory will allow all the data to come to conformity. This is another issue to be solved outside the realm of data mining.

Time to design the new relational data warehouse to hold this data, or is it? Since we are going to mine existing historical data, the details are there in all the old systems, or they could be. There is no different design at this level. So assume we have the logical structure shown in Figure 23.3.

There are two ways to approach this. One is that this data has been moved into warehouses. Another is that we have a tool that allows us to query the data stores in each of the application areas. What matters is that there are tools to do either. The tools that allow access into existing data stores for data mining will extract whatever data is needed, according to the rules of the moment, and move that data into a temporary relational structure prior to the mining processes. If all the claims have been integrated into a warehouse of claims, then the mining process might be easier. The critical business point is to get to the answers now, regardless of where the data is.

At this point, we could use older verification methods, searching for patterns across all four lines, assuming that someone thought there could be a pattern across

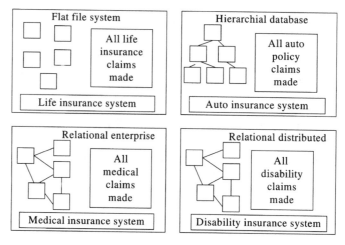

Figure 23.3

There was a higher than normal number of life insurance claims for ages under 60.

There was a higher than normal number of auto accident claims due to drivers losing control due to blackouts.

There was a higher than normal number of disability claims for people under 60.

There was a higher than normal number of medical claims for a toxic disease.

Figure 23.4

all four lines. Given enough SQL queries and enough time, who knows? But if we were to use data mining associate processes like link analysis across all these types of claims, we might find the associations shown in Figure 23.4.

All of these occurred within 200 miles of a town called Townsville in the state of Z. This is a real example and should demonstrate that it is highly unlikely that any group writing queries using the verification method would find this. Verification could have turned up the exceptions in each area, but probably not. Segmentation like 200 miles of a town is not a normal operational attribute, but something that would have to be inferred using additional data. This is not a new fad. It is a complex technology that will have significant business impacts. This example shows a business impact that was perhaps due to outside influences that need to be examined by another enterprise. However, these outside influences are having an adverse business impact on the insurer.

There are many processes taking place in this example. One is the segmentation of the different applications by boundaries, which is not easily determined. Another would be the exception to the rule, perhaps inferred by logic in the individual applications. Figure 23.5 depicts the result.

With these results, we might force the mining process to look beyond the current mileage boundaries, using a lower percentage of occurrence, mixed with a

Claim Counts By Geographic Area with Time Period				
	Boston	Townsville	Worchester	Fairmont
Life insurance claims under 60	17	19	4	5
Auto claims, blackouts	5	11	2	2
Medical claims, toxic disease	11	23	3	0
Disability claims under 60	13	21	9	4
Problem!				

Figure 23.5

higher percentage of occurrence the closer we moved to the town or some location not yet determined. This would require massive amounts of data, perhaps neural logic, and probably massive parallel processing. All of these technologies are just coming together, which is why we are on the cutting edge of data mining and true knowledge engineering. Imagine what the information gathering agencies of any investigative style of business could do if they were able to implement this type of technology.

TOOLS AND TRENDS

Several data mining tools are beginning to appear on the market. Some have already achieved success in certain markets, while some vendors have already disappeared. More frequently, vendors are announcing products in support of some aspect of data mining, a trend that will continue. A few tools are supporting very sophisticated user interfaces but lacking in power. Others have powerful engines but do not support all the platforms. It is still early in the process, and the true parallel hardware environments are just becoming cost effective. It is on these platforms that the tools will succeed. It is impossible to name or suggest any tools at this time. There will be many venues for information regarding the availability and quality of tools.

More important than tool availability is the type of tool. Different applications in data mining need different toolsets. It will be commonplace in businesses to use more than one data mining tool. There are companies that have used their own knowledge and simple repetitive queries to find critical information. In these cases, there have been industry experts who could ascertain the types of patterns required. There is no one approach and no single tool that will provide all the information required. The most important aspect of data mining is to understand its capabilities and to leverage the power to improve the business.

PART FIVE

DATA WAREHOUSE ADMINISTRATION

"We've just begun!"

Anonymous

Planning, designing, and implementing a data warehouse may bring a wonderful feeling of accomplishment to the development team—but it is not over yet. Many issues must be resolved regarding the ongoing management of hardware, software, data, standards, and procedures. Although some shops have managed by the "seat of their pants" with small warehouses, upgrades and modifications in any of these areas can be an administrative nightmare without careful planning. Shops that have effective system and database administration procedures in place for production may still require changes to manage the new environment.

ONCE UPON A TIME

There was a warehouse with horrendous performance problems. A consultant was hired to review the situation. The lead DBA was asked many questions, including "How often do you reorganize your tables?" He replied that they only scheduled reorganizations when end users complained. He also indicated that they did not have the staff needed to review and modify indexing to accommodate query performance problems. In many shops, end users will allow a situation to go on until they are totally frustrated. In this shop, the users had come to the point at which they refused to use the warehouse because performance was so poor. It took considerable effort to modify the design for better performance, improve communication with the users, and convince users that things had improved to the point that the warehouse was usable. It is truly worthwhile to manage performance proactively so that users do not need to complain before tables are properly maintained.

In another shop, there were no backup and recovery procedures. Initially, the warehouse was very small and all tables were reloaded from scratch on a regular basis. After a time, the load jobs became too lengthy and incremental refreshes were implemented. There were still no backup and recovery procedures. The DBA felt that he could always go back to the original extract and load jobs if data was lost. Over a period of time, the size and number of tables grew and the number of users increased. One day, an electrical outage destroyed a large amount of data. Without backup copies, the DBA spent four days extracting and reloading a large amount of data from scratch, and users were irate. They had become dependent on the warehouse, and it was unavailable when they wanted it. The shop implemented a proper backup and recovery process after the experience.

Chapter 24, "Systems Administration" by Brenda Castiel, discusses issues regarding service-level agreements, performance monitoring, evaluation of tools for monitoring performance, storage management, and network management.

Chapter 25, "Database Administration in a Heterogeneous Environment" by Martin Hubel, identifies the database administration issues involved in backup, recovery, designing, and coding for portability and scalability across diverse platforms as well as other traditional database responsibilities.

Chapter 26, "Security in the Data Warehouse" by Martin Hubel, continues with a discussion of user authentication and accountability, password issues, security back doors, physical security, remote access considerations, and a security review checklist.

Chapter 27, "Selecting End-User Tools" by Peter Brooks, outlines a methodology for the selection of end-user tools. End-user tools are an administrative issue in terms of selection, installation, deployment, and performance. In addition, users will require training, support, and analysis of the way in which the tools are used.

Administrative issues can contribute to the failure of an otherwise well-designed data warehouse. This section will help identify the administrative considerations that must be addressed if the warehouse is to be successful.

Systems Administration

Brenda Castiel
Ernst and Young

"This is not the end. It is not even the beginning of the end.
It is, perhaps, the end of the beginning."

Winston Churchill

The focus of most writing about data warehouses is on planning, designing, and building them. But what happens after "happily ever after"? Is that the end? For the DP professional, it is not.

Suppose you have come this far: You have successfully implemented the first data warehouse in your organization, and it is sizable enough that you do not wish to try to manage it by "the seat of your pants." Or else, it may be small, but it is acting as a pilot for additional future undertakings, so it is worthwhile to set up solid procedures for managing this project. You will then be able to test their effectiveness on a smaller scale and improve on them before a much larger number of users has come to depend on the system.

While you may already have some solid systems administration procedures installed at your company, they may need modification or extension for the data warehouse environment. It is possible that they may need to be enhanced to serve the new applications and new users who will be accessing the system, as these folks may have less experience with technology, may have different expectations of service, or may be viewing more massive amounts of data than your other users.

Where transaction rate, high availability, and subsecond response time are the key concerns of operational systems management, other concerns may take their place in a data warehouse environment. The success of this application may be measured by such factors as ability to manage massive amounts of data; the speed with which users can execute their analysis; the timeliness and quality of the data; the ability to manage within a budget for hardware and software; and user satisfaction.

While data administration (the care and feeding of the database itself) is covered elsewhere in this book, this chapter will deal with overall systems management, beyond the boundary of the database.

SERVICE LEVELS

The concept of the service-level agreement (SLA) has become fairly well accepted among large organizations in recent years. It is particularly well entrenched in the financial industry, where technology such as ATMs have demanded a high degree of service. The SLA sets out what users may expect from the systems they use, in terms of such measures as

- Availability (how many hours a day and days of the week the system will be available)
- Target for percentage system availability during the agreed-to hours (for example, 99.5% availability)
- Response time (average time to process a transaction, or what percentage will complete in under n seconds)
- Schedule for completion of batch jobs
- Currency of data
- Disaster recovery measures (for example, the ability to bring the system up in a recovery mode within n business days).

While at first glance it may appear that SLA does not apply to the data warehouse system, most aspects of it are still relevant. Since the organization has invested large amounts of money in this setup, it may fairly expect to see some reliable levels of service. Of the aforementioned items, only response time is difficult to set targets for, due to the variable and unpredictable nature of most data warehouse queries. The other factors, such as hours of availability and currency of data, are still appropriate.

SLAs are often linked to user chargeback. In seems fair that when user departments are asked to pay for application usage, IT also agrees to maintain a specific level of service in return. In a centralized environment, users are typically charged for the amount of CPU resources they use, often with different rates for prime shift and off-shift usage. Other common measures used are megabytes of storage used, pages printed, and tapes mounted.

As organizations have increasingly moved to client/server configurations, they often have changed the paradigm such that user departments own their servers and workstations outright and so are charged only for mainframe CPU resources, or perhaps for their access to help desk or LAN support services. It is tempting to follow this approach for data warehouse (assuming your data is distributed among several locations) because it is less complicated to administer, and users are generally happy to own, and therefore control, their servers. The down side becomes evident after the first couple of implementations: Each server is sized and configured to handle just one group's requirements, and therefore each new user group must purchase an additional machine. No sharing is possible, and economies of scale are out of the question.

The preferred method is to design for sharing of the servers among the user groups who need access to similar data or applications, and to do long-term planning for future growth by purchasing equipment that is easily and incrementally upgradable. This means that the servers are treated as mainframes in the chargeback scheme; that is, each user is charged for actual usage. It also allows IT to keep some control over such tasks as maintenance, backups, repairs, and upgrades.

In general, it is likely that the current SLA may need to be modified only slightly inasmuch as most of the common measures listed previously will still apply. Where the nature of the data queries is unpredictable or varies widely, you may have to dispense with the response time target, at least until sufficient monitoring of the system usage has established some predictable patterns or ranges.

Since the data in a data warehouse has typically undergone extraction, transformation, and some summarization, it is worthwhile to include some measurement of data quality in the SLA. Some of the aspects of data quality are currency, accuracy, completeness, timeliness, security, and retention.

Currency has to do with how quickly real-time updates to the operational data are reflected in the data warehouse. Since data is loaded into the data warehouse at specific intervals, it cannot be as current as the operational data. It might be current as of a daily, weekly, or even monthly refresh.

The accuracy or correctness of the data is naturally of concern to the user community. The integrity of the data comprises business rules, valid values, referential integrity, and correct derivation rules used to build the data warehouse. Data scrubbing of the source data may also be needed to obtain a valid result. Precision may be less of a concern, in that summarized results are often desired, so 100% accuracy may not be a requirement in some environments.

The aspect of completeness reflects whether all the data, from all sources, has been loaded. It is up to the business to determine whether partially loaded data is acceptable for the users to access, or whether it is preferable to wait until it is complete. There are situations when either option may be appropriate. The SLA should include the policy to be followed.

Timeliness is related to the length of time it takes for updates to the data to become known in the data warehouse. With larger databases, the load may take a day or longer to complete, so the lag between the time of the extract and the time the new data is available to users can be elongated.

Security controls are required to ensure that only authorized users see the data in question. Different tools and different classes of data are to be made available to specific users. In some fields, such as health care, confidentiality may be especially important. But when the data is summarized, it becomes more impersonal. Then the security controls that apply in the operational system may be relaxed. However, most organizations allow users to see only the data directly relevant to their jobs (for example, their region's sales, or their part of the company's product line). This specification should be part of the SLA.

Retention is the factor that defines how long historical data will be kept. At some point, data begins to lose all or part of its value, and the organization must determine whether purging the data (deleting it) or archiving it (moving it to a less costly off-line storage medium) is desired. Another option is to remove the detail data that is aged, but to retain summaries of it. Be aware that deleting or moving large volumes of data rows, while maintaining referential integrity among related tables, is not a trivial exercise. This effort must be estimated, planned, and tuned as much as the initial building of the data warehouse. The frequency of purging or archiving, and the speed with which the archived data is to be restored, are also parts of your agreement with the users.

PERFORMANCE MONITORING

In the typical distributed configuration, the systems can become very complex. As a result, neither DBAs nor network administrators know how to spot current or potential problems; nor do they have the right tools to monitor each component. Problems can degrade performance or, at worst, crash the system. The standard network management tools can monitor the infrastructure, the networking devices, but they solve only part of the problem. The missing pieces include the other critical components: clients, application servers, and the database servers.

Monitoring the Server

The health of a database server is critical to the success of your data warehouse setup, because it defines how well the system provides data to its users. Database servers must meet performance expectations consistently. Therefore, tools that monitor database servers should not only provide information to an administrator at any point in time, but also monitor the server over time, providing information along with the analysis tools to obtain useful guidance.

To begin, administrators need to determine their performance expectations. These will likely not be static, as functions and data characteristics can change over time. Not only will historical data accumulate, but new subject areas will be added to the warehouse. As a result, you will need to tune at regular intervals to meet those changing conditions. Tuning alone will not be effective unless you know what problem you are solving. So ongoing monitoring is essential so that you recognize when the server is not meeting the needs of the users or the expectations that have been set.

Performance monitoring is the process of collecting and analyzing performance information. This information reveals the patterns of behavior in the database server (and other system components). Before the system is implemented, however, the system designer and the user should come to an agreement about what constitutes acceptable system performance. Afterward, you monitor the system to determine whether it lives up to the established service levels.

Over time, you can expect the performance to degrade, on average 20% per year. This stems from maintenance on the application software to change or enhance function (such as extraction, transformation, or summarization), as well as database design changes. The biggest source, however, is database growth. Systems administrators must understand where the growth is occurring to be able to optimize and tune for it. To minimize degradation, gather performance statistics over time, and use this data proactively. Use it to model and simulate how the server will respond to future growth and other changes, and then tune the system before the users start to complain. Continue to use the monitoring procedure to ensure that your tuning changes worked.

When it comes to tools, several options exist:

- Performance monitoring tools that come with the database server
- Performance monitoring tools provided with the host operating system
- Tools from a third-party vendor.

The latter category tends to offer more detailed information and provide more assistance in helping to interpret the data collected. These tools operate in various different ways. Some use detailed simulation models to predict performance. This category of tools usually costs more and takes some time to set up correctly. These have predictive value, but are not appropriate for real-time database server monitoring. Some tools use queuing models for performance simulation, but these make assumptions about the system, which may affect the accuracy of the results if the assumptions do not apply to your situation.

Most tools omit the predictive aspect and simply monitor the actual database server activity, gathering data and helping to determine what the data means. They perform real-time monitoring, recent past monitoring, and historical analysis. They reside in the CPU close to the operating system and the DBMS. They allow the analyst to track system behavior through a front-end interface, or console. They measure such data as storage space, looking for free space or fragmentation; buffer activity and I/O performance; and memory management, checking the effectiveness of the buffer cache system and the virtual memory management. These tools provide data collection algorithms made up of a data collector and an analyzer/reporter. The data collector records and accumulates performance information, while the analyzer interprets the data, providing trends, alarms, and subsystem reporting (memory, CPU, disk).

Data collection can take one of two forms: sampling or event driven. Sampling measures system activity at random or predetermined intervals (such as every 10 minutes). This approach will generally have a minimal impact on overall system performance, although it is possible that you will miss small variations in system measures. Event-driven data collection, on the other hand, has functions that trigger a signal to a counter when an event takes place (such as update table or index, search, and so on). This method is more thorough, but it does add an overhead to the system you are trying to optimize and could potentially exacerbate a performance problem.

The sampling approach lets you estimate the characteristics of a population by analyzing only a small subset of the population. The administrator sets the sampling interval to correspond with the level of granularity wanted when measuring the resource utilization of the server. The reliability of the sample information depends on factors such as sample size and variability in the data. A statistical analysis of the data can determine the mean and the variation in the measures, which in turn helps to predict how the data server will run in the future and determine how it is operating now.

Most performance tools store the performance information they have collected on the server itself. Once this data has been collected, the systems administrator can use the analyzer/reporter function in the tool's function set to summarize the data via reports and graphs. Some tools will even provide suggested options for improving database server performance, such as building additional indexes, increasing cache size, or reorganizing the disk drive. Some of the information provided can include

- Server utilization statistics
- Throughput analysis
- Average response time
- Reports on subsystem components (such as I/O, cache, memory, disk).

In addition, trends in the workload and database growth over time can be depicted. With a graphical representation, the administrator and his or her management can examine database performance over time.

Once the tools have assisted with spotting problems before they become too serious, the corrective action is up to you. For example, if a highly fragmented disk has been reported, you need to defragment the disk in question to restore optimal performance. You may wish to check on other heavily utilized disks to see whether they might have a similar problem. Any additional "hot spots" can then be investigated until the problem is isolated. Armed with this information, you can bring the problem areas back into line through appropriate tuning actions.

Some of the actions that might be required would be changing database and operating system parameters, modifying resource allocation practices, or readjusting workload thresholds. Sometimes the issue may be with a third-party query tool that does not access the database efficiently, or a piece of middleware software that does not pass SQL variations (or dialects) correctly. These are difficult to detect but could be just as important to correct as any other system tuning area when it comes to achieving good system throughput.

If the problem comes down to inadequate capacity for the growing needs of the users and their usage of the resources, there may not be any tuning actions that can restore adequate performance. Then it may be time to redistribute workload across additional servers or to upgrade the server. This may mean adding memory, providing additional or faster disks, or adding more processors to a multiprocessor machine.

As businesses become more dependent on their data warehouses for critical information, systems administrators will also find themselves under pressure to maintain a high level of service to their users. As such, they will rely on tools that help manage the environment effectively. With the growth of servers in most large companies, an investment in a solid management infrastructure that prevents service interruptions and lost productivity is a wise one. Such an infrastructure includes procedures, measurements, and reporting, as well as tools. Beginning with an agreement as to what constitutes acceptable performance and ending with an ongoing monitoring process to deliver that level, performance management is a key success factor for the data warehouse environment.

EVALUATING TOOLS FOR PERFORMANCE MANAGEMENT

While there are many performance monitoring tools on the market for a variety of DBMS products, the functionality available may lag behind what IT departments are seeking. Therefore, it is important to be clear on what functions you need and evaluate the tools in question carefully. Do not assume that a feature found in one product is standard across all the similar tools.

While the tools all offer easy to use GUI interfaces, client-resident components, and many other "bells and whistles," they do not always offer everything that is required to ensure good, consistent performance on typical database servers. This section will provide some evaluation criteria based on what systems administrators really need to know. It may be that not every function will be found in a single tool (for example, both a database server monitor and an operating system monitor may be needed to provide the complete range of required information).

The set of information required may be thought of as follows: First, we need to know whether or not there is a performance problem; if yes, what is the nature of the problem—systemwide or particular to one user, one program, or one block of data? Next, we would wish to know which resource is experiencing the problem (e.g., memory, I/O, or other components) and we need to identify the process having (or causing) the problem. Beyond this, we will want enough detailed information to begin identifying what would be necessary to solve the particular problem.

While these classes of information seem simple and basic, they are not uniformly well addressed by the tools available. The most basic function of all is to determine whether there is a performance issue at all. It should be possible to determine this from viewing a small number of high-level screens. Thresholds can be set to trigger or highlight when something is perceived as a problem. If nothing is indicated, the administrator can stop right there.

Assuming that there is a problem of some kind, we will want to distinguish between systemwide problems (that need systemwide fixes) and ones that just affect one subset of the database, one user, or one particular application usage. It may indeed be that one user is causing the problem through unexpected or erroneous query patterns. Either the user is creating runaway queries directly, or a DSS/OLAP query tool is generating the queries from an end-user interface specification. The monitoring tool should help pinpoint this situation. (The solution to the problem may be complex, as neither user re-education nor fixes to inefficient SQL are trivial undertakings.) The specific process or "thread" should be indicated, along with the cause of the problem, such as data contention or excessive CPU usage. The alternative would be tedious manual investigation of each likely cause. The specific resource that is associated with the problem should be identified, whether it be I/O configuration and disk access, memory shortage, database contention, inadequate buffer usage, or other ills. Most tools can easily indicate this type of information by presenting a series of screens for review.

The next step requires more specific information. The tool should display sufficient details that indicate exactly what the problem is and how to resolve it. For example, if inappropriate buffer size is the problem, the tool should show how buffers are allocated and used, the number of buffer hits compared to total data requests, and so on.

Some monitors are more complete in the range of issues they address than others. Furthermore, some offer more guidance to the beleaguered administrator on what are the appropriate actions to take in resolving the problem. A key differentiator between tools is the amount of help and advice offered, in addition to the basic facts presented. The information should be self-explanatory and complete without the need to resort to other manuals or references.

Operation in real time is ideal so that problems can be detected and resolved as quickly as they occur. But since the administrator cannot always be watching, batch reports are necessary, too. The ability selectively to turn on additional levels of tracing and information gathering to track down particularly elusive conditions is important as well. This should be quick and easy to do. Furthermore, the tool should offer some guidance on how much tracing to apply.

In addition to providing the hard information described previously, the tool should offer easy-to-use interfaces. Since you will want the ability to log problems and aggregate them in summaries for later analysis, effective and informative reporting that is customizable is another important factor toward usability. An ideal tool will incorporate tutorials and help functions that can actually educate the tool user on system performance and tuning.

Since we can assume that the organization has many distributed servers to be managed, it would be nice to manage them all, even those at distant locations, from a single point of control. This is not quite the same as location transparency, which means that your operations are completely oblivious to which location you are viewing; as an administrator, you should know which location you are monitoring. But it does mean that your tool should be able to operate on the remote servers as well as the local ones.

In today's diversified technical environment, the ability to support heterogeneous DBMS products is a must. The alternative would be to acquire and learn separate monitors for each DBMS. A single interface to all the database servers is certainly preferable, yet the tool must also understand the different facets of the various DBMSs it monitors and support those sometimes subtle variations. The ideal tool should support "alerts," or the ability to signal the administrator when problems occur. This feature can be leveraged to allow programmed responses to these alerts.

Over time, the performance tools will evolve to provide more of the aforementioned desirable features. But few can afford to wait for the perfect tool. In the meantime, we will need to select carefully the best from what is available, to meet today's needs.

STORAGE MANAGEMENT

The last few years have seen an explosion of information among enterprises. There has been a proliferation of new applications in data warehouses and metadata (data about the data consisting of indexes, repositories, and other descriptors). These applications will add 10% to 25% to the storage capacity requirements of organizations:

- Through additional categories of data being collected
- Due to keeping historical data for longer periods of time
- By storing duplicates of operational data in different formats that promote ease of access.

For these reasons, storage costs are estimated to comprise the largest portion of data warehouse costs, accounting for up to four times the costs of the software. Yet storage is often taken for granted, while other more interesting questions such as data format and content, DBMS and servers, and DSS software, take the lion's share of implementers' attention.

As most performance specialists know, I/O operations are usually the largest component of response time; therefore, tuning I/O is one of the most important facets of performance management, so this task should not be overlooked. Managing the storage system also includes placement, movement, backup, purging, and archiving of data (unless you expect your data to grow forever without bound, plan for an archive/purge strategy).

Among the key success factors in this area are efficiency and reliability, while controlling costs and the ability to manage the storage efficiently are also important. As systems administrator, you will need to be able to predict needs for additional performance and capacity. Keep in mind that additional users, accumulation of historical data over time, and new applications will all place increasing demands on the system. It is unlikely that you will reach a point of stability in the foreseeable future.

Therefore, the technology chosen must accommodate this growth through easy, flexible scalability; this means the ability to add storage with minimum disruption to the existing data. In the event of an upgrade, replacing all the disks would cause considerable downtime and a serious service interruption. Look for modular systems in which volumes can be added while the system is operational.

In a typical distributed configuration, there are multiple servers, each having their own dedicated storage pool. Ideally, data storage systems should provide for the flexibility of connecting multiple servers to a single storage pool to optimize utilization. After all, keeping spare capacity on many servers adds up to a great deal of unused space. You also need to consider configurations options, such as spreading highly accessed data over different volumes to avoid queuing bottlenecks. Since data in a data warehouse is not typically updated, physical placement is done primarily to optimize retrieval operations.

The storage should include high-speed cache and parallel processors to sustain fast retrieval. Large data channels also improve speed of access. Other features to look for include:

- The ability to move data in case of disk errors
- Redundant components to minimize downtime
- On-line maintenance
- Diagnostics that can help prevent service outages.

If your data warehouse strategy calls for frequent data refreshes, backup and restore functions may not be a high priority, as long as the refresh can be accomplished quickly enough to satisfy the users' requirements. If the refresh needs a large processing window, such as a weekend, backup plans should be made that can restore the data in midweek.

Overall, your application needs an intelligent system with enough robustness to meet the demands of the business. It should offer modularity, high performance, high availability, and manageability.

NETWORK MANAGEMENT

If you have a heterogeneous group of platforms for your data warehouse implementation, you will find that network management is one of the most demanding tasks. Not only are new users constantly coming on-line, but users and equipment are invariably moving to new locations. The networking hardware is proliferating with LANs, WANs, hubs, routers, switches, and multiplexors. Lurking behind all this is the next stage—users wanting to access Internet-based data sources along with the corporate data, requiring even greater bandwidth and network management resources. Managing this environment is one challenge; capacity planning for the future is another. If you do not understand the technology, make sure someone in your site does.

Ideally, you will want some integrated tools to assist you in this function. Fortunately, there are several such tools now available, and enhancements are being made with each new release to improve their functionality. Because simple network management protocol (SNMP) is the de facto standard in this area, most vendors concentrate on SNMP-based distributed network management tools.

Here are some of the features to look for in these tools:

- Distributed console support—the ability to access the tool from several different consoles
- Heterogeneous relational database support—the ability to work with many different database management systems, in a mixed environment
- Scalability—the tool can work with an increasing number of servers and platforms without any loss in capability
- Interfaces for alerts (error messages requiring action) from a variety of operating systems
- Security features, such as user ID authentication and auditing of attempted invalid accesses
- Tracking of network utilization in real time and in summary reports
- Measurement of network response time
- Graphical display of key measurements
- Troubleshooting assistance—the ability to provide diagnostics when problems occur
- Identification of underutilized and overutilized resources to permit load balancing and tuning
- Optimization tool to improve overall performance.

Even with the sophisticated tools (that have come a long way in recent years), many sites find that their staff lacks the expertise to exploit them fully. This is, after all, a complex area, and if the staff members do not utilize the tools and associated methods frequently enough, they do not build up enough experience to become experts. So some companies find it cost effective to use outside service providers who specialize in this area to help them identify their best options and, sometimes, implement the recommendations. Such firms can supply network planning, design, implementation, management, and monitoring services, either remotely or on site.

By proactively monitoring the network and resolving any bottleneck issues, you can analyze performance and put a plan in place to be able to support the critical applications. There is no doubt that the new tools and services can provide much better insight into network performance than their predecessors. But it is still the job of the network administrator to maintain network performance and meet the company's objectives.

SECURITY MANAGEMENT

Now that you are opening up your corporate data to an increasing number of new users, providing access while maintaining security may seem to be a contradiction in terms. If you have heterogeneous database platforms for your data warehouse, maintaining appropriate security is a real challenge. Organizations often address security as an afterthought, with no enterprisewide strategy. As a result, many existing implementations have major security exposures. Three classes of security exist: access to the system, via an operating system sign-on, application-level security, and database access, which connects directly to the database manager.

Database Security

The data-level approach ensures that the DBMS has control over data access, and it eliminates the potential for someone to bypass the application's security. It is usually implemented by associating a user with a role or with membership in a group. The user is then allowed to perform certain operations or to view certain classes of data.

In most DBMSs, access is controlled by the use of Grant statements. Because Grants are assigned for each table and for each user, grouping tables together into categories will vastly simplify the administration task. If a more granular level of security than table-level access is required (that is, at the column or row level), you may have to choose between using application-level security or denormalizing tables so the DBMS software will be able to control access.

A better approach is to assign users to roles, where a role comprises a collection of predefined table privileges that end users can manage and control. For example, a few users could have a regional brand management role that allows them to view data pertaining to their own region and product group.

When a user connects to a database at a remote site, the security at the remote database is applied to the transaction. For distributed queries, the user needs to have security privileges to each of the databases involved. Again, to minimize complexity, you should continue to set up roles for the users. By categorizing roles and tables by application group, you create correspondence between a set of tables and a set of access rules. Each application area gets its own role that incorporates all the valid authorizations for the users. The metadata in the data warehouse repository can be the means of documenting the security rules.

Distributed Security

A distributed environment has special considerations because of the complexity of the overall configuration. For one thing, it has multiple entry points. The entry points can be a file server on a LAN, an individual workstation, or any one of the databases linked together in the enterprise. Viruses can enter the system in many ways and be spread at a rapid rate.

The overall security is only as strong as its weakest link in the network. Even if the database is secure, other sources can still introduce problems. One common method of gaining access to a distributed database configuration is to use a PC version of UNIX. Once users have signed on to UNIX, there is often no additional sign-on needed to proceed to the database. Then the user has free access to many data sources.

Unlike a centralized environment, distributed databases let you customize the security for each database in the data warehouse. It is possible to isolate and maintain highly confidential information. Even if unauthorized access is obtained at one node, it would normally be restricted to that one node. (A replication engine could, however, replicate unauthorized changes to other sites.)

If passwords are required for each system component (network sign-on, workstation, database), users will typically choose simple predictable passwords or they write them down in a convenient location, thus subverting the whole scheme. It is preferable to use a tool that permits a single password to control access to many systems. In a systemwide security setup, security tables allow end users to specify their user IDs and sign on once, and the security subsystem automatically manages their access to networks, operating systems, databases, and applications.

To achieve both simplicity and an adequate degree of protection, a few simple rules are suggested:

- Do not use the Grant with Grant option.
- Avoid the Grant with Admin option (special privileges).
- Do not use Grant to Public.
- Prohibit the use of table-level security, using role-level security instead.
- Encourage the use of function/procedure-based security.
- Educate users to keep passwords secret and nontrivial and to follow good practices when working with confidential data.

Auditing the security setup from time to time is a good practice. To audit a distributed database, each site must be checked for unusual Grants and cases in which a user has received privileges from an unauthorized source. An audit file should be produced for the administrator to review. A script can be developed to do this for each database server.

While security management software is improving all the time, the tools are still not as advanced as those that have been available on centralized systems for years. Over time, these packages should improve to the point that administrators can manage heterogeneous platforms as if they were a centralized system.

SUMMARY

While the challenges of managing a data warehouse system may seem daunting, the basic principles of systems management can be applied. Furthermore, when appropriate tools are used, the task becomes more manageable and a smoothly running system is the result.

Database Administration Issues in a Heterogeneous Environment

25

Martin Hubel

Martin Hubel Consulting, Inc.
Toronto, Canada

"Men have become the tools of their tools."

Henry David Thoreau

When data warehouses are built on different platforms from operational data, many issues can surface regarding the management and administration of the data and the database environment on each platform and the interfaces between the products. This chapter will examine the database management function and the special challenges when managing data in a heterogeneous environment. It is assumed that the reader is familiar with the role and responsibilities of the database administrator.

In Figure 25.1, at least three operating environments are shown. The enterprise environment is most likely MVS/ESA, and the servers in departments may run Windows/NT, OS/2, or various types of UNIX. The intelligent workstations may be combinations of Windows, OS/2, or Macintosh. Even if corporate standards are in place to control new hardware and software acquisitions, there may be "islands of technology" that have been purchased by individual departments without the knowledge of IT, perhaps before standards for the data warehouse were developed.

UNDERSTANDING THE HETEROGENEOUS ENVIRONMENT

There are additional challenges facing the DBA when different or multiple environments will be used for the data warehouse. The DBA must understand each environment fully and understand the issues that arise within the interface between

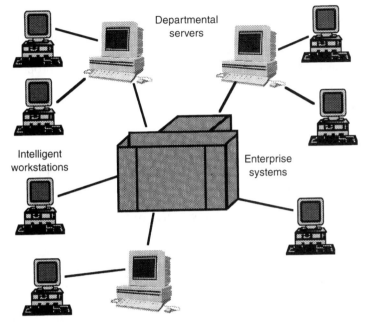

Figure 25.1

two or more products. These issues include usability, portability, performance management, security, recovery, and administration.

These issues may be easier if all DBMSs are from one vendor, such as Oracle™, Informix™, SQL Server™, Sybase™, or IBM™, as there will be fewer considerations between different environments. With different hardware or operating systems, even the same DBMS may have some differences that require the DBA to plan and administer these products differently. Of course, the DBA may not have the final say on which platform, DBMS, or other products are selected. It may be a matter of making other people's decisions work.

In some cases, the same terms are used in multiple environments with different definitions or meaning for each platform. For example, in DB2 for MVS, table spaces are used to store tables and index spaces are used for storing indexes. System managed storage (SMS) is considered the future direction for storage management. By comparison, DB2 Common Server uses table spaces to store both tables and indexes. Database managed storage (DMS) is recommended over SMS for the platforms supported by DB2 Common Server.

DESIGN ISSUES

In designing applications for a heterogeneous environment, it is necessary to be aware of both the similarities and differences between both the DBMS products that will be used and the platforms on which these products will be implemented. Even products of the same name or family may have different levels of compliance with industry standards, or they may physically store data differently based on the operating environment. It is necessary for designers to be aware of the facilities available in each environment and to plan accordingly for their proper implementation.

The SQL Standard

The SQL standard has been embraced by most vendors. While this is critical to most installations, it should be noted that the SQL standard generally only addresses issues for data manipulation language. The standard does not address physical objects or administrative features such as those in DB2 for MVS: storage groups, table spaces, or indexes. These are considered by the standards committee to be implementation dependent. For the DBA, these features are the basis for the physical design.

Extensions have been made by some vendors to support additional functionality within their products. The most interesting of these extensions generally relate to data manipulation, such as outer join and other operators. Data definition extensions include differences in data types to support date and time, and different types of numerical data. Other DDL additions have been added to some products, such as user-defined data types, functions, and triggers.

In a heterogeneous environment, the extensions provided by each vendor may vary. A good example is the differences in the implementation of the outer join. If data or functionality is used in multiple environments, the organization must decide how to convert data structures or applications to run in each environment. Portability should be the governing factor for data and applications that are used in multiple environments. This may not be a problem if a query tool is used that operates in multiple environments and generates the SQL for the user.

It may be difficult to convince the proponents of various products to avoid using extensions in their favorite environment. Provided the application is only used in one environment, this may not pose a problem and may help the efficiency and readability of the SQL used. An important issue will be the portability of skills between environments and the potential maintenance of the application.

Physical Design

Indexes.   In a decision support environment, the number of indexes need not be limited if the number of updates during query processing is few. Indexes should be built to improve the performance of key queries and to anticipate the needs of ad hoc queries. Even using the same DBMS, some parameters in each environment are implementation dependent.

Certain features of indexes may vary greatly between products. For example, a clustering index is defined as being the index in which the physical sequence of the data in the table space matches the order of this index. This results in more efficient I/O when multiple rows are returned for one request. This definition does not vary within the product family, but the implementation is different. In DB2 for MVS/ESA, one index is defined as clustering. This index is used for best-fit inserts, and during table space reorganizations to reestablish proper order of the data. In DB2 Common Server, however, clustering for any one index is established at reorganization time by specifying the index name on the utility command. The clustering index is not used for insert placement by DB2 Common Server.

Cluster in ORACLE has a different meaning. It is an alternate method for storing data within a table space where two tables share the same key. In this case, two tables that are accessed together and share a common key have their rows combined and stored in the same block. Applications that have a one-to-many relationship, such as invoice and invoice detail, may benefit the most from this implementation. A cluster key is required for the column or columns that will automatically cause the building of an index if it is not done manually by the DBA.

Views. Views on tables may make SQL coding easier for end users. It may be desirable to precode some of the views that contain joins, unions, or other summary functions that certain users have trouble coding. In the warehouse environment, almost all views will be used for read-only access.

A major consideration for a heterogeneous environment is the specific restrictions that a particular DBMS implementation may have. For example, some implementations do not allow UNION, ORDER BY, or some column functions to be used in views. Again, the issues are portability and skills transfer between platforms versus the exploitation of valuable features where they are available.

Physical Storage of Information

The physical storage of information and the parameters used by the vendors to control it vary slightly according to the platform requirements and the implementation of the vendor. Some of the differences are merely terminology; if you know one DBMS well, learning the second product is much easier. Many parameters and facilities, however, are important to the efficient implementation of some products. It is also noteworthy that the best parameters to use may not be the vendor default.

System Catalog/Directory Structure

The system catalog contains information about the physical database design. The tables in the catalog are used by the DBMS and by the DBA to determine where data is stored, the information for determining which access path to use, and other physical data management information.

Change is a constant in the data warehouse environment. It may be impractical in a heterogeneous environment to use traditional methods of change management. Existing tools may be stretched when trying to add or change column definitions on multiple platforms. Procedures to receive requests for additional information in the warehouse, such as a new table or just a new column, need to be developed to handle requests from end users. In some environments, there may be only ad hoc queries and no formal application programs running against some tables.

Each DBMS vendor uses and stores this information in different formats. The DBA must learn the catalog structure of each DBMS and develop queries to manage the information stored in each DBMS. The problem is much more difficult when the data structures are in a heterogeneous environment. Parameters can be different based on vendor implementations, and different between implementations of the same DBMS on different platforms.

Independent software vendors (ISVs) are developing tools to address the migration of data and data structures between platforms. The tools for migrating data structures within a given DBMS were identified early by ISVs for the mainframe environment; this concept has also been implemented for other DBMSs on other platforms. Full automation of cross-platform structure migration has not yet been delivered by any vendor for all combinations of platforms. If the same physical table design is to be used on multiple platforms, some intelligence will be required to translate parameters from one DBMS implementation to the next.

Configuring Databases

Each DBMS has parameters to control its configuration. These parameters control the system resources that are made available to the DBMS and each database. These parameters will vary with each DBMS and may vary across implementations if there are controls specific to an operating system environment.

SUPPORTING THE USER COMMUNITY

The two support areas for the data warehouse should be the DBA and the Help Desk. The Help Desk should have procedures in place for handling query problems. The DBA should serve as a backup, but should not be brought in unless the Help Desk is unable to handle the problem. The problems with queries are generally to do with either formulation of complex queries or with query performance. Other warehouse problems that users may ask about generally relate to transferring data out of the warehouse into data marts or personal warehouses.

Query problems relating to poor performance should first be handled by the Help Desk. The Help Desk should use performance analysis tools, such as Explain, to investigate and resolve problems. Additional SQL or query tool training should be available to the users. Problems with the capabilities of query tools, or their handling of queries, may require DBA involvement to resolve these with the vendor. Certain queries may not be efficiently supported by the current database design. In this case, the DBA should be contacted to add indexes or other performance techniques to solve these problems.

It is also important to develop procedures for handling change requests. If a user needs two extra data elements in a table, how will the request be managed? In the warehouse environment, it is important not to have lengthy backlogs and to be able to service requests of this nature in a timely fashion. Procedures used in a traditional OLTP environment are not usually suitable in a warehouse environment. Since most changes will occur in the data structures rather than programs, quality assurance procedures must change to reflect the new environment.

Other support problems require support similar to those techniques used in the production environment. These problems may relate to the transferring and processing of data into the warehouse, unsuitable installation parameters, or problems with data maintenance and regular utilities such as data reorganizations. Standard maintenance procedures with appropriate controls should be developed to reduce problems in these areas.

Loading the Data Warehouse

To populate a data warehouse, regular loading or propagation of data from operational sources will be needed. A schedule for summarizing, loading, and making the information available to the user community should be developed and presented to the user community. For example, weekly summary data may be available by 10 A.M. Monday morning (or the first business day following a holiday), and monthly data will be available on the second business day of the following month. In addition, it is important for users to know if and when the data was actually loaded. If problems occur in the production environment, the load that should have occurred by 10 A.M. on Monday may not actually have occurred until 3 P.M. on Monday. Data regarding actual loads may be made available through metadata in an end-user directory.

It is also necessary to develop procedures for managing the results of a bad load. What if the data loaded by 10 A.M. on Monday is corrupted due to an operational error and the erroneous data is not discovered until 3 P.M.? How will it be reloaded? What will be the impact of reloading during peak hours? User notification regarding corrupted data should be part of the procedure.

Loading substantial amounts of data into the warehouse may require a lot of time. Loads may need to be scheduled for periods in which a sufficient batch window exists if daytime availability is a priority. The amount of data in a data warehouse of moderate size normally favors the use of utilities for loading rather than techniques that simply insert data. These utilities, whether supplied as part of the DBMS or purchased as additional products, provide the benefit of speed, which is often achieved by turning off database logging during the load process.

In other scenarios, an operational data store may be updated periodically, possibly on a continuous basis. Some products, such as Data Propagator/Relational or Sybase Replication Server, allow replication of data from operational systems to the warehouse. The product may support continuous updates in real time, or it may perform updates at certain scheduled times. To move data into the warehouse, it will be necessary to develop and run regular update programs to roll up detailed data into the summary tables in the warehouse and eliminate application-oriented fields. These programs may be required to be run on a daily, weekly, monthly, or yearly basis.

There may be a periodic audit of summary levels to ensure that they are correct. It is very easy for an operator to run an incremental update job twice and add the same amount to a bucket on two occasions. How can we be sure that this has not happened? A health check may be necessary on occasion. Tools that can work in multiple environments provide benefits to DBAs in terms of training and a consistent user interface. Skills may be transferred more easily to other platforms, which can result in reduced orientation time, fewer errors, and more consistent administration. Even when a tool name has the same name in multiple environments, users should be aware that the functionality available and needed by DBAs may vary between platforms.

There are many tools available for analyzing, extracting, cleansing, and transforming data from the legacy environment and moving it efficiently to the data warehouse, and the DBA should take the time to become familiar with the options. The biggest problems in the warehouse are moving data from the legacy systems into the warehouse and moving data from the warehouse into data marts or personal warehouses.

PERFORMANCE MANAGEMENT

Performance levels have long been measured to ensure that they are satisfactory. Tools are available on many platforms to evaluate system and application performance and to help identify and diagnose bottlenecks.

Performance is often stated formally as a requirement by or to user areas, and service-level agreements are put in place. The service levels for a data warehouse are different from those of a transaction workload. Rather than dealing with high availability and fast response time, it may deal more with availability and currency of the data provided. For example, a service level may state that last month's data will be available by the third business day of the following month.

Performance management has long been considered an important activity in the mainframe environment. Vendors now supply tools for other environments, and these tools help with overall system tuning, DBMS tuning, and SQL performance. In a heterogeneous, multiserver environment, there are tools that will automatically monitor the environment and send messages when problems occur. Examples are Patrol™ from BMC Software or ECO™ from Compuware.

In contrast to the mainframe environment, performance measurement may not be an important activity on servers. Rather than spending money on performance management, it may be cheaper just to upgrade hardware when performance is perceived to be slower than is acceptable. When additional hardware costs are $50,000 or less per server, it may be the most cost-effective solution unless a large number of servers are being used. In other words, you may not know if you did the upgrade at the optimal time, when you may need the next upgrade, or if you made the best decision, but the costs of the analysis outweigh the costs of the hardware.

A further discussion of performance and service-level issues is included in Chapter 24.

SECURITY

Security is an important part of relational DBMS administration. A separate chapter on security management is included in this book (Chapter 26). This section summarizes the challenges facing the DBA when administering more than one environment.

Differences in Data Control Language

In terms of the SQL standard, the only privileges included in the SQL2 standard are the GRANT statement for table privileges. Other forms of the GRANT statement and all forms of the REVOKE statement are implementation dependent. Each vendor has various privileges and administrative privileges designed according to their physical design.

Ownership of Objects and Access to Data. The objects in an RDBMS are often owned by their creator. This is necessary from an administrative point of view when loading data into the warehouse and for backup and recovery reasons. The ownership role is often shared between members of the database administration department.

The data itself may be considered to be the property of the line area that created it. In this case, requests for data access to the warehouse may need user management approval before they are processed. In one organization, the data administration area decided that data was important enough that all user access requests should be the responsibility of the president. (In this case, it was delegated to the chief financial officer, who also was working at too high a level to fully understand what he was approving.)

While it may sound appropriate for users to approve access requests, the user manager may not fully understand the significance of their data or be too busy or insufficiently interested in assuming this function. It is important that the user be involved in determining the type of individual who should be granted access and helping to set guidelines for the granting of privileges to various types of users.

Administrative Authorities. Administrative privileges vary from product to product. Some products, such as ORACLE 7™, allow the administrative authorities to be customized through the use of roles. The administrative authorities are normally held only by support personnel for duties such as DBMS software support, database utilities and scheduled maintenance, recovery, and security administration. Depending on the size of the platform and the size of the support staff, the number of individuals performing these duties can vary widely.

The people who provide user support for the warehouse may also be granted more powerful authorities in order to help end users formulate queries in various subject areas of the warehouse. While it may be possible to grant these people select privileges on the dictionary and individual tables, more powerful administrative privileges or roles are granted for reasons of expediency. This situation, while not ideal, may be satisfactory if trust and confidence exist between the support departments.

BACKUP AND RECOVERY

Recovery is often not considered when developing a data warehouse. While many people feel that it is adequate to simply reload the data, when the first failure occurs this may prove to be unsatisfactory. Data volumes, placement, summary and roll-up of data, or other factors, may make the recovery times too long for a full or partial data load. It is better to develop a recovery plan as part of the warehouse development rather than after the first failure has occurred. This plan may have to cover multiple DBMSs and multiple tables that must be recovered to the same point in time. An easy strategy implemented by some shops is to make full disk backups every night and restore to the nightly backup in case of failure.

Recovery Factors

There are several factors that will determine the size and complexity of a recovery plan. The first questions needed to be answered by the user community should include the following:

- What is the required level of availability for the warehouse?
- If a failure occurs, how long can the outage be before it is considered unacceptable? Does this requirement change at certain times of the week, month, or year?

There may be little change to the data after it has been loaded. This type of environment may lead to recovery scenarios in which data is reloaded or pack recoveries are used to re-create data. If the data is summarized or added to existing summaries as part of the load, it is recommended that a backup be done at either the database or disk level to facilitate rebuild data. If data is organized in a fashion that places related data on the same volume or volumes, it may be possible to have parts of the application remain available during the recovery of, perhaps, a failed volume.

It is sometimes assumed that the permanent loss of data is not a factor for a data warehouse. Ultimately, the data could be reconstructed from operational data if other attempts at recovery fail. This may be accurate only if the operational data is kept long enough to allow the reconstruction of historical data in the warehouse.

It is often found that the retention periods for the warehouse are much longer, which makes reconstruction impractical. In addition, the amount of data in the warehouse or the time necessary to recalculate and summarize data could affect the time needed to recover. This may be the deciding factor when considering the recovery strategy. In these cases, it may be better and faster to make copies of the data after loading.

Recovery should be tested and estimates of recovery times should be available for various scenarios. In one shop that started with a small warehouse, the recovery plan was to rerun all initial load jobs. As the database grew, the full nightly reloads of the database were replaced with nightly incremental updates. Unfortunately, they still assumed that the initial extract and load job could be run in an emergency. When an electrical outage occurred, the recovery process took four days. The users had become dependent on the data warehouse and were very annoyed that it was unavailable for such a long time.

Utilities

To protect against a disk failure, pack backups should be taken following the loading of data to each respective disk. This is important when tables and indexes for portions of an application may be spread across multiple disk drives and you want to only restore the data that was affected.

Database-level backups or exports may assist with the restoration of all or part of an application to an earlier point in time. This may be necessary if a refresh of the database is bad or it is necessary for business to use the earlier version of the database. It is important to take the image copies at points to where it may be necessary to restore the database.

Where speed is a concern, faster utilities may be available from other vendors for loading, backing up, and recovering data. These products sometimes provide additional functions during their processing for integrity checking, data conversion, or additional backup capabilities.

Some warehouse environments may not support roll-forward recovery using the database transaction/recovery log. Many products turn logging off during load processing, which will make roll-forward processing impossible. If roll-forward recovery to a previous point in time is needed, this should be included in the evaluation criteria because it may be missing in some products. The use of the log may not be needed, as point-in-time recovery using image copies or disk backups should be sufficient.

Archival of Data

Over the life of the warehouse, it may become normal to remove data that is no longer needed on-line to satisfy user requirements. For example, monthly data may be kept on-line for three years and weekly data for 60 weeks. When this data is removed from the warehouse, the user may need to refer back to it periodically. It may therefore be desirable to archive the data rather than delete it outright.

Archival may also become necessary as the warehouse grows in size. For example, the user may wish to keep five years of historical data on-line, but costs or hardware limitations may make this impractical. In these cases, it may be necessary to incorporate another type of storage media that allows for large, long-term access, or archive the data to an off-line storage media such as tape.

Long-term storage media, if used, may be slower than on-line disk, but using such media may avoid the necessity to delete or archive the data to an off-line storage device. An example is recordable CD. Some types of media may make it possible to have the data available without manual intervention being required to restore or reload the data when it is needed.

The database definitions of tables, indexes, and other features may change over time. It may be necessary to store not only the data, but also the DDL that was used while the data was active. There are software products available that will allow data to be copied in a baseline format that includes the DDL to generate the tables and the rest of the database.

Where release-dependent features of DBMS or other software were used, it may also be necessary to store a copy of the old releases of software to facilitate the re-creation of the database. The alternative may be to convert archived data to a format that is usable by new releases of software.

Database Reorganization

If data is simply replaced, or appended to, during the database load process, database reorganizations may not be necessary. This assumes that the data is preprocessed, perhaps by sorting into the proper order, such that efficient access is assured. Reorganizations may also be avoided if summary information is updated in place. In other cases, real-time or periodic updates may cause the same changes to physical organization that occur in operational databases. This is the case for replication products that create a copy of the operational database. In these cases, it will be necessary to plan for and perform periodic database reorganizations.

MANAGEMENT ISSUES

When organizations move to new platforms from traditional host environments, perceptions exist within the organization about improved cost effectiveness. These perceptions may carry over to the management and administration of these platforms and the heterogeneous environment. In many cases, the support departments may be expected to install and support a client/server environment without a significant increase in staff. While these perceptions exist, the complexity of the heterogeneous environment makes the management more complex.

In establishing the DBA and support role for a data warehouse, there are many organizational factors that should be considered. These factors will affect the number of support personnel, the location of the DBAs both on the organization chart and physically, the number of servers, the number of types of platforms, operating systems, DBMS and gateways implemented, and the responsibilities of each department.

Centralization versus Decentralization

A group of up to 10 DBAs is often better when it is placed together in the organization. A central DBA department provides the opportunity for the DBAs to work together, cross train, and provide backup for each other to support production environments. On occasion, one or more DBAs may be seconded to other areas such as large development projects to provide short-term support. It is easier to develop and enforce standards when all support staff are centralized in one group.

For large applications or special work projects, it is frequently a good idea to relocate people physically to the project area. This allows people to concentrate on project tasks and reduces the interruptions from regular support work. If the project work is done on a part-time basis, a workstation in both areas may be appropriate to allow more focus on the tasks at hand. Without this type of physical location and a specific time commitment each day, day-to-day production responsibility can usurp the project time and the schedule may suffer.

Data Mart Issues

Some end-user departments may have purchased data marts directly from vendors without any involvement from IT personnel during the investigation or implementation. In this situation, IT should make every effort to work with the user area to ensure that corporate standards are followed. Without standard naming conventions, it may be very difficult to integrate information from a nonstandard data mart with other information. There are many examples of data marts that have been implemented with the help of an outside consulting firm using no-standard hardware, operating systems, and software. This is not in the corporate interest.

SUMMARY

Using a solid background from a production environment, the DBA should have little trouble implementing the support procedures for a data warehouse. Where possible, standardization of platforms and DBMS products will ease management and training for staff. The issues of scalabiliy, portability, backup, recovery, data archiving, security, change management, and performance management are obvious issues that must be addressed. With proper procedures, the data warehouse will meet user requirements from an operational point of view and provide a base of integrated, high-quality data that will provide many business benefits.

Security
in the Data Warehouse

26

Martin Hubel

Martin Hubel Consulting, Inc.
Toronto, Canada

"What one man can invent another can discover."

A. Conan Doyle

This chapter covers the security aspects of the data warehouse in a heterogeneous client/server environment. This environment is particularly complex due to the differences in the level of security available in various operating environments and RDBMS security mechanisms. Data security for the data warehouse also has special considerations based on the duration that information may be retained. This is particularly true if the warehouse contains detail information to support any summarized or reduced data.

While many DBAs are aware of, and follow, security policies as part of implementing and administering applications, it has been my experience that security is often ignored during implementation and only addressed after an audit, when the procedures to ensure compliance may be costly and more difficult to implement. With this in mind, a brief review of fundamental security concepts is included. Experienced users may wish to bypass this section, or refer to it as necessary.

BASIC SECURITY CONCEPTS

Most operating systems have security features that enable an administrator to use individual or group authorizations. In some cases, such as IBM's MVS, security must be provided by third-party security software that is used with the operating system.

There are basic security concepts that underlay the controls organizations implement in any environment where corporate data is stored. Most operating systems have security features that enable an administrator to use individual or group authorizations. Procedures are developed by the data security department to secure the operating environment using the facilities available. The audit department ensures compliance with the organizational standards.

To secure a DBMS, it is first necessary to secure the hardware and operating system environment against possible security exposures. Any system that is not in a secure location is especially vulnerable. For example, in an OS/2 system, a user could easily replace the file containing the system userid and password (NET.ACC) file with a different copy, and this could lead to wide-scale compromising of data within the RDBMS. For the DBA implementing a data warehouse on a client/server platform, it will probably be necessary to consider security for the entire environment in addition to the DBMS.

User Authentication and Accountability

The primary function of security software is to ensure that users are authorized to access the computer system. This is normally achieved by a userid and password. This method is common and is well understood. It also provides the basis for establishing individual accountability. It also can be called user sign-on, logon, or login.

The concept of user accountability requires that any user action be traced to only one individual user. This allows certain commands or actions performed by a user to be traced back only to that user. To accomplish this objective, it is required that each user be assigned a unique userid and password.

Having established a userid, system privileges can be given via the system security package. In some environments, these system privileges may extend to the database manager. Thus it is possible that administrative personnel without database responsibilities may hold authorities within the database environment. There may be no practical method to prevent these people from using these privileges; telling them "not to touch anything" may have to suffice.

Password Issues

Choice and Expiry. In popular movies, when a person wants to break into a computer system, they think of an easy password that "everybody" uses or knows that they use to gain access to the system quickly. Fortunately, many computer security systems have methods to prevent this type of access. Security administrators can establish user accountability, password patterns, expiry periods, and the reuse of passwords within these environments. The security system also controls the number of invalid attempts and may report at sign-on the number of unsuccessful attempts since the last successful sign-on.

To ensure user accountability, the password for each userid should be known only by its user. The security or system administrator who assigns userids and passwords should not be placed in the position of being held accountable for possible actions taken by a userid. So, when a userid and password are assigned, the password should be automatically expired by the security system. The user is required to choose and enter a new password when the userid is first used. This is also true when a user forgets his or her password and is assigned a new one by the administrator. An important part of user accountability is an education process to ensure that users understand that userids should never be shared and that passwords are secret and personal. Some security systems store the password internally in an encrypted format to ensure that there is no way for the administrator to determine a user's password.

Password patterns are important to ensure that users choose a password that is not easily guessed by other users. People are encouraged not to use the names of loved ones or other personal information. Security administrators like to have passwords that are at least six characters in length, which often contain numbers as well as letters that presumably would make the password harder to guess. Patterns may be controlled in the some environments by the security software.

In many environments, passwords have expiry periods. After a specified number of days, the password will expire, forcing the user to choose a new password. In other environments, such as User Profile Management in OS/2, the time since each password was last changed is tracked, but it is not necessary to change it. Some security systems prevent the reuse of passwords for a given time (for example, 12 or 18 months).

The security system also controls the number of invalid password attempts. After a certain number of failed attempts, often three, the userid is suspended and must be reset by the security administrator. The number of attempts is controlled by a security software parameter. Following a successful sign-on, the number of invalid attempts since the last successful sign-on is reported to the user. The user should report any unsuccessful attempts that are not accounted for (that is, not accidentally done by the user) to the security administrator in case an attempt was made to gain unauthorized access to the system. In addition, the userid can automatically be suspended if the user does not sign-on within a 30 day period.

Security Back Doors.   When a security system is first installed, a default userid and password may be supplied by the vendor for the initial sign-on. For example, the OS/2 userid and password supplied for DB2 for OS/2 are USERID and PASSWORD. This userid has all authorities available in the system: to access all data, to perform all administrative functions, and to administer system security and assign new passwords. The manual clearly states that this userid should be used to establish another, different administrator userid and then be deleted. Alternatively, the initial userid could be kept if the password is changed to a different value.

Most security exposures caused by people outside the organization (e.g., hackers) are caused by security back doors that are "left open." This is how many DEC systems were hacked in the 1980s, when the default system engineer's password was not changed. It is critical that any, or all, security back doors be identified and closed quickly. Of course, if somebody was to make a movie of a system break-in at your company, they would rely on your leaving the exposure open. Most movie directors would have problems envisioning a movie about computers without somebody using a back door, having an eminently guessable password, or having an unlimited number of invalid access attempts.

PHYSICAL SECURITY

Physical security issues would normally be of interest only to the security department, but they may become important if a departmental server is implemented and it is not managed centrally by computer operations and the other services of the IT department. These issues are fundamental, but they should be well understood by all parties involved. By no means is the information in this section complete; the procedures should be reviewed by the physical and data security people in your organization.

The server should be placed in a room that has limited access for support personnel only. The reasons are obvious, and the consequences perhaps humorous (if it is someone else's machine) if this is not done: for example, if the cleaning personnel shuts off the server to save power, or a clumsy or careless person trips over the power cord during the loading of the database. Of course, the physical environment, such as air conditioning in the server's room, could become a concern.

The machine should have a key lock or some other way to keep an unauthorized person from powering the machine on to gain access. There should also be a way to prevent the system from being booted by diskette, which would then allow access to data, the operating system, and even the security files (which could be erased or replaced).

STAND-ALONE OR SHARED SECURITY

Some organizations have implemented an umbrella security package that allows a single sign-on after which a user can attach to different environments on one or multiple processors. The user may be allowed to connect to one or more environments at once with or without a sign-on being required. Depending on the implementation, the user may be asked to supply a password at the time of logon to the next system. If the password is not required, this situation is sometimes called pass-through. Many organizations require that the password be supplied. This environment requires that the userid be the same across all environments.

Controlling User Connections

In some environments, it is possible to control which users can use DBMS resources. This type of control is somewhat optional, as the security within the relational DBMS will prevent unauthorized access. Privileges must still be granted within the DBMS environment even if this type of connection control is used. The type of control mentioned in this section is meant to be separate from the CONNECT privilege if this is available within the DBMS.

REMOTE ACCESS

When two systems wish to share data, some coordination is needed to ensure appropriate access from each side. These issues include the type of connection used, and whether it is felt that the security measures are sufficient to satisfy the requirements of the most sensitive node in the network. If one node is particularly sensitive, additional security precautions are necessary and should be implemented for that node and for any other node that must use its data.

Trusted versus Nontrusted Nodes

Each node in a network has taken some security precautions (even none could be considered some). When a node wishes to obtain data from another site, the site being accessed may choose to accept the precautions at the other site and allow access freely, or to decide that security at the other site is insufficient and take other measures. These measures may require that the other site provide a userid with an encrypted password each time data is requested.

The Distributed Computing Environment (DCE) from IBM provides services to workstations on a network for many administrative functions including security. The DCE Security Service provides the network with user authentication, access to resources, and user account management. Administration is done from a central control point and a secure link communicates with the workstations. Many organizations use the facilities of DCE to provide a single system image and use the security services to protect the data in the warehouse.

Auth-ID Translation

When there are multiple sites, it is possible that the same userid could be used by different people at different sites. When these sites must communicate and share data, it may be necessary to translate userids to have different values at remote sites. These userids can be translated at the sending site (outbound checking), at the receiving site (inbound checking), or at both sites. Naming conventions for userids between sites are important to facilitate communication between sites.

For certain queries from remote locations, there may be a desire to treat remote from one location as a group. All users during inbound checking would be translated to a common value. This may be possible for other platforms and DBMSs depending on the product and platform. In this case, the translation function would simply convert multiple incoming userids to one value.

Caution should be used when reviewing the security between platforms, and this should be extended to the data warehouse environment. For example, certain environments may lead to the grouping of users in a distributed environment. Depending on the implementation, this could result in the loss of accountability, as a given request would not be able to be traced to an individual user. This is a concern when gateways are used.

RDBMS SECURITY

There are many features in a relational environment that require a separate security mechanism. Some parts relate to the shared use of data, while other parts may have been necessary based on the lack of security within certain environments. Points that the administrator must consider are included in this section.

Object Ownership

RDBMS, object creation, and ownership carry certain privileges that can be nonrevocable by other users. These privileges often include nonrestricted access to objects created by the user and the ability to grant these privileges to other users of the creator's choosing. This can be a cause for concern in production environments. Ownership must be carefully controlled if security is a concern. Sometimes, a different administrator userid is used for the creation of objects that is separate from the normal administrative ID.

In some environments, ownership can be shared through the use of groups set within system security. This will allow users to be granted ownership privileges by adding them to the group. Users can have their privileges revoked by removing their privileges from the group. In this way, even the original creator can lose his or her privileges by being removed from the group.

Data Control Language

The GRANT statement in SQL is used to permit users access to resources within the RDBMS environment. Between RDBMSs, the only commonality lies with the GRANT statement for table privileges. This is the only statement in the SQL standard. The REVOKE statement is not included as part of the standard, although most products support the use of this statement for the removal of privileges.

Each RDBMS requires that an initial powerful userid be granted authority from either system security or from an options module. In DB2 for MVS, these userids are the install SYSADM auth-IDs within the DSNZPARM parameter module. In OS/2, User Profile Management (UPM) sets up the default userid of USERID with a default password of PASSWORD for use during installation and the setup of other administrative userids within UPM.

Most RDBMSs control security at the database level. Users are granted specific authorities or administrative authorities at that level by an administrative ID. The privileges needed for each DBMS and how they function often vary between each vendor and their implementation for various platforms.

The main problem that organizations have when using the RDBMS security mechanism has been termed the "ease of safe use." This refers to the cumbersome nature of using GRANTs and REVOKEs to control a large environment consisting of many objects, privileges, and users. The majority of the administrative burden can be eased if user groups or roles are established, but it is still necessary to document carefully the privileges required by each type of user and to maintain this list as the need for privilege changes.

Differences in Data Control Language

The main differences in data control language (DCL) between products are the forms of the GRANT statement used to support the types of objects and administrative privileges used by the DBMS. The differences between administrative authorities are discussed next. There are other important differences between implementations of RDBMS security.

In most products, the special auth-ID PUBLIC is used to represent a privilege that is granted to all users of the DBMS or database. There are some differences between the implementation of granting and revoking privileges when PUBLIC is used. In SYBASE, it is possible to grant a privilege to public and then revoke the privilege from one or more users to prevent their access. In DB2, to prevent a single user from gaining access, it is necessary to revoke the privilege from public and grant the privilege individually to each user or group of users that need the privilege.

Groups of Users

One of the limitations of granting authorities in RDBMSs is that each authorization ID has to be specified individually in the GRANT statement. Facilities may exist within the environment to allow userids to be placed into a group. Privileges can then be granted to the group using one GRANT statement.

The grouping of users solves the major problem with RDBMS security administration, as most authorization changes involve the administration of users. Users can then gain or lose authority by being added or removed from a group. This can reduce security administration activity by up to 90%. This is especially important in a data warehouse environment with large numbers of users. Except for administrative authorities, some products offer no security grouping for privileges. Other products, such as ORACLE 7, provide the ability to define roles that allow privileges to be grouped together according to the needs of the organization.

No product offers native facilities for dealing with related objects as a group. Of course, the privileges for each object need only be granted to user groups for most products, but it would be preferable to understand which objects go together by establishing a group. This can be done via some administrative products, or by creating a file that contains the objects and privileges to be managed together and using the system editor to edit the userid or group ID to whom the privileges should be granted.

ADMINISTRATIVE AUTHORITIES

The administrative authorities are provided for use by DBA, systems, and security personnel to control the DBMS environment (Table 26.1). These privileges hold

TABLE 26.1   COMPARISON OF ADMINISTRATIVE AUTHORITIES AND OTHER SECURITY FEATURES

DB2 for MVS	ORACLE[*]	SYBASE	DB2 Common Server
SYSADM: All system privileges	DBA: All system privileges	SA: All system privileges	SYSADM
SYSCTRL			
DBADM	RESOURCE	DBO (DB owner)	DBADM
DBCTRL			CONTROL
DBMAINT			
PACKADM			
BINDADD			BINDADD
SYSOPR			
	CONNECT: Access, DML to granted tables, create synonyms and views		
	Extensions for auditing	Public privileges can be revoked from one person— grant select on payroll to public, revoke select on payroll (salary) from public	

[*] ORACLE 7 provides the ability to define roles for granting privileges to users. The large number of system privileges available provides a very fine granularity of security, and these can individually be included in the roles defined by the installation. The Oracle Corporation recommends that this be done.

both explicit and implicit authority for functions vital to the proper maintenance of the RDBMS environment, such as recovery, security, change management, and installation.

One of the strengths of some RDBMS security mechanisms is the ability to control security to a very granular level. It is possible to control the execution of many individual utilities within some RDBMSs. However, one of the weaknesses is that certain administrative groupings may contain many useful privileges but also include privileges that may be undesirable to distribute widely. An example of this, also within DB2 for MVS/ESA, is the REPAIR privilege included with DBADM and DBCTRL, which provide a superzap capability for data.

THE NATURE OF DATA IN THE WAREHOUSE

Data warehouses often contain just summarized data, although this may not always be the case. Detailed data may also be stored for some period of time within the warehouse to support further inquiries after looking at summary data. Data mining tools and techniques should be investigated to ensure that exposures do not occur.

Summary data are not normally considered as sensitive as detailed data. For example, the salary by department may be needed for management reporting and considered less confidential, while the salary of any individual is considered highly confidential. This example is easily implemented using a view containing a GROUP BY DEPARTMENT clause to provide information in summary form.

Security Exposures by Inference

While there may be some feeling of security from giving users access to summary data, there may also be some risk depending on the size of the underlying data. Using the preceding salary example, departments that contain only one or two employees may be more susceptible to the exposure of detailed data. This may also be true for subsets of data, such as a department having 10 employees but only one male or female employee. It may, therefore, be a good idea to restrict the definition of views to include a condition on the grouping using a HAVING clause, as in the following example:

```
SELECT WORKDEPT, SUM(SALARY)
  FROM EMP
  WHERE SEX = 'M'
  GROUP BY WORKDEPT
  HAVING COUNT(*) > 5
```

Some people are concerned that even proper controls on every table within a data warehouse may not be sufficient. While data in each table may be secured properly through the use of views, it may be possible to infer the value of sensitive data through the data mining techniques of reviewing and combining data in multiple tables to produce a result leading to a security exposure. While this concern is real, a concrete example of this type of exposure has not yet been found.

PROTECTING METADATA

The data warehouse can contain many different types of data on many different subject areas. Some subjects may either be confidential or be for the use of certain departments only. The data within the dictionary may need protection to ensure that its existence is not spread to individuals who should not know about it.

The metadata stored in the catalog is often granted to the public. This decision is often made because it is expedient for the security administrator. The knowledge of what data is stored about an entity (that is, the column names), may itself be confidential.

Many DBMSs provide messages that indicate security violations when users attempt SQL against tables for which they are not authorized. The users may receive a message that indicates that the table does not exist. From a metadata security point of view, this is a better message to receive than a message that indicates a lack of authorization. This latter message indicates that the object exists, which means that the user may seek another way to obtain the data.

A SECURITY REVIEW CHECKLIST

The checklist shown in Table 26.2 is meant to summarize and help you understand that a minimum level of security has been achieved with the database environment. Most of these issues were discussed in the preceding sections.

Several important security considerations are discussed in Chapters 24 and 25.

TABLE 26.2   SECURITY REVIEW CHECKLIST

Issue	Notes
Password choices	Establish reasonable, "nonguessable" passwords.
Security backdoors	Change or remove all userids with default passwords.
User sign-on	Provide authentication and accountability.
Remote access	Is the node trusted or not?
Userid translation	For distributed environments, what should the userid be for remote users? Is individual accountability required for remote users?
DDL differences	This is important for a heterogeneous environment.
Administrative authorities	See Organizational Issues.
Object ownership	Identify implicit privileges of owners, if any.
Userid groups/roles	This is useful for security administration.
Physical security	These are issues for departmental servers.

ROLES AND RESPONSIBILITIES

In large environments, the administration of database security may be placed in several locations within the organizational structure. This could be the data security department, DBA, or other administrative area. Segregation of duties is normal in large environments, and it is somewhat necessary based on the size of the environment and the value of the information being stored. On smaller platforms, however, it is normal to have fewer people support the environment. It is possible that security administration on a smaller platform would have to be handled by the software installer or the DBA.

Background Issues

The organizational need and commitment will dictate the level of security required in the organization and the data warehouse. Some industries, such as banks and national defense, require strict security measures by law. Other organizations in other fields may also have legislative requirements; they may face industrial espionage or invasion from computer hackers; or they may simply understand the value of information within their organization.

In determining who should be responsible for DBMS security, and possibly for platform security in a client/server environment, there are several factors that should be considered. The most important of these factors are the skill sets and the knowledge level of both the platform and the DBMS as well as basic security concepts and the standards of the organization.

Another key factor is the staffing levels for the client/server environment. Staffing cutbacks during recent recessions, outsourcing, and mergers often leave organizations with inadequate resources to implement fully the procedures that were developed and supported in years past. The emphasis has been placed on the delivery of systems for the organization to survive with less attention being placed on the operational aspects of these systems. In addition, there is an expectation that smaller platforms should be cheaper to run, so the budget may not be available for the normal levels of security and auditing.

Organizational Issues

Table 26.3 shows the management issues that should be addressed when setting up security for data warehouse.

Responsibility Matrix.   Table 26.4 shows a sample of how privileges could be documented for a warehouse environment. A matrix of this type will allow uniform administration by multiple people and satisfy audit requirements.

Training requirements.   To implement a proper security plan for the data warehouse environment, some training may be required. Some knowledge of security concepts and the security policies of the organization is required if the DBA group is to administer the security for the DBMS and perhaps the system security on a smaller dedicated warehouse platform. If the security department is to take on security, more training is often required. The security department will have to understand the environment and the implications of security within the operating system, DBMS, and the applications to be controlled. This may require formal training in one or all of these topics.

AUDITING REQUIREMENTS

At some point, internal EDP audit departments may want to perform an audit on the DBMS and the applications running on it, including the data warehouse. This

TABLE 26.3 SECURITY MANAGEMENT ISSUES

Issues	Areas of Concern
Number of administrators	Too many people with powerful authority can lead to security exposures. Too few administrators may not provide sufficient coverage to support the environment.
System maintenance and recovery	Software installation and maintenance. Powerful authority is often needed for recovery, particularly for system resources.
Control of administrator userids	Administrator userids can often read all application data, including sensitive corporate data.
Object ownership in production	Similar to administrator IDs, owners have special privileges; they can read or change data and grant these privileges to others.
Emergency fixes to warehouse data	Procedures are required for emergency situations to fix application data or programs in off-hour situations or during vacation time of normal support personnel.
Sensitivity of data within departmental servers	If test data is downloaded to data marts from the warehouse, the security of sensitive data must be considered.
Departmental responsibilities	Refer to the responsibilities matrix in Table 26.4.
Privileges required	Privileges granted to each department/class of user/job function.
"Political" issues	Mandate of departments involved. Interest and commitment to database security. Skill sets of departments and individuals. Audit requirements.

can happen during development or following implementation, depending on the staffing and interest within the audit department.

On the whole, it is better to work with the audit department during development than to wait for an audit following implementation. The mind-set of auditing is different from other parts of the organization; the auditor is trained to evaluate security exposures and to assess the risk of these exposures to the organization. It is better to receive their recommendations early rather than trying to implement required changes sometime after the data warehouse has reached production.

There are two types of audits that are performed: the system audit or systems software support audit, and the application audit. An application audit looks at the inputs and outputs of the system and how well the application controls these relative to the functional design. The distribution of reports is checked to ensure that these are going to the right people. The accuracy of the data itself will also be reviewed. This type of audit is not often needed for the data warehouse.

The systems software support audit is a baseline audit that is done to establish how well the environment has been installed and administered relative to organizational standards. This type of auditing is used to check data for security, accuracy, and quality. It includes auditing of how well the DBMS is set up, what facilities are turned on and off, what privileges have been granted, including special attention to administrative authorities, how data is loaded, and when utilities are run and by whom.

TABLE 26.4 RESPONSIBILITY MATRIX

Responsible Groups	Privileges Needed	Tasks Requiring Privileges
Systems programming	System: Administrator	Backs up, maintains, and installs DBMS software. Runs subsystem utilities.
Security department	System: Administrator	Grants and revokes access. Monitors grants and plans. Grants and revokes temporary access for specials and emergencies.
Help desk/ information center	System: None Database: None Plans: Execute on plans for 4GLs Tables: Select on catalog information for tables, columns, indexes	Helps end users with queries and object creation. Analyzes queries with using available tools such as Explain.
Query tool administrator	System: None Database: None Tables: Access to tables, plans of query tool	Maintains query tool environment.
End user	System: None Database: None Plans: Access to 4GL plans after required training Tables and views: Select access following approval	Queries data warehouse tables. Does possible save of results in DBMS. Saves and maintains SQL queries.

Auditors will often want to see historical information related to security activity. For the RDBMS, this would include GRANT/REVOKE activity, invalid access attempts, and successful data access for particularly sensitive objects. This information should include the data and time of the access or the privilege being granted and the userid of both the grantee and the grantor. The types of audit information vary widely from product to product. While the information provided by all vendors is generally adequate, ORACLE 7 appears to provide the most complete information of any product without further interpretation by other vendor products.

Information regarding the current status of the RDBMS is available from the system catalog/dictionary tables. If the warehouse is installed on hardware that is completely new within the organization, it may be necessary to review the operating environment as well as the DBMS.

SUMMARY

Staffing and budget cutbacks are affecting the commitment to any security within some organizations. This may put the full responsibility for data warehouse security squarely on the shoulders of the DBA. When reading this book, which is filled with many articles on interesting data warehouse topics, there may be readers who choose to postpone or simply ignore the security implications until placed under the scrutiny of the audit department, or until they actually experience a security breach first hand. This is often the first time that security measures are taken seriously. Of course, at this point it is too late for you (if other people in your company find out that you are to blame) or for your company (if the information taken is used by a competitor or the data cannot be reconstructed).

REFERENCES

[1] MARTIN G. HUBEL, "Who Cares about Database Security?," *Database Programming & Design*, November 1995.

CHAPTER 27

Selecting End-User Tools

Peter Brooks

Coopers & Lybrand Consulting
Boston, Massachusetts

'Would you tell me, please, which way I ought to go from here?'

'That depends a good deal on where you want to get to,' said the Cat.

'I don't much care where …' said Alice.

'Then it doesn't matter which way you go,' said the Cat.

'… so long as I get SOMEWHERE,' Alice added as an explanation.

Louis Carroll, "Alice in Wonderland"

How do you choose the right end-user data access tools for your organization? Selecting the best tools to build reports and provide ad hoc access to the information is one of the more visible activities in creating a data warehouse. However, one of the difficulties in choosing this type of tool, unlike for other components of a data warehouse solution, is the large number of available products. There are literally hundreds of tools—ranging from simple ad hoc query products to sophisticated application development suites—that can provide access to data warehouses. Which is the best one for you? How do you cut through the marketing hype to make the best decision? The answer is that a structured, user-centric tool selection methodology is needed to make sure that the best set of end-user data access tools is chosen from among all the products.

This chapter provides a methodology for choosing data warehouse end-user access tools. The methodology is based on

- Real-life tool selections performed over many years
- Published tool selection processes and considerations
- Continuing research.

In the 1980s, most data warehouse access tools were best used by technically astute users, either business analysts with technical abilities or those with an IT background. Executives would use one of the several special EIS tools. There were not many choices available in the marketplace. However, end-user data warehouse access tools proliferated as data warehouses came into vogue and end users became more comfortable with technology. Many products have apparently similar functions and are often marketed to many different types of users. The OLAP tools are examples of end-user tools that appear similar to each other at first glance but are actually significantly different.

In this chapter, the terms *end-user tool* or *tool* will be used to mean a product that allows users to access information in the data warehouse. The term *application* will be used to mean an end-user data warehouse access tool that has been customized to access a particular data warehouse by, for example, defining certain standard reports or general views of data. *Application* does not imply that an application development tool has been used to build the system. A *prototype* is the first iteration of an application. There will probably be several iterations before an application is complete.

A TOOL SELECTION METHODOLOGY: WHY BOTHER?

A project's success or failure can hinge on how easy it is for users to access information in the data warehouse. The data may be cleansed, summarized, and distributed, but if data is difficult to access or use, then the project will not be the success that is first envisioned.

I was once contacted by the IT department of an appliance manufacturer that had developed a sales and marketing analysis data warehouse decision support system. The company had created a system using several tools that were the corporate standards—Microsoft® Excel, Access, and Powerpoint—to present information from corporate relational databases. In addition, Microsoft® Word was provided since it was the corporate word processing standard. Yet when the system was delivered to the sales executives, it was rejected.

After asking several questions, it was to me obvious that the application as it had been designed would never work:

- The end users were not involved in the development. The system was designed and developed by the IT group based on what they "knew" the requirements to be. It was then presented to sales and marketing management. There were little ad hoc query and report customization capabilities.
- It was unclear what problem the system was trying to solve. Standardized reports were created in Powerpoint and Excel. Data was stored in Excel for end-user access.
- The tools were mismatched to the users' skills. The tools required some technical knowledge despite the fact this was the first time some users ever used a PC.

A tool selection methodology that emphasized user involvement and matched the tool functionality to the user skills should have been used. A general software package selection process could have been used, but the unique characteristics of data warehouse solutions would not necessarily have been considered. For the best and quickest results, a tool selection methodology tailored to data warehouse end-user access tools should have been employed.

An end-user tool is often used to build a sense of excitement and validate the data warehouse project to the end users. In one corporation, a rapid application development tool was used to allow access to a simple data warehouse two months after completion of requirements gathering. This was done to show the users how easy it was to satisfy their requirements with the technology. The users were ecstatic at the deliverable, and the developers were very pleased. However, several months later, the end users were restless—where were the follow-on functions? It turned out that the tool chosen was

- One the development staff already knew
- One that could be used to access information quickly in the data warehouse
- One that had scalability problems.

After several more months, developers raised the possibility that the system would have to be redesigned. The IT manager and development team no longer work for the company.

In this case, the developers should have

- Set the users' expectations about the time required to create a "real" system.
- Performed a quick survey of tool capabilities to create a prototype that could be expanded.
- Chosen a tool before building the first prototype or built the prototype so that a different tool could have been switched in. These options would have caused the system to be delivered a little later but would have avoided a "dead end."

One of the difficulties in choosing the right tool or set of tools is in balancing the advantages of creating a custom solution against the advantages of using commercial products that adhere to corporate standards. Custom solutions will usually satisfy nearly 100% of the project requirements, unlike solutions built using commercial products, which satisfy corporate standards. On the other hand, custom solutions will generally cost more and require more time and resources to develop and maintain than standard-based solutions. Benefits and drawbacks are shown in Figure 27.1.

While it is fortunate if the tools that provide the best business functionality are also the tools that work most easily in the existing corporation infrastructure, this is often not the case. The tool selection process should consider the implications of both of these types of needs and make the best overall decision. A tool that supports

Primary driver	Benefit	Benefiting organization	Drawback	Affected organization
Business needs	Best match of tools to business requirements	Business community	Possible difficulty in data access, support, expansion	Information Systems
Alignment with corporate standards	Easiest to implement and support	Information Systems	May not yield the best business benefit compared to other alternatives	Business community

Figure 27.1 Benefits and Drawbacks to Primary Driver Alternatives.

corporate standards but does not provide acceptable business benefits will not be used. Likewise, support and data access problems can also lead to a tool's failure.

TOOL SELECTION METHODOLOGY OVERVIEW

The end-user data access tool selection for a data warehouse project consists of a series of activities that should be integrated with the overall data warehouse plan. Some tool selection steps may naturally occur as part of other data warehouse processes because there are interdependencies between the tool selection phase and key data warehouse decisions. For example, many of the end-user tool requirements can be gathered during other data warehouse requirements and information gathering sessions. The tool and database selection decisions are interdependent—it is just as futile to choose a database for which there is a lack of user access tools as it is to choose a tool that cannot easily access the chosen database.

The overall tool selection methodology consists of the steps shown in Figure 27.2. The tool selection process will often lead to the conclusion that there is no one tool that satisfies all the major requirements. In this case, several tools, a toolset, can be chosen. This toolset will be the combination of tools that best meets the requirements.

Figure 27.3 shows a sample tool selection schedule. The tool selection is performed over a three-month time period, with a review of the decision in the sixth month. Note that this schedule is based on real-life experiences and business pressures in selecting a tool. For example, many activities are overlapped rather than performed one at a time so the selection can be completed as quickly as possible.

The explanation of the following tool selection methodology assumes that you are familiar with the general steps of a software tool selection. The intent is to focus on unique aspects relating to end-user data access tools. Consequently, much detail will be provided for the criteria selection definition process, since the criteria are different for a data warehouse tool selection compared to other types of tool selections. Conversely, there will not be a description of a general prototyping process, but only of prototyping considerations that are unique to the tool selection portion of a data warehouse project.

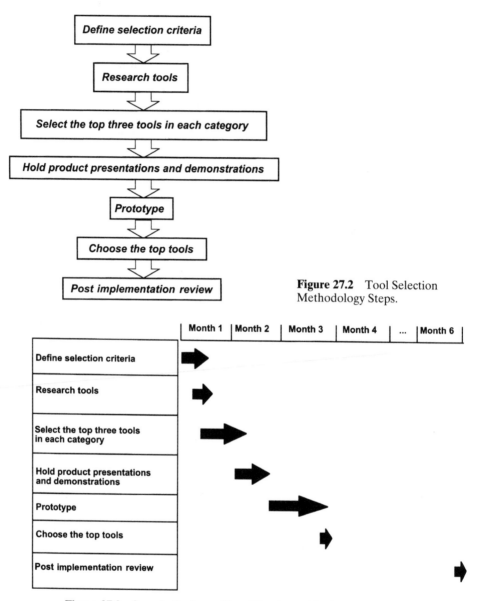

Figure 27.2   Tool Selection Methodology Steps.

Figure 27.3   Sample End-user Data Warehouse Tool Selection Schedule.

An alternative to aforementioned tool selection methodology is to bypass several steps by immediately choosing one or more tools with which the users are already familiar, assuming that the tools seem to satisfy the basic requirements. This has the benefit of significantly reducing the time needed to perform the tool selection by eliminating the Research Tools, Select the Top Three Tools in Each Category, and Hold Product Presentations and Demonstrations activities. Training time may also be minimized. The risk of this alternative, however, is that tools that best satisfy the requirements will not be chosen. The advantage of a shorter selection process must be balanced against the risk of possibly not choosing the best toolset.

Define Selection Criteria

The entire tool selection effort is built on the information captured in the selection criteria definition step. It is important that there be a well-defined methodology for completing this step rather than relying on the selection team's preconceived ideas of the user requirements. Also, selection criteria should not be based on vendor demonstrations. The tool selection process should be driven by user requirements. If it is done otherwise, tools may be chosen that look great but will not be used.

Creating selection criteria for end-user data warehouse access tools is significantly different from other types of end-user or application development tool selections because

- User requirements span the spectrum of flexibility from completely predefined and scheduled reports to wide open ad hoc requests.
- The marketplace contains a wide variety of tools.
- A large amount of accessible data has to be made understandable to users.
- Many different platforms must often be supported.

There are several types of requirements that need to be considered: user, technical, and vendor. User requirements criteria are those functions that provide users the anticipated benefits from implementing a data warehouse. Technical criteria are considerations involving the technical environment—such things as PC or Mac specifications, network configurations, and database connectivity. Vendor criteria include support, pricing, and vendor viability considerations.

There are many ways to select the best tools from among all the criteria. The preferred way is to use a scoring process that works as follows. Figure 27.4 is a sample matrix.

Tool Selection Scoring Procedure

1. As they are gathered, selection criteria should be listed in a spreadsheet or database.

Data Warehouse Tool Selection Criteria	Weighting	Product 1 Score	Product 2 Score	Product 3 Score
Access to operational data	80	00.5	00.9	00.7
Support existing database	70	00.9	00.5	00.3
Average weighted score		51.5	53.5	38.5

Figure 27.4 Sample Criteria Selection Matrix.

2. Once all the criteria are gathered, they should each be ranked in order of importance. Any scale can be used—the result will be the same. A 1 to 100 scale will be used in the following example. For example, if "access to operational data" is an important requirement, it may have a weighting of 80.

3. Each potential product should be scored as to how closely it satisfies each criteria. The scale should be from 0 to 1. A product that "somewhat satisfies" the "access to operational data" requirement could be given a score of 0.5. This is Product 1 in Figure 27.3. A product that "substantially satisfies" the requirement could be given a score of 0.9.

   Sometimes there are certain "required" criteria that must be met by the chosen tool. For example, perhaps the tool must run in a Windows environment. These criteria should be identified, and all tools that do not meet the required criteria can be immediately eliminated from consideration.

4. A weighted score for each product against every criteria should be calculated. For Product 1, the weighted score of the "access to operational data" requirement would be 80 multiplied by 0.5 = 40 and the weighted score of the "support existing database" requirement would be 70 multiplied by 0.9 = 63.

5. To derive the average weighted score of each product, the weighted scores for each product against each criteria should be added together. The sum should be divided by the number of criteria. The average weighted score of Product 1 would be the sum of its weighted scores divided by the number of requirements: $(40 + 63)/2 = 51.5$.

6. The product with the highest average score should be chosen.

As with all methods, a weighted scoring selection process can be manipulated to reach a preconceived result. It is important, therefore, that user, technical, and management representatives all be involved in the ranking of selection criteria and scoring of particular tools against the criteria. This fosters communication and understanding of different perspectives for the weights and should gain buy-in of the ultimate decision by all key constituencies.

In one retail organization, an OS/2-based system was chosen over Windows-based alternatives because it had slightly better end-user interface. However, the organization was primarily a Windows shop. Installing the OS/2 system in this environment resulted in initial and ongoing communications and connectivity problems. (OS/2 was not to blame for the problems.) The Windows-based solution would have been installed in considerably less time and could have been more easily supported. Was the better functionality of the OS/2 system worth the problems it caused?

User Requirement Criteria.   The user requirements can be elicited by using one of three approaches: individual interviews, group interviews, or organization surveys. A structured, interview-based approach is best for a small number of individual interviews or if the requirements may be of a sensitive nature. Group facilitation techniques such as joint application development sessions are best when eliciting requirements from groups of 5 to 20. Surveys are the most appropriate requirements gathering technique when there is a large, dispersed user population. Regardless of technique, as much detail as possible should be gathered in areas such as business goals, comfort with technology, and usefulness of existing reports.

Tool selection questions can often be asked during the overall data warehouse requirements gathering interviews rather than in separate sessions. This strategy has two benefits: It minimizes the interviews required of each user and allows members of the interview team to see the requirements from several different perspectives rather than focusing only on a particular specialty, such as database requirements or communications needs.

The ideal tool selection team has people in the following roles:

- *Executive sponsor:* The executive sponsor and their representative are key participants in the overall data warehouse project. They give direction to team members, answer questions, and resolve management issues that arise.
- *Business subject matter experts:* One or more people extremely knowledgeable in the appropriate business areas.
- *Tool selection expert:* A person familiar with data warehouse end-user access tools and experienced in performed tool selections.
- *Senior technical analyst:* A person extremely knowledgeable in the existing organization infrastructure and technology issues.

User interviews are conducted by one or more business matter subject experts and tool selection experts. The senior technical analyst is an optional member of the interview team.

An amount of information and level of detail that can be used to choose a set of tools must be gathered. Most people who are performing tool selection interviews for the first time tend to ask general questions and receive vague responses. After the first set of interviews, one tool selection team for a retail organization realized they had a general idea of the required sales and marketing information but did not know how the data should be displayed or manipulated. The team was able to create a list of requirements, but failed to remain focused on the purpose of the interviews: Create selection criteria that are detailed enough to differentiate between the various tools. Several executives had to be interviewed again.

A cross section of the users who will eventually access the data warehouse should be identified to create the interview list. There are several fundamental categories of users who will access a data warehouse:

- Executives
- Business analysts
- Power users.

Executives.   Executive users generally log on to the system once a day or so to look at key summary or exception data. Ease of use and display of key performance indicators are most important to these users. Analytic capabilities are not important and are rarely used. Rather than investigate detail, executives will ask their staff to investigate questions. Tools with executive information systems capabilities are most often used to provide executives access to pertinent data warehouse information.

Business Analysts. Business analysts are individuals who need to understand the data and relationships to answer questions and perform analyses. Data drill-down capability is used extensively to identify causes of business problems. Tools with decision support, spreadsheets, and/or statistical analysis capabilities are often used to provide analysts access to data warehouse information. Metadata support may be important to these users so that they may understand the data. There can be both casual usage and high-usage business analysts.

Power Users. Power users take full advantage of the data warehouse capabilities. They can understand and use sophisticated data access tools, are comfortable with SQL, and comprehend the details of data relationships. Power users often have a technical background and may work for IT. Tools with decision support and ad hoc query capabilities are often used to provide power users access to data warehouse information.

Technical Criteria. It does no good to choose a tool that can meet the users' needs but cannot be implemented by an organization. One of the challenges in selecting a tool is to balance the user requirements (which are paramount) with technical criteria, such as those involving corporate standards or connectivity requirements. For one insurance company, an easy-to-use front-end tool was chosen, a quick prototype was built, and then it took three months to get the networking components (PC, LAN server, and host server) working.

There are several categories of technical requirements:

- Desktop
- Connectivity
- Performance.

Desktop criteria deal with the user's system. Considerations include price, type of hardware, memory needs, and operating system. You may wish to constrain the tools to be analyzed to those that will work with existing desktop configurations. Another approach is to leave the desktop criteria fairly open ended and take direction from tool vendors as to what is an appropriate—not minimum—configuration.

Connectivity criteria are those that are required to ensure that the user desktop system will connect with the data warehouse. These criteria are usually not immediately apparent, but they are important to identify early in the process to avoid selecting a tool that is incompatible with the network configuration.

Tools that support common connectivity and data access standards, such as ODBC, can often more easily access disparate database than tools that do not support standards. The advantage of these ODBC compliant tools is that they can access any data source that supports the ODBC standard without requiring vendor code for each source. The use of ODBC compliant tools also allows an organization to switch out one tool more easily and replace it with another because the database connectivity logic should not change from one ODBC compliant tool to another.

Performance criteria include end-to-end performance measurements, not just the speed of the end-user desktop. Bottlenecks can occur in any of the key data warehouse components: database, network, or desktop.

Vendor Criteria.   There are some criteria that involve the vendor organization rather than specific product characteristics. Nonetheless, they must be considered in the tool selection process. These criteria are in the areas such as

- References
- Viability
- Pricing
- Maintenance
- Technical support
- Training
- Product future.

Reference checking is an obvious step to be undertaken in choosing the best solution for an organization. A frequent question clients ask me after seeing several vendor product presentations is, "Now what is the difference between the tools?" It is rare for a vendor to say their tool does not have a particular capability—with enough work, most tools can do most things. Reference checking allows you to see not just if a product can perform a certain function, but how easy it is to do. Performance is another area that should be investigated.

One important consideration is an analysis of vendor stability and viability—whether the vendor will be around in the years ahead. Some organizations would rather choose tools that are supplied by established and financially secure vendors even if less secure vendors have what appear to be tools with better functionality.

Pricing requirements involve more than cash outlay required to purchase the required tool software. What other software is needed, such as special drivers? How much will solution components, such as consulting or training, cost? Are all of these costs included in the tool purchase price?

Maintenance requirements are those that ensure that the tool and its environment can be updated as needed. Questions that should be answered include: How does a new version of the software get distributed? What are the interdependencies of the tool and other installed software? How do software fixes get installed? These questions are especially important for larger organizations that have many locations. Even in smaller organizations, "sneakernet" is becoming less prevalent as software distribution tools become more sophisticated.

Technical support requirements define the need to ask usability or technical questions and receive answers in a timely manner. This category of requirement often includes identification of help desk, installation, and defect support.

Training requirements can exist in many areas: user, installation, configuration, and customization or application development. Although the amount of required training depends on the tool and cannot be known until the tool is chosen, anticipated training needs can be identified in this phase of the tool selection. If it turns out that training in a particular area is not needed, so much the better. Statistical analysis or data mining tools generally have more sophisticated functions and may require end-user training. Regardless of vendors claims, most tools require training to be used most effectively.

Tools from smaller vendors often have the newest and most interesting features. A purchaser can often influence the vendor to add new capabilities to the product set. On the other hand, smaller companies may not have the financial stability or technical and consulting capabilities of larger ones.

Research Tools

Tools can be identified and researched at the same time selection criteria are being defined rather than waiting until the criteria are finalized. In fact, research should begin early in the tool selection process to complete the process as quickly as possible.

Preliminary research can take several days or weeks, and there is often a cost versus time trade-off. For example, it is very easy to request product literature from the vendors, but several weeks of slack time is spent waiting for the free material to be received. On the other hand, much material can be gathered from trade shows, if travel and admission expenses can be incurred.

By spending time in the beginning of the process to initiate the preliminary research and the overlapping activities, as shown in Figure 27.3, an organization will be ready to narrow down the list of tools very soon after the criteria definition is complete. Remember, the intent at this stage is to identify possible tools and gather information about the tools, not to select products.

Although there are well over 150 tools in the marketplace, key search criteria can be used to narrow the field quickly to 10 or 20. There are many sources with which to identify tools in the marketplace:

- Articles and product reviews in the trade press. Some publications, such as *DBMS*, have annual product guides available in print, on CD-ROM, and via the Internet (http://www.dbmsmag.com).
- A guide, such as *The OLAP Report*, by Nigel Pendse and Richard Creeth, published by Business Intelligence.
- Literature searches using products such as ABI/Inform or Computer Select.
- Internet-based information.
- Organizations such as META Group, Gartner Group, or DataPro.

- Attendance at trade shows.
- Peers or consultants experienced in the field.

The goal of performing a tool selection in the quickest possible time should be balanced against the goal of performing the most thorough evaluation of the most tools. To save time and effort, the universe of tools should be narrowed as soon as possible. Even preliminary selection criteria can often be used to narrow the tools under consideration, although the requirements definition is not yet complete. Often, one tool will not satisfy all requirements and several tools will be required, based on the functionality required and level of user.

One approach in the preliminary paring of the list of tools to be investigated is to determine which categories of capabilities are needed. Once the categories are decided on, only tools that provide capability in the chosen category need be investigated. Most tools contain functionality in several categories.

General tool capabilities are as follows:

- *Executive information systems.* These systems emphasize ease of use. They are designed for casual users who generally prefer to look at summary information with some drill-down or multidimensional modeling capabilities.
- *Decision support systems.* These systems provide sophisticated data analysis capabilities, but generally require more expertise to use than executive support systems. OLAP tools that provide "slicing and dicing" of the data have this capability.
- *Report writers.* Report writer tools excel at formatting data for printed or on-screen presentation. They do not have some of the analytic features found in decision support systems but have much richer data formatting capabilities. Titles, headings, and data sorts are easily created.
- *Ad hoc query.* Tools with ad hoc query capability provide for sophisticated querying of data warehouses. Many tools in this category include a user interface that appears to require little or no knowledge of SQL. While this may be true for simple queries against single tables, users will need to understand SQL or risk getting wrong answers when more complicated queries are created.
- *Application development.* Tools that provide a total application development facility can be used to create a user interface that exactly matches user requirements. However, this capability should be balanced against the time and expense needed to build the application, as well as the maintenance that will be required. Application development tools are generally not used to provide user access to data warehouses unless the programming staff is extremely proficient in the chosen tool. Required functionality usually exists in off-the-shelf tools that lead to a less costly project, shorter development time, and lower maintenance needs. Even off-the-shelf tools will require customization in most circumstances.
- *Spreadsheet analysis.* Data from a warehouse is often used to populate spreadsheets for detailed financial or other analysis. Spreadsheets are popular tools

with a ubiquitous user interface. Some technical expertise is needed to take advantage of spreadsheet capabilities, so spreadsheets are appropriate only for certain types of users.

- *Statistical analysis.* Some tools allow for sophisticated statistical analysis of data. Not just simple calculations or trend analyses, these products perform multivariate analysis, regression analysis, and other complex mathematical calculations. Users with a background in statistics are users of tools with this capability, which generally require some training to operate.

- *Data mining.* Tools that provide data mining functionality allow users to discover patterns in large volumes of data. An understanding of the data in the warehouse is needed to use tools with this capability effectively, and a technical background is generally required to utilize data mining products effectively.

Most end-user data access products are strong in one category while having some capabilities in many other categories. Therefore, vendors can usually say that their products can fulfill many types of requirements. That is what makes tool selections both interesting and complicated. This is also why a tool selection methodology that includes prototyping is best—real use of products will cut through all of the marketing claims.

Often, general user interface characteristics can be used to choose a tool category or even some tools within a category. This can be accomplished by understanding which type of user—executive, business analyst, or power user—will be using the tool. Certain categories of tools are more appropriate for certain categories of users. For example, an SQL interface is better suited for power users than executives.

The architecture of the tools under consideration should be consistent with the architecture needed to support the system requirements. Examples of specific architecture requirements that can preclude some tools from being considered are

- Support for users' existing desktop systems
- Ability to "travel well"—work in a laptop computing environment
- Distributed processing capabilities—requirements for particular host or LAN servers
- Client or server operating systems—Windows, UNIX, or OS/2
- Databases to be accessed.

Once the appropriate categories have been chosen and 10 to 20 tools have been identified, literature and demonstration diskettes should be requested from vendors. This should be done even if the requirements have not been totally defined because of the time it can take to receive the material. It is not uncommon for literature to take three to four weeks to arrive.

Select the Top Three Tools in Each Category

After the selection criteria have been defined and documented, tool categories have been chosen, and product material has been received, it is time to create the short list. The short list is created by indicating how well each product under consideration satisfies key selection criteria and creating the weighted score for each product, as previously described. Some vendor contact may be required to clarify specific product features or requirements.

Remember that a short list is being created at this stage of the methodology—the final tool selection will occur later. If only several of the key selection criteria need be used to choose three tools, then by all means choose the top three tools as soon as possible. If there are four or five tools under consideration that appear to be closely matched, more criteria must be evaluated.

The process of choosing the top three tools in each category can be as important as the actual result. End user, IT, and management involvement is important to the process. All involved organizations should be comfortable about the process and decision.

Once the top three tools in each category have been chosen, presentations and demonstrations should be scheduled.

Hold Product Presentations and Demonstrations

The goal of the product presentations and demos is twofold: to determine if the products are a good match for the application requirements and, if so, to determine the resources required to build a proof of concept. A proof of concept is a simple prototype system that is intended to prove the viability of the proposed solution.

Vendors of some of the higher-priced tools will provide presentation and sales support. Most will have several industry "templates" that can be used to start the development process rather than having to start from scratch. Lower-priced tools usually have a CD-ROM or diskette-based presentation and possibly an "evaluation" (limited functionality) copy.

If possible, attempt to gain agreement with the vendor to perform a proof of concept demonstration with your data. Company staff will be required to give vendors direction, provide data, and answer questions, among other activities. If vendor sales support is not available, then you may have to create the demo yourself. Depending on the circumstances and vendors, more than one presentation may be needed for each product. This usually occurs when the data warehouse will be accessed by several user groups in different locations.

The product presentation and demonstration phase consists of several steps:

- Preparation
- Presentation and demonstration
- Postpresentation review.

The most undervalued step in this tool selection phase is the presentation preparation. It is undervalued because many people assume the purpose is to view a vendor presentation and get a general feel for the product. While these are good aims, it is also important that answers be received for any questions and that vendors see the seriousness of your effort. Otherwise, it can be difficult to convince a vendor to create a customized demonstration. Most value will accrue to those tool selection teams that

- Have done background research and have focused and detailed questions. As many questions as possible should have been answered by reading product literature or asking the vendor. This will allow the audience to have focused questions that will require the vendor to answer with specifics. It is much better to ask, as one retail client did, "Can you handle 1000 products, 150 locations, and 20,000 SKUs?" rather than "Do you have category management?"
- Have provided data for the vendor to use in creating a customized demonstration rather than be shown a canned presentation.
- Have provided the presenter a specific business area or scenario that will be first implemented.
- Discuss the product's technology to determine if the technology is compatible with the organization's current or planned infrastructure.
- Come prepared to discuss the next steps.

Once the presentation and demonstration is complete, products should be matched to all of the selection criteria and a score calculated for each product. Based on the score, one or more tools from each appropriate tool category should be chosen for a prototype.

There are pros and cons to prototyping more than one tool from each category: The advantages of prototyping several tools are as follows:

- Better ultimate tool selection decision based on more information from the prototypes.
- Ability to discriminate between two closely ranked products based on experience rather than vendor claims.
- More understanding of the specific user requirements.

The disadvantages of prototyping several tools are as follows:

- More time, effort, and resources are required.
- The final tool selection decision can take longer.
- People can become advocates for the tool they are prototyping rather than looking objectively at all the products under consideration.

Prototype

What is an end-user data warehouse prototype? Is it a souped-up demo? Is it a production system? Does it use real data? Different definitions of prototypes are useful in different circumstances.

For end-user data warehouse access tools, a prototype should be a production prototype that can be delivered in approximately 90 days. A production prototype has limited breadth of function, but the function that is implemented is ready for production. For example, it is better to have a sales reporting prototype access the actual volumes of data in the warehouse (which implies that connectivity to the warehouse is working) than it is to have a sales reporting, marketing, and human resources user interface using small test tables with made-up data.

This type of prototype is used for one of several purposes:

- If users do not understand the benefits of the data warehouse, the prototype can be used to prove or disprove the value.
- If several tools are under consideration, the prototype is a test of the tools or tool suites to see which one is best.
- If one tool has been chosen, the prototype is used to validate the choice.

Data warehouses are complex undertakings. All components of end-user access to the warehouse should be tested in the prototype phase of tool selection. To ensure that all components are tested, the tool selection prototyping activities should be integrated into the overall data warehouse prototyping plan. The prototype should test

- End users actually using the system
- All connectivity components, including the middleware architecture
- Real data, using expected volumes
- Expected performance bottlenecks, such as dial-up access or older-model PCs.

The prototype should be timeboxed to be complete within 90 days. It is generally better to decrease functions in the prototype than increase the time needed to complete the prototype. If additional functions really need to be tested before committing to a particular tool, several prototype iterations, each 90 days, should be built.

User and management expectations should be carefully managed. Developing the end-user data warehouse access using a prototyping process will result in a quicker implementation than using the traditional waterfall application development approach. Particularly, it should be reinforced that problems arising during the prototyping are an expected part of the process. Prototyping allows problems to surface so they can be addressed in a timely manner. All participants must understand the process.

It can be very difficult for the data warehouse sponsors if the prototype is a failure. This is particularly true if user management has not been involved in the tool selection decision or prototyping. While it is unfortunate if the prototype does not succeed, lessons should be learned about the user requirements or system capabilities. It should be expected that not all prototypes will be successful.

Choose the Top Tools

Once the prototype has been built, a final tool decision can be made by updating the selection criteria matrix and calculating scores for each product. A final demonstration of the successful prototype should be held to elicit and resolve any open questions.

If there have been problems during prototyping, the completion of the prototype is a good time to identify and resolve issues. Often, apparent tool problems are really indications of other types of data warehouse implementation problems—particularly data problems. Therefore, often a tool can be chosen at the end of the prototyping even if problems occurred. If there are outstanding issues that are not resolved, a plan for a new prototyping phase to answer the questions should be created.

Post Implementation Review

In conjunction with periodic reviews of the entire data warehouse, there should be reviews of the data warehouse access tools usage. While there is often excitement with the initial system delivery, within one month users will begin to understand the system capabilities and limitations. As data is explored, additional unforeseen requirements will often appear. It is at this stage that the tool delivery organization can show value by understanding that changes will be needed and working with end users to understand additional business requirements and prioritize changes. Participation in a post implementation review should be the last step in the tool selection process.

The purpose of the review is to

- Identify additional requirements.
- Identify system problems.
- Determine the next step in the data warehouse process. Such steps could include
  - Implementing additional requirements.
  - Fixing system problems.
  - Expanding the system scope.
  - Allowing more people to access the system.
- Set up future periodic review sessions.

Both user and technical management and staff should be involved in the review process.

SUMMARY

With over 150 tools to choose from, a structured, user-centric process is needed to choose the best data warehouse end-user access tools for an organization. This chapter provides a methodology that is specifically tailored to choosing such tools. Throughout the process, it is best to keep in mind the principles listed in Figure 27.5. This tool selection methodology, based on real-life experience, can be used to select data warehouse end-user access tools in the quickest time possible.

1. Be business-requirements driven, not tool-features driven.
2. Involve the users.
3. Consider both project and enterprise requirements.
4. Use a structured methodology.
5. Overlap tasks when appropriate.
6. Don't waste time—narrow the search as soon as appropriate.
7. Prototype the solution using real data before making a final decision.
8. Hold a post implementation review.

Figure 27.5   End-user Data Warehouse Access Tool Selection Principles.

PART

TRENDS

"You ain't heard nothin' yet, folks."

Al Jolson, The Jazz Singer

The never-ending quest to provide any information, anywhere, anytime goes on. Gone are the days when information systems could be developed with a narrow-minded vision. The data universe is expanding and technology must follow. Chapter 28, "Trends in Data Warehousing" by Pete Uhrowczik of IBM, discusses the future challenges that we are facing. He discusses issues involving end-user tools, unstructured data, data warehouse architectures, data stores and access enablers, the increasing, changing role of metadata, and problems of data quality with approaches to solving the various problems.

Although there are many challenges ahead, they are not beyond our capabilities. We must step back, see the vision, and reach for it.

Trends in Data Warehousing

28

Pete Uhrowczik

Santa Teresa Laboratory
IBM

"The future is a mirror without any glass in it."

Xavier Forneret

This chapter discusses recent lessons learned in data warehousing and some of the key emerging trends. The topics to be covered include the following:

- Decision making and data warehousing
- Type of decision support tools/applications
- Unstructured data
- Data warehouse architectures
- Data stores and access enablers
- Metadata
- Data quality.

DECISION MAKING AND DATA WAREHOUSING

The following definition was provided by a group of users in 1990 during a requirements study on data warehousing. "A data warehouse is the data, processes, tools, and facilities to manage and deliver complete, timely, accurate, and understandable business information to authorized individuals for effective decision making." This definition continues to be one of the best and most durable expressions of what data warehousing is all about. There are no references to relational data (since any convenient data store would do) or implications that the underlying data had to be structured data (since it could also be unstructured data,[1] such as articles, reports, images, or videos).

Today, most data warehouses[2] consist of internal, enterprise-owned, structured data placed in relational data stores in support of individual business units. The scope of the data is limited to specific types of analyses, such as the sales performance of a product line, which leads to such predictable questions as these:

- How many units of Product X sold last month, worldwide?
- How does this compare to the same month last year?
- Ask the same questions for Japan (and other markets).

Data warehouses that support the solving of such repetitive, predictable types of problems can be called predetermined warehouses. There are, however, other types of problems whose scope is not predictable and require a broader information base. For example, to determine the level of investment for Product X, the questions might be as follows:

- What is the market share of Product X?
- What are the market shares of its competitors?
- What has been the yearly trend in revenue of Product X from inception to present?
- How much has been spent yearly on Product X from inception to present?
- What is the anticipated demand for this type of product in the next year?
- How satisfied are the users of Product X?
- What are the outstanding requirements on Product X?

Each of these question may, in turn, be broken down into smaller questions, possibly forming a hierarchy or network of inquiries. For some questions, the necessary information may exist in the internal organization's data. Other questions may require external data; still other questions may rely on expert opinion (for example, a question about the future of a product could require input from internal and external experts). The information itself may originate from structured or unstructured data. Typically, the decision maker—probably an executive in this example—asks a knowledge worker (perhaps a product manager or staff analyst) to come up with the needed information to support a potential decision.

Although most of today's activity is in building predetermined warehouses (also called functional warehouses or data marts), the trend is toward expanding the scope toward more encompassing ad hoc warehouses.

TYPES OF DECISION SUPPORT TOOLS

Figure 28.1 shows the major components and structure of a data warehouse. The horizontal arrows indicate the denormalization of data for performance reasons,

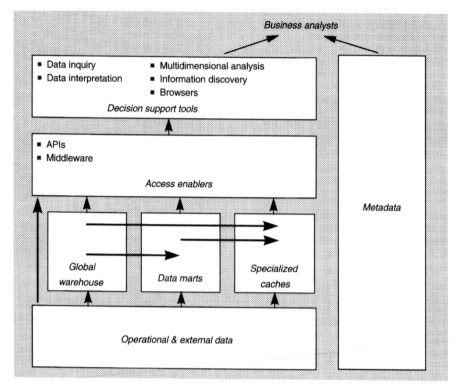

Figure 28.1   Data Warehouse Components and Structure.

while the vertical arrows show the alternatives for the flow of data toward the decision support tools.

This section discusses the decision support tools portion of the structure. These tools (or applications) can be classified as data inquiry, data interpretation, multidimensional analysis, information discovery, and browsers.

- Data inquiry: Typical request for a set of data based on some search criteria
- Data interpretation: Manipulation and visualization of a set of data (for example, statistical analysis)

Data inquiry and interpretation tools are the traditional decision support tools, and most data warehouses use them. Trends for these tools are toward more advanced visualization approaches for interpreting the results and further hiding of data access mechanisms from the end user by providing a business semantics layer on top of relational tables for formulating the queries. As unstructured data becomes more prevalent in corporate databases, these tools will be expanded to support it (for example, by better visualization techniques and searches on unstructured data).

Multidimensional Analysis

This is an analysis of data aggregations from a business point of view (also known as OLAP). Presently, the vast majority of data warehousing users indicate that they need multidimensional analysis. Multidimensional analysis, however, is not a new concept or technology. Two decades ago, some operational database management systems were being used as data stores for aggregated multidimensional data (typically, product, geography, and time dimensions). Likewise, specialized data stores as well as end-user tools for multidimensional analysis entered the market soon thereafter.

The present increase in interest in multidimensional analysis is due to improved workstation technology and tools and the appeal of the spreadsheet paradigm to a vast population of business analysts. In general, multidimensional analysis can be thought of as an n-dimensional spreadsheet analysis. The end-user tools vary from enhanced spreadsheets[3] to integrated data analysis systems.[4] Typically, business analysts use spreadsheets, while executives use more graphical interfaces. There is a degree of predictability to how multidimensional analysis is done with top-sheet analysis (high-level summarizations) as a starting point, followed by pivoting and drill-down analysis. The drill-down can go to lower aggregations or to the detail records themselves (if details exist in relational data stores).

Figure 28.2 shows an existing data warehouse used internally by IBM to perform multidimensional analysis of one of their product lines. Their business analysts primarily use spreadsheets to analyze summaries and details of the internal operational data. Executives and managers use graphical interfaces to analyze the summaries but also have access to competitive data and industry news residing on Web servers. The example is typical of these types of data warehouses, and it can also be used to point to two key trends. One is the need for supporting mobile, disconnected users using laptops containing all the summary data. The size of the data mart and the specialized caches lend themselves well to such a mode of operation, provided the users need not drill down to the details contained in the global warehouse. The second trend is the emerging use of corporate Internet networks—the Intranets.[5] Intranets are proving to be effective for the electronic publication to geographically dispersed and mobile audiences. For example, daily summarizations of warehouse information in both numeric and graphical formats can be captured as bit-maps and placed on a Web page server to be downloaded and displayed by Web browsers (any Web browsers) at the request of the end user.

Information Discovery

This is information discovery without hypothesis (also known as data mining). In typical business data analysis, the end user has specific questions in mind (how many units of Products X were sold in Japan last month) and uses decision support tools to find the appropriate information from the underlying data. Data, however, also contains implicit information that can be discovered by searching for frequently

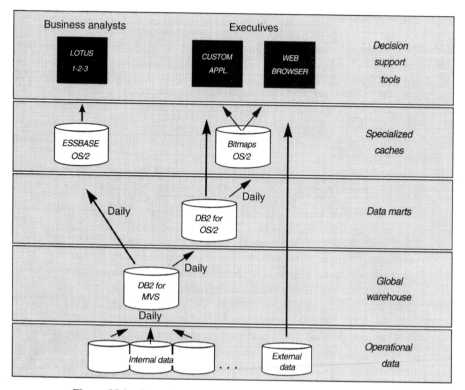

Figure 28.2 Data Warehouse and Multidimensional Analysis.

occurring patterns, identifying trends, etc. For example, patterns of customer behavior or preferences can be discovered from raw transaction records of customer purchases, and fraudulent activities can be detected from transaction records of credit card purchases.

Information discovery tools are frequently being used as part of a discovery service offered by several vendors. The trend, however, is for generalized decision support tools to embed discovery technology into their products. The technology consists of several discovery techniques (for example, associations, sequential patterns, classifiers, clustering[6]) and is frequently called data mining. The term *data mining*, however, is also being used in the industry in a broader sense. For example, a decision support tool for multidimensional analysis may have intelligent agents that, using predetermined criteria, look for exceptional happenings and show them automatically to the end users. In the view of end users, this is also data mining.

Information Catalog Browsers

These involve finding out what information is available by examining the business-oriented metadata in information catalogs (or information directories) with browser tools. The term *browser* is used here as a generic term, not limited to Web browsers.

In the case of functional, predetermined warehouses, business users deal with very specific tasks, such as tracking product sales performance. They may deal with only a few multidimensional hypercubes, perhaps a spreadsheet tool and several dozen preprogrammed queries. For these dedicated users, there is little need to understand what other information is available. However, in data warehouses that support broader, ad hoc problem solving, this need increases significantly. Here, end users need to understand what is available internally and externally, for both data (structured and unstructured) as well as for informational objects (spreadsheets, reports, etc.). This class of end users has a definite need for browser tools.

Several information catalogs (and corresponding browsers) exist in the market, with the most advanced allowing definition of any data or informational object (that is, they are extensible).[7] Open APIs as well as several types of browsing functions, typically keyword searches plus navigation through hierarchical groupings, are included.[8] The users search for some object of interest in the information catalog and, once found, the browser can launch the decision support tool that will be passed to the parameters of the object on which to act.

A second use of information catalogs and their browsers is by technical users building data warehouses. While business users need to find what information is available to solve their business problems, the technical users need to find out what source data is available to build data warehouses. As some information catalogs on the market have the capability to populate themselves from a wide variety of metadata sources, it is anticipated that they will become ideal tools to help these types of users. In fact, the use of information catalogs will likely start in the technical community, followed by the business user community when the data warehouses (especially ad hoc warehouses) have been built.

The World Wide Web will have a major impact in this area. Today, Web browsers and servers are available on virtually every platform, and the low cost of providing access to information by a wide number of users is fueling the growth of Intranets. The use of powerful textual search engines when coupled with the hypertext link paradigm allows for easy filtering and navigating of large quantities of data. This is a natural fit for information catalog browsers. As a result, vendors of information catalogs will likely provide the ability to browse their data with Web browsers. The Web browser paradigm will become the key user interface when searching for "what information is available," whether it is on a local PC, a LAN, a host, a private Intranet, or the external Internet.

Impact of the World Wide Web on Data Warehousing

The Web will have an impact beyond the areas described so far (electronic publication of information and the browsing of information catalogs). It will also play a major role in end-user access to the data warehouse instance data. This is being facilitated by vendors on several fronts.

One is by providing Web gateways that sit between a Web server and a data engine (for example, a RDBMS or an OLAP server). The Web gateway provides the translation from a request in Hypertext Markup Language (HTML) format coming from a Web browser into a specific data engine's API as well as the reverse translation for the answers from the data engine. Once this gateway is provided, the Web browser (any Web browser) can access data on the enabled data engine. It is anticipated that Web gateways will increase in both numbers and sophistication. Vendors of server-centric products with no clients (or only thin clients) will find providing Web gateways most appealing. On the other hand, vendors that depend on fat clients may find it necessary to rearchitect their products (possibly into three-tier architectures) before providing the gateways. The Web gateways could also be used to solve some of the limitations in the Web architecture. Today, a Web server does not retain knowledge of multiple interactions with the Web browsers. As a result, a request for the "next 1000 lines" cannot be handled by the server. Web gateways, on the other hand, could retain the knowledge of the state of multiple interactions.

The second area of vendor activities is in satisfying the large demand for Web development tools for increasingly complex applications (more interactions, increased sophistication in the GUIs). As a result, building blocks such as Java are receiving much attention. An increasing number of software developers are enabling to it, which makes them an early front runner in the race for establishing a new industry standard.

UNSTRUCTURED DATA

Although most data warehouses today deal with structured data, unstructured data—and multimedia in particular—is rapidly increasing in importance.[9] Multimedia provides a new, natural interface for end users of data warehouses. For example, a user may be searching for a specific type of product. Once located, the user may display text and images about it. This information could be enhanced by allowing the user to select a video presentation about the product, which could include examples of usage presented by actual users.

There are a number of issues that are being addressed by some vendors in this area.

Management Systems

One approach is to treat multimedia data as just another data type and simply add it to existing relational tables, which would extend a relational data store's benefits (integrity, single API, etc.) to multimedia data. To achieve this, some relational data stores are being extended with binary large objects (BLOBs), which allow storing of objects up to 2 GB in size and via user-defined types (UDTs) and user-defined functions (UDFs).[10,11] These SQL extensions are originated by the work of SQL standards organizations and are part of the emerging SQL-3 specification. UDFs can be used, for example, as predicates in an SQL search along with traditional search predicates. The UDT/UDF approach is how some relational data store vendors are extending the functionality of their engines—not just for multimedia but also for general functions.[12]

Specialized Servers

It may not be possible to store all multimedia types as part of a relational data store, such as BLOBs. A video clip, for example, needs to be stored on a server capable of supporting the continuous delivery of multiple streams of video at 30 frames/second and synchronized with its corresponding audio. Although these specialized servers are not an integral part of a relational data store, techniques have been developed to link the data in the server with a relational data store so that the data appears to be the value of a column in a relational table.[13]

Search Engines

Because unstructured data types may be images, text (reports), audio, and video, new search engines are being provided. These search engines are invoked from an SQL search statement that uses appropriate UDFs for the specific data type. One example is Query by Image Content,[14] which preindexes images based on shapes, colors, and textures. When more than one image fits the search argument, the engine returns the images in order of the closest match to the visual argument. Another example is a text retrieval engine,[15] which preindexes free-text documents and allows searches by words, phrases, wild cards, proximity operators, Boolean operators, and powerful linguistic capabilities (for example, it will find *mice* even if *mouse* was specified in the query). Although research work is also in progress on audio and video searches, it is anticipated that text search will continue to be the most prevalent search mechanism for unstructured objects, since any such object can be annotated with a textual description.

DATA WAREHOUSE ARCHITECTURES

Although several data warehouse architectures[16] exist today, due to space limitations of this chapter only one of them will be discussed. In 1993, IBM published a generic reference model for a data warehousing architecture.[17] Four different data architectures were discussed: single level, two-level reconciled, two-level derived, and three-level. Figure 28.1 summarizes these alternatives using some of the new terminology in the market today. It should be noted that operational data, as used in this chapter, refers to real-time data (i.e., OLTP data) used by operational/transactional applications. This section describes the four data architectures and the anticipated trends in this area.

Single Level

Data is not "copied" to a data warehouse; instead, decision support tools directly access the operational data. The single-level model is sometimes called a virtual data warehouse and is used in only a small percentage of cases. It is a feasible model when the operational data is "clean" (no need to reconcile), it is stored in a RDBMS, the volume of DSS requests is small, and point-in-time requirements are handled by application design. There is, however, increasing interest in near-real-time data regardless of system size and data status, especially in industries such as consumer retail (e.g., to detect sales increases in a geographic area due to unforeseen ecological or social conditions). Although it is possible that under very favorable conditions some organizations may be successful with a single-level data architecture, it is likely that continuous-flow data warehouses will emerge where technologies such as changed-data replication will maintain "copies" of the real-time operational data with some minimal time lag (e.g., minutes or hours). When dealing with unstructured data, the single-level model will definitely apply—the data will not be copied before being used.

Two Level Reconciled

Appropriate operational data is placed in a reconciled and cleansed global data warehouse, where decision support tools access it. The global warehouse contains detail records (as in the operational level). This model is also used in only a small percentage of cases. As the trend toward ad hoc data warehouses increases, so will the use of this model. One reason is that since ad hoc problem solving occurs less frequently, it may not be justified to place all the data in denormalized data marts instead of accessing the data directly in global warehouses.

Two Level Derived

Operational data is filtered and summarized directly into a derived level, shown in Figure 28.1 as data marts and specialized caches. Decision support tool access is to the derived level. The distinction between a data mart and a specialized cache is that data marts (as well as global warehouses) are typically relational data stores, while specialized caches are special-purpose data stores for specialized data analysis, such as multidimensional databases. This is the most common model of data warehousing today, primarily because of expediency and minimum dependency on IT. Typically, once agreements to extract operational data are reached with IT, work groups can create any additional business views and data subsets on their own.

Three Level

Operational data is first reconciled into a global warehouse and then filtered/summarized into data marts or specialized caches. Decision support tools access the derived level. Proponents of this model stress that data must first be reconciled in a global warehouse before building data marts, to avoid the possibility of getting different answers to the same questions. Today, this model is used in only a minority of cases, although usage is expected to increase as (1) the number of data marts (and possibly data quality problems) increases, and (2) the trend toward ad hoc warehouses accelerates.

To illustrate the use of these data architectures, we use the example of IBM, which today has about 70 internal data warehouses (although the company is building primarily data warehouses for its external customers, this example refers only to IBM's internal, in-house warehouses). Most use the two level derived or three level data models. Where a three-level model is used (one example is shown in Figure 28.2), it does not mean that IBM has a single global warehouse from which functional derived levels are built. There are actually a number of global warehouses, with each major business unit having one or more. Each global warehouse is simply a reconciliation point. In fact, the term *global warehouse* (although widely used) may be misleading as it implies a single warehouse for the enterprise, which is not necessarily true. *Reconciled level* or *reconciled warehouse* may be more accurate terms for this concept. The challenges found in building these warehouses were typical of any large enterprise:

- Large number of heterogeneous legacy systems
- Disappearing knowledge of legacy systems (lack of skills in data sources)
- Source data quality.

While most of these internal data warehouses were built independently of each other to support existing business unit processes, they are increasingly becoming part of IBM's worldwide process reengineering initiative.

DATA STORES AND ACCESS ENABLERS

Today, most data in data warehouses is stored in relational data stores, with SQL as the API. The form of the API is either callable or embedded, and the syntax has many dialects depending on the relational data store. Vendors of relational data stores, desiring to add value to their particular offering, are enhancing their particular SQL dialect with nonstandard enhancements. This makes the effort of application builders (or decision support tools builders) difficult. One solution that has emerged is the least common denominator approach to SQL, as embodied in the ODBC de facto standard. Other approaches take the full SQL syntax of a particular relational data store and map it to a variety of SQL dialects. The mapping is done in a middleware server that connects to the individual relational data stores and performs distributed joins and other functions.[18] The application programmer is unaware of this back-end activity and only deals with the specific SQL (and catalog structure) of the middleware server.

While the preceding examples point to efforts toward a single API, the multi-dimensional tools market is heading in the opposite direction. The reasons are the needs for interactive performance and for specialized API functionality. Four initiatives exist to deal with the problem of how to define APIs as well as where and how to store the data.

Multidimensional Analysis Using Specialized Multidimensional Databases

This is a caching approach (shown in Figure 28.1 as specialized caches) in which data is extracted from operational datastores, global warehouses, or data marts, and then preaggregated and loaded into multidimensional databases residing, typically, on LAN servers.[19] Loading times can be quite long (especially if preaggregation was not done at the source); however, the resulting interactive response time is very appealing. The multidimensional database manages the multidimensional model and provides an API that manipulates the hypercubes and provides functions that facilitate implementations of such problems as "show the ranking of products when comparing sales of this month to the previous month." Proponents of the multidimensional database approach suggest that relational data stores were never intended to solve these types of problems.[20] Each multidimensional database on the market has its own private API, although a group of vendors (the OLAP Council[21]) is trying to agree on an industry standard. The administration of multidimensional databases is done by workgroups with minimum IT dependency.

Multidimensional Analysis on Relational-like Stores

This is also a caching approach in which data from operational stores is copied to a special-purpose (non-OLTP) relational data store.[22] The API is SQL-like, with private extensions, and can handle the type of problems described previously for multidimensional databases. Special indexing to handle access by dimension hierarchies is provided. The approach is used in large database situations and is administered by IT.

Multidimensional Analysis on Relational Data Stores

This is similar to the previous case, but data is in a standard relational data store (OLAP capable as well as OLTP capable). To achieve multidimensional analysis functionality, vendors of client tools provide an extra semantic layer between the client and the relational data store (a three-layer architecture). The extra layer understands the multidimensional structure and its mapping to the relational tables, and generates standard SQL from functional requests from the client. Both details and aggregations are stored at the relational data stores; to improve performance of requests for aggregations directly from detail data, specialized indexes are being introduced by relational data store vendors.[23]

Hybrids

Some vendors of multidimensional analysis tools are combining the aforementioned approaches.[24] The data is stored in relational data stores, but they cache a subset of the data at the client or an intermediate server (this can be dynamic) in a specialized multidimensional data structure that improves performance.

There is considerable debate as to which approach will prevail—multidimensional analysis on multidimensional databases or multidimensional analysis on relational data stores. Relational data store vendors are likely to enhance their APIs[25] (perhaps with UDFs oriented toward multidimensional analysis) to perform middle-layer functions in the relational server in an attempt to decrease the importance of the three-layer architectures. It is also likely that they will continue to provide new indexing approaches because existing B-tree indexes may not be sufficient for this type of processing. The multidimensional data store vendors, on the other hand, will continue to scale up their products in the areas of load performance, number of dimensions, and size of hypercubes.

Regardless of these efforts, it is likely that fundamental differences will remain that will assure a market for both. The multidimensional data stores will continue to appeal to business analysts in functional work groups who wish to do aggregate analysis using primarily a spreadsheet paradigm while remaining independent from IT. The relational approach will be used where the ability to form new hierarchical views is crucial and where dimensions and metrics can be used symmetrically to form new multidimensional views (as in customer relationship marketing and micro-product management applications[26]).

Finally, the emerging field of information discovery also uses specialized caches with their own APIs. All of these developments point to a strong trend toward specialization, in both caches and APIs.

METADATA

Many builders of data warehouses are faced with the challenge of heterogeneous platforms, data, tools, and, therefore, metadata. Figure 28.3 shows the types of metadata of interest.

While CASE deals primarily with the metadata of source data, data warehouse deals with the transformation of this source data into the ultimate business view of data used by informational objects (queries, reports, etc.). Furthermore, data warehouse introduces a new user of metadata, the business analyst, with the corresponding requirement for business metadata.

The transformation of the source data to the business view is a series of source-to-target morphings (represented by the arrows in Figure 28.3). The technical metadata describing the sources, targets, and transformations is contained in different tools, with each tool representing the metadata differently. Ideally, all data warehouse metadata would reside in a single metadata repository with a common

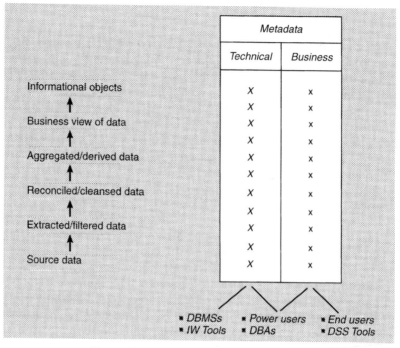

	Metadata	
	Technical	Business
Informational objects	X	x
	X	x
Business view of data	X	x
	X	x
Aggregated/derived data	X	x
	X	x
Reconciled/cleansed data	X	x
	X	x
Extracted/filtered data	X	x
	X	x
Source data	X	x

• DBMSs   • Power users   • End users
• IW Tools   • DBAs   • DSS Tools

Figure 28.3   Data Warehousing Metadata.

representation (information model) and commonly accessed by database management systems software, data warehouse tools, database administrators, and business analysts, with performance acceptable to all. The reality is that due to lack of agreement on common representation and different performance requirements of each type of user, there are hundreds of different metadata stores in use (CASE, relational catalogs, copy libraries, data warehouse morphing tools, and decision support tools, to name a few). To address these problems, several trends are emerging, including integration of componentry, standardized metadata interchange, synchronized metadata interchange, and the building of business metadata.

Integrated Components

A major benefit to users is meaningful integration of both the functions and metadata of the different components needed to build a data warehouse. The ideal approach is to define an information model for a data warehouse, place it in a common metadata repository, and have all the components use it.[27] This, of course, is possible if the vendor owns or controls the components to be integrated. As few vendors own the necessary components for building a complete data warehouse, many are entering into partnerships, alliances, and acquisitions. Some of these alliances include up to 50 vendors, which raises the question of the practicality of such a wide integration objective. Other alliances have fewer members and more specific integration objectives. It is left up to the users to assess the likelihood of success of each of these initiatives. The benefits of significant integration may be substantial. One view of the cost of data warehouses is that for every $1 in software, there are $2 in design/services/consulting and $3 in hardware. Some of the $2 is spent in integration, so this expenditure may be somewhat reduced. More significantly, the time to implement a data warehouse as well as errors during operations may be substantially reduced.

Standardized Metadata Interchange

When integration of function and metadata around a common information model and metadata repository is not feasible, a more modest but realistic approach is to standardize the metadata interchange. The goal is metadata reuse ("enter metadata only once"). Here, the components keep their particular information model and metadata repository, but they agree on (1) an interchange information model and (2) an interchange syntax.[28] Each component (i.e., tool) agrees on extracting metadata from its information model into the agreed interchange model and also on importing from this common interchange model into its private model using the common interchange syntax mechanism. The same approach applies to private agreement for interchange between as few as two tools. The appeal of this approach is that individual tools do not have to change their own information models, metadata repositories, or administration.

An example of such an initiative is the Metadata Council,[29] established in 1995 by a group of vendors of data warehousing components. The Council delegates the actual standards work to the Metadata Coalition, which consists of vendors and users. The Council has, already agreed on an interchange information model and an interchange syntax. The interchange model consists of the most commonly shared metadata objects, such as tables, and the interchange syntax is Tag-language based. There is a great deal of user interest in this initiative. Because the effort by vendors to enable to this standard is relatively modest and the user interest is high, this initiative has a good potential of succeeding.

Synchronized Metadata Interchange

While interchange standardization is important, the real value to users will come when the metadata interchange is achieved in an automatic manner. The synchronization may be initiated by an administrator request, time, changes in metadata, etc. The trend is toward increased capabilities in this area, with some vendors providing solutions supporting only their toolset and others providing solutions in which any tool can participate.

Building of Business Metadata

While technical metadata exists in many sources (it has to exist for software to run), business metadata in most cases simply does not exist. Existing information catalogs have self-population mechanisms that rely on extracting data from metadata sources that contain largely technical metadata. Although some technical metadata also applies to business users, most of it does not. For example, the transformation description of some source data to business views may exist as SQL-based filters and COBOL programs that may be comprehensible to a technician but not to business analysts. The technical declaratives need to be transformed into free-text descriptions since no declarative language exists today that is general enough to describe all forms of transformations in a manner comprehensible to business analysts. For the foreseeable future, building of business metadata will remain largely a staff analyst's task. Although not a big problem for users of individual predetermined warehouses, the need for business metadata will increase as data warehouses move into ad hoc areas supporting users with interest in a wide number of information resources (including multiple data marts).

DATA QUALITY

Data placed in a data warehouse may be consolidated from heterogeneous sources, such as operational data, external files, and historical data. This consolidation is often faced with many obstacles. For example, they may be

- No common keys to build consolidated views
- Conflicting data values (for example, different forms of the "name" attribute for the same data instance)
- Incomplete or missing metadata descriptions (common in legacy systems)
- Unclean data values (for example, gender with 10 values).

Some analysts suggest that the only way to clean this data is to make changes to the source application systems where the data originates. However, source systems were, in most cases, not designed as integrated systems, and the data shows the resulting differences. To solve this, major redesign may be necessary. If one adds to this situation the short time allotted for building data warehouses, it is unlikely that source application systems will be redesigned before the data warehouse is built. Therefore, it is anticipated that data cleansing and reconciliation will continue to be done primarily as a data preprocessing step when building the data warehouse. On the other hand, enterprises embarking on reengineering as the primary objective will consider data warehouses as an integral part of the process.

The question is who will provide the preprocessing step. Two overall approaches are followed. In one, the assumption is that only the owners of the source application systems know the source data; therefore, they are to provide the data in a specific format and semantic. Here, although the data is delivered and the warehouses are built, the warehouse owners never really know what is being provided. On the other hand, if the warehouse builders assume the responsibility of the preprocessing, they face the problem of their own lack of knowledge about the source data. Data modeling of the source and target data as well as data cleansing will continue to be prerequisites to solving these problems.

Today, some cleansing is done by specialized service bureaus or off-the-shelf specialized packages for specific problems with some type of data (typically free text), such as names and addresses. A second approach is with generalized tools that preanalyze data using pattern processing, lexical analysis, and statistical matching to understand the structure of the data. Based on such analysis, these tools are capable of generating code that provides reconciled data. These types of tools will likely gain in popularity, not only as preprocessors for data warehousing but also as general reengineering tools. A third approach is custom programming of the cleansing process; although it is the most common technique used today, it is also the most expensive, thus the aforementioned reengineering tool will gain in popularity.

Finally, there is the question of data quality as it applies to external data such as information on the World Wide Web or market information databases offered for sale by a number of organizations. Here the context of *quality* has an additional dimension to the one discussed previously. It deals with reliability and credibility of the data. For example, in a survey of present uses of PCs or a forecast of future uses of PCs, end users will need to understand such information as the size of the sample, the randomness of the sample, how the data was collected, the total population, and the statistical error of the sample used. Such descriptors will become a requirement, with service organizations offering quality ratings for some types of information resources.

SUMMARY

This chapter described the following major trends:

- Although most data warehouses today support predetermined types of questions, warehouses providing answers to broad, ad hoc questions from a great variety of source data will grow substantially.
- Two types of decision support tools will show the strongest gains: multidimensional analysis and data mining tools.
- The World Wide Web will have a major impact on data warehousing, both as access to information catalogs as well as widespread access to data in data warehouses.
- Increased use of multimedia data is accelerating the need for specialized servers and search algorithms, ideally within the context of SQL.

- Middleware providers will continue to add functionality on top of RDBMS, while RDBMS vendors will improve the performance of their engines to compete better in the multidimensional analysis market.
- Metadata interchange and synchronization may be the most likely approach to succeed in the area of metadata integration.
- Data quality will remain one of the most challenging problems in data warehousing. Tools that help in this area will see significant gains in the market.

REFERENCES

[1] For simplicity, articles and reports are included as unstructured data, although, of course, they do have structures.

[2] Some early references to the concept of data warehouse are Martin Hubel, *"Data Base and the Data Warehousing Concept,"* Presentation at the Insurance Accounting and Systems Association, October 30, 1986; B. A. Devlin and P. T. Murphy, *"An Architecture for a Business and Information System,"* IBM Systems Journal, Vol. 27, No. 1, 1988.

[3] For example, Lotus 1-2-3™ and MS Excel.

[4] For example, IBM Data Interpretation System (DIS) and Information Advantage Decision Suite.

[5] ALLISON L. SPROUT, "The Internet Inside Your Company," *Fortune,* November 27, 1995.

[6] For a more detailed discussion of this technology, see "Data Mining: Extending the IBM Information Warehouse Framework," http://www.software.ibm.com/software/data.html

[7] For example, DataGuide,™ http://www.software.ibm.com/software/data.html

[8] COLIN WHITE, "Data Warehousing: The Role of the Information Directory," white paper by DataBase Associates International, November 1995.

[9] In this chapter, unstructured data is documents (static) and multimedia (animated) data.

[10] For a more detailed discussion, see "Object Support and the DB2™ Family," http://www.software.ibm.com/software/data.html

[11] C. J. BONTEMPO and C. M. SARACCO, *Database Management: Principles and Products,"* Englewood Cliffs, NJ, Prentice Hall, 1995.

[12] For a more detailed discussion, see "DB2™ Relational Extenders," http://www.software.ibm.com./software/data.html.

[13] For a more detailed discussion, see "Multimedia and the DB2™ Family," http://www.software.ibm.com/software/data.html.

[14] For a more detailed discussion, see "Ultimedia™ Manager," http://www.software.ibm.com/software/data.html.

[15] For example, IBM Search Manager/2™ or Oracle ConText Option.

[16] Some examples of data warehouse architectures are Chapter 7 of this book and H. S. GILL and P. C. RAO, "The Official Guide to Data Warehousing," *Que,* 1996. This describes a reference architecture for data warehousing.

[17] *Information Warehouse™ Architecture I*, SC26-3244, IBM Corporation; available through IBM branch offices.

18 For a more detailed discussion, see "DataJoiner™—A Multidatabase Server," http://www.software.ibm.com/software/data.html.

19 For example, Arbor Essbase or Pilot Lightship Server.

20 E. F. CODD, S. B. CODD, and C. T. SALLEY, "Beyond Decision Support," *Computerworld*, July 26, 1993.

21 The OLAP Council was established in January 1995 to serve as an industry guide and customer advocacy group for the multidimensional database technology.

22 For example, Red Brick Warehouse.

23 For example, Sybase IQ Accelerator.

24 For example, Cognos PowerPlay or BusinessObjects Mercury.

25 R. KIMBALL, K. STREHLO, "Why Decision Support Fails and How to Fix It," *Datamation*, June 1, 1994

26 For a more detailed discussion, see "Multidimensional Analysis: Extending the IBM Information Warehouse Framework," http://www.software.ibm.com/software/data.html

27 For example, IBM Visual Warehouse and PRISM Warehouse Manager.

28 An example of an interchange syntax is the IBM DataGuide™ Tag Language.

29 For more information about the Metadata Council and their work, see http://www.metadata.org.

Glossary

Access Path The path selected by the database management system to locate and retrieve required data.

Ad Hoc Query A query that has not been anticipated, usually run just once. It consists of dynamic SQL that has been prepared by a query tool.

Administrative Data Data that will be used by a warehouse administrator in managing all aspects of the warehouse. Examples: Date that a particular table was last updated, name of the job used for incrementally refreshing a particular table or set of tables.

Alert A process of notification when a particular event exceeds a predetermined threshold.

ANSI American National Standards Institute. An organization created for the purpose of establishing industry standards.

API Application Program Interface.

APPC Advanced Program-to-Program Communication.

Atomic Level Data Data elements representing a low level of detail.

Architecture A framework for organizing the planning and implementation of data resources. The set of data, processes, and technologies that an enterprise has selected for the creation and operation of information systems.

Anomaly (Data) A permutation of the standard. A data anomaly occurs when a data field defined for one purpose is used for another. For example, a currently unused, but defined, field is used for some purpose totally unrelated to its original intent. A clever programmer may put a negative value in this field (which is always supposed to be positive) as a switch.

Attribute A characteristic or data element describing something about an entity in business terms (e.g., name, type scale, owner, function, etc.). Example: Employee name, order quantity, department number.

Back End Typically a server running a DBMS that provides data to front-end applications.

402

Base Tables   A table that physically exists in one or more datasets.

BSP   Business Systems Planning.

Business Data   Data related to the people, places, and things that are needed to operate a business.

Business Model   A model or representation of the business showing the processes or functions of the departments or business units, their relationships, and the data they use at a particular point in time.

Business Strategic Plan   A plan to support the strategic goals of the business.

CASE   Computer Aided Software Engineering. The use of computer tools to assist in software engineering. These tools might include a pretested database of sub-routines, code generators, data flow analysis tools, self-documenting compiles and techniques, library organizers, specialized design tools, and integrated on-line debuggers. CASE tools provide benefits in the requirements, analysis, design, and code generation phases of the development life cycle.

Cardinality   (1) The number of unique values of a key or column. (2) The number of occurrences that can participate in a relationship. Example: A savings system with 100,000 accounts has an account cardinality of 100,000 since all account numbers are unique. A personnel system has a sex cardinality of two (male and female).

Catalog   A component of a data dictionary that contains a listing of DBMS objects and their attributes.

Centralized Data Warehouse   A style of data warehousing in which all warehouse data is located and managed from a single, central location.

Change Data Capture   The process of capturing changes to production data and consolidating them so that they can be added to the data warehouse.

Client/Server Computing   A distributed approach to building applications in the result to the client. The server may manage communications, provide database services, etc. The client handles individual user functions, such as the desktop interface, help functions, etc.

Cooperative Processing   A type of processing in which the presentation, application logic, and data management may be divided between two or more platforms. In cooperative processing, functions are invoked through the exchange of parameter-driven messages.

Composite Key   A key that is a combination of attributes. An ordered collection of columns in the same table. Example: A checking account number would have the composite key of the branch number and an account number unique only to that branch.

Constraint   A policy imposed by the business. Example: All bank withdrawals over $100,000 must be verified with the customer.

Copy Management   The process of taking a snapshot of data from a source and copying it to a target environment.

Corporate Data Model   A data model that incorporates all, or at least the most important, aspects of an enterprise's data architecture. It contains entities, attributes, relationships, rules, and definitions in business terms.

Cost-Benefit Analysis   An analysis of the business benefits to be derived from the implementation of an application, database, query tool, etc.

COTS   Commercial Off-the-Shelf application software.

Critical Success Factor   Activities or factors in which favorable results must be achieved to achieve an objective.

Crosstab   A process that summarizes or combines data and presents it in a different format for reporting or analysis.

Custodianship   Physical responsibility for databases.

Data   A fact and its meaning. It is the "raw material" of information and a fundamental element in any organization.

Data Analysis   The systematic study of data so that its meaning, structure, relationships, representation, validity, controls, volume, and origins are understood.

Data Administration (DA)   The organization that has the overall responsibility for the enterprise's data resources and for the administration, control and coordination of all data related activities. The DA has the responsibility for planning and defining the conceptual framework for the overall data environment. The functions of the DA typically include requirements definition, logical design, logical to physical mapping, maintenance of inventory of the current system, data analysis, data definition, administration of the corporate data dictionary, support of the application data dictionary, and business planning support.

Database   (1) A repository for stored data that is integrated and shared. (2) A data collection that is organized for computer processing so as to optimize storage and increase the independence of the stored data structure from the processing programs. (3) A formal, computerized method for storing details of interest to a business so that it may be accessed and manipulated.

Database Corruption   The loss of the integrity of the data usually as a result of incomplete data validation, lack of either application or system referential integrity, or incorrect data specifications when loading or updating the data.

Database Management System (DBMS)   A computerized software system for creating, maintaining, and protecting databases.

Data Constraints   Rules that assure the integrity, consistency, and shareability of data. Example: The only two allowable values for gender are male and female.

Data Dictionary   A data dictionary is a catalog and a cross reference of available development data in the enterprise that provides business meaning to the end user and IT. It is a database of data about data (metadata). It is a tool for the collection, specification, and management of the enterprise data resources. The data dictionary serves as a repository for information about data, including identifying characteristics, relationships, ownership, sources of data, authorities, complete definitions, and data characteristics (size and data types).

Data Driven   An approach to design that begins with the data. The data becomes the central node of the design, and the process is derived from this model. The approach should produce subject databases.

Data Element   The most basic unit of data that is defined in a dictionary or repository.

Data Flow Diagram   A diagram that shows the flow of data between data stores and business processes.

Data Independence   A property of data that enables it to be processed independently of access mode, storage method, or arrangement. A high degree of data independence reduces the need to modify application programs when data storage or access methods are modified.

Data Integrity   The ability to preserve the accuracy, currency, and completeness of the data; the ability to produce results that are correct to a predefined level. Loss of data integrity means that the data is wrong, old, or incomplete and the information derived from this data could produce inaccurate results.

Data Loading   The process of populating a data warehouse. It may be accomplished by utilities, user-written programs, or specialized software from independent vendors.

Data Management   The function of organizing, cataloging, locating, storing, retrieving, and maintaining data. Data management attempts to optimize the use of the data asset.

Data Mapping   The process of identifying a source data element for each data element in the target environment.

Data Mart   A collection of related data designed to meet the needs of a specific group of users. It is often a subset of the data warehouse. Although it often consists of highly summarized data, it may also contain detail data, depending on the needs of the specific group of users. It may or may not have been designed with corporate standards in mind.

Data Mining   A process of analyzing large amount of data to identify patterns, trends, activities, and data content relationships.

Data Model   A data model is a set of diagrams and definitions that represents the enterprise data and their interrelationships in a specific and consistent way. It is a definition of the structure, rules, and constraints on data required by an enterprise to conduct all of its business functions. The data model contains entities, attributes, relationships, primary and foreign keys, and rules governing the data. Data modeling is the practice of analyzing and representing the data in a meaningful fashion, easily understood by nearly anyone in the enterprise.

Data Owner   The individual responsible for the definition and content of data.

Data Pivoting   The process of rotating a view of data.

Data Propagation   A process of distributing data from source systems to target systems according to established rules.

Data Replication   The process of copying data from one environment to another and keeping the sources and targets synchronized.

Data Repository   A database used to store metadata.

Data Scrubbing   The process of analyzing, merging, decoding, translating, and validating data for the data warehouse.

Data Sharing   The ability to share information, rather than requiring identical data items to be entered or stored multiple times in the system.

Data Steward   The person responsible for the quality of the business data; an information expert about a particular data subject area.

Data Store   A place in which data views are temporarily or permanently kept. An example is a file cabinet for documents or a direct access device.

Data Transformation   See DATA SCRUBBING.

Data Warehouse   A data warehouse is a collection of integrated, subject-oriented databases designed to support the DSS (decision support systems) function, where each unit of data is relevant to some moment of time.

Data Warehouse Infrastructure   The combination of technologies, skill sets, and tools needed to implement a successful warehouse.

Data Warehouse Technology   A set of methods, techniques, and tools that may be leveraged together to produce a vehicle that delivers data to end users and integrated platforms.

Decision Support System   A database designed to meet the needs of end users for information and analysis to facilitate decision making by enterprise management.

DBMS   Database Management System.

DD   Data Dictionary.

DDBMS   Distributed Database Management System.

DDL   Data Definition Language.

Denormalized Data   Data that does not conform to the rules of normalization.

Derived Data   Data that is the result of computation, aggregation, or relating one or more data elements to an external business rule.

Distributed Data   Data that is stored in more than one system in a network and is available to remote users and application programs.

Distributed Data Processing   The dispersion of computing functions and data at nodes electronically interconnected on a coordinated basis, geographical dispersion not being a requirement in every case.

Distributed Relational Database (DRDB)   A collection of relational data that is stored in more than one system in a network and is accessible as though it were in a local system.

Distributed Relational Database Architecture (DRDA)   An open architecture for distributed relational database processing that is issued by IBM's relational database products and can be implemented by other products. DRDA comprises connection protocols for communication between application and a remote RDBMS and communication between RDBMSs.

DM   Data Modeling.

DML   Data Manipulation Language.

Drill-Down   The process of dipping down into detailed data from summary data. This also includes the process of moving through various types of metadata from more general metadata to more specific metadata, and possibly to the launching of an application from a Data Directory.

DSS   Decision Support System.

DW   Data Warehouse.

EIS   Executive Information System.

End User   A user of an enterprise's computer system. Sometimes called a knowledge worker or business professional. To IT, the end user is their client.

Enhanced Data   Data used by knowledge workers to track, report, and analyze in support of the decision-making process. It is usually a subset of operational data that has been summarized, aggregated, or derived.

Enterprise Data   Operational plus informational data. All nonprivate data in the enterprise.

Entity   An object about which we wish to record business information.

ER   Entity Relationship.

ERD   Entity Relationship Diagram.

Extract   A set of data pulled from a production file. Often used for Decision Support Systems.

Filters   A set of criteria that specifies a subset of information from the data warehouse.

First Normal Form   The first normal form does not allow for any groups that could repeat within a record.

Foreign Key   These keys are attributes that define relationships between entities. A key that is part of a definition of a referential constraint. A foreign key points to a primary key in the same table or another table. Foreign keys establish relationships between tables.

4GL   Fourth-generation Language.

Front End   An application that runs on a workstation, usually for query purposes, that can access a back-end processor that holds the server data.

FTP   File Transfer Program.

Gateway   A software product that allows SQL-based queries to access data in relational and nonrelational sources.

GUI   Graphical User Interface.

Hashing   A method of storing data for easy retrieval. The application of an algorithm to the records in a data set to obtain an even distribution of the records across the available storage space. All records that fall into similar groups are placed in the same bucket. In an indexed data set, the process of transforming a record into an index value for storing and retrieving a record.

Hash Total   A technique for ensuring that data moving from one portion of an information system to another is transmitted totally, without the loss of data or integrity. Any numeric field is accumulated (such as zip code). This total is transmitted along with the data, and the numeric field is "hashed" again at the receiving point. The hash totals are then compared.

IE   Information Engineering.

IS   Information Services.

IT   Information Technology.

IWS   Intelligent Workstation.

Information   Data in context. Data that has meaning to someone in the organization.

Information Warehouse   A set of DBMSs, interfaces, processes, tools, and facilities to manage and deliver complete, timely, accurate, and understandable business information to authorized individuals for effective decision making.

Informational Data Data that is used primarily for decision support purposes. This data can be accessed on an ad hoc or on a regularly scheduled basis.

Integrity Rule/Policy Integrity rules express business rules and govern data manipulation. An algorithm that defines the criteria for acceptability of data. Example: A rule/policy may require data keyed into a particular field to have a value less than 20,000 or to be character data only.

JAD Joint Application Design.

Join A cross match of any two columns in two or more tables.

Key One or more columns that are part of the definition of a table, an index, or a referential constraint that serve to identify the row.

Key Attribute The attribute selected to identify an entity uniquely.

KPI Key Performance Indicator.

LAN Local Area Network.

Legacy Can refer to either systems, applications, or data. Those old production systems, applications, or data on which the business depends.

Local Data Directory A data directory that has been propagated from the main repository to a local server.

Lock An operator that prevents other programs from changing an object concurrently in use by another program. Locks are used to prevent loss of data integrity due to concurrent update to the same data by more than one program.

Log A set of data that records the changes to a database including the time of change. A log has whatever data is necessary for a DBMS to recover or restore the integrity of the database.

Logical The view that is seen from the perspective of the programmer or end user. It is not the physical manifestation.

Lower CASE Tools Those CASE tools that provide code generation, screen painting, report generation, and testing facilities.

LU 6.2 A program-to-program communication protocol defining a rich set of interprogram communication services.

LUW Logical Unit of Work.

Metadata Data about data.

Middleware A layer of communication that allows applications to interact across diverse hardware and software environments; software that shields end users and developers from differences in the services and resources used by applications.

Model   A representation of the real thing.

Normalization   Normalization allows the database designer to represent data and relationships of that data in a table format allowing easy access to the data. Those accessing the data do not have to be concerned about the mode of access but only need to know what data they need. Normalization is a database design process that attempts to simplify data structures by decomposing them into simpler structures to reduce anomalies in update, insert, and delete operations.

ODS   Operational Data Store (see Operational Data Store).

Ordered   A predetermined relationship or scheme, or a defined sequence (sorted).

Operational Data   Production files or databases updated by on-line or batch production programs.

Operational Data Store   A database to provide an interim step for near-real-time data to informational and operational queries. It minimizes the impact on production or operational systems while providing as current live data as possible. Can also serve as a data staging area for processing data into the data warehouse.

Partitioning   The division of a database (usually one that is very large) into pieces. The object of partitioning includes improved performance, higher availability, and more granularity for control purposes.

Platform   A combination of hardware and operating system. It is the platform on which applications run.

Policy   Statements of constraints on data.

Portability   A form of integration that allows applications and data to be moved from one platform to another.

Primary Index   An index that enforces the uniqueness of the primary key.

Primary Key   Primary keys are attributes or sets of attributes that uniquely identify entities such as bank account number or social security number. A primary key can be pointed to by a foreign key.

Protocol   The conventions that govern communication between processes. The format and content of material to be exchanged are specified by a protocol.

Prototype   A process in which a working model or representation of a system or its components is developed. For information systems, the working model usually evolves iteratively from a simple representation through more complex, working models.

Query   A request for information from decision support systems. As opposed to a transaction, a query usually accesses multiple rows of data in a data warehouse, often provides summary information, and is used for management purposes.

Query Governor   A facility that monitors resource usage of queries and terminates them when they reach a predetermined threshold.

Quality   The absence of any defect. The characteristic of a system that conforms to the original design. A system of quality would have the following characteristics: (1) maintainability (easy to add new functions), (2) conformance to specifications (fulfilling end-user requirements), (3) long mean-time to failure (few bugs and ABENDS), (4) performance that is adequate or as expected, (5) well tested for functionality, user interface, and performance, (6) well documented, (7) easy to use, (8) uses standard interfaces.

ODBC   Microsoft's Open Database Connectivity.

OLAP   On-line Analytical Processing.

OLTP   On-line Transaction Processing.

Operational Applications   The applications that create, update, and access operational data. They do not access or update informational data.

Operational Data   Production files or databases updated by on-line or batch production programs.

PC   Personal Computer.

QMF   Query Management Facility.

RDBMS   Relational Database Management System.

Referential Constraint   The assertion that non-null values of a designated foreign key are valid only if they also appear as values of the primary key of a designated table.

Referential Integrity   The concept of certain relationships between tables, based on the definition of a primary key and foreign key. The enforcement of referential constraints on load, insert, update, and delete operations.

Repeating Groups   Data items that are repeated within a record.

Replication   Storing the same data in more than one place.

Roll-Up Queries   Queries that summarize data at a higher level.

RPC   Remote Procedure Call.

Scalability   The ability to support larger or smaller numbers of users in cost-effective increments with minimal impact on the business.

SDLC   System Development Life Cycle.

SDM   System Development Methodology.

Second Normal Form   For a table to be in second normal form, each column that is not a key must contain some information that is dependent on the entire key of the table.

Security Access and update control.

Server A computer that provides (serves up) data to another computer.

Slice and Dice The process of viewing data from different perspectives at different levels of detail; a capability usually provided by multidimensional database products.

Snapshot An image of a database or file at a specific point in time. Generally used for reporting purposes.

Source Database A production or operational database that feeds a data warehouse.

SQL Structured Query Language.

SQL Compliant Specifies that a particular dialect of SQL complies with a particular level of the ANSI standard SQL.

Star Schema (or Star Join Schema) "A specific organization of a database in which a fact table with a composite key is joined to a number of single-level dimension tables, each with a single, primary key."[1]

Subject-oriented Database A database that contains data related to one or more logical subjects.

Summary Data Data that has been aggregated to meet the needs of users.

System Development Life Cycle (SDLC) The course of development changes through which a system passes from its conception to the system running in production mode. The steps include planning and requirements specification, analysis, design, coding, testing, and maintenance.

System Development Methodology (SDM) The procedures that are followed in the System Development Life Cycle. These procedures are documented and followed by those developing, implementing, and maintaining systems.

Target Database The database into which data will be loaded from a source database.

Third Normal Form A database has been normalized to third normal form if each attribute in the relationship is a fact about the key, the whole key, and nothing but the key. Having a database in third normal form minimizes future changes in the database as a result of new requirements. In relational tables, data design must meet three rules:

- At the crossing of a column and a row, there is only one value.
- Every attribute that is not part of the key is dependent on the whole primary key, not only on a part of the primary key.
- There are no functional dependencies between attributes that do not belong to the primary key.

[1] Kimball, Ralph, *Data Warehouse Toolkit*, New York: John Wiley & Sons, 1996.

Token-ring Network   Consists of a wiring system, a set of communication adapters (stations), and an access protocol that controls the sharing of the physical medium by the stations attached to the LAN.

Traditional Data Warehouse Development   The process of building a data warehouse with the following steps:

- Create an enterprise data model.
- Create a system data model based on the enterprise data model.
- Define a warehouse architecture.
- Design, build, and populate the physical databases.

Transaction   An on-line process in which a program or set of programs perform a well-defined and limited process. Usually involves the access and often update of data. Differentiated from a query that is read only and for which the amount of data accessed cannot be anticipated.

Trigger   An action to take when a database-related event occurs.

Two-Phase Commit   The process will ensure that a transaction can commit all data before any are committed. It is only required if there are multiple updates in the same transaction.

Update Anomaly   Inconsistent data, or a loss of data integrity when data is changed in one location but not in another.

Update Rule   A policy that controls the allowable conditions that change the values of a row or record.

Upper CASE Tool   Those tools that have been developed to meet the needs and requirements of business experts and analysts early in the application development life cycle, such as creating specifications, building models, and capturing the requirements of the business.

VSAM   Virtual Sequential Access Method.

View   An alternative representation of data from one or more tables. A view can include all or some of the columns contained in tables on which it is distributed.

VLDB   Very large database.

Author Profiles

Sid Adelman

Sid has been actively consulting and working with a number of organizations over the past seven years architecting, planning, developing, and implementing decision support systems and data warehouses. He is an internationally known lecturer, presenting at DAMA, GUIDE, and SHARE/GUIDE in the United States, Australia, the Philippines, and Hong Kong. He presented at Data Warehouse Conferences in Holland, Germany, the United Kingdom, and the United States, at the Catalog Network Symposium, and at the Customer Information System Users and Technical Conference.

Sid has published articles in *Data Base Management Magazine, Computer-World*, and *Database Programming and Design*. He is the coauthor of *PlanXpert for Data Warehouse*, a data warehouse methodology and project planning tool. Sid Adelman was with IBM for over 24 years. His last positions were Consulting Systems Engineer and Senior Consultant. He has an MBA in Business Economics from UCLA and is a member of the Life Office Management Association with a specialty in Data Processing. He may be reached at sidadelman@aol.com

Ted Alexander

Ted, Senior Partner and Co-Founder of the Praxium Group, Inc., has consulted internationally on data warehousing, database design, client/server architectures, application design, application tuning, risk management, and customer relationship management. He has worked in data warehousing, database, and other areas in the financial, government, retail, manufacturing, legal, and entertainment industries. Ted has participated in all phases of data warehouse development, including measuring client impact, building a new client infrastructure, architecture, design, planning, review, and implementation. He has provided research and input into many articles and is an active reviewer for technical publications.

Ted has served on the board of the Atlanta DB2 User Group for the past seven years and is currently its president. He has been active in many regional

414

groups and is a member of the IBM Gold Consultants Group, a group of 25 world-wide, hand-selected consultants who are provided with special information and products as well as current and future products and directions. He may be reached at tedalex@ix.netcom.com

Joyce Bischoff

Joyce, President of Bischoff Consulting, Inc., has consulted and lectured in the United States, Europe, and Canada on database design, performance, and design methodologies. She has been involved in planning, designing, performing design reviews, and implementing numerous data warehouses in the chemical, pharmaceutical, insurance, financial, banking, oil refining, and hospital industries.

Joyce is the author of numerous articles and a chapter in the *Handbook of Data Management*, published by Auerbach. She was the founding Chairperson of the Delaware Valley DB2 User Group, served as Leader of the Guide Task Force on DB2 Standards for Performance, and served on the Conference Planning Committee for IDUG and WRAD conferences. She was awarded the Quality Service Award by Guide International in 1989 and received the Keith McGrath Service Award from the Delaware Valley DB2 User Group in 1990. She is listed in *Who's Who in America* and was elected to the New York Academy of Sciences in 1992. She has made presentations for IDUG, DPMA, ACM, WRAD, and many data warehouse conferences. She may be reached at 75330.3705@compuserve.com or by phone at 302-239-7202.

Peter Brooks

Peter is a management consultant with the Advanced Technology Group of Coopers & Lybrand Consulting, where he specializes in leading organizations to achieve business advantage by applying strategic and innovative technologies such as data warehousing. Data warehouses are used in conjunction with strategic alignment, business process analysis, and organization design principles to improve organizations' decision-making capabilities.

Peter has over 17 years of management and consulting experience in a variety of industries. Before joining Coopers & Lybrand, Peter worked at IBM in a variety of capacities, the last of which was as a senior consultant in the Executive and Decision Support Systems practice of the IBM Consulting Group. He is well known in the data warehousing field. He has presented at DCI's Data Warehouse World and been quoted in *The OLAP Report, Beyond Computing*, and *WebWeek*. He has been published in magazines such as *DBMS, Data Management Review*, and *WebMaster*. He is based in Boston and can be reached at 74477.3043@compuserve.com

Marie Buretta

Marie is an internationally known consultant, instructor, and lecturer. She is president of Marie Buretta, Inc., a consulting and training firm specializing in client/server application development, technologies for achieving data consistency (such as replication and messaging), data warehousing and OLAP technologies, and database performance and tuning. As a senior consultant, she has developed a methodology for designing databases in a distributed environment that addresses maintaining integrity, performance, availability, and consistency across multiple sites. She specializes in implementing data replication solutions in heterogeneous database environments. This includes using replication within and across OLTP and OLAP systems. She conducts training sessions on replication technologies and approaches for establishing global replication services within firms.

In the past, as a partner with Computer Science Corporation/Partners, Marie specialized in database conversions, performance tuning, and training. She has held positions as database administrator, project manager, performance analyst, and standards development analyst. She is a past Project Manager for GUIDE's DB2 Technology Development Project. She can be reached on the Internet at www.mburetta.com

Brenda Castiel

Brenda has over 20 years of data processing experience. She was a Senior Systems Engineer and Database specialist with IBM Canada for several years, where she was involved in an early data warehouse project. She was responsible for supporting a large telecommunications company in implementing numerous DB2 applications. In addition, she worked on an IBM "red book" on distributed database. Currently, she is a Senior Manager with Ernst & Young in Los Angeles, working on a large custom development project, where she is responsible for infrastructure issues, data conversion, and performance. She is a frequent speaker at technical conferences and local user groups, and has published several articles. She can be reached at Brenda.Castiel@ey.com or 102131.1764@Compuserve.com

Howard Fosdick

Howard is both an industry analyst and hands-on practitioner. He has written over a hundred articles and six books, founded several national user groups, and is frequently quoted in the industry trade press. He has survived several data warehouse projects. Fosdick is an independent consultant and can be reached via Fosdick Consulting, Inc., 49 N. Princeton, Suite 100, Villa Park, IL 60181, or at 75403.1772@compuserve.com

Susan Gausden

Susan, Director of Brooklands Technology Limited, Weybridge, Surrey, England, is a computer systems consultant with over 15 years of experience, specializing in client/server architecture and information warehouse technologies. Bringing with her a wealth of knowledge from a decision support software vendor environment as a Technical Manager and Technology Specialist, she is an authority on the connectivity issues inherent in heterogeneous software and hardware mixes. Susan is a Physics graduate from McGill University in Montreal. She can be contacted at 104564.62@compuserve.com

Dave Gleason

Dave is a Senior Manager for Consulting and Offerings with PLATINUM Information Management Consulting (PIMC), a unit of PLATINUM Technology, Inc. He specializes in the planning, design, and development of data warehouses and meta-data solutions. Dave has worked with numerous clients to assist them in all phases of data warehouse planning and development, including companies in industries as diverse as banking, financial services, healthcare, pharmaceuticals, telecommunications, and public utilities. He has worked with clients located throughout the United States, and has done extensive work in many foreign countries. His responsibilities at PIMC include oversight of the consulting group's data warehouse efforts, including methodology and training. Additionally, he plays active roles on many of the firm's data warehouse projects, getting involved in hands-on data warehouse planning and construction tasks. Dave has over seven years' experience in the information systems field. His previous work experience includes RELTECH Services, a division of RELTECH Group Inc., and Andersen Consulting.

Paul Hessinger

Paul is the Managing Director of Vision UnlimITed, an Atlanta-based management advisory and IT research practice. He is widely known and respected as a pragmatic industry analyst and visionary, motivational IT strategist. He has consulted with a number of leading IT users and vendors. He conducts over 50 executive briefings and workshops around the world each year. In the fall of 1995, he began conducting UnlimITed Vision Leadership RetreatSM programs for IT and business process management teams, which expose them to a small but accomplished group of facilitators who have extensive technology, process, and change management expertise. He has over 20 years of industry experience. He has held senior executive positions with Computer Task Group (for 17 years from 1974 to 1991, 10 as Chief Technology Officer; Buffalo, NY), BMW/Softlab (1992 in Munich, Germany as a Senior Vice President), Knowledgeware (1993 as Executive Vice President, Atlanta, GA), and DYNASTY Technologies (in 1994 as Executive Vice President). He resides in

Atlanta, GA and Hilton Head Island, SC. He can be reached via the Internet at HESSPR @ AOL.com

Martin Hubel

Martin, an independent consultant, has worked extensively with relational database since 1985. Martin develops and teaches advanced DB2 courses and is recognized as a leading authority in the field. He is a member of the Gold Consultants Program sponsored by the IBM Response Center in Somers, NY.

Martin has been using DB2 for OS/2 for several years and participated in the beta test program for DB2 Common Server. He has made numerous presentations for GUIDE International, International DB2 Users Group, Insurance Accounting and Systems Association, Canadian Information Processing Society, CMG Canada, EDP Audit Association, Computer Security Institute, and many regional user groups.

Martin has an extensive background in computer systems, including software design and development, project management, disaster recovery planning, data security, systems programming, capacity planning and performance, operations support, teaching, charge-back systems, end-user support, data administration, and database administration. He can be reached at 75201.2767@compuserve.com

Denis Kosar

Denis currently works for the Chase Manhattan Bank as the Vice President of Enterprise Information Architecture. He is responsible for the establishment of the Enterprise Data Warehousing Strategy, Life Cycle and Tool Guidelines. He has been responsible for the analysis and design of a major data warehouse, which was implemented in the Wholesale Bank to support Customer Profitability. He has also played a role in the development of the Chase's Corporate Data Model, which has been a valuable part of the Chase Data Architecture.

Denis has been a frequent speaker at the International DB2 Users Group (IDUG) and has recently participated in the Data Warehousing Panel for the 1995 IDUG conference. He is currently a member of the IDUG Conference Planning Board and holds a position on the Data Administration Management Association (DAMA-NY) Board. He has a B.B.A. in Management from Baruch College and an M.B.A. in Executive Management from St. John's University. He can be reached at 76345.2142@compuserve.com

John Ladley

John is currently a Program Director at Meta Group, specializing in Data Warehouse and Organizational Issues. Prior to Meta Group, he was Director of Information Management for Alliance Blue Cross & Blue Shield, St. Louis, MO, where he was responsible for defining and providing the corporate data and decision-making environment. John's 18 plus years of experience in information technology range from the Department of Defense to the health care industry. He has been involved with data warehouse technology since 1989 and has completed four data warehouse projects. John also writes and speaks frequently in the data warehouse field. He can be reached at John_Ladley@Metagroup.com or JLADLEY@aol.com

Trina LaRue

Trina specializes in relational database design, implementation, and performance and tuning in both mainframe and alternate platform environments. She supports many major telecommunication billing/credit card/data warehouse applications with tables up to 750 million rows. She has extensive experience in performance and tuning of relational database systems. Trina has provided database tuning and SQL code reviews that resulted in significant performance gains.

Trina functions as a Senior Database Consultant at AT&T, as a resource to many different applications. She is an active member of a team in the process of moving customer data into a heterogeneous environment. She is a member of the Business Unit that won the Malcolm Baldridge Award this past year for excellence. Trina has worked with DB2 since its initial release. Over the years, she has written a number of articles on SQL code reviews and backup and recovery. She is an author of a chapter in the *Handbook of Data Management*, published by Auerbach. She is a frequent presenter to many international and local user groups. She can be reached at cardinal!tbeyer@buzzard.attmail.com

Jay Marquez

Jay, Senior Partner and Co-Founder of The Praxium Group, Inc., has consulted internationally on data warehousing architectures, database design, performance tuning, client/server architectures, application design and tuning, and lecturing and teaching on various database, client/server, and object-oriented issues. He was one of the founders of the Atlanta DB2 Users' Group and served as the first Vice President and later was elected as the President. He also served as President of the Georgia Sybase User Group and was a member of the Planning Committee of the International DB2 Users Group (IDUG) for four years.

Jay has presented at IDUG, IEEE, and regional user groups on subjects related to database tools and object-oriented practices. He participated on the Client/Server Panel and was the Special Interest Group (SIG) leader for Data Warehousing SIG at IDUG. He has reviewed books and articles for different authors, including Chris Gane's book entitled *Rapid Application Development*. He has written articles and product reviews for various newsletters and magazines. He may be contacted at 70413.246@compuserve.com

Terry Mason

Terry, Director of Brooklands Technology Limited, Weybridge, Surrey, England, is a computer systems consultant with over 25 years of experience, specializing in information warehouse performance and migration of legacy database technology to relational database technology. As such, he is fully conversant with the optimization and multidatabase access issues of data warehousing. Having spoken internationally on database technology and authored commentaries on DB2 and database tools, he has become a recognized authority in the database technology arena. He is a member of a worldwide group of independent consultants participating in IBM's elite Gold Consultants Program for Data Management. He may be reached at 104564.62@compuserve.com

Edward M. Peters

Edward is Vice President and General Manager of the DataDirect Division of INTERSOLV, Inc., a major independent software company located in Rockville, MD. Prior to joining INTERSOLV, he held various management positions, including Managing Director at ILS, Inc., a management and information technology consulting firm located in McLean, VA, and Vice President, Strategic Technology & Research, Manufacturers Hanover Trust, NY. Edward is the recipient of the fourth R/A/D International Award for Excellence in Repository-based Application Development and the GUIDE International president's Award. He may be reached at ed_peters@intersolv.com

Jack Sweeney

Jack is currently the President and CEO of Intellidex Systems, located in Winthrop, MA. Intellidex develops and markets a suite of software products called the "Data Warehouse Management System," which manages a data warehouse environment. He has spent 29 years in the IS industry and is a recognized leader in the segments associated with the decision support, data warehousing, expert systems, and client/server development. He has spoken around the world on these topics to audiences of over 500 professionals on dozens of occasions. He has been interviewed and publicly quoted on the subjects of data warehousing and expert systems by several leading publications, including *Computerworld, Business Investor's Daily*, IBM's *Think Magazine, Open Computing, Datamation, Bank Systems and Technology*, and *American Banker*.

Before cofounding Intellidex with his partner, Mark Grise, Jack was the Director of Information Management Resources at a large international bank. There he created the vision, staffed the organization, and marketed the benefits for building a corporatewide data warehouse. He may be reached at jack@intellidex.com

Pete Uhrowczik

Pete is a Senior Technical Staff Member at IBM's Santa Teresa Laboratory. He is the lead architect for IBM's Information Warehouse (IBM's name for the data warehousing solution). Pete joined IBM in 1963 and has been involved with database management systems since 1970. During the 1970s he supported customers in the design and implementation of DBMS-based applications as well as in the usage of data dictionaries/directories. In 1979 he joined the Santa Teresa Development Laboratory, and his work included technical planning as well as Management of IMS Strategic Planning.

Pete developed the present Coexistence Strategy for IMS-DB and DB2 and later the IBM Information Warehouse Architecture. Recently, he has been involved in defining how multimedia data is to be handled in IBM's RDBMSs, solutions for multidimensional analysis, and integration of metadata in data warehousing. He may be reached at uhro@us.ibm.com

Colin White

Colin is president of DataBase Associates International, a leading information technology consulting and education company. As an analyst and consultant, he specializes in distributed computing and data warehousing and is the editor of *InfoDB,* a technical journal covering developments in information technology. He is also well known as the conference director for DB/EXPO, the leading U.S. database and client/server exposition and conference. He is a regular columnist for several trade journals and has written numerous articles and lectured throughout the world on the subject of database, client/server, and distributed computing.

Richard Yevich

Richard is an internationally recognized consultant, lecturer, and teacher, known for his expertise in enterprise information systems and DB2. He specializes in client/server, warehouse, and distributed relational systems across multiple platforms and in establishing proper design to achieve high performance and high availability. Richard is widely published and writes the column "Enterprise Trends and Directions" for *Data Management Review,* and a column on DB2 for the magazine *IDUG Solutions Journal.* He is a regular guest speaker at conventions and user groups in the United States, Australia, Japan, and Europe and has won best speaker awards for many of these. He is a member of the IBM Gold Consultants program. Formerly a senior consultant with Codd and Date Inc., Richard is currently a principal with RYC Inc., a firm specializing in information technology, data modeling, performance tuning, and advanced education. He can be reached at Richard_Yevich@ibm.net or by phone at 305-361-8585.

Index